STUDIES IN THE HISTORY OF CHRISTIAN MISSIONS

R. E. Frykenberg
Brian Stanley
General Editors

STUDIES IN THE HISTORY OF CHRISTIAN MISSIONS

Judith M. Brown and Robert Eric Frykenberg, *Editors*
Christians, Cultural Interactions, and India's Religious Traditions

Robert Eric Frykenberg
Christians and Missionaries in India: Cross-Cultural Communication since 1500

Susan Billington Harper
In the Shadow of the Mahatma: Bishop V. S. Azariah and the Travails of Christianity in British India

D. Dennis Hudson
Protestant Origins in India: Tamil Evangelical Christians, 1706-1835

Jon Miller
Missionary Zeal and Institutional Control: Organizational Contradictions in the Basel Mission on the Gold Coast, 1828-1917

Andrew Porter, *Editor*
The Imperial Horizons of British Protestant Missions, 1880-1914

Brian Stanley, *Editor*
Christian Missions and the Enlightenment

Brian Stanley, *Editor*
Missions, Nationalism, and the End of Empire

Kevin Ward and Brian Stanley, *Editors*
The Church Mission Society and World Christianity, 1799-1999

MISSIONS, NATIONALISM, *and the* END *of* EMPIRE

Edited by

Brian Stanley

Associate Editor

Alaine Low

William B. Eerdmans Publishing Company
Grand Rapids, Michigan / Cambridge, U.K.

Published 2003 by
Wm. B. Eerdmans Publishing Co.
255 Jefferson Ave. S.E., Grand Rapids, Michigan 49503 /
P.O. Box 163, Cambridge CB3 9PU U.K.

Printed in the United States of America

08 07 06 05 04 03   7 6 5 4 3 2 1

Library of Congress Cataloging-in-Publication Data

Missions, nationalism, and the end of empire /
edited by Brian Stanley; associate editor, Alaine Low.
p. cm. — (Studies in the history of Christian missions)
Includes bibliographical references and index.
ISBN 0-8028-2116-2 (pbk.: alk. paper)
1. Missions — History — 20th century — Congresses.
2. Nationalim — History — 20th century — Congresses.
3. Decolonization — History — 20th century — Congresses.
I. Stanley, Brian, 1953- II. Low, Alaine M. III. Series.

BV2120.M58 2003
266′.009′04 — dc22

2003062358

www.eerdmans.com

Contents

Contributors

Daniel H. Bays is Professor of History, Emeritus, at the University of Kansas and Spoelhof Chair and Professor of History at Calvin College, Grand Rapids, where he is also Director of the Asian Studies Program. He is author of several articles on twentieth-century Chinese Protestantism and editor of *Christianity in China: From the Eighteenth Century to the Present* (1996).

Philip Boobbyer is Lecturer in Modern European History at the University of Kent at Canterbury, U.K. His main work is in modern Russian history, and his publications include *S. L. Frank: The Life and Work of a Russian Philosopher, 1877-1950* (1995). He is editor of two collections of addresses by the Scottish religious writer and scientist Henry Drummond: *The Greatest Thing in the World* (1997) and *The Changed Life* (2000).

Judith M. Brown is Beit Professor of Commonwealth History in the University of Oxford and Professorial Fellow of Balliol College. Previously she held posts in the Universities of Cambridge and Manchester. Her main interests are modern Indian history and politics, South Asian migration, and contemporary Hinduism. She has published on Indian history and politics, focusing particularly on the career of Gandhi, and was coeditor of the twentieth-century volume of *The Oxford History of the British Empire* (1999). Her latest book is *Nehru: A Political Biography.*

Richard Elphick is Professor of History at Wesleyan University, Middletown, Connecticut. His early writings concerned the origins of the racial hierarchy in colonial South Africa. More recently he has edited, with Rodney Davenport, *Christianity in South Africa: A Political, Social, and Cultural History*

(1997). He is now completing "The Premise of Equality: Protestant Missions and Racial Politics in South Africa."

Deborah Gaitskell is Senior Research Associate of the History Department at the School of Oriental and African Studies (SOAS), University of London. She has also taught at Birkbeck and Goldsmiths Colleges and in the Study of Religions at SOAS. Her published work focuses on mission domesticity, African girls' education, and churchwomen's groups. She is completing a study of women missionaries for this series, and editing a collection on indigenous female evangelists in Asia and Africa.

Adrian Hastings was Emeritus Professor of Theology at the University of Leeds. His many publications in history and theology include *A History of African Christianity, 1950-1975* (1979); *The Church in Africa, 1450-1950* (1994); *The Construction of Nationhood* (1997); and *Oliver Tomkins: The Ecumenical Enterprise, 1908-1992* (2001). He also edited *A World History of Christianity* (1999) and was for many years the editor of the *Journal of Religion in Africa.* Professor Hastings died in May 2001.

Caroline Howell completed her D.Phil. thesis, "Church and State in Decolonisation: The Case of Buganda, 1939-1962," at the University of Oxford, where she was a member of St. Cross College.

Ka-che Yip is Professor of History at the University of Maryland, Baltimore County. He is author of *Religion, Nationalism, and Chinese Students: The Anti-Christian Movement of 1922-1927* and *Health and National Reconstruction in Nationalist China: The Development of Modern Health Services, 1928-1937.* He is writing a book about the development of medicine and health care, which includes the role played by missionaries and mission institutions during the Sino-Japanese War of 1937-45.

Ogbu U. Kalu is Henry Winters Professor of World Christianity and Missions at McCormick Theological Seminary, Chicago. He was a Professor of Church History at the University of Nigeria, Nsukka, until 2001. His publications include *African Church Historiography: An Ecumenical Perspective* (1988); *The Embattled Gods: Christianization of Ogboland, 1841-1991* (1996); and *Power, Poverty, and Prayer: The Challenges of Poverty and Pluralism in African Christianity, 1960-1996* (2000).

Hartmut Lehmann is Director at the Max-Planck-Institut für Geschichte in Göttingen and Adjunct Professor of History at the Universities of Göttingen and Kiel. His recent publications include *Max Webers Protestantische Ethik*

(1996); *Protestantische Weltsichten* (1998); and *Protestantisches Christentum im Prozeß der Säkularisierung* (2001).

Derek Peterson is Assistant Professor of History at the College of New Jersey. He is editor of *The Invention of Religion: Rethinking Belief in Politics and History* (2002) and author of a forthcoming book, *Creative Writing: Translation, Bookkeeping, and the Work of Imagination in Colonial Kenya.*

Andrew Porter is Rhodes Professor of Imperial History in the University of London and teaches at King's College. His books include *Victorian Shipping, Business and Imperial Policy* (1986); *European Imperialism, 1860-1914* (1914); and, as editor and contributor, *The Oxford History of the British Empire,* vol. 3, *The Nineteenth Century* (1999). He has published extensively on missions, for instance, in the *Journal of Imperial and Commonwealth History,* and has a forthcoming book from Manchester University Press on British Protestant missions and imperial expansion, 1763-1914.

Brian Stanley is Director of the Henry Martyn Centre for the Study of Mission and World Christianity and a fellow of St. Edmund's College, University of Cambridge. He was formerly the Director of the Currents in World Christianity Project, under whose auspices this volume was produced. His publications include *The Bible and the Flag* (1990); *The History of the Baptist Missionary Society, 1792-1992* (1992); and *Christian Missions and the Enlightenment* (2001).

John Stuart is temporary Lecturer in Imperial and Commonwealth History at the Department of History, King's College, University of London. His forthcoming Ph.D. thesis, "Race, Politics and Evangelisation: British Protestant Missionaries and African Colonial Affairs, 1940-63," examines the response of British Protestant missions to political developments in eastern and central Africa during this period.

INTRODUCTION

Christianity and the End of Empire

BRIAN STANLEY

The twentieth century witnessed first the apogee and then the demise of the system of global dominance constructed by the Western colonial powers during the Victorian period. Increasingly the disintegration of that system and its replacement by an internationalism founded on the principle of the territorial integrity of the sovereign nation-state is being interpreted as the most significant episode in world history since 1945. The vogue in literary and cultural studies of "postcolonial" theory supplies further evidence of how fundamental and far-reaching this shift in the alignment of global politics is deemed to be, necessitating a revolution in intellectual framework throughout the disciplines of the humanities. A trend that has attracted rather less attention has been the almost simultaneous reconfiguration of the religious geography of the world. Religions which were formerly the preserve of the subject peoples of colonial rule — Hinduism, Buddhism, and Islam — now have large and growing constituencies in the Western world, and not simply as a result of migration flows. Conversely, Christianity, which in 1900 appeared to be primarily a religion of the very same Western nations that controlled the colonial system, has propagated itself in the former colonial territories and diversified to the extent that it is now in numerical terms more a religion of the South and East than of the North and West, regions in which it is generally in decline.

What the tangled connections may be between these two processes of change is an intriguing question that has scarcely begun to attract the attention of scholars. This volume is concerned with one important aspect of the question, namely, the nature of the linkages in the mid–twentieth century between the Christian churches (and in particular their missionary bodies) and the dynamics of anticolonial nationalism and decolonization in the non-Western world. Christian missions in the twentieth century, despite their more extended geographical scope and much greater numerical weight than in the nineteenth century, have to date received only a fraction of the scholarly attention that has been lavished on the Victorian mission enterprise. Although the volume of historical inquiry devoted to the process of decolonization has increased rapidly since the 1980s, the contribution of churches and missions in assisting, retarding, or simply responding to that process is still largely unexplored. While the twentieth-century volume in the recent *Oxford History of the British Empire* identifies the role of missionaries in the empire as one of the seven integrating themes that recur both in that volume and throughout the five volumes of the *Oxford History*, the theme makes little or no appearance in the sections concerned with the end of empire.[1] The standard introductions to European decolonization are largely silent about the part churches and missionary bodies may have played. Their absence from the narrative may be indicative of an assumption that they were at best marginal to a series of events that was instigated by fundamental structural readjustments in the multiple contracts of material interest on which the survival of empire depended. Insofar as religion makes fleeting appearances on the stage of these narratives of decolonization, the religion concerned tends not to be that of the missionaries or the Christian adherents of the mission churches. Revivals in Asia of Buddhism or Islam, or spasmodic outbreaks in Africa of popular messianism such as the Watchtower movement in Nyasaland in 1914-15, receive some notice as evidence of a growing cultural and spiritual alienation between the Western and non-Western worlds that began to "clog the machine" of European imperial dominance in the two decades before the Second World War.[2] Yet orthodox Christianity, which supplied, whether willingly or unwillingly, much of the moral vocabulary and rhetoric undergirding the civilizing mission of empire, is seen, strangely, to be irrelevant to its end.

The chapters in this book were all originally presented as papers at a conference entitled "Missions, Nationalism, and the End of Empire" held at Queens' College, Cambridge, from 6 to 9 September 2000. The conference

1. Judith M. Brown and Wm. Roger Louis, eds., *The Oxford History of the British Empire*, vol. 4, *The Twentieth Century* (Oxford and New York, 1999), pp. 17-18, and see index, s.v. "missions, missionaries."

2. R. F. Holland, *European Decolonization, 1918-1981: An Introductory Survey* (Basingstoke, 1985), pp. 8-11. See also John Darwin, *Britain and Decolonisation: The Retreat from Empire in the Post-War World* (Basingstoke, 1988); Darwin, *The End of the British Empire: The Historical Debate* (Oxford, 1991).

was organized by the Currents in World Christianity Project, hosted by the Centre for Advanced Religious and Theological Studies, Faculty of Divinity, University of Cambridge, and generously funded by the Pew Charitable Trusts of Philadelphia. The 115 delegates hailed from all over the globe and represented a variety of disciplines — history, sociology, anthropology, missiology, and theology. The seven main papers and thirty-one shorter communications delivered covered a great variety of topics and all continents, and the thirteen chapters that follow are only a representative selection of the contributions to the conference.

The papers given at the Cambridge conference illuminated the complex fashion in which mission movements have juxtaposed elements of nationalism and universalism. Under the heading "Missionary Traditions, National Loyalties, and the Universal Gospel," part I of this volume examines a number of European missionary traditions from the perspective of how far (if at all) they reconciled the universality intrinsic to Christian theology with varying degrees of adherence to nationalist ideology and differing responses to the rapidly changing political context of the non-Western world in the twentieth century. Chapter 1 was delivered as the opening lecture of the conference, and is one of the last pieces of writing from the pen of Adrian Hastings, whose death on 30 May 2001 deprived the history of Christian missions (not to speak of other fields of historical and theological scholarship) of one of its most penetrating commentators. Hastings notes the strength of missionary nationalism, not simply where one might expect it — among German, British, South African, and American Protestants — but also, more surprisingly, among Portuguese, French, Belgian, and (in the 1930s) Italian Catholics. In practice, and despite periodic castigation from the Vatican, Catholics seemed as prone to uncatholic distortions of Christian universality as Protestants, whose ecclesiology of national churches, often founded on theologically dubious appropriations of the Old Testament image of the redeemer nation, might be supposed to give them more of an excuse for such aberrations. Hastings identifies the Congregation de Propaganda Fide and the International Missionary Council, followed by the World Council of Churches, as the bodies primarily responsible for recalling Christians in the West from these nationalist preoccupations to a truly catholic understanding of the universality of the church. Yet the conclusion of Hastings's chapter warns against those contemporary (and predominantly American) forms of Christian universalism that claim to be universalism pure and simple but are in fact highly particular "nationalist" expressions of the universal missionary imperative.

Hastings's chapter lends further weight to the case, already advanced persuasively in his *Construction of Nationhood* (1997), that modernist explanations of nationalism that exclude the role of historic religious identities and specifically the formative power of vernacular scriptures or liturgy fail to convince.[3] If this is so, the relevance of changing Christian beliefs and assumptions to the decline of national empires in the tropical world is at least worthy of investigation, whether this decline is interpreted as constituting evidence of the waning power of nationalism in Europe or, contrariwise, as the result of the successful transplantation of nationalism from North to South and West to East.

It is not however clear that the form of Christian imperialism so evident in the Protestant missionary movement in the late Victorian or Edwardian period can *simply* be labeled "nationalistic." British Protestant missions in the high imperial era proved capable of combining distressingly crude expressions of imperial pride and racial prejudice with a quite genuine and continuing evangelical internationalism that reached its peak at the World Missionary Conference in Edinburgh in 1910. While that internationalism was dealt a severe blow by the outbreak of war in 1914, the point to notice is surely the horror that the prospect of Christendom at war with itself aroused in the leadership of Protestant missions: for J. H. Oldham, for example, the outbreak of war was a "catastrophe," a "terrible blow" that gravely imperiled "the international fellowship and love which we began to learn at Edinburgh."[4] British Protestant imperialism was never purely nationalistic, but rather a form of Christian expansionism that idealized British power primarily because it was perceived to be a providential instrument for achieving the universalistic goal of winning all nations for Christ.

German missionary enthusiasm was perhaps more directly vulnerable to an unqualified nationalist tendency founded on romantic notions of the *Volk*, though German missiology was at the same time considerably more wary than its British or American counterpart of yoking the Christian message to the partial Anglo-American slogans of civilization and progress. The "Appeal to Evangelical Christians Abroad" issued by German church and mission leaders in September 1914, despite its crudely nationalist expressions, also lamented the fact that the mission fields in central Africa and eastern Asia that Edinburgh had indicated as being of the highest priority were "now becoming the scenes of embittered struggles between peoples who bore in a special degree the responsibility for the fulfilment of the Great Commission in these

3. Adrian Hastings, *The Construction of Nationhood: Ethnicity, Religion, and Nationalism* (Cambridge, 1997).

4. Keith Clements, *Faith on the Frontier: A Life of J. H. Oldham* (Edinburgh, 1999), p. 123.

lands."[5] Only after the disappearance of German colonies during the First World War, as Hartmut Lehmann shows in chapter 2, did a significant section of the German mission movement redirect its enthusiasm toward the narrow nationalistic aim of consolidating the ethnic identity of German communities abroad. Yet even in the 1930s German Protestant missionary leaders such as Julius Richter and Siegfried Knak endeavored to combine allegiance to the principle of the *Volk* with an insistence on the universal mission of the church.

Similarly, in South Africa, the archetypal representative of Afrikaner missionary enthusiasm in the interwar period, Johannes du Plessis, as expounded by Richard Elphick in chapter 3, was no Afrikaner nationalist. At the same time, he believed the Dutch Reformed Church had a particular divine calling to evangelize Africa. For du Plessis, white supremacist though he was, universal mission was the very heart of Christianity, though particular national sections of the church had distinctive callings within that overall commission. Elphick shows that there were other sections of the Afrikaner mission community, notably in the Orange Free State, that foreshadowed the later dogmas of apartheid in their emphatic opposition to any mingling of the races. Nevertheless, even this crudely nationalistic variant of mission Christianity retained, at least in theory, an official commitment to the equal value in God's sight of all human beings, black and white. However powerful the forces impelling Christian missions in a nationalistic direction in the early to mid–twentieth century, missiology could not capitulate entirely to such forces without imperiling a principle that is integral to Christian doctrine.

This last observation may yield some comfort for Christians, but the paradoxical and distinctly unpalatable reality about the history of Christian mission seems to be that its commitment to universality — the insistence that the gospel of Christ is a truly universal ethic that must be proclaimed to all nations — has been at its strongest when combined with a lively sense of the calling of particular peoples — whether Britain, or Germany, or Portugal, or France, or South Africa, or the United States — to take a leading role in discharging that responsibility. In terms of Christian theology this is not surprising, since the concepts of universalism and election are so closely intertwined in the Bible, especially in the Old Testament. But once former colonial powers have, for reasons good or bad, lost confidence in their supposed particular divine calling within the world, their Christian populations have begun to weaken in their conviction that the Christian message contains within it an

5. Clements, pp. 126-27.

inescapably universal obligation. The local and the universal, the national and the international, are hence more often to be found in ambiguous and subtle combination than in simple binary opposition. The current missionary dilemma of the churches in the West is how to recover the compelling sense of universal missionary obligation that earlier generations understood at least partially in national terms and reattach that compulsion to where, theologically, it ought to be fixed — to the Christian doctrine of the church itself. The distinctive challenge this material raises for Christians is thus *not* to move from nationalism to universalism, but to find a way of abandoning nationalism *without also* weakening universalism.

The challenge part I issues to imperial historians is to suggest that the finer points of theology and missiology may have rather more relevance to their study of political and racial attitudes than they might suppose. Elphick's chapter is an extended apologia for the political and ideological significance in twentieth-century South Africa of bodies of apparently arcane missiological theory. Andrew Porter's study of the Universities' Mission to Central Africa (UMCA) in chapter 4 argues that a form of conservative, even sectarian Anglo-Catholicism that uniquely stressed the prerogatives of the clergy and the need for obedience to the apostolic authority of the episcopate proved a liability for the UMCA when confronted by the challenges of the need for devolution and preparation for the end of empire. The evidence for the cash value of theology is not, of course, all in one direction. Conservative evangelical missions with their own brand of sectarian resistance to modernity could be just as resistant to the urbanization of Africans, just as reluctant to devolve authority to indigenous leaders, and just as unaware of which way the political wind was blowing as was the UMCA. The particular way a church or mission constructs its religious search for holiness or power does have immense ramifications, but those ramifications are not uniformly predictable.

The chapters in part II supply further evidence that no simple correlations can be drawn between theological perspectives and political responses. Nevertheless, they also permit us to posit some general conclusions about contrasting patterns of Christian identity. In much of sub-Saharan Africa — for example, in Ghana, Zambia, Uganda, or Tanzania (though not, of course, in Islamic Sudan or northern Nigeria) — there has generally been little difficulty about affirming both Christian and emerging "national" identity. In countries of white settlement the tensions were for a time greater, as in Kenya in the era of Mau Mau or Zimbabwe under white minority rule. Yet even in colonial Kenya Christian words, in the hands of Kikuyu readers or converts participating in often unofficial processes of biblical translation, as Derek Peterson emphasizes in chapter 8, supplied a grammar and vocabulary for a new popular politics, enabling the young to challenge the wisdom of the old and wealthy and to articulate anticolonial sentiments through identification with the subjects of biblical narratives. Although in sub-Saharan Africa Christianity was the religion of the colonial power, there has been in Africa no lasting contradiction between Christian and national allegiance.

In India and China, as the chapters by Judith Brown, Ka-che Yip, and Daniel Bays make clear, such a ready identification between Christian profession and nationalist sympathies has not been possible. In India, partly because of the logic of the caste system and partly as a result of the British encouragement of separate religious electorates, political alignments became irretrievably entangled with questions of fundamental religious identity. As a result, nationalist opposition to Christian missions focused not, as in Africa, on questions of defining cultural boundaries or on challenging missionary control of the church, but on the even more fundamental issue of the acceptability of religious conversion. For the members of the Christian community, the independence and partition of India in 1947 simply accentuated the problems inherited from the colonial era of how to affirm and defend their "Indianness."

In China, as in India and later in Africa, Christian missions contributed substantially to the emergence of nationalism through the introduction of Western education, social reforms, and political ideas. Missionaries in both the late Qing and Republican periods saw themselves as proponents of an authentic and reforming Chinese nationalism, shorn of any antiforeign elements, that would enable China to hold her head high as a modern nation that need not fear domination by Japan. The two principal architects of Nationalist China — Sun Yat-sen and Chiang Kai-shek — were personally very far from being anti-Christian. Yet, as Ka-che Yip argues in chapter 6, missionary hopes that Christianity and Chinese nationalism could achieve harmonious coexistence proved illusory. The claim of the state under the Guomindang to be the final arbiter of morals and ideology undermined the central rationale for the heavy investment of China missions in education and resulted in the antimission reaction of 1920-28. Increasingly allegiance to missionary Christianity came to be associated with cultural and political disloyalty to the new China, an association that became peculiarly sharp after 1949. The resulting dilemmas were acute for Christians of all theological persuasions. As Daniel Bays shows in chapter 7, those whose theology was conservative did not necessarily view the claims of the Communist state as incompatible with their faith. Chen Chonggui's long quest for spiritual autonomy from missionary tutelage led him ultimately to espouse the goals of the Three-Self

Patriotic Movement, even though that movement subjugated the church to another external authority, the totalitarian power of the Communist state. Questions of how churches whose origins lie in Western missions should respond to newly defined or newly enhanced national identity in the non-Western world have not, of course, been confined to the early and mid–twentieth century.

Part III of this volume grounds some of the general themes explored in parts I and II in a series of case studies of Christian responses to particular crises that occurred either in the terminal phase or in the aftermath of empire. John Stuart's study in chapter 9 of missionary responses to nationalist politics in central Africa in the years following the Second World War highlights the danger of generalizing about missionaries' political attitudes. Stuart's conclusion, which coheres with Porter's arguments in chapter 4, is that the Anglo-Catholic UMCA was generally wary of any involvement with African politics, but lost its initial confidence in the plans for central African federation as the true extent of settler ambitions became clear. Scottish missionaries in Northern Rhodesia and Nyasaland found themselves driven sooner and further by the logic of their context toward support for "nationalist" political objectives. The Church Missionary Society (CMS), under the astute guidance of the leading missionary statesman Max Warren, pursued a carefully crafted tactical middle way that sought to keep lines of communication open with Africans, settlers, and colonial officials alike. The CMS, probably more than any other missionary body, was a significant player in the politics of the end of empire in Anglophone Africa. Caroline Howell, in chapter 10, in a detailed study of the society's role in the crisis over the deposition of the Kabaka of Buganda suggests however that its contribution to the reinstatement of the Kabaka in 1955 was both more subtly qualified and rather more limited in its effect than earlier accounts have implied. Where the influence of the Anglican Church, and the CMS in particular, was crucial, was in the brokering of the Ugandan constitutional settlement of 1954, which for the first time in the colonial history of eastern and central Africa laid the foundations of a primarily African state. The further significance of this episode lies in its illumination of the problematic ambiguities of the term "nationalism" when applied to anticolonial politics in Africa. Bugandan nationalism was a traditionalist and frequently divisive force within Ugandan politics. Although the CMS had played a unique part in the modern history of Buganda, it could not permit itself to be identified with Bugandan interests to the exclusion of those of the other peoples of Uganda with whom it was also associated. As Adrian Hastings has pointed out, what much Western liberal opinion of the day disparaged as "tribalism" or "separatism" should properly be denominated nationalism, while much of what has traditionally been labeled "nationalism" bore little relation to any real political or ethnic community.[6]

Most of the chapters in this book deal with the role of Christian missions in either contributing or responding to episodes in the history of the end of empire. Chapter 11 is concerned by contrast with the contribution of one particular "missionary" organization — Moral Re-Armament (MRA) — toward the amelioration of some of the human tensions endemic in the processes of decolonization in Africa. While MRA was not a mission society nor even exclusively Christian, it was rooted in an evangelical tradition and in the 1950s and 1960s propagated in Africa a missionary message of repentance and reconciliation between black and white that was heavily dependent on Christian theological motifs and vocabulary. Philip Boobbyer's account illuminates the particular importance of plays, musicals, and films in spreading the gospel of interracial forgiveness. In certain contexts, notably Morocco, Tunisia, and Zimbabwe, the political impact of the MRA message appears to have been quite significant.

The end of empire confronted leaders of missionary organizations with the policy challenges thrown up by a radically transformed political context. But it is important to remember that those organizations were made up of individual women and men, many of them people of no great political sophistication. For some the direction and sheer pace of change were bewildering, as Barbara Kingsolver's novel *The Poisonwood Bible*, depicting the impact on an American Baptist family of the turbulent transition to independence in the Belgian Congo, has graphically, if rather unreliably, illustrated.[7] Hartmut Lehmann's exploration in chapter 2 of the vocational pathways taken by German missionaries after the abrupt termination of their new missionary careers brought about by the First World War suggests that similarly illuminating investigations could be undertaken of the routes taken by former China missionaries after the exodus of 1949-52, or by former India missionaries following the gradual closing of the door to expatriate missionaries by the Indian government after November 1966.[8] For missionaries in Africa the end of

6. Hastings, p. 162.

7. Barbara Kingsolver, *The Poisonwood Bible* (New York, 1998). For a review pointing out some of the historical inauthenticities in the novel, see *International Bulletin of Missionary Research* 24, no. 3 (July 2000): 138.

8. A suggestive outline of such research for former British missionaries in China is to be found in George Hood, *Neither Bang nor Whimper: The End of a Missionary Era in China* (Singapore, 1991), pp. 142-57. For a brief study of how the changing political context in India affected one British missionary society, see Brian Stanley, *The History of the Baptist Missionary Society, 1792-1992* (Edinburgh, 1992), pp. 422-27.

colonialism did not usually imply a termination of their careers on the continent. For a few, independent Africa brought a stimulus and freedom of opportunity they had not known under white rule. In chapter 12 Deborah Gaitskell presents a case study of one such woman, Hannah Stanton. Stanton's experience encompassed both Anglican mission work with the black urban church in Pretoria from 1956 to 1960, culminating in her imprisonment under the State of Emergency, and work of a very different kind with university women in independent Uganda from 1962 to 1970. In this latter role, as warden of the women's residence at Makerere University, she was not formally part of the missionary community, although undoubtedly still conceiving her vocation of educational empowerment as one of Christian service within Africa. Gaitskell suggests, however, that those who remained in Kampala working with the Ugandan church as official "missionaries" may have been slower to adjust to service under African leadership. Even Stanton herself, a dangerous liberal from the perspective of the South African regime, found elements of paternalism in her own responses to the working environment of an African university in which power no longer lay in white hands.

The coming of political independence thus did not imply an automatic end to the subservience of African churches to missionary control. Ogbu Kalu's study of Nigeria in the years 1967-75 in the final chapter of this volume powerfully makes the point that, in the ecclesiastical sphere, "decolonization" has often followed a different and more protracted timetable from that which applied in the sphere of constitutional law and politics. The agents of such decolonization of church life have not always been predictable. Kalu identifies a group of high school and university students of Nigeria as an example of those who "sabotaged" missionary attempts to retain control of the postcolonial African church, but they did so through a charismatic search for powerful religiosity that drew heavily on American cultural patterns. Those who, from one perspective, were prey to the globalizing power of American religion of which Adrian Hastings warns at the end of his chapter, were, from another perspective, key figures in the liberation of Nigerian Protestantism to be authentically African.

John Darwin has recently protested against the tendency of historians for whom the concept of informal empire is now a truism to persist in defining decolonization in narrow terms as the end of formal territorial rule.[9] The title of this volume refers to the end of empire, but it should not be taken to imply that the notion of a conclusion to imperialism, either as a structure of West-

9. John Darwin, "Diplomacy and Decolonization," *Journal of Imperial and Commonwealth History* 28, no. 3 (Sept. 2000): 6.

ern dominance or as a more general phenomenon, is beyond contestation. In Asia the beginning of the end of empire should be dated as early as the 1920s; in Africa the timetable was later; in the Pacific decolonization did not gather momentum until the 1970s. But in none of these cases ought the assumption that we have seen the end of the end of empire be accepted uncritically. Thus Ogbu Kalu properly insists that "decolonization did not imply a radical change of socioeconomic structure. . . . The goal of decolonization was to return to informal empire where former rulers would retain sufficient economic and technological resources to exercise powerful influence upon future development."[10] The advantage of informal empire for those who exercise it is that it is both economically more advantageous and politically far more difficult to assail. During the era of formal empire, Christian missions occupied a privileged position from which to challenge the conduct of empire from the standpoint of Christian humanitarian principle. In the present, supposedly "postcolonial" and globalized age, the poor in the nations of the Southern hemisphere are at least as vulnerable, if not more so, to the impact of economic forces beyond their control as they were during the era of formal rule by the Western powers. In such a context the churches and their mission bodies are arguably finding it more, not less, difficult to exercise the prophetic role that is integral to their Christian missionary vocation.

10. See below, p. 259.

"Context and Conversion"

Lesslie Newbigin

sodality

[illegible]

PART I

Missionary Traditions, National Loyalties, and the Universal Gospel

CHAPTER 1

The Clash of Nationalism and Universalism within Twentieth-Century Missionary Christianity

ADRIAN HASTINGS

In 1919 Pope Benedict XV published the first of the missionary encyclicals of the twentieth century, *Maximum Illud.* One of its most striking features was its denunciation of missionary nationalism. Taking as his text Psalm 45, verse 10, "Forget thy people and thy father's house," he declared that it "would be deplorable" if missionaries were to be "so forgetful of their dignity that they should think rather of their earthly country than that of the heavenly, being unduly desirous to widen its influence and to extend its glory above all else." He continued:

> Should [a missionary] in any way follow worldly considerations and not conduct himself altogether as an apostolic man, but should seem to be engaged in doing the business of his own country, at once his whole work is suspected by the multitude; and the people may easily be led to conclude that the Christian religion is the religion peculiar to some foreign nation, and that any one who embraces it is to be considered as having put himself under the protection and the orders of some foreign state, and to have renounced the citizenship of his own.
>
> We have been greatly grieved by certain publications on the subject of Missions, which have appeared in the last few years, in which less desire is apparent for the increase of the Kingdom of God than for the influence of the writer's own country; and we are amazed that these authors seem not to care how much these views alienate the minds of the heathen.[1]

1. Benedict XV, *The Missions* [*Maximum Illud*], *Apostolic Letter . . . to . . . the Patriarchs, Primates, Archbishops, and Bishops of the Catholic World on the Propagation of*

Benedict is likely to have had Portuguese, Belgian, but most of all French missionaries principally in mind. Spanish missionary nationalism had largely ceased with the loss of Spain's American territories in the opening years of the nineteenth century, but the Portuguese *Padroado* remained a thorn in the side of Rome, of Propaganda Fide in particular, all the more so because it was by papal authority that the *Padroado* had initially been instituted. Indeed, until the time of Benedict XV Rome appeared to worry very little about the close political links between Catholic missionaries and their home country, so striking in not only the Portuguese but also the French case. What distressed Rome in the Portuguese case was not the link but the ineffectualness of the work achieved. Moreover, as there were extremely few Portuguese missionaries and Portuguese governments were perennially anticlerical, Portuguese missionary nationalism offered almost no advantages to offset its preoccupation that the churches in its overseas territories should remain committed above all to an exercise in "Portugalization." Even the diocese of Bombay, which had for centuries been ceded to Britain, was torn apart by an ongoing battle between supporters of the *Padroado,* dependent on the patriarch of Goa, and supporters of Propaganda. This remained the case throughout the first decades of the twentieth century.[2] In 1933 Dr. Salazar's Colonial Act continued to describe Portuguese missions as "Instruments of national civilization and influence." While from Rome's point of view one of the chief gains of the 1940 Concordat and Missionary Agreement would be to allow non-Portuguese missionaries to work in Portuguese territories, this was only contrived through acceptance of the integration of missionary activities into the colonial state structures. Moreover, the Missionary Statute of 1941 made it absolutely clear that all the bishops must be Portuguese, that "in principle missionary staff shall be of Portuguese nationality," and that, when foreign missionaries were allowed in, it was only as "part of the missions of the Portuguese missionary organization."[3]

The French case was rather different, as France provided a very high proportion of the total Catholic missionary force. French governments too had frequently been anticlerical, although for the most part, in the nineteenth century, they abided by Gambetta's famous words that "anticlericalism is not for export." That adage was thrown into question with the new anticlerical campaign of the Waldeck-Rousseau government after 1899, which led to the

---

the Catholic Faith throughout the World, trans. Catholic Truth Society (London, 1936), pp. 12-13. In the Vulgate, the text is in v. 11.

2. See the account in David Abner Hurn, *Archbishop Roberts, SJ* (London, 1966).

3. Adrian Hastings, *Wiriyamu* (London, 1974), app. I, pp. 137-53.

formal dissolution of the bond between church and state in 1905. Antoine Klobukowski, governor-general of French Indo-China from 1908 to 1910, declared before leaving France that "clericalism is not for export," but on arrival in Tonkin he still assured Bishop Gendreau that "anticlericalism is not for export."[4] Whatever the sentiment in Paris, the reality remained that missionaries were too useful to be flung overboard, and at home the French Foreign Ministry, the Quai d'Orsay, felt the same. Thus the determination of the French state to maintain its position as protector of the Christian missions in China and to prevent any direct relationship between the government of China and the Vatican remained unchanged. When in 1918 Benedict XV actually appointed a nuncio to China, the French minister in Peking (Beijing) succeeded in having the plan quashed. The yearbook of the Missions catholiques de Chine et du Japon for 1919 included a statement by Fr. Planchet of the French case including the claim that "the protectorate over the Catholics depended not on the pope but on a clause in the treaty of 1858" (the Treaty of Tientsin). Planchet's piece may well have been one of the recent mission accounts referred to in *Maximum Illud.* Missionary nationalism was quite as much a characteristic of French missionaries themselves as of the French government. "Pour Dieu, pour la France," the characteristic motivation of Mgr. Augouard, the pioneer Holy Ghost Father on the Congo, remained that of numerous French missionaries in the era of the "scramble" and long after. You can count on it, declared Augouard to the local French officer, that if you withdraw I will keep the flag of France flying here. It is ironic that in due course the Congo was handed over to King Leopold, who insisted on the withdrawal of the French Holy Ghost Fathers and their replacement by Belgian Jesuits. But French missionary nationalism had been ubiquitous. Missionaries in Saigon, declared its bishop, Mgr. Mossard, in 1908, "only have one desire: to serve the influence and interests of France to the best of their ability."[5] In 1902 the Jesuit J. B. Piolet published a massive survey "in collaboration with all the Missionary Societies," entitled *Les Missions catholiques françaises au xixe siècle,* which concluded with some words of the academician Ferdinand Brunetière:

> I shall not claim that the Reverend Father Piolet was literally "inspired" when he gave to his history of *French Catholic Missions* the more general title *France Overseas,* but merely that in these two words he has summed

4. Patrick Tuck, *French Catholic Missionaries and the Politics of Imperialism in Vietnam, 1857-1914: A Documentary Survey* (Liverpool, 1987), p. 287.

5. Tuck, p. 291.

> up the situation in a nutshell. Wherever our missionaries have gone, they have indeed "planted," as we used to say, love of France alongside the faith. It was due to them that in the East and the Far East, in China for example, France long held the preponderant and privileged position which could and should be hers still, which could and will be hers again, once our government comprehends that aid and support for Catholic action overseas is a means of extending, expanding and consolidating the influence of France.[6]

Missionary nationalism could take a variety of forms. By the 1920s the age of annexations was over and that of what one may call a League of Nations–led benevolence was just beginning, if rather ineffectually. It was, anyway, a mood that penetrated some Catholic missionary societies fairly slowly. One form missionary nationalism now took, a form always troublesome for Rome, was the anxiety to retain a given "field" for one's own country and religious order. This was a particularly French disease: French missionaries had an almost complete monopoly of work in the vast areas of French West Africa, as also in Indo-China, as well as being the dominant group in China. Nevertheless, they bitterly resented being forced to hand over mission areas here and there in China to Americans of various orders, pressed into going there often unwillingly by the Vatican. While theoretically the Catholic missionary army was a highly international one, this seldom was true on the ground. Even totally international orders, such as the Jesuits or Dominicans, were firmly divided at home into national provinces, and it was a province, rather than a society as a whole, which had responsibility for, and manned, a particular mission. While the White Fathers were unusual in refusing to divide their work in this way, in practice even they were forced by colonial governments to do so quite considerably. Thus only Belgian White Fathers were sent to the Belgian Congo, almost only French ones to French West Africa. Of the colonial powers, Britain alone was generally happy to accept missionaries of any nation into its colonies, even at episcopal level: the mixed religious condition of Britain itself, the sheer size of its empire, the strength of liberal opinion at home to criticize apparent discrimination, but above all a prudent realization that the cause of empire could best be served by religious neutrality had all helped bring this about. Hence "Protestant" Britain was actually Rome's best, because most accommodating, partner.

Perhaps the most pervasive and damaging form of missionary national-

6. Jean Bruls, "From Missions to 'Young Churches,'" in *The Church in a Secularised Society,* ed. Roger Aubert (London, 1978), p. 412.

ism in the post–World War I period, however, was its ingrained hostility to any local sentiment of nationalism or to the promotion of indigenous priests to positions of authority. It had become in fact an "antinationalism," manifested very notably in suspicion of the indigenous clergy. This was for long more noticeable in Asia than in Africa because there were both more indigenous nationalism in the former and also a much more numerous local clergy. It was, moreover, a nationalism (if we may still call it so) shared, with few exceptions, by missionaries of almost all national backgrounds, involving an often aggressive shared contempt for the non-European. It could even pervade the lives of people who had given themselves entirely to serving the non-European world, but in their own terms, not those of the locals. Thus a young American Maryknoller, newly arrived in China in 1918, learned the word for "thanks" in Chinese and "proudly sprung it on the Chink who brought my laundry." He was at once corrected by one of the French Fathers with the words "We never say that to the Chinese, it is only for equals."[7] The dominant attitude of British missionaries in India was very similar. In China missionaries, whether French, British, German, or American, were caught within the nefarious network of the unequal treaties providing sources of information for their consulates, an excuse for sending in gunboats and marines to provide protection, and demands for reparations when their property was damaged.

By the 1920s none of this was working. China was in chaos, swept by an increasingly bitter antiforeign nationalism. While Rome objected to missionaries applying to their home governments to pursue reparation cases and wanted them to remain at their stations in unsettled circumstances, their national consuls continued to insist on the opposite. The missionaries themselves often preferred the consular line. When in 1924 at an American Passionist mission in Hunan the American flag was fired on, the father in charge wrote to his consul that if reparations were not made, "America and Americans will not have the respect of even the local Chinese."[8] When in 1929 some missions staffed by Chinese clergy were damaged in the American Vincentian Vicariate of Genzhou and the local authorities argued that "no residence of the foreign missionaries had been burned," its bishop, Mgr. O'Shea, retorted that everything in the mission was "foreign property," regardless of who was using it. "It is only *per accidens* that native clergymen happened to be conducting those missions at the time they were burned.

7. Thomas A. Breslin, *China, American Catholicism, and the Missionary* (University Park, Pa., and London, 1980), p. 45.

8. Breslin, p. 48.

They are, and will remain, foreign property."[9] "The best that can be expected from the natives is that they do not cause trouble," wrote the American Mgr. Misner of his Chinese priests in 1938.[10] In missionary terms these were all devoted, selfless men furthering the kingdom of God. That the entire missionary movement had engendered a profound antiforeignism both in Chinese society generally and among the Chinese clergy merely demonstrated in missionary eyes how perverse the Chinese were, how unworthy to take control of their own church.

The papal appointment of the first six Chinese bishops in 1926 and fourteen more in the following seven years was done in the teeth of missionary opposition. Similarly when, twelve years later, Rome was moving to appoint the first African bishop in Uganda, the first anywhere in black Africa, local missionaries attempted to stop it with every possible argument: "In all the Buddu missions entrusted to African clergy," they reported in 1938, "we have observed an evil spirit. Priests manifest nationalism. They want to be on their own, manage their own affairs and be free from the control of whites."[11]

What one sees in the 1920s and 1930s, all across the missionary field from China to Uganda, is a continuing clash between two nationalisms. On one side was that of the white missionaries (a diverse mix of Northern hemisphere nationalisms, increasingly fused together as white racialism), on the other that of the non-Europeans themselves, and particularly of those most influenced by Christianity, a nationalism with deep historical roots and rapidly growing in the intensity of its expression. Between the two, in the Catholic Church, stood Rome. The Congregation of Propaganda Fide had never cared for any form of nationalism that went with missionary independence from Roman control. In this period Propaganda was renewed in vigor under the leadership of the Dutch Cardinal Van Rossum, appointed prefect by Benedict in 1918 and sometimes described as Propaganda's second founder. It was during Van Rossum's fourteen-year tenure that Rome's missionary policy was vigorously renewed in almost all its aspects. *Maximum Illud* represented an assertion of Van Rossum's priorities. Nationalism was recognized as a threat to the whole Catholic missionary endeavor, and as its most powerful form was now French, it is unsurprising that Van Rossum was perceived as hostile to France. Nevertheless, the French state's anticlerical campaign did in fact do much to transform the French missionary mind, particularly perhaps in a firmly French-controlled area like the interior of West Africa, freeing it from a

9. Breslin, pp. 62-63.

10. Breslin, p. 95.

11. John Waliggo, *A History of African Priests* (Katigondo, Uganda, 1988), p. 134.

sense of close alliance with the colonial state.[12] The impact of nationalism, for Van Rossum, was to be overcome by hastening the education of a local clergy and its advancement to the episcopate, a development singularly uncongenial to most missionaries. For the latter it was inopportune. Only a very rare missionary, such as Mgr. Henri Streicher in Uganda, who had prepared the way for an African-led diocese in Uganda, or the Belgian Vincent Lebbe in China, was able to see things differently. Lebbe in particular, one of the few great missionary visionaries of the twentieth-century church, saw to the heart of the matter. Already in 1908 he set out to a friend his "personal vision of breaking with the past as quickly as possible and turning our Christians into Chinese Christians with a *totally* indigenous priesthood," and in 1917 he wrote to his bishop that "The time has come to found a living, fertile, national Church, to be the leaven in the lump, flesh of the people's flesh, blood of the people's blood, sanctified in Christo, the only Church with a hope of survival."[13] Sent back to Europe on account of his outspoken views, he was called by Van Rossum for consultation. Fortunately for once, Rome listened to a visionary. When the appointment of a nuncio in Beijing was thwarted, Rome appointed instead its first apostolic delegate, Celso Costantini, who would share Lebbe's ideas and develop an official missionary strategy to escape nationalist entrapment, though in the eyes of most missionaries it constituted rather a sellout to the new nationalism of the non-European world.

The Protestant struggle to escape that entrapment was little easier. Indeed, the absence of any central authoritative body comparable to a Roman Congregation might have made it, in theory, a great deal harder. Almost every nineteenth-century Protestant missionary body had a strongly national character and base. If the Church Missionary Society's early recruitment of Germans was a remarkable exception, representing what Paul Jenkins has called "the Protestant internationalism"[14] of the early nineteenth century, it did not last beyond 1860. Apart from American-British faith missions, Protestant missionary activity at the beginning of the twentieth century was as intensely national as it was denominational. Nevertheless, the World Missionary Conference of Edinburgh in 1910 had set the scene for change, less in what it said than in the construction, through its Continuation Committee, of a new sort of international leadership, something at that time well-nigh unique in the

12. Joseph-Roger Benoist, *Église et pouvoir coloniale au Soudan Français* (Paris, 1987).

13. Bruls, pp. 397-98.

14. Paul Jenkins, "The Church Missionary Society and the Basel Mission: An Early Experiment in Inter-European Cooperation," in *The Church Mission Society and World Christianity, 1799-1999*, ed. Kevin Ward and Brian Stanley (Grand Rapids and Richmond, Surrey, U.K., 2000), pp. 43-65.

Protestant world. Its leadership consisted initially of Joe Oldham and John Mott, whom William Paton later joined. They largely controlled the International Missionary Council (IMC) when it came into existence in 1921, and further engineered the establishment of two immensely significant bodies, in relation to our theme, the National Christian Council of India in 1922 and that of China in 1923. Paton became the principal secretary of the former before returning to London to assist and then succeed Oldham as secretary of the IMC, but it was the high proportion of Chinese and Indian members of those councils that mattered most. Missionary dominance was at last being broken. Oldham, always prescient in the articulation of new challenges, wrote an important article, "Nationality and Mission," in 1920 for the *International Review of Missions,* which he had founded the year after Edinburgh and continued to edit. In consequence of these efforts, Protestantism by the 1920s had a central guiding body reshaping missionary strategy not too unlike Propaganda Fide and its policies on the Catholic side.

Yet during the First World War the maintenance of a spirit of internationalism within the missionary world had seemed next to impossible. Even Mott, symbol of missionary internationality and chairman of Edinburgh's Continuation Committee, had been persuaded, after America entered the war, to take part in a mission to Russia whose aim was to persuade the provisional government to continue the struggle against Germany. In Petrograd he even addressed a congress of Cossack officers supporting a new offensive. Oldham had enthusiastically supported Mott's membership of the mission. It is hard to understand how either of them could have imagined this to be consonant with the cause to which they had engaged their lives, and the German bitterness it produced was profound. The expulsion of German missionaries from what had hitherto been German colonies, and indeed, from other territories such as India, resulted in the claim in German mission circles that the Anglo-Americans, who dominated the Continuation Committee and then the IMC, were far from committed to "the supranational character of the Church of Christ"[15] because they had made no protest at the expulsions. While Oldham replied that he regretted what had happened, he regarded it as inevitable in the circumstances. "Supranationality," to which both sides appealed, became a bone of contention. Given the immense contribution Germany had made to Protestant mission worldwide, the removal of its missionaries from India, Africa, and elsewhere appeared a major disaster for world Protestantism. Furthermore, it stimulated a bitterness in German missionary circles not easily

15. Keith Clements, *Faith on the Frontier: A Life of J. H. Oldham* (Edinburgh, 1999), p. 144.

assuaged when, after the war, German missionaries were not permitted to return to work for a number of years.

Through most of the nineteenth century, while the British missionary world had shared enthusiastically enough in the advantages provided by the British Empire,[16] German missionary thought (with no German empire in existence) had enjoyed a natural sense of "supranationality." This greatly altered with the emergence of the Bismarckian empire and Wilhelmine nationalism. Moreover, the shift had a theological building block of sorts, which was lacking on the British side, in the long-standing German Protestant preoccupation with *Volk* and the *Volkskirche.* This was carried across into mission theory through the teaching of the leading German missiologist, Gustav Warneck, and implemented in the field by missionaries such as Bruno Gutmann in Tanganyika and Christian Keysser in New Guinea.[17] There was nothing Nazi or even German nationalist in such approaches; nevertheless, it is clear how easily such *volkisch* lines of thought could cohabit with a resurgent German nationalism in the interwar period, and Keysser, it seems, was one of the many who welcomed the advent of National Socialism. While by the 1930s British missionary theorists were becoming increasingly ecumenical and antinationalist, German theorists such as Walter Freytag, Martin Schlunk, and Diedrich Westermann were moving in the opposite direction in an attempt to develop a theory of Christian mission that could somehow fit within the dream of a German National Socialist colony. As early as 1932 Freytag defined the role of German mission as providing the core of opposition to the "victory of international culture and Bolshevism," and even in 1940 he could insist that while "we make no secret of the fact that we see differences in the value of the races, yet we emphasize that each race has its own purpose and its own value in the entirety of mankind."[18] Given Nazi treatment of Jews, gypsies, and others at that time, it is hard to include such racialist views within a history of missionary thought, but Freytag was both then, and in the postwar world, a highly influential figure particularly within World Council of Churches circles. His colleague Westermann had also been a close friend and ally of Oldham whom one might single out as principal proponent of the new missionary internationalism. An adequate intellectual

16. Brian Stanley, *The Bible and the Flag: Protestant Missions and British Imperialism in the Nineteenth and Twentieth Centuries* (Leicester, 1990).

17. Timothy Yates, *Christian Mission in the Twentieth Century* (Cambridge, 1994), pp. 34-56.

18. Werner Ustorf, "'Survival of the Fittest': German Protestant Missions, Nazism and Neocolonialism, 1933-1945," *Journal of Religion in Africa* 28, no. 1 (1998): 97; Ustorf, *Sailing on the Next Tide: Missions, Missiology, and the Third Reich* (Frankfurt am Main, 2000).

history of the twentieth-century missionary movement, comprising its many eddies and unexpected relationships, remains to be written.

While the entire history of Germany from Bismarck to Hitler exacerbated the theological and missionary nationalism inherent in belief in the providential role of German *volkisch* Protestantism, developments in Britain, whose colonies were never threatened until Japan struck in 1941, helped keep her missionary nationalism covert enough, yet it had plainly existed in the era of the "scramble," and it survived, especially in the Anglican sphere, with the pursuit of what Max Warren called a "quasi-establishment."[19] One must remember that even in 1950 there was not a single black Anglican diocesan bishop in Africa. It is noteworthy too that insofar as Anglican mission theory progressed beyond an "ecclesiastical expansion of England" view of things (to quote the title of a late Victorian study),[20] it was still viewed, notably by Henry Venn, in essentially national terms. There was to be an "accession of national churches" reflecting "national peculiarities" and making a "national profession of faith," to quote from a paper of Venn, "On Nationality," presented as early as 1868.[21] Doubtless for Venn "national" meant little more than local or native, but it reflected an ecclesiology that could hardly think except in terms of a "national church." Anglican missionary nationalism was fortified by conviction of the providential role of the British Empire for the worldwide spread of Christianity, but it came to be fiercely challenged precisely by some of the most sensitive Anglican missionaries of the twentieth century, notably C. F. Andrews and Arthur Shearly Cripps. While Oldham represented in principle the quintessence of Christian "supranationality," in practice he distrusted such extremists. Andrews was in his way the Lebbe of India who, already in 1906, declared in a public lecture in Lahore "how wholeheartedly as a Christian missionary and an Englishman I sympathise with the higher aspirations of Indian nationalism today."[22] He became the closest of friends of Gandhi and Tagore. Oldham, on the other hand, preferred to work hand in glove with the British Colonial Office. Perhaps his approach was not so dissimilar from the desperate efforts of Westermann and Freytag to provide some input into a National Socialist colonial policy. The implementation of supranationality remained conditioned by the practicalities of an imperialist and white-dominated world for Oldham, but not for Andrews.

19. Max Warren, *Social History and Christian Mission* (London, 1967), chap. 1, "Church and State in the British Colonial Empire from Palmerston to Macmillan."

20. Cf. Ward and Stanley, p. 346.

21. Ward and Stanley, pp. 164-65.

22. Constance M. Millington, *Whether We Be Many or Few: A History of the Cambridge Delhi Brotherhood* (Bangalore, 1999), p. 97.

If the Nazis themselves never had the opportunity to put into practice their colonial dreams, the implementation of some of them was attempted in South Africa in the heyday of apartheid, after the victory of the Nationalist Party in 1948, particularly by its principal ideologue Hendrik Verwoerd, the son of a missionary and deeply influenced by Nazi ideas. "The struggle for racial purity," as he formulated, it represented well enough what Nazi colonial policy might have been like with one difference — the claim to be Christian. Apartheid, Verwoerd believed — and the Dutch Reformed Churches in the main shared in his belief — was designed to defend "everything which has been built up since the days of Christ . . . for the salvation of mankind."[23] Afrikaner nationalism provided an almost classic case of the processes I attempted to describe in *The Construction of Nationhood* (1997). The impact of the Old Testament was continuous at the level of image making, a migration was central to its own mythology, while the defensive nature of the trek, an escape from British imperialism, led rapidly to the offensiveness of subduing black Africans into a permanently servile class. The latter's separation was justified in terms of biblical accounts both of Babel and of the treatment of Canaan. *Volk* and *Kerk* were almost identified, together constituting South Africa's chosen race, destined to inherit its land. What most effectively constructed this new nation, however, was the development of Afrikaans as a separate literary language. Afrikaner nationalism, like Ulster's Unionist nationalism and Serbia's Orthodox nationalism, demonstrates that white European nationalism of a classical sort could still flourish in the later twentieth century, though all three would be in a state of crisis or collapse by its close.

At the same time that a late wave of nationalist missionary thinking was breaking the surface in German Protestant circles, a less sophisticated, more popularist, and — temporarily — effective outbreak was affecting Italian Catholicism, delighted, as it was, with Mussolini's conquest of Ethiopia. Nationalism was a very widespread characteristic of Catholic life in the interwar years in Spain, France, and Latin America. Hitherto Italian missionaries had remained largely free of the nationalist "virus," but in the 1930s both they and Vatican policy became deeply contaminated by fascism. Unfortunately the papacy of Pius XI and, later, Pius XII remained bewitched by the attractions of a privileged ecclesiastical status, theoretically guaranteed by concordat, even when concluded with the most nationalist and unreliable of regimes. Concordats with Italy, Germany, and Portugal were seen as a way of protect-

23. Wolfram Kistner, "The Sixteenth of December in the Context of Nationalistic Thinking," in *Church and Nationalism in South Africa,* ed. T. Sundermeier (Johannesburg, 1975), pp. 85-86.

ing and extending the pastoral and missionary work of the institutional church. After the successful conclusion of an extraordinarily barbaric campaign in Ethiopia and the execution of the head of its Orthodox church, all non-Italian missionaries were expelled, including the aged French bishop Jarousseau, who had worked there for forty years and was much loved by its people. It is deeply regrettable that the Vatican immediately acquiesced in this, agreeing in 1937 to reserve Ethiopia to Italian missionaries and even recognizing the king of Italy as emperor of Ethiopia. The Ethiopian war had been enthusiastically supported by numerous Italian bishops, notably Cardinal Schuster of Milan. Here was almost the last, as well as one of the worst, expressions of Catholic missionary nationalism. Doubtless Pius XI did not really like it, and that summer of 1937, addressing the students of the College of Propaganda Fide at Castel Gandolfo, he lamented that nationalism "is a veritable curse of sterility." Yet he and the church of Italy had in fact just encouraged, or at the very least unprotestingly acquiesced in, a particularly nasty expression of the "exaggerated nationalism" he condemned when speaking to the students of the Catholic Church's principal international missionary college. In the words of J. Bruls, it was "one of the most flagrant examples of damaging compromise. Many Italian bishops openly supported the venture and the pope did nothing to restrain them. The demeanour of the Vatican suggested on the contrary that there was great rejoicing at the opportunities the Fascist conquest opened up for Catholicism."[24] Yet Pius XI is hailed as, par excellence, the "missionary pope."

The defeat of Nazism and Fascism in the Second World War brought with it a profound reevaluation of nationalism in Europe both by society in general and by the churches. A repudiation of the historic nationalist legacy, closely linked with that of the Reformation, can be seen in the 1937 Oxford Conference entitled "Church, Community, and State," so carefully planned by Oldham, at which the formation of the World Council of Churches (WCC) was agreed upon. But it was in the WCC itself, from its first conference at Amsterdam in 1948 onward, that the shift away from a nationalist to a Catholic or universalist reference can be seen most clearly. Most post–World War II missionary work flows out, in consequence, from a vision of the church and Christianity extraordinarily different from that of previous generations. It is true that it would be mistaken to discern any fundamental alteration in Rome at this time, at least in Propaganda Fide. The policies of Rome, however, had long been divided between, on the one hand, those traditional to Propaganda, deeply opposed to the effects of European nationalisms, and, on the other,

24. Bruls, p. 415.

those of the Secretariat of State whose preoccupations were more juridical and amenable to doing a deal with any currently powerful nationalist regime. Yet such a contrast must not be overplayed. Van Rossum was himself the closest of collaborators with Pius XI's secretary of state, Cardinal Gasparri. Undoubtedly Pius XII was a quintessential representative of the Secretariat of State, the man who had personally negotiated the concordat with Hitler and then, as pope, effectively ratified Portuguese missionary nationalism with the concordat of 1940. If, after the Second World War, his always excruciatingly careful affirmations distanced the church somewhat from its long compromise with European colonial nationalism, a more wholehearted endorsement of the postcolonial age would only come with John XXIII. But even in Catholic missionary circles the mind-set had changed profoundly. Propaganda Fide itself had Costantini as its secretary from 1935. He was the true heir of Van Rossum with a personal experience greatly enriched by his years in China, while in France, Belgium, and elsewhere missiology grew more alive than it had been for generations. The Semaines Missiologiques, held annually in Louvain from 1925 under the guidance of the Jesuit Pierre Charles, provided one focal point. Another was the circle of Lebbe's followers who formed the Societé des Auxiliaires des Missions (SAM) and founded after the war a dynamic new missionary journal, *Eglise Vivante.* The nationalism that had so dominated Catholic missionary attitudes was appearing at last both archaic and highly reprehensible.

At the same time, the victory of nationalism across Asia and its rapid rise in significance and vehemence in Africa raised a new series of questions. Disillusioned as missionaries might be, for good reasons and bad, with the European nationalisms of the past, they could still find it hard to stomach the claims of non-European nationalisms — again for bad reasons and good. Many continued to affirm that the time was simply not ripe for any general transfer of authority to nonwhite bishops: by and large the Asian and African clergy was still not mature enough, it was claimed, to be trusted. The establishment of a Chinese hierarchy and creation of a first Chinese cardinal, Archbishop Tien of Peking (Beijing), in 1946 delighted local clergy but, mild-mannered as Tien was, dismayed many missionaries. If nationalism was after all to be recognized as a bad thing in Europe, how could it be a good thing anywhere else? The few clerical enthusiasts who welcomed what was happening unreservedly were thus put into something of a theological quandary.

An article written in 1946, only a year after the war ended, by Pierre Jean de Menasce, the Dominican professor of missiology at the University of Fribourg, represents one of the earliest but also finest expressions of the new thinking. It appeared in the *Neue Zeitschrift für Missionswissenschaft,* a journal he had recently helped found, and it was appropriate that it was published in Switzerland, a country with no nationalist axe to grind and, in consequence, a usefully disinterested tradition of missionary activity. De Menasce himself, as a converted Alexandrian Jew with a profound knowledge of east Mediterranean and Iranian culture, could face the issues with a breadth of vision and serenity available to few. He focused his whole discussion on the simultaneous existence in both Israel and the church of a supernatural universalism and a supernatural particularism together with an analogy of each in the natural order. Contrasting those who saw "the reawakening of the nations of Asia and Africa as the prelude to a general apostasy in missionary countries" with those who wanted Christians to take the lead in every national reawakening, he admitted that "there is a great deal of talk about nationalism which suggests that the very exaggerations which, after causing so much damage, have come to be condemned in Europe are transformed into quasi-virtues when they appear in missionary countries and are practised by Asiatics and Africans." The real challenge, he insisted, all the same, is not to attack or ridicule the extent to which Afro-Asian movements actually imitate European ways even when denouncing them, but is instead "to help them to escape that hypertrophied patriotism which we call nationalism, and which is no more to be encouraged when it is Chinese or Indonesian than when it is French or German." Instead of merely humoring the particularist sentiment of young churches, he suggested that the time might already be ripe to encourage them to become missionaries to their neighbors, yet in ways that avoided the cultural imperialism to which European missionaries had so largely succumbed.[25]

Every year in Rome in the early 1950s a *giornata missionaria* was held at which many hundreds of ecclesiastical students gathered to study some major current topic. In February 1955 the topic chosen was nationalism, and I was invited to give the principal address on nationalism in Africa. I was at the time a student in theology at the College of Propaganda Fide and had the previous year both written a pamphlet entitled *White Domination or Racial Peace?* which Michael Scott and Mary Benson at the Africa Bureau had published, and become involved in a controversy over Goa with representatives of the Portuguese government. Scott was one of the Anglican mavericks who did so much in those years to rewrite the relationships between the churches and

25. Pierre de Menasce, "Nationalisme en pays de mission," *Neue Zeitschrift für Missionswissenschaft* 3, no. 1 (1947), trans. into English as "Nationalism in Missionary Countries," *Worldmission* 5 (1954): 267-78; see Adrian Hastings, "The Legacy of Pierre Jean de Menasce," *International Bulletin of Missionary Research* 21, no. 4 (1999): 168-72.

the movement for African political advancement. Banned from South Africa in 1950, he was trusted and loved by African leaders not only there but in Botswana and Namibia. In 1954 the Africa Bureau was just getting into its stride, and they were delighted to publish a contribution from a Catholic. My little pamphlet thus provided a sort of preface for a much longer exercise in African missionary rethinking involving such works as Trevor Huddleston's *Naught for Your Comfort* (1956), John V. Taylor's *Christianity and Politics in Africa* (1957), and Scott's own *A Time to Speak* (1958).

The Goan affair was more intriguing. There had been a good deal of whipping up of support for Portugal's retention of Goa in the British Catholic papers, and after discussing the issue with some Goan students in the college, I had written to the *Catholic Herald*[26] protesting that this was not a religious issue and much that was said on behalf of the Portuguese position was simply untrue. The address on my letter was the College of Propaganda Fide. This produced a furious reaction in Portugal, including a quite remarkable attack on the Congregation of Propaganda delivered by Salazar when opening parliament that autumn. Propaganda Fide correctly denied all responsibility for my letters — I was not "Mgr. Hastings," a *minutante* in the Congregation as the ambassador had imagined, but a mere student in the College! Radio Delhi, on the other hand, promoted me to "Professor Hastings" at Propaganda's university and quoted me as backing the Indian cause. In December, furthermore, the *Tablet* published two articles on Goa side by side.[27] The first, entitled "The Portuguese View," was by Salazar — the relevant section of his address in parliament; the second, entitled "A Roman View," was by me. Officially I was in no way a spokesman of Propaganda Fide, but looking back on it forty-five years later, I am struck not just by the amused tolerance with which the Roman authorities viewed my activities but, still more, that I should have been invited soon after to address so public and semiofficial a gathering as the Twelfth Roman Missionary Day, a gathering graced by the presence of Archbishop Pietro Sigismondi, only recently appointed secretary of the Congregation after some years as apostolic delegate in the Belgian Congo. It represented a remarkable endorsement of the position I had taken, a position so swiftly denounced by the ruler of Portugal who, only fourteen years earlier, had signed a concordat and missionary agreement with the Vatican.

In my lecture I endeavored to cover three separate forms of nationalism in Africa: colonialist nationalism, Afrikaner nationalism, and black nationalism. I had recently read de Menasce's article and been much impressed by it, so

26. 3 Sept. 1954.
27. *Tablet*, 11 Dec. 1954, pp. 575-76.

what I said reflected and even quoted from his work. I contrasted Pius XI's 1929 assertion that "Nationalism has always been a scourge for the missions, indeed it is not exaggerated to call it a curse" with Salazar's Colonial Act and a 1954 remark of a Portuguese Holy Ghost Father summing up missionary work in Angola: "Thus Angola is in process of becoming more and more Christian and Portuguese." I asserted, correctly enough, that colonialism, especially in British Africa, was "nearly dead, though its effects survive." I remarked that nationalisms are often at war with one another and that some have a quite transitory character: "The nationalisms of today may be history tomorrow." I deplored particularly any form of nationalism that is specifically racialist while insisting that "a nationalistic spirit being largely the fruit of Europe's bad example, Europeans above all have no right to throw the first stone." I hailed the desire of all people to be ruled by men of their own land as an aspect of nationalism in modern Africa that Catholic priests have "a real duty not only to approve of, but to encourage. . . . It should never be suggested that the movement for self government is to be condemned or avoided." It is right to oppose the color bar but wrong to oppose plans for independence. At the same time, "it would be a tragedy if now when Western Europe is at long last endeavouring to transcend its nationalist divisions and return to some sort of union, Africa should insist on creating a series of antagonistic nation states." What is needed is instead the ability to transcend local and racial ties in a new internationalism reflecting "an authentic Catholicism." My lecture, together with the entire proceedings of the *giornata,* was published in a booklet by the International Secretariat of the Missionary Union of the Clergy, with the same title as my lecture.[28] It included a further *nota di conclusione* of mine, responding to various objections, but ended with an address by Sigismondi and was illustrated by two photographs of the archbishop attending the *giornata.* Fuller endorsement one could hardly have received. My lecture was then reprinted twice in Italian — in a popular magazine and a book — and once in English, in Archbishop Fulton Sheen's *Worldmission.* All of which leads me to conclude that this was not just a matter of a lively student expressing relatively radical views — views deeply disquieting for most Catholic missionaries at the time — but a quite significant, if subtle, indication of a shift of position by the Catholic Church's principal missionary authority.

28. "Il nazionalismo e la chiesa in Africa oggi," in *Il nationalismo e la chiesa in Africa oggi, Atti della XII Giornata Missionaria per gli studenti ecclesiastici degli Atenei Romani'* (Rome, 1955), pp. 22-35; reprinted in *Oltremare* (May and June 1955), and in Vittorio Dellagiacomo, ed., *Il Destino dell'Africa* (Bologna, 1956), pp. 39-53; English version, "Africa's Many Nationalisms," *Worldmission* 6, no. 3 (Fall 1955): 343-54.

The mid-1950s constitute something of a hinge moment. Europe's Asian empires had mostly disappeared; China was firmly communist and its missionaries expelled. David Paton's trenchant *Christian Missions and the Judgement of God* had been published in 1953. The foreword by K. H. Ting to its second edition describes it as "a book of prophetic vision, which came just in time for initiating a reevaluation."[29] While principally concerned with China, Paton found place to call for "a theological as well as a scientific evaluation both of British colonial policy and of African nationalism, and a critical appreciation of the relation to them both, not only of the mission . . . but of the African church."[30] I did not know until much later of Paton's book — so separate were Catholics and Protestants at that time — but, clearly, we were attempting something similar and so was Propaganda itself, at probably its most radical twentieth-century moment. Perhaps the Secretariat of State did not much approve, but there was at the time no secretary of state and the pope was old. In theory, according to official circles in London or Brussels, colonialism in Africa had still a long life before it, but those who believed this were diminishing rapidly in number. Many missionaries remained intensely alarmed by the advance of nationalist movements that they saw as communism in disguise and hoped that colonial regimes would last as long as possible. In the College of Propaganda the Indian students were slightly smug. They had their national independence and a leader of worldwide standing in Nehru but not communism. China, on the other hand, was communist, and its surviving clergy in Rome mixed their deep antimissionary sentiment with recognition that, for them, real national independence was fused with communism. The large Vietnamese group were in a still more painful situation. As bitter as they mostly felt about French missionaries and French colonial policy, their Catholic community was now embroiled in a fearful civil war with the communist Vietcong, a struggle they could only hope to sustain with French or American assistance. Everywhere the tendency remained strong to identify the nationalist as communist or anti-Christian. But there was just time "for initiating a reevaluation" for breaking out of the whole traditional missionary syndrome so as to free young churches able to live with the inevitable nationalism of the independence struggle but also able to think more than nationalistically. With the help, some years later, of John XXIII and Vatican II, we largely succeeded.

Part of my own time in my last years at Propaganda, those rather stagnant

29. David Macdonald Paton, *Christian Missions and the Judgement of God*, 2nd ed. (Grand Rapids, 1996), p. ix.

30. Paton, p. 56.

final years of the pontificate of Pius XII, was spent editing a symposium, *The Church and the Nations,* inspired by the internationality of the College, an attempt, as explained in my introduction, to show through case studies that "The Church is both universal and national. . . . No nation has a unique or primary claim to the title of Catholic."[31] I remember Sigismondi being intrigued when I explained the theme. Even he found the idea of a diversity of "national" or local churches in the plural, all sharing in the catholicity of the one church, slightly alarming. It was not a terminology they were accustomed to, he remarked tolerantly. In fact, of course, if Propaganda Fide was the enemy of missionary nationalism, its own tradition had been decidedly Roman imperialist, something that could be quite as stifling of legitimate diversity. Yet the college in my time, flourishing under the benign rectorship of Mgr. Cenci, gave a different impression. It seemed to be alive through recognition of the legitimate diversity of national traditions of Christianity and local churches, an idea that hardly received formal sanction before the final sessions of Vatican II and its insistence, as in chapter 3 of the Decree on Missionary Activity, on the nature and rights of "Particular Churches."

What none of us anticipated at that time was that the gravest nationalist threat to Christianity by the late twentieth century might come from the United States, essentially a rehash of the traditional Christian imperialism of western European countries. It is just the latest example of a self-appointed "chosen people" carrying forth a gospel message reshaped by its own values and bonded to its own political expansion. I do recall sometime in the mid-1950s overhearing a conversation between Archbishop Fulton Sheen and an African bishop. Sheen represented American Catholic nationalism at its most earnestly international. As director in the United States of the Association for the Propagation of the Faith, he brought annually to Rome sums of money without which the missionary activities supported by Propaganda Fide could quickly have collapsed. His commitment to the missionary cause was immense, but so was his belief in the American way of life as supreme expression of Christianity. The future he held out to the African bishop, a century or two ahead, to my shocked amusement, was that of becoming like America.

In one of his most perceptive remarks about the relationship between universality and particularity, Jean de Menasce pointed out that some European cultures have an almost universal character and that most missionaries come from them: "A Swiss or Belgian missionary is immune to the temptation which assails a Frenchman to impose around him an extremely French brand of universalism which he regards as simply universalism itself. Very se-

31. Adrian Hastings, ed., *The Church and the Nations* (London and New York, 1959).

vere judgements are passed, outside France, on the ways in which this instinct manifests itself; Frenchmen, in turn, can see it perfectly well, and in quite a different light, when it is German or Spanish."[32] The dual temptation of late-twentieth-century America, basking in a prosperity and imperial power beyond anything hitherto known, has been to see itself in terms of God's preferred people and to see the American brand of universalism "as simply universalism itself." This is particularly true of the conservative, fundamentalist, charismatic, and televangelist wing of American Protestant Christianity, and is much assisted by the latest universalist form of the mass media, the video, the Internet. The linkage with the American government and state policy could be illustrated at almost every level, including at the top, where in 1998 Robert Seiple, the president of World Vision, largest of America's evangelical agencies, was appointed to the State Department as principal advisor to the president and special representative to the secretary of state for international religious freedom — freedom that chiefly means for American missionaries to carry American policies, linked with the gospel, wherever they choose to go. *Exporting the American Gospel*,[33] to use the title of an influential recent account of it, is a historical phenomenon central both to the missionary history of the last half-century and to the ongoing story of nationalism and its interaction with religion. An account of that interaction that stopped short of its most potent contemporary example would do a grave injustice to its subject, but the global scale of its impact, its relationship to American capitalism and foreign policy, the demonstration that this particular form of Christianity is indeed a "made in the USA" expression of missionary nationalism would require analysis well beyond what is possible here. One has simply to insist that the story of white imperialist nationalism and its relationship to missionary Christianity is one that did not end around 1960, the "Year of Africa." It merely shifted its shape.

32. De Menasce, "Nationalism in Missionary Countries," p. 272.

33. Steve Brouwer, Paul Gifford, and Susan D. Rose, eds., *Exporting the American Gospel: Global Christian Fundamentalism* (London, 1996).

CHAPTER 2

Missionaries without Empire: German Protestant Missionary Efforts in the Interwar Period (1919-1939)

HARTMUT LEHMANN

Before addressing my topic, a few explanatory, or cautionary, remarks seem necessary. First I should like to point out that little research has been done on how German Protestants understood missionary activities after the German Reich had lost all its colonies early on in the First World War. The same is true for the history of German foreign missions between the two world wars.[1] Certainly there is a wealth of material, but not much of this has been worked

1. Ernst Damman, "Ausblick: Die deutsche Mission in den ehemaligen deutschen Kolonien zwischen den Weltkriegen," in *Imperialismus und Kolonialmission. Kaiserliches Deutschland und koloniales Imperium,* ed. Klaus J. Bade (Wiesbaden, 1982), pp. 289-305; Brian Digre, *Imperialism's New Clothes: The Repartition of Tropical Africa, 1914-1919* (New York, 1990); Klaus Fiedler, *Christentum und afrikanische Kultur. Konservative deutsche Missionare in Tanzania 1900-1940* (Gütersloh, 1983); Hans-Werner Gensichen, "German Protestant Missions," in *Missionary Ideologies in the Imperialist Era, 1880-1920,* ed. Torben Christensen and William R. Hutchison (Aarhus, 1982), pp. 181-90; Arno Lehmann, "Der deutsche Beitrag," in *Weltmission in Ökumenischer Zeit,* ed. Gerhard Brennecke (Stuttgart, 1961), pp. 153-65; Wm. Roger Louis, *Great Britain and Germany's Lost Colonies, 1914-1919* (Oxford, 1967); Richard V. Pierard, "John R. Mott and the Rift in the Ecumenical Movement during World War I," *Journal of Ecumenical Studies* 23 (1986): 601-19; Pierard, "Allied Treatment of Protestant Missionaries in German East Africa in World War I," *Africa Journal of Evangelical Theology* 12 (1993): 4-17; Pierard, "Shaking the Foundations: World War I, the Western Allies, and German Protestant Missions," *International Bulletin of Missionary Research* (1998): 13-19; Marcia Wright, *German Missions to Tanganyika, 1891-1941: Lutherans and Moravians in the Southern Highlands* (Oxford, 1971), chaps. 7–9, pp. 137-207.

on. What I am able to offer, therefore, is not, and at this point could not be, a comprehensive picture based on extensive new research. Rather, I plan to restrict myself to two specific issues: the debate about the future of German missions abroad, which was lively and controversial during the First World War, and the missionary activities of a few prominent German missionary societies between 1919 and 1939, namely, the Berliner Missionsgesellschaft, founded in 1824; the Rheinische Missionsgesellschaft, founded in 1828; the Norddeutsche Missionsgesellschaft, in Bremen, and the Leipziger Missionsgesellschaft, both established in 1836.

I will not look in detail at the missionary activities of the Moravians, or Herrnhuter Brüdergemeine, which began in 1732 and which in the interwar period were also part of an international network of Moravian settlements and communities located in the Netherlands, Great Britain, and the United States, nor will I discuss the work of the famous Basler Missionsgesellschaft, founded in 1815. This was certainly one of the most influential German-speaking missionary societies. Most of the personnel of the Basel mission were recruited in southern Germany, but the center of this mission was located outside of the German Reich in Switzerland. The history of the Basel mission after the Franco-Prussian War of 1870-71 and the foundation of the German Reich in 1871 would be a most worthwhile topic in itself because, although the Basel mission was closely linked to German missionary circles, the leaders of this mission never identified themselves with the political aims of the German Reich, in particular during the period of imperialism when it acquired colonies in Africa and in the Far East. In addition, I cannot discuss here the activities of some of the smaller German Protestant missionary societies,[2] nor the German Catholic missions in the interwar period.[3]

2. See, for example, the Goßnersche Missionsgesellschaft (founded in 1836), the Frauenverein für christliche Bildung des weiblichen Geschlechts im Morgenlande (1842), the Hermannsburger Missionsgesellschaft (1849), the Berliner Frauenmissionverein für China (1850), the Jerusalemsverein (1852), the Schleswig-Holsteinische evangelisch-lutherische Missionsgesellschaft in Breklum (1877), the Neukirchner Missionsgesellschaft (1881), the Deutsche Evangelische Missionsgesellschaft für Deutsch-Ostafrika (1886), the Deutsche China-Allianz-Mission (1889), the Deutsche Blindenmission unter dem weiblichen Geschlecht in China (1890), the Mission der Hannoverschen evangelisch-lutherischen Freikirche (1892), the Pilgermission von St. Chrischona (1895), the Liebenzeller Mission (1899), the Kieler China-Mission (1899), the Sudan-Pionier-Mission (1900), the Deutsche Orient-Mission Potsdam (1900), and the Missionsgesellschaft der Siebenten-Tags-Adventisten in Hamburg (1903).

3. German Catholic missions were almost as large as German Protestant missions. Catholic missions in the period from the First to the Second World War have also not attracted much scholarly attention.

I

Less than a year after the outbreak of the First World War, most German colonies were severely endangered. A year later most of them had been lost and were occupied by troops of the Entente powers. Although some German missionaries managed to flee, most were assigned to internment camps or expelled. Missionary activity was completely interrupted, unless native preachers were able to take over and continue the work, as happened, for example, in Togo. For German missionaries stationed in British or French colonies, such as British India, the Gold Coast, British East Africa, or South Africa, the situation was no better. In India, the largest mission field, German missionary activities had come to a complete standstill by 1916, and the same was true for the Near East, that is, Turkish Palestine, and the Far East, that is, New Guinea and Kaiochow. Even in places such as the Dutch Indies (Indonesia) or China, which were not directly involved in the war and where German missionaries were allowed to continue, conditions of work rapidly deteriorated as contacts with the mother country were few or were severed completely. By 1917, of the sixteen hundred German Protestant missionaries working abroad, more than three-quarters were unable to perform their duties.[4] By 1918 or 1919 most of them had decided to return to Germany.

For all German missionary societies the First World War was a catastrophe. As a result, between 1915 and 1919 leading officials of German missionary societies and some German Protestant theologians discussed the future of German foreign missions.[5] The debate was opened by Julius Richter, secretary of the Deutsche Evangelische Missionshilfe, a foundation for the support of German missionary work created in 1913 on the twenty-fifth anniversary of the coronation of Emperor William II. In a pamphlet entitled *Der deutsche Krieg und die deutsche evangelische Mission* (The German war and German Protestant missions), Richter attacked what he called the lies of Allied war propaganda. He praised the courage of German soldiers and protested loudly

4. More than a third of the German missionaries abroad, according to the "Direktor der Deutschen Evangelischen Missions-Hilfe," A. W. Schreiber, that is, 593 of 1,637, had been stationed in British colonies or in territories under British sovereignty. A. W. Schreiber, *Die Wirkungen des Weltkriegs auf die deutschen Missionsgesellschaften* (Leipzig, 1915), p. 11.

5. As Richard V. Pierard pointed out in the response to my paper at the Cambridge conference, there was a sharply worded exchange of public statements between a number of German and British missionary officials in the fall of 1914. More than anything else, this exchange was both the expression of mutual disappointment and of propaganda efforts in order to influence public opinion in both countries as well as in the United States.

against British policies in the mission fields that were directed against German missionaries, including their wives and children.

After a survey of the situation in the various mission fields, Richter explained that it was necessary that the German people develop a much clearer vision of their unique national character. Because the Germans were a Christian nation, he pleaded for a continuation of German missionary work worldwide as a sacred duty. He wished that the great and strong "Germania" should retain her good Christian heart and never turn into a greedy shopkeeper (*gieriger Krämer,* alluding to the British), nor a violent conqueror (*gewalttätiger Eroberer,* like the Russians), nor a gluttonous weakling (*weichlicher Schlemmer,* such as the French). Old Testament Israel could teach the Germans a lesson, Richter explained. Tiny Israel had faced the world powers of Assyria, Babylon, Persia, Syria, and Egypt and feared it would lose its national existence. Out of that obstinate, undecided, wavering Israel, according to Richter, God had forged the pure, genuine gold of true servants of God. Now in his own time, Richter claimed, the German people were going through a similar process of purification. Therefore he believed in a great future for the German people and in the prophetic mission of Germany for humankind.[6]

In a sermon delivered in 1915, August Cordes, a theologian from Leipzig, supported Richter's arguments. After the war, he said, the Germans should strive for a leading position in world missions because they represented the leading culture of the world. For Cordes the propagation of Protestant ideas and of German values were two sides of the same coin.[7] Similar arguments were propagated in sermons and public speeches by Karl Axenfeld,[8] Johan-

6. Julius Richter, "Der deutsche Krieg und die deutsche evangelische Mission," *Flugschriften der Deutschen Evangelischen Missionshilfe* (hereafter *FDEM*) 1 (1915). See also Richter, "Die Mission in dem gegenwärtigen Weltkriege. Berlin," *Biblische Zeit- und Streitfragen zur Aufklärung der Gebildeten* 10, no. 3 (1915). In this pamphlet Richter calls the war a special examination of the Germans ordered by God, an "examen rigorosum," that is, the oral examination of doctoral candidates (pp. 21, 37). Furthermore, he speaks of the Russian pan-Slavist arrogance of power ("Rußlands panslawistische Herrschsucht"), of French irreconcilable spirit of revenge ("Frankreichs unversöhnlicher Revanchegeist"), and of British jealousy and envy vis-à-vis Germans ("Englands Neid und Eifersucht auf Deutschland"), p. 44.

7. August Cordes, "Der christliche Gedanke in der Welt," *FDEM* 2 (1915).

8. Karl Axenfeld, "Vaterland und Mission," in *Mission und Vaterland. Deutsch-Christliche Reden in schwerer Zeit,* ed. Ernst von Dryander and Karl Axenfeld (Berlin, 1914). In this speech Axenfeld asked that his listeners thank God because they had not only been born white people and Christians but also Germans (p. 13); he sharply criticized British politicians who followed business interests single-mindedly and permitted that the home

nes Warneck,[9] A. W. Schreiber,[10] Martin Schlunk,[11] and Wilhelm Studemund.[12]

By contrast the editor of the *Evangelische Missions-Magazin*, Friedrich Würz, a Swiss-German member of the Basel missionary society, was somewhat more cautious. In 1915 he also noted that several classes of future missionaries had lost their lives in combat and that, as a result of the war, the ecumenical solidarity of all missionaries had been destroyed. For Würz, what was necessary was complete trust in God's divine rule.[13]

The speakers at a conference in Herrnhut in October 1915, on the national and international character of missionary work, also resorted to a somewhat different approach. Wilhelm Lütgert, a theologian from Halle, explained in his sermon that each people possessed special gifts, and in doing missionary work notions of national Christianity should not prevail, although they were always present. For Richter, who also spoke at Herrnhut, it was a mistake to equate the world-power status, which the Germans might be able to gain after the war, with a special role in God's plan of salvation for humankind. For Richter more power meant more responsibility, and what was needed, in his view, was a strengthening of domestic missionary work *(heimatliche*

---

of the Reformation and of European civilization would be destroyed by Russian hordes (p. 15); Axenfeld also praised the community of prayer among Germans that would lead to a rebirth of Germany and prepare the Germans for a leading role in world missions (pp. 16-17).

9. Johannes Warneck, "Weltkrieg und Weltmission," *Das neue Zeitalter* 3 (1915). For Warneck it is Great Britain that has destroyed international cooperation (pp. 11-14); also Warneck claims for the Germans, whose qualities he praises, new responsibilities in world missions (pp. 20-31).

10. Schreiber, *Die Wirkungen des Weltkrieges auf die deutschen Missionsgesellschaften.* According to Schreiber, by 1 Feb. 1915, 384 German missionaries served in the German army: 3 teachers from seminaries, 65 missionaries, and 316 students. Of these, during the first six months of the war, 50 had been wounded, 27 were killed in action, 17 had become prisoners, and 19 had received medals of honor (p. 5).

11. Martin Schlunk, "Die Misssionsprobleme des Weltkriegs," *Bremer Missionsschriften* 39 (1915). While Schlunk argued that because of the war Bremen missionaries felt more German than ever before, he warned against feelings of hatred. Rather the missionaries should, like all Germans, strive for religious renewal (pp. 3-5).

12. Wilhelm Studemund, *Der Weltkrieg und die deutsche evangelische Mission. Für unsere evangelischen Missionsgemeinden dargestellt* (Schwerin, 1915). Like his colleagues, Studemund is extremely critical of what he calls British lies (p. 25) and wonders whether God may have great plans for the Germans after the war. In this sense, for Studemund the war was a blessing for the Germans (p. 37).

13. Friedrich Würz, "Menschengedanken und Gottesgedanken über die Mission im Weltkriege," *FDEM* 3 (1915).

Missionsarbeit) as a precondition for success in foreign missionary efforts. Richter also argued that the time had gone when the Germans were simply loyal servants within British and American missionary empires. According to him, world missions should be freed from what he called the unhealthy amalgamation with world politics and world trade, and German missionary work should be based solely on pure religious motives.[14]

In 1916 the Leipzig theologian Albert Hauck introduced new arguments into the discourse on the national aspects of missionary work. With brute force the British had trampled the tender plant of German missionary work, he wrote. Since hatred and unreasonableness ruled in Great Britain, he expected no improvement in the near future. That Christians of all nations would cooperate in world missions had been nothing but a beautiful dream. Although missionary work was always a religious and never a political task, according to Hauck, one could not separate missionary work from national character, and the national character of the Germans had been defined during the Reformation. For Hauck this meant that the Germans had an obligation to lead the congregations and churches on the mission fields to full independence. Only through independence would they be able to become truly Christian.[15] Another suggestion Hauck made is worth mentioning. He pleaded for a concentration of German missionary efforts in the Near East. Through this, he argued, German missionary societies would best serve Christianity and the interests of the German nation.[16]

In a speech delivered in 1916, Gustav Kawerau, a member of the Berlin consistory, compared what he called the idealistic German approach to missionary work with the British approach that, in his view, was determined completely by considerations of power. For Kawerau the Christianization of humankind could not be achieved through political means. Like his colleague Hauck, Kawerau believed the unique character of German missionary work was service for the kingdom of God without any political implications.[17]

14. In *Nationalität und Internationalität der Mission. Vorträge auf der sechsten Herrnhuter Missionswoche im Oktober 1915* (Herrnhut, 1915), see esp. Wilhelm Lütgert, "Mission und Nation" (pp. 4-8); Julius Richter, "Besteht eine Gefahr der Verweltlichung unseres Missionslebens" (pp. 43-46).

15. Schlunk, in his treatise "Die Missionsprobleme des Weltkriegs," had discussed the same problem in 1915. While he recognized that many of the congregations in the mission fields were now required to fend for themselves, he doubted that there were enough qualified indigenous preachers (pp. 8-10).

16. Albert Hauck, "Evangelische Mission und deutsches Christentum," *FDEM* 4 (1916). See also Theodor Devaranne, *Deutsches Christentum und sein Weltberuf* (Berlin, 1916).

17. Gustav Kawerau, "Reich Gottes und Mission," *FDEM* 5 (1916).

In the course of 1917, the turning point of the First World War, the debate about the future of German missionary work became more agitated. Like Hauck, Carl Mirbt, a theologian from Göttingen, argued in a speech delivered in Berlin that it was the legacy of the German Reformation to combine missionary work with the education of the peoples abroad. Missionary congregations should be founded on native structures and thus become the basis for national indigenous churches. In retrospect, the tactical dimension of Mirbt's argument seems obvious: as hope for regaining the German colonies dwindled, he attempted to devise a strategy through which all colonial powers, including the British, would lose control over the churches in Africa and Asia.[18]

For all German Protestants the First World War was an *Eiserne Zeit,* a time of trial. In 1917, in a speech labeled "Eiserne Zeit," Carl Meinhof, a professor from Hamburg, argued that what mattered was the inner disposition of people. For the Germans this meant, as he wrote, that they confront British arrogance with a sober sense of duty and sacrifice. This should be the attitude of German soldiers as well as German missionaries. If this attitude prevailed, Meinhof argued, then as a result of the war the German missionary societies would gain enormously in inner strength and would be well equipped for the future. No longer would they be intimidated by what he called empty British talk and British phantoms.[19] For Julius Richter and Karl Axenfeld, the German missionaries had to suffer in many countries of the world not because they were missionaries, but because they were Germans.[20]

In discussing the future of German missionary work, Pastor Erich Meyer from Frankfurt, who had formerly served in Alexandria, came to a startling new conclusion. For Meyer, who wrote for a series published by the Evangelische Bund in 1917, German missions had always been closely connected with German cultural and economic activities abroad. Because the British side plotted to destroy German influence throughout the world, it was high time, he argued, to strengthen the connections between German missionary work and the German settlements abroad. In the past, ties between the *Auslandsdeutsche* (the settlements of ethnic Germans living abroad) and German missionaries had been rather loose, he wrote. The war, however, had cre-

18. Carl Mirbt, "Mission und Reformation," *FDEM* 7 (1917).

19. Carl Meinhof, "Eiserne Zeit," *FDEM* 8 (1917). See also Heinrich Frick, *Nationalität und Internationalität der christlichen Mission* (Gütersloh, 1917); Ludwig Weichert, *Der Weltkrieg der Mission. Ein Missionsgruß an unsere Feldgrauen draußen und daheim* (Gütersloh, 1917).

20. Karl Axenfeld and Julius Richter, *Das Kriegserlebnis der deutschen Mission im Lichte der Heiligen Schrift. Eine Handreichung für die deutsche Missionsgemeinde* (Berlin, 1917), pp. 15, 35.

ated a new kind of closeness and better mutual understanding. Both German missionaries and *Auslandsdeutsche* had been interned in the same camps and had suffered the same kind of pain. According to Meyer, both had been despised because they were German. Consequently, German technicians and merchants abroad should come to recognize the values of Protestant Christianity. At the same time, German missionaries should acknowledge the need to support the settlements of Germans living abroad with the aim of maintaining the German character of these settlements. In other words, Meyer proposed a remarkable reorientation of German missionary work. Rather than continuing the work to convert the natives of Asia and Africa, Meyer pleaded for work among ethnic Germans abroad in order to stop their assimilation into their host societies.[21]

In 1918 Carl Paul, the director of the Leipzig missionary society, discussed the same question, that is, the connection between *Mission und Auslandsdeutschtum*. More Germans lived abroad than members of any other nation, he argued, and many of them had been lost to the German fatherland because Germans tended to be assimilated very quickly. For too long Germans who lived abroad had ignored the efforts of German missionaries, Paul contended, while missionaries, as a rule, had not been eager to serve German communities abroad. Paul's conclusion was the same as Meyer's: for the rebirth of Germany after the war, Germans living in other countries could play a crucial role. It was necessary, therefore, to strengthen both missionary work abroad and the German diaspora, and moreover, to increase the cooperation between the two. According to Paul, the combination of pure German Protestant faith and pure "Germanness" among those living abroad would guarantee a better future for the whole of Germany.[22]

After the war, the revolution of November 1918, and the downfall of the Hohenzollern monarchy, a further argument emerged about German foreign missions. Meyer and Paul had urged missionaries to help in the spiritual regeneration of Germans abroad. Some Protestant officials now applied the same thinking to the German domestic scene. This idea was best expressed in the phrase "Die Heidenmission im Dienst der Volksmission," that is, foreign missionary experience in the service of German missionary work at home. In 1919 Georg Beyer, the director of the Berlin Missionary Society, argued that missionaries knew best how to convert irreligious people to true Christianity, and in his view conversion to true Christianity was what the German people

21. Erich Meyer, "Die Mission und der Weltkrieg," *Volksschriften zum großen Krieg* 114/115.

22. Carl Paul, "Mission und Auslandsdeutschtum," *FDEM* 9 (1918).

needed more than anything else after the defeat. The war had been lost, Beyer assumed, because the Germans had fallen away from Christian faith.[23]

In 1920 Beyer's Berlin colleague Gustav Knak, while stressing the need of both foreign missions and home missions, insisted that in his time *Volksmission* was the first and foremost task of Protestant missionaries. Like Beyer, Knak believed missionaries who had returned from foreign mission fields were ideally suited to help those engaged in the difficult yet extremely important task of missionary work at home. For Knak, as for many of his colleagues, the Christian rebirth of Germany had priority over any other aim.[24]

II

Article 438 of the Treaty of Versailles (1919) stated that the Allied and associated powers would guarantee that the work in former German mission fields could continue. For this purpose they would be obliged to appoint administrative councils to protect the property of the missionary societies. Such councils were to consist of persons of the same faith as the former missions. The German government was asked to approve of all actions taken by these administrative councils.[25] In the period immediately after the war, the leaders of German missionary societies did not notice, or at least did not discuss, the positive aspects of this rather generous arrangement. They were bitter and very disappointed that they had lost the Great War and, along with Germany's colonies, most of their mission fields. Anti-British feelings persisted long after the war had ended.

As a result of the discussion about the future of German missionary work during and shortly after the war, one can conclude that from 1919 to 1920 German missionary leaders identified four options:

- Hope for a renewal of the German colonial empire. Considering the outcome of the war, this was not a very realistic basis on which to base their plans.
- Employ some, or most, of the missionaries who had lost their place of service abroad and place them in some institution, or society, devoted to missionary work at home. During the war a number of missionaries who

23. Georg Beyer, "Die Heidenmission im Dienst der Volksmission," in *Handbuch der Volksmission,* ed. Gerhard Füllkrug (Schwerin, 1919), pp. 121-48.

24. Siegfried Knak, "Völkermission und Volksmission," *FDEM* 11 (1920).

25. *Der Friedensvertrag von Versailles* (Berlin, 1925), pp. 238-39.

had returned to Germany had been filling in for pastors who were serving as military chaplains.

- Former missionaries could be sent to serve as pastors or teachers in German settlements abroad, as messengers of Protestantism and "Germanness."
- The attempt could be made to send some of the former missionaries back to their mission fields under the conditions spelled out by the Treaty of Versailles.

Whereas the first three options were clearly meant to serve the national regeneration of the German people, that is, the political, economic, cultural, and religious rebirth of Germany, only the fourth option was in line with the traditional international character of missionary work.

III

I will now examine, on the basis of available statistical material, the policies of some German missionary societies with regard to these four options. First I shall consider the Norddeutsche Missionsgesellschaft in Bremen. Early on in the war the Bremen-based society had lost its mission field among the Ewe in Togo. Although some missionaries managed to return to Bremen, most spent the war in internment camps under British or French supervision. Information about the subsequent employment of twenty missionaries who returned to Germany between 1916 and 1924 is available.[26] Of the twenty whose professional careers can be traced, eight entered regular service of the church as pastors; the same number started to work in some institution, or society, of the home mission *(Innere Mission);* three began careers as teachers or university professors; and only one, just one, became active as a pastor in a community of Germans living abroad.

After 1918 the leaders of the Norddeutsche Missionsgesellschaft never gave up the hope of being able to return to Togo one day. In 1923 three Bremen missionaries were able to do so, not in the name of their mother institution, but under the protection of the missionary society of the United Free Church of Scotland. A year later, with the help of the International Missionary Coun-

26. The following information is from the *Monatsblatt der Norddeutschen Missionsgesellschaft* 75 (1914); 100 (1939). See also Wilhelm Oehler, *Geschichte der deutschen evangelischen Mission,* vol. 2, *Reife und Bewährung der deutschen evangelischen Mission 1885-1950* (Baden-Baden, 1951), pp. 103-6, 283, 319-21.

cil, the Bremen society was officially recognized by British colonial authorities in Togo. In 1926 seven Bremen missionaries returned to Togo. There can be no doubt, however, that the Bremen engagement in Togo remained limited in the 1920s and 1930s. In 1913 thirty-four Bremen missionaries had been stationed there. By contrast just five missionaries and four women lay workers were still in Togo in 1938.[27] Although one of the missionaries served as head of the church, or *Präses,* most of the pastoral work in the Protestant congregations of the Ewe was done by native preachers. In retrospect, it seems that in the interwar period in Togo the Norddeutsche Missionsgesellschaft followed the advice given by Albert Hauck and Carl Mirbt during the First World War, namely, to lead the indigenous Christian churches to full independence. As regards the other options listed above, the early 1930s seem to be of special interest because during this period the Bremen society sent several missionaries as preachers to various places in northern Germany. Their task was *Evangelisation* and *Volksmission,* that is, missionary work among Germans who had lost contact with Christendom. Ten years after the end of the First World War, the need to stem the tide of secularization and to become engaged in campaigns of home mission seemed as urgent as ever.

My second example is the Berliner Missionsgesellschaft. Before 1914, 184 of its missionaries had been working abroad, mainly in the German colony of East Africa, in the Transvaal and other parts of South Africa, and in China.[28] As a result of the war, many of these missionaries needed a new place of service. Whereas 84 had been stationed in the various regions of South Africa in 1913, as far as I can tell, only 52 were left by 1921. By the mid-1930s this number had risen to over 80. In 1921, of the 50-plus missionaries from Berlin who had been working in German East Africa, not one was left. By 1936, 5 Berlin missionaries had returned; and they cooperated with a larger number of indigenous preachers. Twenty-five had been stationed in China and 6 in Kiautschou in 1913, and in 1921, 15 were still active in China and 3 in Kiautschou. In 1936, it would seem, the number was the same.

Given the material available, it is particularly difficult to trace the career of those Berlin missionaries who were forced to return to Germany. This much seems clear, however: by 1921, 13 of the missionaries who had returned from China and East Africa had found new positions in German settlements in Lithuania or Poland, while 2 had entered new service in German commu-

27. See Oehler, 2:426-27.

28. The following information is from *Missions-Berichte der Berliner Missionsgesellschaft,* 1914-21; *Berliner Missionsbericht,* 1922-29 and 1936-40. Cf. also Julius Richter, *Geschichte der Berliner Missionsgesellschaft 1824-1924* (Berlin, 1924); Oehler, 2:279, 327-29, 333-34, 342-44, 399.

nities in Brazil and Paraguay. By contrast, in 1936, 7 former Berlin missionaries were still working in German communities in east-central Europe, while 4 had entered new employment in Brazil and Argentina and 1 in the United States. Most of the Berlin missionaries who returned to Germany, however, found new positions in institutions or societies devoted to home missionary work, to *Volksmission* and *Innere Mission.* In addition, a fair number seem not to have been fully employed in the 1920s and 1930s. They were on what was called extended home leave, or they were staying in the mission center in Berlin.

The Berlin Missionary Society seems to have been even more nationalistic than the Bremen society. During the war several Berlin missionaries served as military chaplains or as officers. Anti-British polemics were extremely strong during the war, and thereafter. In 1919 Berlin missionaries took up arms on the side of the counterrevolution in fighting leftist workers and soldiers. Throughout the 1920s the Berlin society used its publications to denounce the Treaty of Versailles as an intolerable injustice. Time and again the demand for the return of the former German colonies was propagated vehemently. During the 1920s and into the 1930s, missionary work on the home front was understood as a battle against the forces of evil, such as atheism, materialism, socialism, bolshevism, communism, and other variations of secularization. It was only during the Jerusalem Conference of 1928 that the head of the Berlin mission, Siegfried Knak, showed a somewhat more conciliatory attitude. It is more telling, however, that several leaders of the Berlin mission were early members of the Nazi Party, as, for example, the superintendent of missions Ludwig Weichert. It is likely that Weichert initiated a special evangelization campaign in Lithuania and in parts of Poland in the mid-1930s. I will return to the significance of the Nazi rise to power for German missionary work.

Before 1914 my third example, the Rheinische Missionsgesellschaft, had been the largest of all the German missionary societies.[29] In 1913 the Barmen-based society had sent out almost two hundred missionaries, even more than the Berlin Missionary Society or the Herrnhuter. Of the German-speaking missionary societies, only the Basler Missionsgesellschaft was larger. Barmen missionaries were stationed in the Dutch East Indies, in China, in South Africa, in the German colony of German Southwest Africa, and in New Guinea. In addition, the society possessed a strong network of local missionary sup-

29. The following information is from the *Berichte der Rheinischen Missionsgesellschaft* 71 (1914) to 96 (1939), and the *Jahresbericht der Rheinischen Missionsgesellschaft* 89 (1918/19) to 110 (1939/40). See also Eduard Kriele, *Geschichte der Rheinischen Mission,* vol. 1, *Die Rheinische Mission in der Heimat* (Barmen, 1928), pp. 342-99, and Oehler, 2:324-26, 362-64, 367-69, 375-77, 402, 409.

port groups, mainly in the Protestant parts of the Rhineland and in Westphalia. A special superintendent for missionary work at home had been appointed in April 1914.

In August 1914 22 of the 33 students in the Barmen Seminary joined the German army. In the course of the war, 28 Barmen students as well as some 50 sons of Barmen missionaries lost their lives in combat.[30] After 1914, as in the other German missionary societies, contact with the missionaries abroad became increasingly difficult, but the Barmen society managed to carry on. Before the end of the war, only a few stations had to be abandoned, for example, those in Hong Kong, in Tsingtau, and in Amboland, that is, in the border region between Portuguese Angola and the German colony of Southwest Africa. After 1918, however, financial constraints meant that the mission field in Borneo had to be handed over to the Basel mission. This was done in a friendly manner. The Barmen society was deeply hurt, however, when in 1921 the Australian government, which had taken over New Guinea as a protectorate, postulated that Barmen missionaries had to decide whether they wanted to leave or continue work under the Lutheran Mission of the United Evangelical Lutheran Church of Australia or the Lutheran Synod of Iowa.

The Rheinische Missionsgesellschaft suffered a major crisis, not during the First World War, but immediately after. Debts were rising, while the number of missionaries dropped to barely over a hundred. In 1925, after ninety-nine years, the *Barmen Missionsblatt* had to be discontinued. By 1926 the number of active missionaries was down to 80. Recovery began in 1927. Between May and August of that year the number of missionaries who could be sent abroad rose from 78 to 100. By 1938 more than 200 missionaries, male and female, were engaged in the service of the Barmen society abroad: in South Africa; in the Dutch East Indies, mainly Sumatra; in former German Southwest Africa; and in the Kwangtung province of China. Although many Barmen missionaries had been unemployed in the 1920s, most had found new places of work in the 1930s.

Some information is available about the Barmen missionaries who returned to Germany. In the 1920s many of them joined some branch of *Innere Mission,* that is, some kind of service in the home mission. In 1928, 89 former Barmen missionaries lived and worked abroad, 43 of them in the United States, 14 in Brazil, 12 in the Dutch East Indies, 10 in Canada, and between 1 and 3 each in South Africa, former Southwest Africa, Lithuania, Switzerland, and Norway. About half had been in these countries before 1914, whereas the

30. Kriele, 1:343 n. 18.

other half had returned from the Dutch East Indies, former German Southwest Africa, and New Guinea in the early 1920s and had been relocated. Most of the returnees decided to go to either the United States or Brazil. In 1936, 74 former Barmen missionaries had found new jobs in Germany, while 81 had engagements abroad. The distribution of countries was about the same as in 1928.

A word of caution is necessary here. Much more detailed research is needed before exact numbers can be established. At present only trends can be described.[31] Furthermore, one would like to know much more about the exact kind of work that some of these Barmen missionaries were doing, for example, in the United States or in the Rio Grande do Sul province of Brazil. Did they really serve in congregations of German emigrants? Did they really attempt to uphold "Germanness" in these communities as messengers of the German fatherland? What were the feelings of those missionaries who had been assigned a new task? How much pressure was used in sending them to new places of service? Was the new task an obligation owed to the missionary society, grudgingly accepted, or something for which they volunteered? How strong was their motivation, their enthusiasm? In a few cases only are details known. Heinrich Hunsche, for example, a former missionary of the Barmen society, was a very active member of the German congregation, the *Auslandsdeutsche Gemeinde,* in Rio Grande do Sul in the 1930s,[32] but many more cases have to be studied in detail before a general assessment can be attempted.

The Leipziger Missionsgesellschaft had been engaged, in the main, in two mission fields before 1914: in East Africa and in India.[33] Both mission fields were badly hurt in the course of the First World War. Many Leipzig missionaries spent time in internment camps, and most returned to Germany after the war. Of the forty returnees from India whose careers I have been able to trace, seventeen became pastors in parishes somewhere in Germany; seven retired; two worked for the domestic missions, as teachers; and two became pastors in German congregations in Poland. Ten returned to India in the late

31. There is some reason to assume that the figures in the journals of the various missionary societies are not complete. In order to check and, if necessary, also to correct these figures, one would have to go through the piles of unpublished, handwritten material in the missionary societies' archives.

32. Cf. Martin N. Dreher, *Kirche und Deutschtum in der Entwicklung der Evangelischen Kirche lutherischen Bekenntnisses in Brasilien* (Göttingen, 1978), pp. 88-89.

33. For details see *Evangelisch-Lutherisches Missionsblatt,* 1914-33; and Oehler, 2:337-41, 347, 354-56, 272-73, 426-27; see also Paul Fleisch, *Hundert Jahre lutherischer Mission* (Leipzig, 1936), pp. 309-454.

1920s. Of the thirty-three missionaries who returned from East Africa, eleven had the chance to become pastors, six took over a pastorate temporarily and returned to East Africa in the late 1920s and early 1930s, two began to work in a Christian publishing house, another two died, and the others went into retirement.

In the mid-1920s, in both India and in East Africa, the Leipzig society made a new beginning. Only a few Leipzig missionaries decided to go back to India, however, while efforts were concentrated on the missions in East Africa. Between 1923 and 1933 no fewer than twenty-three new missionaries were sent to East Africa from Leipzig. As a result, the total number of Leipzig missionaries abroad rose considerably. In 1913 the Leipzig society had stationed about a hundred missionaries abroad; twenty-five years later, in 1938, the number of active Leipzig missionaries abroad had again reached ninety-one. As compared to the Rheinische Missionsgesellschaft, only very few former Leipzig missionaries became involved, in one way or another, in communities of Germans abroad. This fact should not be interpreted, however, as an indication of a more conciliatory political outlook. For the Leipzig society, as with others, the future of the German people played a critical role. Accordingly, they organized campaigns for the evangelization of Germans who had lost their faith, they attempted to strengthen Protestant communities in the diaspora, and they maintained close contacts with German congregations in east-central Europe.

IV

In trying to analyze the data about the placement of personnel by the various missionary organizations and about their political outlook in the interwar period in a systematic way, one has to begin by looking at the situation immediately after the war. As many examples demonstrate, in the early years of the Weimar Republic, German missionary societies were confronted with the fact that dozens upon dozens, and in total hundreds upon hundreds, of missionaries returned home and expected help. Societies like the one in Leipzig with traditionally good relations with some of the German Protestant churches were able to secure appointments for some of their returning missionaries as pastors, although very often only in a temporary or auxiliary capacity.[34] Because most of the returnees had not been officially ordained, it was often difficult to entrust them with regular parishes. Other societies, such as the one

34. See Fleisch, pp. 312-13.

in Barmen, which had long-standing, excellent relations to church bodies in North America and Latin America, managed to find new assignments in those places at least for some. For all the German missionary societies, the institutions and agencies in the various branches of the home mission, the *Innere Mission,* provided the best opportunities for new employment for returning missionaries. Even those who had not been ordained could serve in some capacity in home missionary work. Moreover, they could be asked to serve in campaigns of evangelization, or *Volksmission.* There is no doubt, however, that at least for some of the time many of the returning missionaries were unemployed.

Even if one considers the difficulties of finding proper employment for the returning missionaries, the argument that the German missionary societies had various options in 1918-19 seems significant and relevant for future research. The main decision the leaders of the German missionary societies had to make after the war was whether they were prepared to steer a pragmatic course with regard to missionary work abroad or wanted to attack the Treaty of Versailles and refuse to recognize the possibilities for foreign missions laid down therein. Perhaps it would have asked too much of German missionary leaders to state publicly that they were prepared to continue missionary work in the countries of Africa and Asia that were British, French, Dutch, and Portuguese colonies or were entrusted by the League of Nations as Mandates to the governments of Great Britain, France, Australia, and South Africa. Very clearly, however, from the mid-1920s some of the German missionary societies silently took a pragmatic course in this matter, in particular the societies in Bremen and in Leipzig. As a result, they began to abstain from anti-British polemics and to enter into working relations with the missionary societies of the former Entente powers. By the early 1920s contacts with the National Lutheran Council, a joint body of American Lutherans, had been resumed. In the late 1920s relations between German Lutheran missionary societies and Swedish Lutherans were being intensified.[35]

No doubt financial constraints and inflation made missionary activities abroad especially difficult in the early 1920s. After 1918, moreover, a career in the mission field seems not to have been very attractive for young German Protestants. Further research is needed to discover which young Germans did in fact enter the seminaries of the German missionary societies in the 1920s and 1930s. What was their background? What were their aims? Were they thinking of traditional missionary work? Were they hoping to serve in some German community abroad in order to help the cause of *Auslandsdeutschtum*

35. Fleisch, pp. 314, 392-94.

and preserve "Germanness" among German emigrants, or were they planning to be trained and later become missionaries on the home front? There is some indication that, in the 1920s at least, some young men who might have become missionaries in former years decided to become teachers and serve in German communities abroad in that capacity. In this way they hoped to combine work for the preservation of Germanness in these communities with cultural activities abroad *(Auswärtige Kulturarbeit)*.[36]

V

With the Nazi rise to power the dream was revived among German Protestant missionaries that the former German colonies could be regained and they would be able to return to their old mission fields. In German Protestant circles, moreover, one aspect of the hope for a general political and Christian reawakening of the German people was a revival of interest in German communities abroad. In the election campaigns of the early 1930s, among German Protestants the polemics against the peace settlement sounded as shrill as ever. Leaders of the German missionary community were soon to find out, however, that their relationship with the Nazi movement was a very difficult one.[37]

As early as 1932 some German missionaries had voiced support for the Nazi Party. For Walter Braun, for example, the mission inspector from Berlin,

36. Cf., for example, the career of Erich Fausel, author of D. Dr. Rotermund, *Ein Kampf um Recht und Richtung des evangelischen Deutschtums in Südbrasilien* (Sao Leopoldo, 1936). Like his older brother Heinrich, Erich Fausel was supposed to become a pastor, or like some other members of his family, a missionary. But he changed from the study of theology to history and modern languages. His dissertation was on a small German settlement in Czechoslovakia. In 1931 he decided to go to Rio Grande do Sul as a teacher. See also *Deutsche Evangelische Auslands-Diaspora und Deutscher Evangelischer Kirchenbund. Sonderdruck aus dem Tätigkeitsbericht des Deutschen Evangelischen Kirchenausschusses und den Verhandlungen des Deutschen Evangelischen Kirchentags von 1924, 1927 und 1930* (Berlin-Charlottenburg, 1930), pp. 82-97; Franz Thierfelder, *Die wirtschaftliche Bedeutung des Auslandsdeutschtums* (Stuttgart, 1934); Ernst Ritter, *Das Deutsche Auslands-Institut in Stuttgart 1917-1945. Ein Beispiel deutscher Volkstumsarbeit zwischen den Weltkriegen* (Wiesbaden, 1976).

37. For the following see also Doris Bergen, "'What God Has Put Asunder Let No Man Join Together': Overseas Missions and the German Christian View of Race," in *Remembrance, Repentance, Reconciliation: The Twenty-Fifth Anniversary Volume of the Annual Scholars' Conference on the Holocaust and the Churches*, ed. Douglas F. Tobler (Lanham, Md., 1998), pp. 5-17; Bergen, *Twisted Cross: The German Christian Movement in the Third Reich* (Chapel Hill, N.C., 1996), pp. 29-31.

the National Socialist movement promised the genuine rebirth of the German people for which people had been waiting so long. It was necessary, however, he argued, to use the experience of doing foreign missionary work in the process of German reawakening. Most certainly, he wrote, the hour had come to preach the gospel to the Germans. This the National Socialists too would have to learn, just as they would have to learn the importance of foreign missionary work for the recovery of Germany. Furthermore, the Nazi view of the peoples in Africa and Asia was too negative, Braun contended, and so was their attitude toward the Old Testament. According to Braun, what the Hitler party needed were strong Protestant leaders. For Braun, who listed in his bibliography works by Nazi authors, including Rosenberg and Hitler, the case was clear: German Protestants, and especially Protestant missionaries, should support the Nazi movement with the intention of converting the Nazis to a policy of the Christian rebirth of Germany. Such a policy would serve the needs of the German people best, he argued, and also help the Christians in Africa and Asia.[38]

A year later, in 1933, Siegfried Knak, director of the Berliner Missionsgesellschaft, saw matters in much the same way. Out of ignorance and because of their views of racial difference, many National Socialists were too critical of foreign missionary work, Knak argued. It was the task of all Protestant Christians, therefore, to become engaged in politics and to see to it that true Christian attitudes prevailed in the Nazi movement.[39]

It is obvious that German Protestant missionary leaders such as Braun or Knak were in a rather difficult position. On the one hand, they hoped for the rebirth of a strong Germany and they genuinely believed in Hitler as a political leader.[40] On the other hand, they had to realize that a tension existed between the nationalistic egoism of National Socialist foreign policy and their own commitment to missionary work for the sake of building the kingdom of God worldwide. For Knak, as well as for Julius Richter, who addressed the problem of foreign missionary work under Nazi rule in 1934,[41] the solution was a policy through which Christianity among all peoples would be embedded in genuine *Volkstum*. Feelings of genuine Germanness and of true Prot-

38. Walter Braun, *Heidenmission und Nationalsozialismus* (Berlin, 1932).

39. Siegfried Knak, "Mission und nationale Bewegung," *Brennende Fragen der Frauenmission* 6/7 (1933).

40. Hartmut Lehmann, "Hitlers evangelische Wähler," in Hartmut Lehmann, *Protestantische Weltsichten. Transformationen seit dem 17. Jahrhundert* (Göttingen, 1998), pp. 130-52.

41. Julius Richter, "In der Krisis der Weltmission," *Allgemeine Missions-Studien* (1934): 17.

estant faith should be the basis of Protestantism in Germany, they thought, and the indigenous churches in Africa and Asia should be built on strong national beliefs in a similar manner.[42] But what if a majority of leading Nazis refused to accept this argument?

In 1935 Julius Richter published a comprehensive volume on German missions *(Das Buch der deutschen Weltmission)*.[43] In his article "Mission und Rassen" Martin Schlunk explained that all races were part of God's creation. They should coexist, "each race with her own gifts and tasks, with her own rights and limitations"; but races should not be mingled.[44] In the political context of 1935, despite Schlunk's request for racial segregation, this could be read as a criticism of Nazi policies. In the article "Mission und Kirche im Dritten Reich," Knak stated soberly: "Up until now, the relationship between Church missionary work and the Third Reich has not been clarified." Like Richter and many of his colleagues, Knak hoped it would be possible to convince the Nazi leadership of the political, ethical, and religious value of German missionary work among other peoples. Like others, Knak explained that the aim of these endeavors was the creation of genuine indigenous churches *(artechte Volkskirchen)* like their own German Lutheran churches.[45] Georg Hammitzsch, from the Leipzig missionary society, expressed the same thoughts in a work also published in 1935. Because they cherished service and sacrifice, according to Hammitzsch, National Socialism and missionary work abroad belonged together.[46]

By 1934 or 1935 the struggle between the German Christians and the Con-

42. Within German Protestantism there is a long tradition of discussing the attractiveness of a theology that addresses the collective ethnic body called the *Volk*. See Johannes Christian Hoekendijk, *Kirche und Volk in der deutschen Missionswissenschaft* (Munich, 1967; Dutch original, Amsterdam, 1948); Wolfgang Tilgner, *Volksnomostheologie und Schöpfungsglaube. Ein Beitrag zur Geschichte des Kirchenkampfes* (Göttingen, 1966); Ernst Jaeschke, *Bruno Gutmann: His Life, His Thoughts, and His Work* (Erlangen, 1985); see also Gensichen, pp. 187-88; Christian Keysser, *Altes Testament und heutige Zeit* (Neundettelsau, 1934); Richard V. Pierard, "Volkisch Thought and Christian Missions in the Early Twentieth Century," in *Essays in Religious Studies for Andrew Walls*, ed. James Thrower (Aberdeen, 1986), pp. 136-54; Werner Ustorf, "Anti-Americanism in German Missiology," *Mission Studies* 11 (1989): 23-34. It is interesting to note that there are some similarities between the theological positions of the German Christians and Bruno Gutmann's attempt to incorporate indigenous African traditions into the life of Christian churches in Africa.

43. Julius Richter, ed., *Das Buch der deutschen Weltmission* (Gotha, 1935).

44. Richter, pp. 135-38.

45. Richter, pp. 240-44.

46. Georg Hammitzsch, "Die Grundlagen des Dritten Reiches und die Heidenmission," *Leipziger Missionstudien N.F. Heft* 7 (1935): 17-20, 25-27.

fessing Church had torn German Protestantism apart. German Protestant missionaries could be found on both sides of the divide.[47] There were other, perhaps not less troubling problems for the German missionary community.[48] As part of a fiscal policy of strict autonomy, the Nazis prohibited the transfer of money to foreign countries, including mission fields. The Nazis also claimed the sole right to collect money on the streets, a practice that had traditionally provided at least part of the income of German missionary societies. African preachers who were invited to Germany in the mid-1930s and asked to preach were attacked by Nazis in a most vicious manner. Before any of these matters could be resolved in a way that would have suited German missionary societies, Hitler had started another war. The story of German foreign missions during the Second World War is another matter,[49] as is the role of German foreign missions after 1945.

47. Some former missionaries, like Jakob Wilhelm Hauer, had completely drifted away from Christendom and attempted to formulate their own religion, in his case the Deutschgläubige Bewegung, a strange mixture of Germanic mythology, mysticism, and the pre-1914 youth movement.

48. Cf. Oehler, 2:307-11; Arno Lehmann, "Die deutsche evangelische Mission in der Zeit des Kirchenkampfes," *Evangelische Missionszeitschrift* 31 (1974): 105-10.

49. See Paul H. von Tucher, *Nationalism: Case and Crisis in Missions: German Missions in British India, 1939-1946* (Erlangen, 1980); Siegfried Knak, *Mission im Kriege* (Berlin, 1940), esp. the section "Der Christ und sein Volk," in which Knak once again spells out the principles of "*volkisch* theology." "It is something great," Knak writes, "that after the turbulences and the desperation in the years after the war [First World War], our people has now regained a strong will and has rediscovered its historical mission" (p. 14).

CHAPTER 3

Missions and Afrikaner Nationalism: Soundings in the Prehistory of Apartheid

RICHARD ELPHICK

"The National Party, anxious to stimulate active Christianising enterprise among the non-Whites, will gladly support the efforts of mission churches. Churches and missions, however, which frustrate the policy of apartheid or which propagate foreign doctrines, will not be tolerated."[1] These sentences formed part of the manifesto of the (Re-united) National Party, South Africa's official opposition, when, in the election of 1948, it made its case to the overwhelmingly white electorate. This "mission policy" was more than a rhetorical sop to the Dutch Reformed Church, the spiritual home of almost all Afrikaners. It was integral to the party's plan to recast South African society in the mold of "apartheid," an ideology recently fashioned by Afrikaner churchmen, intellectuals, journalists, and politicians.

The year before, Daniel François Malan, the Nationalists' leader, had formed a commission to articulate the party's "color policy." The "Sauer Report" (named after its chair, P. O. Sauer) presented the principles of apartheid, followed by a "mission policy," and finally a list of concrete measures. By inserting mission policy between principles and implementation, the commissioners declared their conviction that Christian missions were a uniquely powerful engine for social change. On the one hand, missions could foster assimilation of the races. Many were already doing this, thus, in the commissioners' view,

1. "Race Relations Policy of the National Party," in *South African Parties and Policies, 1910-1960: A Select Source Book,* ed. D. W. Krüger (London, 1960), p. 403.

I am grateful to Jeffrey Butler, Hermann Giliomee, Eugene Klaaren, and Pieter Verster for perceptive comments on earlier drafts.

imperiling white domination. Alternatively missions could encourage whites and blacks to develop in separate areas, to their mutual benefit. The National Party wanted "non-whites to be actively and powerfully led to make the Christian Religion the foundation of their whole life, so that a healthy Christian-National life-view is also built up among them." It would accordingly promote "healthy" missions with "all possible means and support." Yet the party would also be vigilant against "such activities of Church, Societies, and Movements that undermine the power of the Government, propagate confusing and alien viewpoints, and undervalue the principle of separate development."[2]

The Sauer commission consisted of four Nationalist members of Parliament, along with one nonpolitician — G. B. A. Gerdener, the professor of missions at Stellenbosch University and arguably South Africa's leading missiologist. Gerdener was responsible for articulating a missiological perspective in the innermost circles of the National Party. He apparently encountered little resistance from his more secular colleagues. One lay member of the commission who had long been active in shaping apartheid thought was M. D. C. de Wet Nel, leader of the National Party's "color group" in Parliament. Once when asked, "How can I make the greatest contribution to the welfare of South Africa?" De Wet Nel answered without hesitation, "Become a missionary."[3]

Afrikaners and Missions: A Story of Attraction and Repulsion

Since 1652, when white settlement began in South Africa, the overwhelming majority of Dutch-speaking settlers, and their Afrikaner descendants, have been members of the Dutch Reformed Church (DRC). (More accurately, since the 1860s they have been members of one of four Dutch Reformed *Churches,* one in each province.)[4] The DRC, for much of its history, has been

2. "Verslag van die Kleurvraagstuk-Kommissie van die Herenigde Nasionale Party" (1947), sec. C.

3. N. J. Rhoodie and H. J. Venter, *Apartheid: A Socio-Historical Exposition of the Origin and Development of the Apartheid Idea* (Cape Town and Pretoria, 1960), p. 167; G. B. A. Gerdener, *Die Afrikaner en die sending* (Cape Town and Pretoria, 1959), p. 127.

4. The Cape Colony (later Cape Province), the Orange Free State, the Transvaal, and Natal. Following widespread convention, even among DRC clergy, I refer to the Dutch Reformed Church in the singular, except in contexts where the plural is clearly called for. The four churches had a seminary (Stellenbosch) and a periodical *(Die Kerkbode)* in common. They cooperated closely on many issues, especially through the Council of Churches (Raad van die Kerke), founded in 1907. On some issues, race policy among them, sharp divisions occasionally arose among the churches. Technically the four churches should be called the Federated Dutch Reformed Churches in South Africa until they united in 1962.

profoundly committed to missions, a commitment that has frequently conflicted with its role as the spiritual home of most (white) Afrikaners.[5] At the beginning of the nineteenth century many Dutch-speaking settlers regarded Reformed Christianity as an emblem of their white identity, a boundary marker separating them from the dark-skinned indigenes and slaves among whom they lived. Yet from the 1790s onward, certain DRC ministers preached an evangelical, revivalist gospel that led many Dutch-speaking settlers to undergo a personal conversion to Christ and frequently to acquire a commitment to missions as well. Some settlers supported the missionaries of the Moravian Brethren and the London Missionary Society (LMS), who were arriving from Europe in the same period. But when several LMS missionaries, among them John Philip, the mission's superintendent from 1822 to 1851, publicly campaigned against the oppression of blacks in the colony,[6] many settlers blamed missionaries for poisoning the British government against the colonists. Dutch-speaking settlers accumulated a long list of grievances against missionaries, which dogged DRC mission advocates deep into the twentieth century.

The DRC decided to establish its own missions in 1824, and these rapidly gained a measure of success. Black converts began to appear in formerly all-white congregations, requesting access to Holy Communion and the right to hold church weddings. Some settlers, for whom a DRC church was the temple of their cultural and racial identity, bitterly opposed such measures and looked askance at missions in their neighborhoods. In 1857 the DRC synod passed a resolution introduced by Andrew Murray Sr., an eminent evangelical, to the effect that it was "desirable and scriptural" that black converts be incorporated into white congregations, but that where "this rule, because of the weakness of some, should stand in the way of the advancement of Christ's cause among the Heathen, the congregations raised up, or to be raised up, from the Heathen, shall enjoy their Christian rights in a separate building or institution."[7] This resolution was intended only as a stopgap measure to overcome local whites' resistance to missions. Yet it enabled the rapid formation of separate black congregations. In 1881

5. There are two much smaller bodies, the Hervormde and the Gereformeerde churches. The latter played a formative role in the shaping of Afrikaner nationalism, but neither were much active in missions. For simplicity's sake I omit them in this narrative.

6. Here I use "black" to refer to all people of color. In reference to the modern period the term embraces (mixed-race) Coloureds and Indians, along with the African majority.

7. C. J. Kriel, *Die geskiedenis van die Nederduitse Gereformeerde Sendingkerk in Suid-Afrika, 1881-1956* (Paarl, 1963), p. 59.

the DRC grouped twenty-three of these congregations into the Dutch Reformed Mission Church in South Africa, a distinct body with its own synod but subordinate to the white synod, on whom it depended for clergy and financial support.

Ecclesiastical segregation, henceforth a hallmark of DRC missions, helped overcome much of the antimissionary sentiment among Afrikaners. Inspired by revivals in the 1860s, and again early in the twentieth century, DRC missions grew, prospered, and became objects of pride for many church leaders. By 1925 the DRC supported 194 missionaries working inside South Africa (and a number in central Africa and Nigeria). Although DRC missionaries constituted only one-tenth of the Protestant missionary force in South Africa, this was a respectable number for a church whose membership was relatively poor and often suspicious of missions, especially missions providing education to blacks. DRC missions were disproportionately strong among Coloureds (people of mixed race) and weak among Africans (then often called "natives" or "Bantu"),[8] the largest and, for much of the century, the fastest-growing segment of the South African population. By the 1950s the DRC laid claim to 45.3 percent of the whites and 30.6 percent of the Coloureds, but a mere 3.2 percent of the Africans.[9] The last figure was a matter of grave concern to DRC mission leaders.

Johannes du Plessis and the Justification of a Missionary Church

In the years after 1910, when four British-ruled colonies had united to form the Union of South Africa, many whites became convinced that the "native question" required urgent thought and action. Black poverty, already deepening in rural areas, was exacerbated by the segregationist Natives Land Act of 1913. Several strikes broke out among black workers in the mines and in the cities. Increased resentment was apparent, too, among the mission-educated black middle class, many of whom had recently formed the South African Native National Congress (later renamed the African National Congress). In

8. "Native" was used widely before the 1930s and was not usually regarded as pejorative. For a brief period some Africans referred to themselves as "Bantu," but in the apartheid era this term was used by the government and rejected by most Africans and liberal whites. From the early 1920s the preferred term among African leaders was "African."

9. C. H. Badenhorst, "Die ontwikkeling van die Bantoe op godsdienstige en maatskaplike gebied: Soos uit die oogpunt van die drie Afrikaanse Kerke gesien," in *Volkskongres oor die toekoms van die Bantoe: Referate en besluite: Volkskongres, Bloemfontein, 28-30 Junie 1956* (Stellenbosch, 1956), tab. I, p. 89.

this tense period the DRC came under fire from black leaders. The eminent African journalist Sol Plaatje charged that "the calculatingly outrageous treatment of the coloured races of South Africa by the Boer [Afrikaner] section of the community is mainly due to the sanction it receives from the Dutch Reformed Church." D. D. T. Jabavu, an African lecturer in African languages and Latin at the South African Native College (Fort Hare) and a close collaborator with missionaries, labeled the DRC "an anti-Native church."[10] Such statements alarmed mission-minded members of the DRC: "In spite of good work done by the D. R. Church for the last 30 years, the idea remains in the Natives' minds that this Church is opposed to their upward striving for more knowledge and enlightenment."[11]

The DRC response to these attacks was framed largely by Johannes du Plessis, since 1916 the professor of missions and New Testament at the DRC seminary at Stellenbosch. A staunch advocate of the evangelical tradition of the Cape Church, du Plessis had published, in 1919, a sympathetic biography of Andrew Murray, Jr., his church's towering evangelical figure and passionate supporter of missions. Never a missionary himself, du Plessis crossed Africa three times in a trek of some 16,781 miles, meeting between three hundred and four hundred missionaries in western and central Africa.[12] His account of this journey, published in English as *Thrice through the Dark Continent* (1917), along with his earlier *History of Christian Missions in South Africa* (1911), still the standard survey of the subject, propelled him into national and international prominence as a mission expert. In South Africa he participated actively in the General Missionary Conferences, serving in 1909 as conference secretary. In 1921 he attended the founding of the International Missionary Council (IMC) at Lake Mohonk, New York.[13] At Stellenbosch he devoted more time to biblical studies (and to the public controversies they generated) than to missiology. Yet he found time to publish a major study of missions in central Africa and, in 1932, *Wie sal gaan? Of, Die sending in teorie en praktyk* (Who shall go? Or, Mission in theory and practice), probably the most im-

10. Sol T. Plaatje, *Native Life in South Africa: Before and Since the European War and the Boer Rebellion* (London, 1916; reprint, Johannesburg, 1982), pp. 148-49; D. D. T. Jabavu, "Native Unrest: Its Cause and Cure," in *The Black Problem: Papers and Addresses on Various Native Problems* (Lovedale, 1920), pp. 4-5.

11. The Reverend D. G. Malan of Cape Town, quoted in "'De Kerkbode' and Native Education," *Christian Express,* 1 June 1921, p. 92; G. B. A. Gerdener, "Du Plessis, Johannes," in *Dictionary of South African Biography,* ed. W. J. De Kock, 4 vols. (Cape Town, 1968-81), 1:263.

12. G. B. A. Gerdener, *Die Boodskap van 'n man: Lewenskets van prof. J. du Plessis* (Stellenbosch, 1943), p. 122.

13. Gerdener, *Boodskap van 'n man,* pp. 61, 142-43.

pressive work of missiology published in South Africa before David Bosch's writings late in the century. Bosch himself called du Plessis "the founder of South African missiology."[14]

To respond to their critics, ten DRC mission leaders, led by du Plessis, wrote *The Dutch Reformed Church and the Native Problem* (1921). This document presented statistics on what the DRC was "doing for the Natives," but admitted that the church's efforts had been inadequate in some respects. The authors asserted that the DRC, more than other mission societies, had to take white prejudices into account: "Of all the missionary enterprises in South Africa, ours is the only one of any magnitude that is supported solely by funds raised in South Africa from people who are, and have been for generations, in immediate contact with the native races. There is still a large amount of deeply-rooted prejudice against mission work generally, and against educational mission work in particular."[15] The missionary leaders asserted without apology that the "white race is and must remain the ruling race," but also claimed that blacks had rights to "equal opportunities . . . to develop themselves along their own national lines, and in accordance with the highest ideals which their national consciousness, suffused and transformed by the spirit of Christianity, shall create for them."[16] The DRC writers regarded racial segregation as a "most excellent theory." Yet, ironically in view of later DRC stances, they showed themselves more aware of the ambiguities, contradictions, and pitfalls of segregation than many English-speaking theorists and missionaries of the time did, and possibly more than many blacks.[17] It was not, however, their vague and conventional segregationist sentiments but their forthright demands on behalf of blacks that were striking. They insisted on expanded secondary education for blacks, university education to create a black professional class, and greater funding for black education at all levels. Distancing themselves from those who demanded job color bars, they claimed to see "no immediate danger" to white workers from "the competition of Bantu tradesmen," even if blacks might come to monopolize certain trades. Pass laws that constrained the movements of black people ought either to be "abolished altogether, or so re-adjusted that their incidence falls only on the raw native." The DRC mission leaders also demanded higher wages for blacks, a right to strike equal to that of whites, better housing and

14. David J. Bosch, "Johannes du Plessis as sendingkundige," *Theologia Evangelica* 19, no. 1 (Mar. 1986): 67.

15. J. du Plessis et al., *The Dutch Reformed Church and the Native Problem* (n.p., [1921]), pp. 6-10.

16. J. du Plessis et al., *Dutch Reformed Church*, pp. 11-13.

17. J. du Plessis et al., *Dutch Reformed Church*, pp. 19-22.

sanitation for blacks in towns, and more lands to support a growing black population in the countryside.[18]

In the wake of this document, which was remarkably progressive for its time, the Federal Council of the DR Churches called a conference of twenty-nine African leaders and thirty-four white leaders from a broad array of churches and missions to debate the "native question." Du Plessis was the principal DRC speaker. Contemporary observers regarded this as the most important conference on black-white relations held to this time in South Africa. There were tense moments as black indignation clashed with white paternalism, but the conference ended on a surprisingly congenial note. The most significant conference resolutions had been drafted by Edgar Brookes, perhaps the leading English-speaking theorist of segregation. These called for the "differential development of the Bantu" and some segregation on the land, but rejected "complete segregation" and did not comment on political segregation (separate voting rolls for Africans), which African conferees had already rejected.[19] This conference marked perhaps the highest level of consensus that Africans, English-speaking whites, and Afrikaners would ever attain on segregation.

The DRC was lavishly praised for presiding over such a successful conference. Jabavu, whose criticisms had first stung du Plessis and his colleagues into action, declared the conference a "milestone" in interracial understanding. Z. R. Mahabane of the African National Congress said it had "restored the confidence of the Bantu people in the ruling race, and removed the causes of suspicion and unrest." For their part DRC mission leaders exploited the glowing publicity to stir up support for DRC missions and to exhort Afrikaners to treat blacks more equitably. They plunged, too, into ecumenical activities, taking a leading role at the 1925 (South African) General Missionary Conference and sending four delegates to the 1926 conference on Africa held by the IMC in Le Zoute, Belgium.[20]

Du Plessis and other DRC mission leaders struggled to hold together the loose network of Afrikaners, moderate blacks, and English-speaking whites

18. J. du Plessis et al., *Dutch Reformed Church,* pp. 22-29.

19. *European and Bantu: Being Papers and Addresses Read at the Conference on Native Affairs Held under the Auspices of the Federal Council of the D. R. Churches* (Cape Town, Stellenbosch, and Lovedale, 1924), p. 44.

20. "De Johannesburgse Konferensie: Indrukken van verscheidene voormannen," *Kerkbode,* 19 Oct. 1923, p. 373. *The Evangelisation of South Africa: Being a Report of the Sixth General Missionary Conference* (Cape Town, 1925), pp. 5, 181; Edwin W. Smith, *The Christian Mission in Africa: A Study Based on the Work of the International Conference at Le Zoute, Belgium, September 14th to 21st, 1926* (London, 1926), p. 186.

that had been forged in 1923. This became increasingly difficult when, in 1926, Parliament passed the Mines and Works Amendment (or "Colour Bar") Act, which in effect transferred many skilled jobs from Africans to whites. In the same year the prime minister, J. B. M. Hertzog, offered four "Native Bills" for public comment. The most contentious of these would remove Africans from the common voter rolls in the Cape Province, thus rescinding a right that dated from colonial times and was entrenched in the constitution. Segregation, heretofore a nebulous concept with uncertain consequences, now appeared unmistakably damaging to African interests. Jabavu and Brookes, devout Christians who had toyed with segregation, now renounced it.[21] Du Plessis, however, moved in the opposite direction. At the 1923 conference he had said, "Develop your own educational system, my native friends, hold by your own social traditions, advance along your own economic lines and work out your own political salvation."[22] He now appeared before a parliamentary committee to support the abolition of the Cape franchise, clashing publicly with the Anglican archbishop of Cape Town, who declared that "the right way to proceed is to give the native equal rights with the white man."[23] Yet the coalition held together long enough for the DRC, with du Plessis as the driving force, to hold another interracial conference at Cape Town in 1927. This conference, though less harmonious than its 1923 predecessor, agreed to demand some significant revisions to Hertzog's proposed legislation. By now, however, that leadership of the DRC was losing faith in du Plessis's policy of coalition building and advocacy on behalf of blacks. The Federal Council of the DR Churches pointedly refused to act on the Cape Town resolutions.[24]

The coalition unraveled further as du Plessis became embroiled in the so-called *kerksaak* (church case). For reasons only remotely connected to his missiology and ecumenical involvement, some of du Plessis's colleagues at Stellenbosch accused him of propagating theological modernism in his teaching and writing. Du Plessis vigorously contested the charges. The case became a public sensation as it wound its way through presbyteries, synods, and civil courts, until finally, in 1932, the Cape Supreme Court ruled in du

21. Paul B. Rich, *White Power and the Liberal Conscience: Racial Segregation and South African Liberalism, 1921-60* (Johannesburg, 1984), pp. 33-34; D. D. T. Jabavu, "The Segregation Fallacy," in *The Segregation Fallacy and Other Papers* (Lovedale, 1928) pp. 1-16.

22. *European and Bantu*, p. 15.

23. Union of South Africa, *Report of the Select Committee on the Subject of the Union Native Council Bill, Coloured Persons Rights Bill, Representation of Natives in Parliament Bill, and Natives Land (Amendment) Bill* (Cape Town, 1927), pp. 346-56; quotation on p. 356.

24. Dutch Reformed Church, *Handelingen . . . Raad der Kerken* (1927), pp. 11-12.

Plessis's favor. By then, however, his reputation was irretrievably damaged among conservatives in the church. He consented to leaving his academic post and died soon after, in 1935.[25]

As the DRC's principal spokesman on race during the 1920s, du Plessis never camouflaged his belief that whites must remain the ruling race. Yet he insisted that blacks did have a right to "protection, impartial justice and righteous treatment at our hands." They should be encouraged to "develop themselves along their own national lines," and segregation (though not total segregation) was the best way to accomplish this end.[26] On two cardinal issues — the black franchise and job color bars — du Plessis took strong stands repugnant to different members of his coalition. Because he rejected racial equality, he also opposed common citizenship for blacks and whites and a common franchise. "Natives," he said, "must refrain from always agitating for more political influence, and in particular, for the right to send their own representatives to our Parliament." Instead, "educated blacks, voting in separate constituencies in all provinces, should elect their own members of parliament."[27] But while the franchise was for du Plessis a "right," which Africans could not claim, economic freedom was an "opportunity" to which justice entitled them. No African should "be prevented by legislation from asking and getting the highest salary." When the Colour Bar Bill was before Parliament, he argued that the "artificial regulations" envisaged by the bill would "sooner or later give way to the quiet operation of economic laws," such as the law that "equal efficiency tends to be paid for at equal rates." He denied that white workers needed color bars to protect them from Africans willing to work for low wages. "The virtues and abilities the Caucasians have hoarded up, not over one or two generations, but over many centuries," would protect them.[28]

Though he differed with his black associates and some white "liberals" on the common franchise, and with many Afrikaners on color bars, du Plessis's political views were in the broad mainstream of informed white opinion of

25. Gerdener, *Boodskap van 'n man,* pp. 217-31.

26. J. du Plessis et al., *Dutch Reformed Church,* pp. 11-13, 19-22; J. du Plessis, "The South African Problem: Second Paper," *International Review of Missions: Special Double Africa Number* (July 1926): 366-70.

27. J. du Plessis et al., *Dutch Reformed Church,* p. 26; see also "Het naturellenvraagstuk," *Kerkbode,* 4 July 1923, p. 901; "Die Naturelle-Vraagstuk," *Kerkbode,* 14 July 1926, p. 50; "The South African Problem," p. 371; J. du Plessis, *Wie sal gaan? Of, Die sending in teorie en praktyk* (Cape Town, 1932), pp. 194-95.

28. J. du Plessis et al., *Dutch Reformed Church,* p. 27; see also "Maandkroniek: De Kleurslagboom," *Zoeklicht* 3, no. 7 (July 1925): 193-96.

the 1920s. He was no more a forerunner of apartheid than many other thinkers, most of them non-Afrikaners, who flirted with segregation. Moreover, unlike the apartheid theorists who would follow him, du Plessis was no Afrikaner nationalist. Though he loved the Afrikaans language and was deeply distressed by the plight of impoverished Afrikaners, his education, his reading, and his associates were largely in the evangelical, Anglo-American world. He believed, and rejoiced, that Afrikaners and English speakers were forging a common white South African culture.[29] He deplored Afrikaner nationalist theorists who claimed that Afrikaners had a distinctive "Calvinist worldview" based on their "Christian-National volk tradition." Du Plessis argued instead for a broadly conceived "Christian" worldview.[30]

Du Plessis did, however, believe that God had called the DRC to evangelize Africa. "To that end, religious persecution drove us to the Southern shore; to that end, Divine Providence prepared us over two and a half centuries; to that end, we stand here today, a beacon in the South, established by the divine Hand."[31] Yet this view should not be confused with slogans of the 1940s that called for an Afrikaner "salvation deed," a self-sacrificing campaign to reshape South African society. For du Plessis it was the Afrikaner church, not the *volk,* that was called by God, and it was called principally to preach the gospel to the heathen, only secondarily to engage in social engineering. Still his work, more than that of any other thinker, consolidated the intellectual platform from which later, more grandiose national projects could be launched. He was at pains to show that the Old and New Testaments were shot through with the necessity of mission.[32] "The Gospel of Christ does not include the idea of missions, but it *is* the idea of missions, and nothing else." "Missions cannot be taken away from Christianity without tearing its heart from its body."[33]

Because he so closely identified church and mission, du Plessis believed mission was an "activity that the *Church* as such must undertake and must control by means of commissions that it appoints itself." Less desirable were missions undertaken by interdenominational missionary societies, by local congregations, or by voluntary commissions only loosely linked to a church. Du Plessis emphatically ratified the DRC's long-entrenched tradition of centralized missions, coordinated and directed by powerful synods and by mis-

29. Gerdener, *Boodskap van 'n man,* p. 205.

30. "Maandkroniek: 'n Kalvinisties kongres," *Zoeklicht* 8, no. 7 (July 1929): 197-201.

31. Gerdener, *Boodskap van 'n man,* pp. 126-27.

32. J. du Plessis, *Gaat dan henen! Eenvoudige handleiding tot de studie der zending,* 2nd ed. (Amsterdam and Cape Town, 1911), pp. 22-34; J. du Plessis, *Wie sal gaan?* pp. 11-17.

33. J. du Plessis, *Wie sal gaan?* pp. 6-7, 21-23.

sion commissions under their control.[34] Although he did not contribute directly to the notion that Afrikaners were an intrinsically missionary *volk*, he did lay the intellectual groundwork for the idea that the DRC was an intrinsically missionary church with a broad social responsibility. He himself lived out his belief that missiologists and church synods should help shape the racial policies of South Africa. When the DRC, which overlapped almost exactly with the Afrikaner *volk*, was later captured by the theology of Christian nationalism, du Plessis's ideas of mission were readily appropriated by the leaders of the mobilized *volk* and, after 1948, by the rulers of South Africa.

J. G. Strydom and the Calling of a Missionary Nation

As du Plessis's influence was declining, an alternate school of DRC missiology arose in the Orange Free State, a province less Anglicized and less liberal than du Plessis's base in the western Cape. In 1929, at a Free State DRC conference on "the native question," the Reverend J. G. Strydom (not to be confused with the later prime minister, J. G. Strijdom) warned that Africans in the province were rejecting Christianity while some were converting to Islam. On the political front, white "negrophilists" and "Negroes in America" were enflaming Africans with the false claim that Africa should belong to Africans. More than two hundred churches and sects, "wolves in sheep's clothing," were corrupting the souls and behavior of Africans, as was the Roman Catholic Church, which was building churches and schools for blacks all over the Free State. For Strydom the gospel was Christendom's "only means of rescue from these and other dangers." Afrikaners must preach the gospel not only because Jesus commanded it, but also because it "serves as a blessing to ourselves and salvation for *volk* and fatherland."[35] Speaker after speaker echoed Strydom's alarm. We must "do *good* to the heathen or he shall end up doing *bad* to us," said one. The conference called for the founding of a mission journal to be the Free State church's "information office and means of propaganda." It decided, too, that it was time for "our Church clearly to express its standpoint in regard to relations with the native, and responsibility for him, in the religious as well as the social sphere."[36] With these mandates Strydom immediately joined with

34. J. du Plessis, *Wie sal gaan?* pp. 18-19, 42-53, 246.

35. J. G. Strydom, "Die gevare wat die naturelle regstreeks bedreig en ons onregstreeks," in *Die N.G. Kerk in die O.V.S. en die naturelle-vraagstuk* (Bloemfontein, 1929), pp. 75-81; quotation on p. 81.

36. Strydom, "Die gevare wat die naturelle regstreeks bedreig en ons onregstreeks," pp. 84, 94, 27.

other colleagues to found *Die Basuin* (the *Trumpet*), a journal of mission opinion, and to draft a mission policy, which the Synod of the Free State DRC adopted in 1931.

Johannes Gerhardus Strydom had been a pioneer missionary, from 1912 to 1919, among the Tiv of Nigeria. Returning to South Africa with a damaged heart, he began a new career, first as a minister, then, after 1926, as mission secretary of the Orange Free State DRC, a post he would hold for twenty-three years. Strydom at first found Free Staters little inclined to support missions — particularly missions within their own province, or missions that included education. Defying the danger to his weak heart, and paying some of his expenses from his own pocket, he traveled incessantly on second-class trains throughout the Free State, preaching the imperative of missions, raising funds, supervising missionaries and African evangelists, and founding black congregations. Every Afrikaner must support missions, Strydom said, as he depicted the "dark future for the white man in Africa if he does not follow Christ and also bring the heathen around him to the light."[37]

Strydom's views, as reflected in *Die Basuin* and the Free State church's mission policy, were distinctive in content and combative in tone. He turned his back on the ecumenical activities of du Plessis and did little to cultivate good relations with missionaries who did not share his views.[38] The Free State's mission policy emphatically repudiated tendencies to *gelykstelling* (equalization of the races) and "race degeneration and bastardization," which it declared to be "psychologically unsound," "denationalizing," and an abomination to "every right-minded white and native." Yet, in a striking juxtaposition of ideas, the Free State Mission Policy also proclaimed, in its first sentences, that "our church bases its relations with the native on the teaching of God's word that teaches that the Native is a human being with similar emotions to ours and that his soul is of equal value in the eyes of God as that of any other human being. He has the same right as we have to lay claim to the rights and privileges that are in principle bound to Christian civilization. Our view is that a sacred responsibility rests with us, as a Christian civilized people . . . to raise the native out of the poverty and misery of barbarism." To reconcile its hostility to *gelykstelling* with its conviction that blacks and whites were equal in Christ, the policy declared that the DRC would uplift Africans on their "own terrain, separated and apart" (the same idea repeated three times),

37. Lala Badenhorst, *Dienskneg* (published by the author, 1981), pp. 23-70, 76, 97-100, 103; quotation on p. 100.

38. See J. G. Strydom, "Die Afrikaner se sendingbeleid," *Basuin*, Mar. 1945, p. 3, for a typical critique of other missions.

striving "to build up the natives into a Christian people that through its own Christian virtue, energy, resourcefulness, and organization shall take care of its economic life apart from, yet, where possible, in cooperation with the white community." More concretely, the Free State church would assist Africans in founding their own economic organizations and insist that they received fair wages. But equal economic opportunities would exist only within races, and only in separate spheres. "Whites cannot demand [equality] in the natives' sphere, nor, on the other hand, can the natives demand it in the whites' sphere."[39]

In advocating "equality" while rejecting "equalization" in white areas, and in advocating black development in areas from which whites would be excluded, the Free State Mission Policy (1931) foreshadowed themes that would become prominent in the apartheid era. In fact, Jan Christoffel du Plessis, a minister at Bethlehem West and later a member of the *Basuin* editorial board, in his speech to the 1929 Kroonstad congress twice described DRC policy as "apartheid," six years before the term was used in political circles.[40] Du Plessis (not to be confused with the more famous Johannes du Plessis) profoundly shaped the economic passages in the Free State Mission Policy. He also embedded his "apartheid" views in a theory of conflicting nationalisms. Missions, he believed, had roused large parts of the African population from their "age-long Rip-van-Winkel slumber" to an "awakening national feeling of self and purposefulness." The South African problem had to be studied "from the viewpoint of the national aspirations of both races," a theme that would later come into its own in the era of Verwoerd. Taking his cue from the Native Economic Commission (1932), du Plessis argued vigorously for economic devel-

39. "Die Sendingbeleid van die Nederduitse Gereformeerde Kerk van die Oranje-Vrystaat, 1931," app. I, Johan Andries Lombard, "Ontwikkeling in die sendingbeleid en -praktyk van die Nederduitse Gereformeerde Kerk gedurende die tydperk 1932 tot 1962" (D.Th. thesis, University of the North, 1985), p. 306.

40. I have not found evidence that his usage influenced anyone else directly. J. C. du Plessis, "Die ideale van ons kerk in verband met sendingwerk," in *Die N.G. Kerk in die O.V.S.* "The explanation for the spirit of *apartheid,* which has always marked our line of conduct, and for which some, through misunderstanding, censure us, is in this foundational idea of Mission work [the notion of developing culturally specific forms of Christianity among Africans], and not in racial prejudice" (p. 22). "Segregation so meant is consequently not *apartheid* on the basis of prejudice but is just another word for concentrating on everything that is distinctive [to the African] and on everything that fosters 'being-oneself' ['*selfsyn*']' (p. 25). In 1951 du Plessis would write to "Dawie," the *Burger* columnist, to draw attention to his use of the term in 1929: *Dawie, 1946-1964; 'n Bloemlesing uit die geskrifte van Die Burger se politieke kommentator,* ed. Louis Louw (Cape Town, 1965), p. 49. I am grateful to Hermann Giliomee for this last reference.

opment of the reserves (rural areas exclusively for African occupation). Such development would attract Africans back from the city, lessen competition with whites, and lay the foundations for a healthy African nation.[41]

To set South Africa on the proper course, the Free Staters wanted drastically to reform African education. J. P. Wessels, a missionary from Harrismith, had asserted at Kroonstad that in the Free State, where 90 percent of whites were members of the DRC, "it goes without saying that native education . . . should be cast in a pure Afrikaans mold." Wessels asked, "Who is today the best friend of the white man in this land? The native who got his education from the DR Church. He is the greatest opponent of the political agitators."[42] The speakers at Kroonstad had agreed that the DRC must vigorously propagate an educational policy beneficial to both whites and blacks; it must educate blacks to "know their own language, people, and history," and not to "hate the white man."[43] The Free State Mission Policy, elaborating on this theme, asserted that education must make the African "suited for his land and people," no mere "follower and imitator of white civilization." An educated African, retaining his "racial identity" and his "racial connection" to his society, must gain an opportunity, in his separate sphere, "to reach the highest rung of an educated life that he possibly can." He should, in addition, learn Afrikaans as well as English.[44]

Most of these ideas had been expressed before — more hesitantly and tentatively — by English-speaking segregationists and by Cape DRC figures like Johannes du Plessis. Yet the combination of ideas — racial equality in principle, no white rights in black spheres, no black rights in white spheres, unlimited "advancement" of blacks along a separate track, emerging African nations, generous offers of Christian tutelage and assistance to blacks — was so emphatic (despite rather sloppy drafting) and so fundamental to the document that one can say that it adumbrated, in the most general terms, the apartheid ideology almost two decades before a South African government would adopt it as official policy.

41. J. C. du Plessis, "Die ideale van ons kerk in verband met sendingwerk," p. 20; J. C. du Plessis, "Ethiopianisme en die naturelle probleem," *Basuin,* Nov. 1934, pp. 11-13; "Die Uitwerking van Ethiopianisme op sending beleid en naturelle opvoeding," *Basuin,* Apr. 1936, pp. 14-15; "Ethiopianisme en die economiese sy van die naturelle probleem," *Basuin,* Aug. 1936, pp. 17-19, and Oct. 1936, pp. 17-18.

42. J. P. Wessels, "Ons deel in die onderwys van die naturel op dorpe en plase en die gevaar as ons terugstaan," in *Die N.G. Kerk in die O.V.S.,* pp. 34-35.

43. Dan P. van der Merwe, "Afrikaans in naturelle skole," in *Die N.G. Kerk in die O.V.S.,* pp. 60-61; C. J. van R. Smit, "Hulpmiddels daarteen," in *Die N.G. Kerk in die O.V.S.,* p. 72.

44. Lombard, "Sendingbeleid," pp. 304-5.

Perhaps in part to temper Free State radicalism, the Cape DRC adopted its own mission policy in 1932. This document bore virtually no resemblance to the Free State's, apart from its (briefer and more tactful) rejection of "race mixture and social equality." While the Free State had begun with the "duty" of "a Christian, civilized *volk*" to spread the gospel, the Cape, in traditional evangelical fashion, began with Jesus' Great Commission to the *church.* The Cape document stuck with the vaguely segregationist language of the 1920s but gave it little emphasis. In stark contrast to the Free State document, it paid considerable attention to the DRC's need to cooperate with "other recognized Protestant churches and mission societies."[45]

By the early 1930s the dialogue between whites and blacks had passed from the control of the DRC into the hands of secular institutions like the South African Institute of Race Relations, founded in 1929. To regain the initiative, but on lines distinct from those of Johannes du Plessis, the Federal Council of the DR Churches arranged for the crafting of a federal mission policy. After widespread consultation among white DRC leaders, Strydom of the Free State and Johannes Reyneke (formerly of the Cape church, but from 1934 mission secretary of the Transvaal church) and others produced a draft. They had initially intended to consult black leaders "under our influence," but never did. Giving almost equal weight to Free State and Cape concerns, the document fudged the issue of which Afrikaner body was to fulfill Jesus' Great Commission: the *volk* or the church. It said *both* that God had arranged for "the first white inhabitants of this southern corner of Dark Africa" to evangelize "the heathen nations of this continent," *and* that it was "the particular privilege and responsibility of the DR Church of South Africa . . . to bring the Gospel to the Heathen of this land." The federal policy incorporated most of the Cape church's friendly gestures toward other Protestants. On *gelykstelling* and "racial mixing," it was firmer and more elaborate than the Cape's, vaguer and less inflammatory than the Free State's. It adopted the essence of the Free State's economic policy, shearing it of its most negative expressions. It stressed, instead, the positive economic development of blacks: "as far as possible separate [*apart*] from whites," but with whites helping and encouraging, and "providing work and opportunity for development and granting [Africans] reasonable compensation for services." The federal educational policy stressed African culture, opposed Africans "imitating Westerners," and insisted that Africans learn Afrikaans as well as English — all themes based closely on the Free State document.

45. Lombard, "Sendingbeleid," app. II, "Die sendingbeleid van die Nederduitse Gereformeerde Kerk in Suid-Afrika, 1932," pp. 308-13.

In several respects, then, in 1935 the federated Dutch Reformed churches entangled their mission enterprises with the agenda of an increasingly mobilized *volk,* but not as closely as the Free State Mission Policy had done. Also, the federal policy adopted, in temperate language, the Free State's proto-apartheid vision as one of its themes. In a small but potentially significant deviation from the Free State text, it said "the Native and the Coloured must be assisted to develop into self-respecting Christian nations" *(volke)* rather than a single "Christian people" as the Free State document had put it. While this new wording may have been devised merely to distinguish Coloureds from Africans, it was compatible with the policy of separate African nations later adopted by Prime Minister Verwoerd.[46]

G. B. A. Gerdener and the Ideology of a Missionary Government

Though Strydom and the Free State church had goaded the federated Dutch Reformed churches to adopt a mission policy and had profoundly affected its content, it was chiefly through the efforts of the more moderate Cape church that the policy made its way into the National Party's apartheid agenda. In the late 1940s and early 1950s the key link between DRC missions and Afrikaner politicians was Gustav Bernhard August Gerdener, the son of a German missionary and, from 1937 to 1955, Johannes du Plessis's successor as professor of missions at Stellenbosch. Gerdener, like du Plessis, moved in ecumenical Protestant circles both in South Africa and overseas. He attended the 1910 missionary conference at Edinburgh and the 1948 founding of the World Council of Churches (WCC) in Amsterdam. Many of his writings were in English, and in a conciliatory spirit he frequently called English-speaking whites "English-speaking Afrikaners."[47] His theological idiom, like du Plessis's, was evangelical. Like du Plessis, he was a prolific writer on the history of DRC missions and a strong partisan of the DRC's tradition of racially separate churches — in 1932 he had supervised the founding of a church for Africans in the Transvaal. In the theological faculty at Stellenbosch, bitterly divided in the wake of the *kerksaak,* Gerdener was apparently regarded as a du Plessis sympathizer.[48] In

46. Lombard, "Sendingbeleid," app. III, "Die Sendingbeleid van die Gefedereerde Nederduitse Gereformeerde Kerke van Suid-Afrika, 1935," pp. 314-17.

47. Gerdener, *Die Afrikaner en die sending,* pp. 3-4.

48. This is the most likely meaning of F. E. O'Brien Geldenhuys, *In die stroomversnellings: Vyftig jaar van die NG Kerk* (Cape Town, 1982), p. 10. See also Gideon van der Watt, "GBA Gerdener: Koersaanwyser in die Nederduitse Gereformeerde Kerk in Sending en Ekumene" (D.Th. thesis, University of the Orange Free State, 1990), pp. 50-51.

fact, well before the wounds of the church had completely healed, he wrote a long biography of du Plessis, which dealt only cursorily with the *kerksaak* but provocatively portrayed his subject as a model son of the DRC, a viewpoint that "did not meet with universal approval."[49] In 1958 he published *Recent Developments in the South African Mission Field,* a thoroughly ecumenical update of the *History of Christian Missions in South Africa* that his "illustrious friend" du Plessis had published in 1911.[50]

Replicating du Plessis's political activities, Gerdener tried to ally DRC stalwarts with black and English-speaking white Christians in order to address the burning questions of race. He defended the DRC before non-Afrikaner audiences by expounding the federal mission policy. To encourage debate and refinement of this policy, in 1939 he founded *Op die Horison,* a more moderate missionary journal than the Free State's *Basuin,* and continued to edit it until 1950. From as early as 1943, *Op die Horison* published black authors, to the consternation of some DRC readers, and regularly gave space to DRC and non-DRC writers troubled by aspects of the emerging apartheid policy. Gerdener frequently exhorted the Dutch Reformed churches to cooperate with other Protestants and join the ecumenical Christian Council of South Africa. He was critical both of the neo-Calvinist "Christian-National" theologies flourishing in some DRC circles by the late 1940s and of the petulant nationalist Strydom, whom he accused of chaotic thinking, exaggeration, and an "obsession against English church bodies."[51]

More than du Plessis, Gerdener had a powerful institutional platform for rallying Afrikaners to missions and also for lobbying governments. In 1942 he founded and chaired the Federal Mission Council (FMC), a body of the four Dutch Reformed churches charged to attend to "missionary matters of Union scope," including all "racial, social and economic questions." From its founding the FMC vigorously lobbied government ministers for such issues as a ban on racially mixed marriages, and more positively, for black universities, one of Gerdener's own enthusiasms.[52] Strydom was also an active member of

49. Gerdener, *Boodskap van 'n man;* D. Crafford, *Aan God die dank: Geskiedenis van die sending van die Ned. Geref. Kerk binne die Republiek van Suid-Afrika en enkele aangrensende buurstate* (Pretoria, 1982), 2, p. 466.

50. G. B. A. Gerdener, *Recent Developments in the South African Mission Field* (Cape Town and Pretoria, 1958), pp. 7-8.

51. G. B. A. Gerdener, "Boekbespreking," *Op die horison* (hereafter *OdH*) 3 (1941): 144.

52. DRC Archives, Cape Town (hereafter DRC), SA(A) 4 1/1, G. B. A. Gerdener, "Iets oor die voorgeskiedenis van die Kommissie vir Naturellesake van die Raad der Kerke, waaruit gebore is die Sendingraad van die Nederduitse Gereformeerde Kerke in S.A.," pp. 1-4; Minutes of the FMC, 1 Oct. 1942, pp. 21-24; Minutes of the FMC, 19 Aug. 1943, pp. 52-54.

the FMC, and sometimes its chair. He and Gerdener frequently clashed. Strydom demanded a forthright proclamation of DRC policies, while Gerdener pleaded for positive actions to convince blacks that the promises of its mission policy would be fulfilled.[53]

In the early and mid-1940s Gerdener favored relatively mild forms of segregation, which he believed had not yet been seriously implemented.[54] But, more than earlier DRC leaders, he stressed the positive side of segregation, the need to help Africans "develop" in their own areas. He never became comfortable with the new term "apartheid," though he sometimes used it. Believing its connotations were negative, he preferred such terms as "separate development" *(aparte ontwikkeling* or *eiesoortige ontwikkeling)* and "independent development" *(selfstandige ontwikkeling),* which he thought sounded progressive and fair.[55] From an early date he emphatically asserted that segregation and Christianization must lead not to perpetuating the subordination of blacks, but eventually to "an equivalent grade of independence as we [whites] aspire to in the rank of nations." Gerdener was chiefly responsible for revisions to the 1935 mission policy made by the FMC in 1945. The new version, which was subsequently ratified by the Dutch Reformed synods, was much more forthright than its predecessor in asserting that "the church is in favour of co-equal education and instruction, in their own sphere, of the Coloured and Native with what the European enjoys," and "desires to co-operate with the State and the people themselves in respect of economic justice, better housing, health services and general social uplift."[56]

In 1943 when three academics at Stellenbosch University began to advocate "absolute and total segregation," Gerdener declared their viewpoint "too dogmatic" and unfeasible. He also dissented from their authoritarian and hyper-nationalist belief that South Africa could solve its race problem only through a "common action of the *volk,* borne on a united *volk* spirit, carried out by a powerful *volk* movement . . . led and ruled by a powerful government sympathetic to the *volk.*"[57] Within a few years, however, Gerdener had partially reversed himself on both issues, advocating separation severe enough to

53. E.g., DRC, SA(A) 4 1/1(a), Minutes of 11 Mar. 1944, p. 38.

54. "Van die redaksie," *OdH* 4, no. 4 (Dec. 1942): 145-46.

55. "Van die redaksie," *OdH* 5, no. 1 (Mar. 1943): 2; "Van die redaksie: Nog 'n S.O.S.," *OdH* 5, no. 2 (June 1943): 53; "'n Verduideliking," *OdH* 5, no. 3 (Sept. 1943): 99.

56. Gerdener, *Recent Developments,* pp. 272-73. I have quoted the English translation that Gerdener himself used to convey the mission policy to the non-Afrikaans world.

57. "Oraloor," *OdH* 2, no. 3 (Sept. 1940): 141; "Van die redaksie," *OdH* 5, no. 1 (Mar. 1943): 1-3; editorial comments on "Oplossing van die naturellevraagstuk," by P. J. Coertze, F. J. Language, and B. I. C. van Eeden in *OdH* 5, no. 2 (June 1943), pp. 92-93.

inflict heavy economic sacrifices on whites and cooperating closely with the Nationalist government elected in 1948 to implement his separatist vision. But he and contributors to his journal frequently worried that apartheid or separate development would be undermined by whites' unwillingness to sacrifice. "What are our motives for the proposed policy of separate treatment?" he asked. "Is it really equivalent and autonomous development, or is it merely a cheap and easy way to steer clear of the question?" Gerdener frequently permitted authors to vent their doubts about apartheid. B. J. Marais, for example, writing for *Op die horison* in the year before the Nationalist electoral victory, asserted that for apartheid to be justified, it must be inspired by "Christian love and not by racial egotism or a feeling of racial superiority." Whites would have to pay an enormously high price for true apartheid, said Marais, and face opposition from "ninety per cent of those who today are supporters of segregation or apartheid."[58]

In 1946 and 1947, just before the Nationalist electoral victory, South Africa faced a barrage of criticism at the newly founded United Nations, particularly over its treatment of Indians and its administration of the League of Nations Mandate in South-West Africa. Gerdener was among the first to argue that South Africans, now dragged into an international spotlight, must "summon all our powers to justify ourselves to the world and to prove our good faith." Though he claimed that the United Nations' hostility was largely misinformed and irrational, he believed vigorous publicity of the DRC mission policy and the theory of separate development could deflect at least some of it. South Africa's policies, he said, were not based on skin color alone, as was falsely charged in New York, but on "colour paired with another social structure, with another language, tradition, and lifestyle." He called on Afrikaners "with all their might to win the full trust of the non-whites — or to re-win it where we have perhaps lost it. . . . The day of the master-servant relationship is quickly passing. But in more than one area the trustee-minor relationship is also over. And then comes the relationship of equals in separate terrains, fellow citizens of a constituted confederation, the precise structure of which we cannot now foresee."[59]

After the victory of the National Party, whose "color policy" he had helped draft, Gerdener, now almost seventy, approached the pinnacle of his influence. He sat on the Eiselen commission, 1949-51, whose recommendations on African education laid the basis for the bitterly contested Bantu Education

58. "Van die redaksie," *OdH* 9, no. 1 (Mar. 1947): 2; B. J. Marais, "'n Kritiese beoordeling van die standpunt van ons Kerk insake rasseverhoudings met die oog op die gebeure oorsee," *OdH* 9, no. 2 (June 1947): 76-79.

59. [Gerdener], "Ons rassevraagstuk gesien in die lig van die gebeurtenisse oorsee," *OdH* 9, no. 1 (Mar. 1947): 12-18.

Act of 1953, the death knell of mission schools. In 1950 he was founding member of the South African Bureau of Race Relations (SABRA), a secular think tank established to refine apartheid thought and counter the more liberal South African Institute of Race Relations (one of whose eight founders, ironically, had been Gerdener's mentor, Johannes du Plessis). The high point in Gerdener's public career was reached in 1950 when the FMC held a church congress on the "race question" attended by representatives of dozens of DRC mission bodies. Gerdener chaired the conference, edited its papers, and used it as a platform to address Afrikaners over the radio, calling them to prove to blacks that "by apartheid we do not mean negative separation and indifference but positive development and progress."[60] In an era when Afrikaner organizations convened major congresses almost every year, the 1950 church congress was exceptional in the scope, detail, and careful presentation of its recommendations. It also attracted unusually extensive coverage from the English-language press. Long before delivery, all speeches had been stringently edited and coordinated by an oversight committee that included such secular apartheid theorists as P. J. Coertze, along with the active political figures W. W. M. Eiselen, Nico Diederichs, and De Wet Nel.[61] Gerdener was clearly the principal drafter of the conference resolutions, which closely reflected his views. The conference called on the state to take leadership in racial matters, to take control of black schools and hospitals, and to provide separate universities for blacks. It envisaged close ties between the state, the DRC's missions, and SABRA. It stressed the positive aspects of apartheid (frequently using Gerdener's term "separate development," years before the government adopted it), above all the necessity of providing "homelands" for blacks in the reserves. In line with much DRC thinking, and with missionary thinking generally, the conference demanded more land for blacks, better housing and amenities for blacks on white farms and in the cities; it even decried the effects of job color bars on blacks. As a solution to South Africa's problems, it advocated "eventual total separation" of the races.[62]

60. G. B. A. Gerdener, "Radiobookskap," in *Die Naturellevraagstuk: Referate gelewer op die Kerklike Kongres van die Gefedereerde Ned. Geref. Kerke in Suid Afrika, byeengeroep deur die Federale Sendingraad* (Bloemfontein, 1950), p. 178.

61. "Voorberig," in *Die Naturellevraagstuk*, pp. 2-3; DRC, SA(A) 1/1, Minutes of the FMC, 1-3 Oct. 1949, p. 224.

62. *Die Naturellevraagstuk*, pp. 20-21, 42-45, 81-83, 116-19, 170-71. The minutes of the conference are in DRC, SA(A) 1/1 Notule van die Kerklike Kongres . . . 4-6 Apr. 1950, pp. 215-30. The paper givers were Gerdener, C. H. Badenhorst, A. A. van Schalkwyk, P. J. Coertze, M. C. de Wet Nel (replacing C. A. van Niekerk), D. F. de Beer (replacing N. Diedrichs), and J. H. Rauch.

The FMC immediately sent a deputation to present the conference's resolutions to government ministers. The minister of education said he was too busy to meet them, while the minister of health expressed vague concurrence with their ideas. But the more important minister of native affairs told the delegation that "the implementation of the policy of apartheid" was "impractical," asserting that white farmers and industries had serious objections to any policy that would shrink their already inadequate African work force. The unkindest cut came from the prime minister, D. F. Malan (himself a DRC clergyman and mission enthusiast before he entered politics in 1915), who told the delegates that "apartheid as envisaged by the congress [was] an ideal that in practice is not at present feasible. [But] the path the Government now follows is not incompatible with eventual separation [of the races]."[63]

However much the missionary leaders of the DRC might have helped fashion the apartheid doctrine, the new "apartheid" regime wanted no further advice from the church if it meant implementing the policy's more generous and costly dimensions. (Three years earlier, before his electoral victory, Malan had similarly rebuffed Strydom, telling him "he doubted the wisdom of holding out the prospect of full independence [for blacks] already, while the non-white races clearly will not be ready for it for many years.")[64] The FMC apparently took the hint. It veered away from politics and attended instead to traditional missionary matters, such as the regulation of African marriage. Gerdener for his part continued to pursue his goals in a more secular setting, taking over the chairmanship of SABRA in 1951, a post he held until 1955. During his years at SABRA's helm, he repeatedly called on whites to advance toward total apartheid by gradually weaning themselves from their reliance on cheap African labor: "One fears," he said, "that the ruling motive among the great majority of whites in South Africa for supporting apartheid or segregation is egotistical and not altruistic." Not all members of SABRA supported him on this issue, which was eventually rejected by Verwoerd and Eiselen, respectively the minister and secretary of native affairs.[65] Gerdener also remained active in the missionary councils of the DRC, defending the DRC's mission policy and the government's policy to black and English-speaking Christians and to the rest of the world. In 1951 and 1952 he organized four conferences for black church leaders in the DRC. In 1953 he organized and chaired a conference with leaders of English-speaking churches. This meeting was polarized, not only between

63. DRC, SA(A) 1/1 (a), Minutes of the Executive Committee of the FMC, 4 May 1950, pp. 241-42.

64. Badenhorst, *Dienskneg*, pp. 149-50.

65. John Lazar, "Conformity and Conflict: Afrikaner Nationalist Politics in South Africa, 1948-1961" (D.Phil. thesis, University of Oxford, 1987), pp. 174-85; quotation on p. 180.

the DRC and the other churches, but also between DRC delegates who believed apartheid to be biblically mandated and those who regarded it as a practical measure only. Pronouncing such contentious conferences a waste of time, the churches of the Free State and Natal refused to attend an interracial conference called in 1954 by the Transvaal Dutch Reformed Church, with Gerdener as a principal speaker.[66] This conference formed a continuing committee to plan even more conferences throughout the 1950s. Gerdener, however, now seventy-four, was increasingly overshadowed by younger leaders in the enterprise of selling the mission policy and apartheid. This campaign would receive an almost fatal blow in 1960 when, during a "consultation" organized by the WCC at Cottesloe, the DRC delegates acquiesced in a number of criticisms of apartheid, only to be vehemently assailed by the South African government and then repudiated by their own church synods.[67]

Missions and the Innovations of Apartheid

In the 1940s and 1950s advocates and enemies of apartheid agreed that the ideology was somehow rooted in Afrikaners' religion, particularly in their "Calvinism." Though in subsequent decades historians have disagreed on the exact nature of the Calvinism-apartheid link, and though some have denied it altogether, two lines of investigation have met with some success. First, Afrikaners' attachment to racial purity and hostility to *gelykstelling* have been traced in part to Reformed baptismal theologies of the early colonial period.[68] (The view that early colonists came to believe themselves a *volk* with a divine calling has, however, been discredited.)[69] Second, it has been shown

66. R. T. J. Lombard, *Die Nederduitse Gereformeerde Kerke en rassepolitiek: Met speciale verwysing na die jare 1948-1961* (Silverton, 1981), pp. 104-9.

67. A. H. Lückhoff, *Cottesloe* (Cape Town, 1978), passim.

68. Jonathan Neil Gerstner, *The Thousand Generation Covenant: Dutch Reformed Covenant Theology and Group Identity in Colonial South Africa, 1652-1814* (Leiden, New York, Copenhagen, and Cologne, 1991); Robert C.-H. Shell, *Children of Bondage: A Social History of the Slave Society at the Cape of Good Hope, 1652-1838* (Hanover and Middletown, Conn., 1994), pp. 330-70.

69. Chiefly by André du Toit in "No Chosen People: The Myth of the Calvinist Origins of Afrikaner Nationalism and Racial Ideology," *American Historical Review* 88, no. 4 (Oct. 1983): esp. 920-28; "Captive to the Nationalist Paradigm: Prof. F. A. van Jaarsveld and the Historical Evidence for the Afrikaner's Ideas on His Calling and Mission," *South African Historical Journal* 16 (1984): 49-80; "Puritans in Africa? Afrikaner 'Calvinism' and Kuyperian Neo-Calvinism in Late Nineteenth-Century South Africa," *Comparative Studies in Society and History* 27, no. 2 (1985): 209-40.

how intellectual elites of the 1930s and 1940s, many of them "neo-Calvinists" at Potchefstroom, a university linked to the tiny Gereformeerde Church, created a "Christian-National" ideology, which they successfully marketed, first to many clergy of the massive DRC and later to Afrikanerdom as a whole.[70] Constrained by space, I have alluded only briefly to anti-*gelykstelling* and Christian Nationalism, though I believe both to be crucial components of the Calvinism-apartheid nexus. Instead I have followed a third trail, one carefully blazed by Dutch Reformed writers[71] but ignored by secular historians, the role of the missionary leaders of the DRC.

In the 1920s DRC missionary leaders joined discussions on the "native question" that were already under way among African Christians, white "liberals," and government officials.[72] Johannes du Plessis managed briefly to gain some mastery over this discussion by adopting, with a slightly distinctive spin, conventional segregationist ideas long put into circulation by non-Afrikaners. His career as a political activist suggested the power DRC missions might come to exert over social policy, while his missiological writings uncovered the sources of this power: centrally controlled missions, powerful synods, and a church closely identified with an awakening nation.

After du Plessis's fall, younger DRC missionary leaders campaigned to transmute the nebulous, fragmented notions of segregation into a plan for thorough social transformation. Apartheid appealed to Afrikaners in part because it fused Afrikaner nationalism — with its exalted emotions, intellectual rationale, and elaborate organization — with the grab bag of segregationist notions formerly of interest only to a handful of missionaries, politicians, and theorists. The Free State Church had aligned mission and nationalism rather brazenly in 1931. The federated DRC did so, more circumspectly, in 1935. It was not until December 1934 that the Afrikaner Bond vir

70. T. Dunbar Moodie, *The Rise of Afrikanerdom: Power, Apartheid, and the Afrikaner Civil Religion* (Berkeley, Los Angeles, and London, 1975); Charles Bloomberg, *Christian-Nationalism and the Rise of the Afrikaner Broederbond in South Africa, 1918-48*, ed. Saul Dubow (Bloomington and Indianapolis, 1989).

71. Lombard, *Die Nederduitse Gereformeerde Kerke en rassepolitiek;* J. C. Adonis, *Die afgebreekte skeidsmuur weer opgebou: Die verstrengeling van die sendingbeleid van die Nederduitse Gereformeerde Kerk in Suid-Afrika met die praktyk en ideologie van die Apartheid in historiese perspektief* (Amsterdam, 1982); Lombard, "Sendingbeleid"; Andries Johannes Botha, *Die evolusie van'n volksteologie* (Bellville, 1986); *Die NG Kerk en apartheid*, ed. Johann Kinghorn (Johannesburg, 1986); J. A. Loubser, *The Apartheid Bible: A Critical Review of Racial Theology in South Africa* (Cape Town, 1987).

72. Richard Elphick, "Mission Christianity and Interwar Liberalism," in *Democratic Liberalism in South Africa: Its History and Prospect*, ed. R. Elphick, J. Butler, and D. Welsh (Middletown, Conn., Cape Town, and Johannesburg, 1987), pp. 64-80.

Rassestudie, the first secular body to address race policy from a distinctly Afrikaans perspective, began to meet. In any event, it apparently soon petered out.[73] The Potchefstroom intellectuals, who had been honing an ideology of Christian Nationalism since the 1920s, did publish a few articles on race and on African education in the 1930s, but did not present a full-orbed exposition of apartheid to a wide audience before 1940.[74] Academics based in secular universities published their first book-length expositions of apartheid in 1943 and 1945.[75] Yet from the mid-1930s DRC leaders had been propagating their church's mission policy, and its apartheid extensions, to broad and influential audiences.

Apartheid, as the DRC expounded it by 1945, differed from segregation not so much in its specifics as in its totalistic vision (complete racial separation, withdrawal of black labor, promise of a final solution) and in its stress on the positive "development" of blacks (through state-run schools, the encouragement of black nationalism[s], and the provision of black homelands that would acquire autonomy or even independence). DRC mission leaders were among the first to rework segregation into apartheid and to propagate the new vision among Afrikaners. Among them, Strydom was a key figure, though he was no theologian or missiologist and his influence waned after 1935. Ironically Gerdener — only a moderate nationalist and a late convert to total segregation — was the most prominent mission spokesman. His career exemplified not only the importance of the mission impulse, but also its gradual secularization, as he carried the idealistic notions of "positive apartheid" or "separate development" out of the churches, where they had been ripening for a decade, into the National Party program, and on into SABRA, a secular think tank.

Apartheid enjoyed great success as a political slogan because it tapped into whites' grassroots racism, their fear of *gelykstelling,* and their desire to escape daily frictions *(wrywing)* with members of other races; and also because

73. Rhoodie and Venter, p. 145; Lombard, *Die Nederduitse Gereformeerde Kerke en rassepolitiek,* pp. 49-50, 119.

74. Statement based on an analysis of *Wagtoring* (in 1933 renamed *Koers*), the principal neo-Calvinist journal, between 1928 and 1940. Significantly, the first major compendium of neo-Calvinist thought published in South Africa, H. G. Stoker and F. J. M. Potgieter, eds., *Koers in die krisis* (Stellenbosch, 1935), devoted only two of its forty-two articles to racial matters. The second volume of *Koers in die krisis* (1940), however, had a weighty article by L. J. du Plessis, "Liberalistiese en Calvinistiese naturelle politiek."

75. P. J. Coertze, F. J. Language, and B. I. C. van Eeden, *Die oplossing van die naturellevraagstuk in Suid-Afrika* (Johannesburg, 1943); G. Cronjé, *'n Tuiste vir die nageslag: Die blyvende oplossing van Suid-Afrika se rassevraagstukke* (Johannesburg, 1945).

it played into the emotions and objectives of an aroused Afrikaner *volk*. To varying degrees the DRC missionary leaders shared or at least accommodated both racism and nationalism. Yet they were determined to inject an element of self-sacrificing idealism, to make their scheme for Afrikaner survival acceptable to a Christian conscience. Their determination led the DRC into disaster. In time racism and nationalism would triumph over idealism, and the idealists in the DRC, many of them mission leaders, would find themselves powerless to redirect government policy. Yet, enthralled by their utopian vision, they would persist in explaining the inexplicable, and justifying the unjustifiable, to a skeptical and increasingly hostile world.

CHAPTER 4

The Universities' Mission to Central Africa: Anglo-Catholicism and the Twentieth-Century Colonial Encounter

ANDREW PORTER

A recent attempt to explain that the history of the Universities' Mission to Central Africa (UMCA) might provide for reflection on the themes of missions and the end of empire met with immediate skepticism. It was suggested that the mission was both the merest of minnows set alongside those blue whales of the missionary world, the London Missionary Society (LMS) or Council for World Mission, and the Church Missionary — now Mission — Society (CMS). On the Richter scale of missionary protest or agitation, it registered far lower than, say, the Scottish missions. Did not its limited resources simply demonstrate that its theology, ecclesiology, and liturgy represented a comparatively unimportant strand in Britain's Christian tradition, and in consequence carried little political weight? Its demise by absorption into the Society for the Propagation of the Gospel to form the United Society for the Propagation of the Gospel in 1964-65 might be seen as evidence of the comparative ease with which, unlike other mission societies, it was overwhelmed by the main currents of modernity — professionalization, secularization, racial and nationalist politics, and the multilayered transfers of power associated with the end of the European empires.

These suggestions of insignificance or weakness, an appearance of being on the losing side, and the possibility of alternative analytical approaches may well, and from some angles even rightly, cast doubt on the value of the enterprise. It is not only historians of Africa and decolonization who, generally paying little or no attention to the missionary dimension of their subject, might feel inclined to overlook the UMCA.[1] Awash with antiquarian relics, missionary historiography is also likely to benefit far more from a substantial injection of analytical comparisons than the multiplication of minor case studies. I would like to suggest, however, that the record of the UMCA deserves our attention precisely because its difficulties and distinctive features provoke important comparative questions. In particular, an investigation of the UMCA certainly raises, and may help to illuminate, that most central of issues, the extent to which the theology and ecclesiastical traditions of particular missionary societies either helped or hindered them in approaching the transition from the world of colonial rule to that of the newly independent nation-state. In following this particular line of investigation, I do not of course intend to suggest that other perspectives are less deserving of study. Most obviously in this respect, the mission's involvement at different times with the German and Portuguese colonial authorities; its shifting relationships with the different white settler communities throughout eastern and central Africa, to whom, as well as to Africans, its members also ministered; and its long-term contribution to the postindependence development of Anglican Christianity, in which women have also played a vital role, all spring to mind.[2]

I

The significance of varieties of Christian belief or theology for the development of missionary strategy and mission-influenced approaches to colonial politics is still frequently ignored. This may be variously explained. In an increasingly secular academic profession, historians have often found the subject itself uncongenial, and have abandoned it as the private preserve of missiologists. In the context of imperial rule they have commonly portrayed

1. The UMCA features most significantly in Terence Ranger, "Missionary Adaptation of African Religious Institutions: The Masasi Case," in *The Historical Study of African Religion, with Special Reference to East and Central Africa,* ed. T. O. Ranger and I. N. Kimambo (London, 1972), pp. 231-51, and in John Weller, "The Influence on National Affairs of Alston May, Bishop of Northern Rhodesia, 1914-40," in *Themes in the Christian History of Central Africa,* ed. T. O. Ranger and John Weller (London, 1975), pp. 195-211. Most recently Daniel O'Connor et al., *Three Centuries of Mission: The United Society for the Propagation of the Gospel, 1701-2000* (London, 2000), esp. pt. 1, chap. 12, and pt. 2, chap. 8.

2. As was stressed by Deborah Gaitskell, as commentator on this paper at the Cambridge conference. I am much indebted to her, the Reverend Dr. Gavin White, and John Stuart for comments and information.

missionaries as the captive agents of the colonial state, perhaps as the representatives of a more broadly based humanitarian tradition, or as Western "cultural imperialists." They have also assumed that the question itself is misconceived, such intellectual developments being shaped by, rather than actively shaping, colonial conditions. As historians of the extra-European world, they have frequently admitted the general importance of religion as an ingredient in the growth of local political identities and indigenous nationalisms, but have regarded the missionary dimension as relevant only to the internal history of Europe. As is well known, many religious and ecclesiastical historians of Britain have completely neglected the widespread outpouring of missionary enthusiasm, not only since the 1920s but even when it was at its height before 1914.

This situation has begun to change, notably in the last decade.[3] Little of the detailed research, however, has so far been done on the missionary enterprise in the mid–twentieth century that would enable us to understand how far older traditional beliefs and habits continued to characterize societies in the rapidly changing world after 1945 and to assess their implications for responses to decolonization. So it is that, in his recent book *The Transformation of Anglicanism,* William Sachs could write of "the end of empire" in the following terms:

> The loss of colonial identity became the primary feature of Anglican life during the 1950s and 1960s. South Africa represented the tensions Anglicans experienced as the British Empire contracted. The independence of India in 1947 began the process of spawning new nations in Asia and Africa. . . . Anglicans recognized the approach of independence as the logical end of their work. By the end of the Second World War they understood that a new political moment was at hand, and they positioned the Church well for this development. The church's schools helped to groom future national leaders, and increasing numbers of indigenous

3. Brian Stanley, *The Bible and the Flag: Protestant Missions and British Imperialism in the Nineteenth and Twentieth Centuries* (Leicester, 1990); Stanley, *The History of the Baptist Missionary Society, 1792-1992* (Edinburgh, 1992); Adrian Hastings, *The Church in Africa, 1450-1950* (Oxford, 1994); John Wolffe, *God and Greater Britain: Religion and National Life in Britain and Ireland, 1843-1945* (London, 1994); David Hempton, *Religion and Political Culture in Britain and Ireland: From the Glorious Revolution to the Decline of Empire* (Cambridge, 1996); Gerald Studdert-Kennedy, *Providence and the Raj: Imperial Mission and Missionary Imperialism* (New Delhi and London, 1998); Kevin Ward and Brian Stanley, eds., *The Church Mission Society and World Christianity, 1799-1999* (Grand Rapids and Richmond, Surrey, U.K., 2000).

> clergy abetted a process of training for national leadership. The Church's synodical structures . . . gave a theoretical basis for self-governance. Anglicans encouraged peaceful transitions of power which were achieved in many instances.

Citing central African examples, he argues the general point that "Anglicans retained historic forms of ministry and worship while making this ethos familiar to local cultures. Indigenous leadership was followed by deepening reliance upon translations of the Bible and Prayer Book, and use of local music to accompany worship. The importance of worship and music increased as means of identifying the Church and assuring its authentically local character."[4] Notwithstanding the considerable interest of Sachs's book, his arguments conflict seriously with those of other scholars. In common with many others in 1945, few Anglicans "understood that a new political moment" was upon them, and even if they recognized "the approach of independence," fewer still were happy to accept it as "the logical end of their work" at least in the immediate future. The upheavals of the 1940s may have ensured that "like other sectors of British society, evangelical Christians had become more observant and perceptively critical of colonial rule," but leaders such as CMS General Secretary Max Warren were still significantly in advance of much missionary thinking in their understanding of the rapidity with which colonial empire would unravel.[5] Sachs's suggestion that Anglicans were not only moving forward but were moving together across a broad front is also in danger of blurring important distinctions that existed both between different sections of the Anglican Church and within the broader British missionary community.[6]

This seems particularly strange when set alongside Sachs's emphasis elsewhere in his book on the distinct contribution made by the Anglo-Catholic tradition to Anglican missionary endeavor. This contribution, he argues, took the form of a "sustained legacy of protest against Anglican accommodation to

4. William L. Sachs, *The Transformation of Anglicanism: From State Church to Global Communion* (Cambridge, 1993), pp. 319-20.

5. Andrew N. Porter, "War, Colonialism and the British Experience: The Redefinition of Christian Missionary Policy, 1938-1952," *Kirchliche Zeitgeschichte* 5, no. 2 (1992): 269-88.

6. John V. Taylor and Dorothea A. Lehmann, *Christians of the Copperbelt: The Growth of the Church in Northern Rhodesia* (London, 1961), suggest that from 1942 to 1943 missionaries on the ground were becoming increasingly equivocal in their responses to African ambitions, chap. 7, esp. pp. 161-63; John Stuart, "'A Measure of Disquiet': British Missionary Responses to African Colonial Issues, 1945-53," *NAMP/CWC Position Paper* (Cambridge, 2000), does much to highlight the divisions and indecision of missionary leaders.

the modern world."[7] Did the UMCA, confronted with the pressures toward political decolonization, then abandon that tradition of protest or find at last some way of reconciling its traditions with "modernity"? Sachs goes on to suggest that the "church's ability to become a prominent social force outside the western world" owed much to Anglican "dynamism." It "attested to the flexibility of Anglican forms of authority and Church life . . . throughout the Anglican world, a sense of a global Church was solidified by new forms of consultation and mission."[8] Here Sachs again avoids the direct question, and certainly seems to offer no explanation, as to when and how the angularity of Anglo-Catholic traditions, so overtly manifested in a missionary society such as the UMCA, was overcome in the process of creating this essentially Whiggish Anglican consensus. A closer look at the history of the UMCA can throw at least some light on these aspects of Anglicanism's missionary expansion.

II

The mission originated in the widespread outburst of humanitarian and evangelical enthusiasm that attended David Livingstone's visit to Cambridge in 1857. This was seized on by Robert Gray, bishop of Cape Town, to set up a committee for a mission to the Zambezi that was eventually able to secure the consecration of Charles Mackenzie in January 1861. Gray's role, however, also points to the mission's roots from the start in Anglican party divisions. "Nothing," wrote its second bishop, William Tozer, "can be more unsatisfactory than the whole length and breadth of our present mission organization, C.M.S. plainly anti-episcopal, S.P.G. great with factions and dry as dust."[9] Known at first as the Oxford and Cambridge Mission to Central Africa, and then as either the Central Africa Mission or, from 1865, the UMCA, the new venture was always identified with the High Church Anglo-Catholic interest. This section overlapped with that substantial body of Anglicans anxious to establish episcopal authority and direction over the missionary activity of the Church of England. This included at its beginning prominent figures such as the bishop of Oxford, Samuel Wilberforce. After defeats at the hands of evangelicals in Parliament earlier in the 1850s, Wilberforce and his allies were concerned to see the bishop in Africa as head of the mission, free from what they

7. Sachs, p. 121.

8. Sachs, p. 336.

9. W. G. Tozer to Edward Steere, 21 Mar. 1871, quoted in D. R. J. Neave, "Aspects of the History of the Universities' Mission to Central Africa, 1858-1900" (M.Phil. thesis, University of York, 1974), p. 6.

saw as the essentially improper control characteristic of the CMS, namely, that of "a paternal committee in London — Episcopal in name, but too often Presbyterian in fact."[10]

However theologically sound, episcopal direction in all aspects of the mission's life had its practical disadvantages, as the UMCA's early history and Mackenzie's career demonstrated. Based in Zanzibar from 1863, the mission nevertheless made headway, slowly giving substance to the originally hopeful designation of its leaders as "Missionary Bishop to the tribes dwelling in the neighbourhood of Lake Nyasa and the River Shire."[11] In its early days it received much support from members of the Society for the Propagation of the Gospel in Foreign Parts (SPG), for example through the management of its finances as a special fund, the provision of publicity, and help with office space. However, relations became steadily more acrimonious and were finally broken off in 1881. The narrowly Anglo-Catholic character of the mission was thus steadily strengthened, and its base moved out of the universities into the parishes especially of London and the south of England. Simultaneously it expanded significantly on the mainland under Bishop Steere (1874-82), and in 1892 was divided into two with the creation of the diocese of Nyasaland. The extension of stations and schools, the growth of an African clergy and indigenous evangelists provided the necessary bulwarks for institutionalized additions to the UMCA preserve. A new diocese for Northern Rhodesia in 1910 was followed by the further division of Zanzibar to form the dioceses of Masasi in 1926 and southwest Tanganyika in 1952.

Variable accounting practices and differences in the categorization of mission staff make precise comparisons between societies very difficult, but the following figures offer some sense of the relative scale of UMCA activity. The annual income of the CMS immediately before the First World War averaged £375,000 (1910-13), compared with a UMCA revenue of £43,500 (1902-5). European missionaries employed by the CMS fell in number from 1,360 in 1910 to 1,088 by 1942, while as a consequence of the swing away from Asia numbers employed in Africa rose from 253 to 450. The UMCA by contrast employed

10. Tozer, quoted in Neave, p. 63.

11. Principal sources for the history of the UMCA are Neave, "Aspects of the Universities' Mission to Central Africa, 1858-1900"; Jerome T. Moriyama, "The Evolution of an African Ministry in the Work of the Universities' Mission to Central Africa in Tanzania, 1864-1909" (Ph.D. diss., University of London, 1984), and his essay "Building a Home-Grown Church," in O'Connor et al., pp. 330-42; A. E. M. Anderson-Morshead, *The History of the Universities' Mission to Central Africa, 1859-1909*, new rev. ed. (London, 1909); A. G. Blood, *The History of the Universities' Mission to Central Africa*, vol. 2 (1910-32), vol. 3 (1933-57) (London, 1957, 1962); Owen Chadwick, *Mackenzie's Grave* (London, 1959).

218 European men and women in 1939, and only 178 by 1957.[12] Despite these falling totals, however, by 1955 the UMCA was responsible for a striking range of activities beyond the narrowly ecclesiastical. Its members ran twenty-five small hospitals, thirty-three dispensaries, and sixteen leper clinics, as well as four teacher-training colleges, one senior and five junior secondary schools, forty middle schools, and 360 primary schools.[13]

Although these figures show that the UMCA never attained the stature of those missionary societies operating on a global scale, they nonetheless demonstrate that the mission by midcentury had established itself as a substantial regional presence in five dioceses of eastern and east-central Africa.

III

The values that dominated the mission and its work in the mid–twentieth century were in many respects essentially those that informed the career of Frank Weston, bishop of Zanzibar from 1908 until his death in 1924. Weston's powerful presence and significant public impact established his place as the most notable of all in the pantheon of UMCA bishops. As one of the mission's historians wrote, "this remarkable man made a greater impression on his contemporaries, European and African, than any other member of the Mission staff has ever done."[14] As a result, Weston became a common reference point, a yardstick by which in later decades members of the mission frequently measured themselves. For a mission concerned with the history of the early church, and which constantly looked back to the apostolic age, it was also natural to recall the achievements of those members who had most evidently embodied apostolic virtues and vigorously upheld apostolic traditions.[15]

Weston was born in south London, in 1871, the fourth son and fifth child of Robert Gibbs Weston, a tea broker in Mincing Lane. His father came from a Leicestershire family, but three of his grandparents were Scots, and he was proud of his descent from two seventeenth-century bishops of Brechin. He was educated as a day boy at Dulwich College, and at Trinity College, Oxford,

12. Gordon Hewitt, *The Problems of Success: A History of the Church Missionary Society, 1910-1942*, 2 vols. (London, 1971), vol. 1, app. 3 and p. xiv; Neave, app. 3.

13. Gerald W. Broomfield, *Towards Freedom* (London, 1957), pp. 48-49. The Reverend Canon Gerald Broomfield was general secretary of the UMCA (1937-61).

14. G. H. Wilson, *The History of the Universities Mission to Central Africa* (London, 1936), p. 134.

15. For instance, *Central Africa*, Aug. 1949, p. 106; Oct. 1949, p. 145; Nov. 1949, pp. 157-59; 1952, p. 15; 1953, pp. 186-87.

where he obtained first-class honors in theology in 1893. He was ordained deacon in 1894, and a year later priest by the bishop of St. Alban's. He then took two curacies in London's slums, the first (1894-96) in Stratford East, the second at St. Matthew's, Westminster (1896-98).

A fervent Christian Socialist, Weston moved at university in High Church Anglican circles, and committed himself to a celibate vocation as a missionary in response to Bishop Smythies' appeal in Oxford on behalf of the UMCA in 1892. Despite reservations about his health, he eventually joined the UMCA in 1898, and for nine years was stationed at Zanzibar. As chaplain (1898-99) and principal (1901-8) of the school at St. Andrew's Training College, Kiungani, and spells in running St. Mark's Theological College (1899-1901 and 1906-8), which he had established, his work was chiefly educational. His career was marked by his distaste for European race consciousness, which he viewed as the great obstacle to African advancement, by his doubts as to the "civilizing" impact of European trade on Africa, and by his conviction that missionaries should identify themselves with Africans' own ideals, lifestyles, and traditions. Only education in such a spirit could help develop an African-led church. An intensely energetic man with too few colleagues, he also functioned as a canon of Christ Church cathedral in Zanzibar and chancellor of the diocese. Somehow he found time to gain a B.D. degree in 1906, a qualification he felt was demanded by the chancellorship, and published *The One Christ* (1907) to the general approval of theologians such as Bishop Gore, Canon Scott Holland, and his former Oxford tutor, Professor Sanday.

Notwithstanding his lack of direct exposure to the varied currents of Anglicanism, his single-mindedness and limited ability for compromise, Weston was in other respects an obvious successor to Dr. E. J. Hine, who resigned as bishop of Zanzibar in 1908. Having declined the bishopric of Mashonaland in 1907, Weston was consecrated in Southwark Cathedral in October 1908. In the fashion of the peripatetic bishops of the UMCA, he immediately set about traversing and reorganizing his diocese, spending only about three months of each year in Zanzibar itself. He worried in particular about the "debased civilization" of the European-run plantations and the corrupting impact on African family life of the commercial society of coastal towns. These he thought quite as threatening as the omnipresent expansion of Islam and the practices of "witchcraft." Zanzibar, he wrote, "is more and more immoral — Piccadilly, Sodom, and a public bar!"[16] Impatient of anthropological findings and insisting on high standards for Africans as for Europeans, he fretted at the fragility

16. H. Maynard Smith, *Frank Bishop of Zanzibar: Life of Frank Weston, D.D., 1871-1924* (London, 1926), pp. 96, 187.

of African Christianity in such a setting. Sensitive to the mission's overwhelming dependence on the efforts of African Christians, he struggled endlessly to balance the need for trust in his clergy with the dangers of "a premature grant of home rule" to local churches.[17] His commitment to the ideals of celibacy and the "religious life," lived out in a closely knit religious community, embraced not only men but women. He drew on his acquaintance with British female orders to establish, in 1910, the Community of the Sacred Passion, which was, above all, to contact African women in their own homes.

It was, however, Weston's highly critical reaction to the proceedings of the Kikuyu missionary conference of 1913 that made him widely known in British church circles. Kikuyu was the latest of several conferences held since 1904 between CMS and other Protestant missionaries. Presided over by the bishops of Mombasa and Uganda, and designed to foster their common cause against Roman Catholicism and Islam, the conference drew up proposals for an ecclesiastical federation and intercommunion under Anglican leadership. This apparent blurring of denominational divisions came at a time when, against the background of modernist criticism, Anglo-Catholics in Britain itself were increasingly fearful for the coherence of the Church of England and its doctrines.[18] Weston denounced the scheme, appealed to the archbishop of Canterbury, and simultaneously developed his wider views on the nature of the church in *Ecclesia Anglicana: For What Does She Stand?* (1913). A great stir ensued, and Weston was summoned home to explain his impulsive, exaggerated claims of heresy and schism. His polemical, passionate, and abstract arguments alienated as many as they enthused, but Archbishop Davidson's skillful diplomacy and published decision of 1915 were together sufficient to calm all parties.[19] Thinking many of his questions unanswered, however, Weston thereafter continued to write as a powerful exponent of both the Anglo-Catholic position within the Anglican Church and of alternative plans for co-operation and unity. These included, for example, a Central Missionary Council of Episcopal and Non-Episcopal Churches in East Africa.[20]

At the beginning of the 1914-18 war, being still on leave in England, Weston was spared internment with his mainland colleagues in German East

17. Smith, p. 88.

18. Blood, vol. 2, chap. 8, esp. pp. 68, 80; Neave, pp. 125, 132-33.

19. Most recently on the Kikuyu controversy, Stuart P. Mews, "Kikuyu and Edinburgh: The Interaction of Attitudes to Two Conferences," in G. J. Cuming and Derek Baker, eds., Councils and Assemblies. Studies in Church History, 7 (Cambridge, 1971), pp. 345-59; Gavin White, "Frank Weston and the Kikuyu Crisis," *Bulletin of the Scottish Institute of Missionary Studies,* n.s., 8-9 (1992-93): 48-55.

20. Blood, 2:74.

Africa. After returning to Zanzibar, where the military campaigns seriously disrupted his diocese, he was appalled at the methods used to compel Africans to assist Allied forces. In 1916 he therefore took up the challenge to recruit a Carrier Corps of his own. Remarkably, as a major commanding some twenty-five hundred men, he suffered no casualties, and was awarded an OBE. This commitment to the well-being of Africans echoed both his missionary concern and his earlier Christian Socialism. It also led him into wartime propaganda, with his indictment of German colonial practice in *The Black Slaves of Prussia* (1917), and prompted his vigorous attack, after the war, on Britain's approach to labor recruitment in the East African colonies, *The Serfs of Great Britain* (1920). "We regard forced labour," he wrote, "as in itself immoral; and we hold that forcing Africans to work in the interests of European civilization is a betrayal of the weaker to the financial interests of the stronger race."[21] He played an important role in the successful political campaign by humanitarians and churchmen to change imperial policy.

In 1920 Weston attended the Lambeth Conference as well as the first Anglo-Catholic Congress. On this occasion, despite his reputation for uncompromising advocacy, he surprised many present by his warmth and goodwill even to doctrinal foes such as Hensley Henson, and he made a significant contribution to Lambeth's Appeal to all Christian People with its renewed approach to questions of Christian unity. Tall, imposing, a brilliant and gifted speaker equally capable of holding an audience of thousands in the Albert Hall as of fascinating a handful of African children, Weston's presence on this occasion was later represented by the archbishop, Randall Davidson, as an "extraordinary mixture of generosity and menace."[22] Often naive, prone to feelings of insecurity, and lacking much practical sense of the evolving history of the church, Weston in Britain was widely seen as unreliable and unpredictable. His last major public appearance in Britain, as president of the Anglo-Catholic Congress of 1923, seemed to bear this out. His telegram of greetings from the congress to the pope prompted widespread disquiet and outrage, scarcely helpful to Anglo-Catholic interests. Archbishop Davidson regretfully wrote of him as "a source and centre of real danger to the Church at present owing to the unguarded way in which he writes and speaks."[23]

Weston returned to Zanzibar in September 1923, wearied from his exertions rather than fresh from the change of scene. He immediately resumed the

21. Quotation from Hewitt, 1:165.

22. G. K. A. Bell, *Randall Davidson Archbishop of Canterbury*, 3rd ed. (London, 1952), p. 1010.

23. Bell, p. 1277.

administration of his expanding diocese. A year later, suffering from blood poisoning after mistreating a carbuncle, he died at Msalabani on 2 November. The memorial fund appeal attracted a large sum for the Zanzibar diocese, and provided a memorial altar and tablet in St. Matthew's, Westminster.

IV

Central to the Anglo-Catholicism of the UMCA was its members' belief in the unquestioned authority of its bishops in all matters of faith and church order. Unlike other Protestant missions, the home committee, or General Council of the UMCA, from a very early date had virtually no say in the running of the mission. It served as an agency, marshaling funds and potential recruits for the bishops in Africa (as head of the mission) to use as they thought best. Such influence as it exercised only came through its power to divide finances between the two dioceses created in 1892. Moreover, after 1892 the archbishop of Canterbury, and no longer the committee, chose the UMCA bishops. This was felt to accord with the apostolic commission; it reflected members' understanding of apostolic practice; and it embodied the pronounced anti-Erastianism of the Oxford Movement. As Frank Weston put it, "The Episcopate then is essential to the Church's life, and Bishops are the organs through which the mystical Body functions."[24]

Although twentieth-century colonial expansion increasingly posed obstacles to the pursuit of this ideal, the mission field continued to be widely regarded as an arena in which apostolic tradition in its Anglo-Catholic form could not merely survive but flourish. Episcopal order and hierarchy were preserved through an emphasis on the threefold orders of bishops, priests, and deacons, together forming a clerical elite. At least in theory bishops conducted all business in concert with their clergy, supposedly in the manner of the early church; in practice, as Weston and his successors frequently demonstrated, unilateral action was common, albeit tempered occasionally by wider consultation in diocesan synods with their constitutional provision for lay representation. The UMCA's general secretary summed up the dilemma over authority that confronted the mission when he explained how "The government of the Church cannot be democratic in the normal sense, because the ministry was instituted and commissioned by Christ. But it must be constitutional, because the Church also has an authority derived from Him."[25]

24. Smith, p. 165.
25. Gerald Broomfield, *Constitutional Episcopacy* (London, 1944), pp. 3-4.

Episcopal power and authority were also moderated, or their impact perhaps made more bearable, by the importance attached in the mission to the missionary vocation. After more than thirty years it was recalled how, in response to one man's refusal of "an invitation to help in Zanzibar on the ground that he did not think he could live very long in such conditions," Weston had replied, "I did not ask you to do that."[26] If few were altogether as rigorous as Bishop Frank, members of the UMCA saw themselves as called to the religious life, and readily accepted the obligations of poverty, chastity, and obedience embodied in their promises. Missionaries received no salaries, and from the earliest days until the 1940s aimed at living simply, as far as possible like Africans. They committed themselves to celibacy, and promised to obey their bishop as head of the mission and those he placed in authority over them.

Adherence to one's vocation and pursuit of the communal ideals of the religious life were themselves aided in turn by the regular practices of confession and penance. They depended on the intertwined notions of service, obedience, and discipline, all of which relied on active membership of a close, well-functioning community, whether church, chapter, brotherhood, college, school, or family. In his conviction that "our fundamental danger is individualism," Weston was touching a chord that had earlier led the bishop of Likoma (Nyasaland), Chauncy Maples, to define heathenism in nonracial terms as "a simple working out in every possible detail of self-indulgence."[27] Emphasis on the communal character of Anglo-Catholic life, both at home and in Africa, provided the strongest possible defense against such personal defaults. As Weston told the Anglo-Catholic Congress in 1923, it was impossible "to make . . . Christ real to the world, unless religion can be presented to people as a matter of discipline. Ideally we move in an atmosphere of self-sacrificing obedience."[28]

Anglo-Catholic commitment for the UMCA involved the transfer of this institutionalized system of belief from England to Africa. In the words of one member, the mission was setting up Christ's church "in its completeness and compactness of apostolical organization . . . in the richness of its sacramental life," "the Person of Christ given to Africa . . . to bind [all] into one social and living organism."[29] Commitment was frequently driven by both a powerful

26. Broomfield, *Towards Freedom,* p. 4.

27. Smith, p. 139; Ellen Maples, *Chauncy Maples D.D., F.R.G.S. Pioneer Missionary in East Central Africa* (London, 1897), p. 150.

28. Frank Weston, *In Defence of the English Catholic* (London, 1923), p. 33.

29. Chauncy Maples, *The African Church and its Claims upon the Universities* (Cambridge, 1879), p. 15.

dislike of the consequences of modern urban civilization at home and abroad, and a determination to protect Africans from its impact. Many UMCA recruits seem to have derived this from their Christian Socialism or their work in urban slum parishes, especially in London. For others attachment to the rhythms of rural English life or the world of the theological colleges such as Cuddesdon or Westcott House induced a similar aversion. Consciously or unconsciously, missionary work offered British missionaries of all denominations the possibility of escape from an industrial urban society whose failures were becoming more and more apparent to contemporaries. Far more strongly than most British African missions, the UMCA welcomed this release. Once in Africa, members increasingly rejected the "civilizing mission" that others, less critical, still widely understood and promoted as the Westernization of African societies. Returning on furlough in 1901, Weston for example only found his reservations confirmed: "England seems more worldly and on the surface than ever, and there is an absence of real life which makes me very pessimistic." Back in Tanganyika, he deplored more than ever "the development of plantations" with "its debased civilization" as "a sore trial to our people and a hindrance to the Gospel."[30]

The UMCA was not so unrealistic as to think that these processes could be halted. "We cannot keep our men out of the commercial movement if we would; the coast town will always claim many, and in claiming their bodies will enchain their souls."[31] Nevertheless, it became the goal of the mission to prevent the urban drift and to sustain a "traditional," essentially rural, African society with its families, tribes, and community life as far as possible. Weston shared Maples's view that "the European must become an African to win Africans,"[32] adopting local lifestyles, living simply and ascetically, avoiding any suggestion, as a white man, of superiority or standing on one's dignity. He told the European missionary, "If you want to help African women, go and live in their villages and share their life."[33] Pastoral practice was in turn to be supported by institutional provision. In deepening the structure of the church, converts were generally discouraged from leaving their villages and new archdeaconries were linked to individual tribes.[34]

Despite the accent on equality and commonality, this process of blending Anglo-Catholic Christianity with indigenous ways intensified the UMCA's

30. Smith, pp. 41, 96.

31. Smith, p. 96.

32. Ellen Maples, ed., *Journals and Papers of Chauncy Maples D.D., F.R.G.S., Late Bishop of Likoma Lake Nyasa, Africa* (London, 1899), p. 186.

33. Smith, p. 137.

34. Smith, p. 96; Wilson, p. 189.

theologically informed emphasis on authority, obedience, and discipline. This had two dimensions, the first concerning the lives of ordinary African Christians, the other that of African priests.

Regarding converts, Weston found his tour of July 1909 "very fruitful in cases of discipline; in fact, I did nothing else all day long for a whole month but interview Christians who were in trouble of some sort or another."[35] Often the bishop felt his "chief job seems to be listening to the words of the wicked."[36] In dealing with moral lapses, which meant above all infringements of church teaching on marriage, it was doubtless a relief for him, as earlier for Maples, that "Here we are perfectly able to restore the ancient discipline of the Church, to the great and inestimable benefit of the body of the faithful." In a "solemn excommunication," "the power of the Church as a spiritual institution is emphasised and realised."[37]

Discipline was the response to disobedience, to the failure of conformity with the requirements and regulations of the church community, and to disrespect for its authority. While missionaries everywhere grappled with disciplinary problems, its implications for African priests of the UMCA were especially stringent. This reflected not least Anglo-Catholic preoccupation with the training of priests, whose elevated status within the hierarchy of the church not only demanded particularly high levels of scholarly attainment but left less room for tolerance of other shortcomings. Weston "was most anxious that the African priest should not become Europeanised," but was at the same time "convinced that a very hard self-discipline was necessary for Africans."[38] These requirements were not easily reconciled, especially when his own experience seemed to confirm that most Africans had very little idea of discipline. "No one at home can quite grasp the situation in Africa, the exact condition of the native church, the morality which seems to hang on a thread, and the faith which has so little resistance — always quick to reach out but weak against opposition, like St. Peter's early faith."[39]

An African sense of vocation also seemed to be in short supply, and his conclusion was to remain characteristic of the UMCA: "I am most anxious that we should not lose confidence in the African ministry. Many members

35. Blood, 2:19.

36. Smith, p. 87.

37. Ellen Maples, *Chauncy Maples D.D., F.R.G.S. Pioneer Missionary in East Central Africa*, p. 241.

38. Ellen Maples, *Chauncy Maples D.D., F.R.G.S. Pioneer Missionary in East Central Africa*, p. 36.

39. Ellen Maples, *Chauncy Maples D.D., F.R.G.S. Pioneer Missionary in East Central Africa*, p. 86.

have proved themselves most zealous and able ministers of the Word and Sacraments: but . . . [as events in the diocese of Masasi had demonstrated] the increase of the native ministry must for years involve us in the increase of our European staff."[40]

The UMCA predilection for building from the clerical pinnacle downward in a world where communal support was limited imbued the mission with an episcopal authoritarianism no less real for being expressed in terms of service and the Christian family of Anglo-Catholic theology. An insistence on the need for more English workers to supervise ordained Africans, and to train them further in "the powers of an individual Christian conscience," "poverty," and "self-sacrifice," was well established by 1914. Notwithstanding some later relaxation, the UMCA as a consequence remained behind the other missions in the promotion of an African ministry through to independence in the 1960s.[41] This shortfall was further exacerbated by persistently poor clerical salaries.

V

It is of course necessary to beware of identifying Anglo-Catholic theology and ecclesiology with no more than the thinking and writings of Bishop Weston. His biographer, for example, acknowledges both his periodic unfairness to members of other denominations and his tendency to write "as if formal logic ruled the world." Later historians have pointed to his weak historical sense, his naïveté, insecurity, and impulsiveness.[42] Nevertheless, we are concerned here less with Weston's eccentricities or the finer points of his theological expositions than with the persistent characteristics of a particular missionary tradition. The forcefulness, at times the acerbity, of Weston's comments and the energetic practice of his years in East Africa highlight central features of that tradition. Together with the clarity and vigor of his comments on missionary matters, these continued to dominate the work of the mission and, as will be seen below, helped delay any significant response by the UMCA to the issues of the decolonizing decades of the midcentury.

The 1920s and 1930s have been represented as the most self-confident,

40. Ellen Maples, *Chauncy Maples D.D., F.R.G.S. Pioneer Missionary in East Central Africa,* pp. 87-88.

41. Moriyama, "Evolution," pp. 235-41, 285, and epilogue; O'Connor et al., pp. 128-30.

42. Smith, p. 168; White, "Frank Weston," passim.

even triumphalist, period of the Anglo-Catholic movement's history.[43] To most missionaries between the wars, but perhaps not least to a missionary body emphasizing the institution of the church and referring to its roots in the apostolic age, time was not only necessary but available. In 1939 the UMCA's monthly magazine, *Central Africa,* reviewing the eighty years since the mission's foundation, commented in terms reminiscent of the early nineteenth century. "It is a long span in human life . . . but how short in God's own time. . . . Why then should we grow impatient at the apparently slow progress of man's achievement in the mission field? Rather should we be filled with joy at the progress made in this short period." Even after the disturbances on Northern Rhodesia's Copper Belt in the mid-1930s, the fact that "the future of Africa is in the melting-pot" was a source of satisfaction and hope, not of undue concern.[44] Even at the end of the war, the apocalyptic tone of a review of "Africa emergent" by the secretary of the Conference of British Missionary Societies elicited a sympathetic but overwhelmingly irenic response from the UMCA's general secretary. Broomfield explained that he was not

> overwhelmed . . . so much as you seem to be, because the whole future of the Church, of Christianity and of civilization has, at various times in its history and in various countries, appeared just as much in jeopardy as it does now in Africa, and yet the Church has always survived, and I believe it always will just because it is a divine institution. This of course is no kind of reason why we should be excused from making the very maximum efforts of which we are capable, but it does mean that, if we are doing our best, we need not be over-anxious about the results.[45]

Continual reminders that the unstoppable spread of European ways was eating away at customary forms of African society seem to have reinforced

43. See W. S. F. Pickering, "Anglo-Catholicism: Some Sociological Observations," in *Tradition Renewed: The Oxford Movement Conference Papers,* ed. Geoffrey Rowell (London, 1986), pp. 153-72. For a valuable expression of interwar attitudes, see E. R. Morgan, ed., *Essays Catholic and Missionary* (London, 1928).

44. *Central Africa,* Jan. 1939, pp. 1-2. For the troubles, Elena L. Berger, *Labour Race and Colonial Rule: The Copperbelt from 1924 to Independence* (Oxford, 1974); R. I. Rotberg, *The Rise of Nationalism in Central Africa: The Making of Malawi and Zambia, 1873-1964* (Cambridge, Mass., 1966).

45. Rhodes House Library, Oxford, UMCA Papers, SF 27/XI/A, G. W. Broomfield to H. M. Grace, 8 Jan. 1946. This was Broomfield's reply to Grace's letter to him, Confidential, 3 Jan. 1946, finally issued in Grace's pamphlet *The Church in Africa* (London, 1946).

throughout the 1930s and 1940s the UMCA's commitment to its preservation wherever possible. This was to be achieved by the infusion of Christian ideals and practice via the churches and schools. Indeed, "Only the missions can save the situation. . . . We look forward to an African civilization which, while incorporating the best that the white man can contribute, will be no mere imitation of what is European, but in a real sense a product of the genius of Africa, giving permanent form to what is valuable in African life and thought, and recognised by the African as their own."

The new type of community would be one "bound by links no less spiritual than the clan"; incorporating an individualism that was not selfishness; preserving a reverence for spiritual values; and more firmly based than the old on moral obligations.[46] Although there were already Africans "who sincerely desire . . . to take their share in building up a new civilization for their country and were realizing the true meaning of liberty," there could be no doubt that this would take a long time, a point reinforced by the republication of Broomfield's pamphlet thirteen years later in 1951.[47]

Appeals were therefore made for women teachers to work in Nyasaland's villages, where they could enjoy "freedom from the worries of 'civilization.'" In the setting of the Second World War, the "new civilization" for which the UMCA was working was presented as "one of those things upon which the future peace of the world depends."[48] British colonial rule itself was often brought in to assist the UMCA's efforts. In 1942, contrary to the changing current of official thinking at the Colonial Office, which was worried about its conservative impact, indirect rule — "self determination applied to native tribes" — was felt to be working well in Northern Rhodesia, generating a "sense of responsibility and initiative" that could "be brought to the service of the Church."[49] In such circumstances missionaries felt justified in concentrating on "the practical application of Christian principles to African customs (the chief business, after all, of our work in Africa)."[50]

Rapid change south of the Zambezi in the Union of South Africa only

46. Canon [G. W.] Broomfield, *Education in Central Africa: The Church's Task* (London, 1938), p. 5.

47. Canon R. M. Gibbons, "African Leadership," *Central Africa*, July 1939, p. 164. The second edition (1951) of Broomfield's *Education in Central Africa* was changed only in very minor details.

48. Canon Hicks, "Education in Nyasaland," *Central Africa*, July 1939, pp. 158-59; Hicks, "Carrying On," *Central Africa*, Oct. 1939, pp. 219-20.

49. A. G. Rogers, "Indirect Rule at Msoro," *Central Africa*, Sept. 1942, pp. 81-82.

50. L. P. H[arries], "The Mission and Bantu Scholarship," *Central Africa*, Oct. 1942, p. 119.

seemed to reinforce the UMCA's reservations about industrial urban society. "It establishes the importance of mission work in the rural areas, which, after all, are the cradle of African life."[51] Newcomers to the mission field were therefore warned against being overhasty where time was needed for a painstaking search for aspects of life "adaptable to the Christian religion." To guide its members, and to reinforce what had long been preferred policy among the leaders of the mission, the UMCA published in 1949 Bishop Vincent Lucas's work *The Christian Approach to Non-Christian Customs.* It is somehow fitting to find a speaker at the anniversary meeting in 1942 referring to "we of the UMCA Tribe."[52] Such views of modern civilization were still characteristic of the older missionaries at the beginning of the 1960s.[53]

Preservation of a customary Africa closely paralleled the UMCA's own struggles to protect its own identity as an Anglo-Catholic body. Church and tribe were similarly viewed as the embodiments of fundamental communities under attack. The sense of embattlement had characterized the UMCA from the start, and Bishop Weston felt it no less in Africa than at home. Writing home in 1923, he complained at the aggressiveness of other denominations. "On the one hand British Nonconformity invades our diocese without notice; on the other hand, the C.M.S. diocese of Uganda refuses us, deliberately and synodically, the right hand of fellowship."[54] Such disputes did not die with Weston. They continued in response to both CMS influence in the dioceses of Mombasa and Uganda and further pressure for church unions. In 1933, for example, anxious inquiries from the UMCA head office sought confirmation that the Anglo-Catholic members of the Standing Committee of East African Bishops were standing firm, like Weston at Kikuyu in 1913, against the latest reform proposals.[55]

In these continuing debates about church union, stimulated by the establishment in 1947 of the United Church of South India, the UMCA consistently rejected the bland, not to say crude and potentially troublesome, theo-

51. L. P. H[arries], "North of the Zambezi," *Central Africa,* Sept. 1942, p. 83; also D. J. Hitchman, "Men Manners and Morals in Northern Rhodesia," *Central Africa,* Oct. 1942, p. 122.

52. "The Greater Spirit," *Central Africa,* Mar. 1942, p. 27; William Vincent Lucas, *Christianity and Native Rites* (London, 1949); Canon E. P. Walker, *Central Africa,* July 1942. On the conditions for Lucas's success based on his ideas worked out in practice between 1910 and 1930, see Ranger, "Missionary Adaptation of African Religious Institutions," and O'Connor et al., pp. 112-13.

53. Information from Dr. Gavin White, in a letter to the author, 16 Oct. 2000.

54. UMCA Papers, SF 15/I, Weston to Secretary, 26 Feb. [1923?].

55. UMCA Papers, SF 15/VIII, E. F. Spanton (secretary) to bishop of Zanzibar, 14 Sept. 1933.

logical compromises that union and intercommunion schemes seemed to embody. The UMCA's bishops had declared themselves against the constitution of the Church of South India in 1942, as "diverging widely from the Catholic Faith and Order as maintained in the Anglican Communion," and in 1947 refused it intercommunion.[56] Central to the Anglo-Catholic stand were the nature of the church and its sacraments, the sources of authority and doctrine, and the significance of episcopacy.[57] Reunions, it was insisted, should not be allowed to make bishops in the last resort "subject to synods containing a large majority of priests and laity even in matters of faith and order."[58]

The belief among UMCA members that they were the true guardians of church order and authority merged easily with their conviction that the Catholic sense of "the just balance" between individual and community in the family of the church was well attuned to Africans' own concern for family obligations.[59] Broomfield developed publicly this argument: "That Africans are at home in their religion is not due to any adaptation made for their benefit, but fundamentally to the fact that Catholic Christianity itself fulfils their needs." It addressed "their profound sense of community" and their feeling for "a community embracing both the living and the dead." The sacraments of the church tended to their linkage of the material and spiritual worlds. "Their sense of the numinous is hallowed in the mystery of Catholic worship, and the need for confession, recognised as necessary in some circumstances in tribal life, is satisfied at a deeper level in the sacrament of penance."[60] The UMCA was thus not only far better able theologically than Protestant denominations to undertake the reformation of the African's spiritual world. It was also well equipped institutionally to sustain that achievement, not least by protecting converts against the denominational scheming that constituted yet another undesirable aspect of modernity.

This self-confident and conservative, albeit often defensive, pattern of

56. Blood, 3:136. Joseph Barker, C.R., "Intercommunion: Is There Any Objection?" was commended (*Central Africa,* Feb. 1942, p. 24) for setting "out clearly and charitably some of the reasons why we cannot rightly accept such proposals. Truth must always come before what may appear expedient or friendly, and the sacraments are not ours to do as we like with, but are a sacred trust to be handed on intact."

57. J. J. Willis, J. W. Arthur, S. C. Neill, G. W. Broomfield, and R. K. Orchard, *Towards a United Church, 1913-1947* (London, 1947). Broomfield contributed part III, 1, "An Anglo-Catholic View," pp. 149-75.

58. Broomfield, *Constitutional Episcopacy,* pp. 21-22.

59. Hitchman, pp. 121-22.

60. Broomfield, *Towards Freedom,* pp. 116, 12, 84, and chap. 9, "Through the Church and the Mission," passim.

thinking within the UMCA was nevertheless difficult to sustain in the face of mounting change. The many-sided impact of the Second World War; the continuing expansion of the industrial economy in central and South Africa; the reshaping of colonial rule in association with government initiatives, in development and welfare policies, bringing about the "second colonial occupation"; and the beginnings of the significant African political organization did not go unnoticed in the UMCA. Of particular importance in the UMCA's own sphere was the issue of race relations, to debate on which the general secretary made serious contributions from 1940 onward.[61] By 1953 the melting pot of 1939 had produced an alarming mix. "The future is in the balance: the future of all the peoples of Africa: the future of the Church in Africa. The mounting tension and distrust between the races, the reversion to barbarism in Kenya, the threat of violence elsewhere, the increase of materialism and self-seeking, the resurgence of Islam, the disappointment of many hopes — it is a sombre picture." Despite some encouraging signs, Broomfield felt "there never was a time of greater anxiety."[62]

VI

There was one immediate and conventional response to these changes on which all sections of the mission could agree. In the editorial just quoted, Broomfield had ended with a traditional appeal for funds: "this Church in Africa, upon which so much depends, is cabined, cribbed, confined by the shortage of its resources."[63] Relative poverty throughout the UMCA's existence had, in a sense, both discouraged critical self-examination and stunted imagination. The way forward lay simply in tapping fresh resources — colonial government grants, increased African self-support, and increased giving at home — so that existing lines of work could be extended. Little change of outlook or direction was called for.

This of course appealed to busy bishops, not always good at delegation and with little time or inclination for fresh reflection.[64] There were, moreover, strong grounds for emphasizing financial needs. Like all missions, UMCA

61. Gerald Webb Broomfield, *Colour Conflict: Race Relations in Africa* (London, 1943), written at the request of the United Council for Missionary Education in consultation with the Conference of British Missionary Societies; Broomfield, *The Chosen People or the Bible, Christianity and Race* (London, 1954).

62. Broomfield, "Africa's Future in the Balance," *Central Africa*, Mar. 1953, pp. 76-77.

63. Broomfield, "Africa's Future," pp. 76-77.

64. UMCA Papers, SF 96/VI, Guy Carleton to Broomfield, 18 May 1948.

found it hard to provide salaries for teachers at the level of civil pay scales; competitive salaries for educated ministers were all but impossible to afford. Even the national insurance contributions obligatory under new British welfare legislation were a serious drain, costing the UMCA in 1950 more than the previous year's increase in general funds.[65] In order to meet government standards in medical and educational provision, to expand opportunities for African women, and to benefit from economies of scale, smaller stations were closed or amalgamated. The bishop of South-West Tanganyika wrote in 1953: "the day of small centres has gone."[66] Capital expenditure was almost impossible as costs of living and every activity steadily rose, "obstructing every idea of a forward movement in the Church's work."[67]

Nevertheless, inside and outside the UMCA there were those who realized that more fundamental problems were hampering the mission. Above all, there was its tendency under the leadership of the clergy in Africa to operate increasingly as a sect intent on self-preservation. As Archdeacon Capper expressed it: "We have too many people serving U.M.C.A. who think that U.M.C.A. religion is their peculiar expression of Anglicanism and as such needs protecting — and they are suspicious that an attempt is being made to breach the wall. . . . The position is serious as . . . African support of the Church has not improved over the last ten years — this is the tragedy of our work."[68]

The defensive isolationism of Anglo-Catholicism, seen so clearly in Weston, was again — one might say still — strong in the two decades after 1945. It was demonstrated, for instance, in discussions of liturgical reform. The bishops, much against Broomfield's better judgment, pressed for usages which would set them apart from the entire Anglican Communion, and for the use of Greek in place of the vernacular.[69] Strong clerical pressure for adoption of the complete Roman Mass surfaced in reports reaching Central Africa House. There was persistent reluctance even to request approval from the archbishop of Canterbury for any liturgical changes. As an irritated

65. Blood, 3:210; Bishop of Nyasaland, "African Wages," *Central Africa*, Sept. 1949, p. 125. SF 15/XIII, William Zanzibar to Broomfield, 28 Jan. 1949; SF 15/XIII, General Secretary to UMCA Bishops, 17 Feb. 1950; SF 27/XI/A-B, Broomfield to H. M. Grace (CBMS secretary), copy, 4 Mar. 1949; SF 15/XV, UMCA Papers, Ven. H. R. Sydenham and copy to UMCA Bishops, 20 Oct. 1959.

66. Blood, 3:290.

67. Blood, 3:370, and 210, 236, 292, 324-25, 329.

68. UMCA Papers, SF 102, E. M. H. Capper to Broomfield, 30 Oct. 1961.

69. UMCA Papers, SF 15/XIII, Broomfield to UMCA Bishops, 11 Nov. and 20 Dec. 1949.

Broomfield pointed out, this went considerably beyond even Weston's recalcitrance.[70]

The defense of Anglo-Catholic identity ranged from the natural or innocuous to the positively destructive. *Central Africa* carried a report of how, in the church at Machambe that was overrun by ants, "at mass it was necessary to have a server sweeping them off the altar, and, even so, some found their way on to the corporal."[71] Mbeya's new church, dedicated in 1954, was built to a "neo-Byzantine design," and the new cathedral at Lusaka in 1957 on "the traditional ground plan of a basilica" rather than to local patterns.[72] The Guild of St. Athanasius was launched in 1956 by the bishop of South-West Tanganyika to encourage new candidates for the ministry; and from London, Broomfield pressed for the restoration of Simon of Cyrene to the calendar, because a "large number of keen UMCA supporters, who are bound to pray regularly for the Mission, are banded together in the Companionship of Simon the Cyrenian."[73]

Other issues were more problematical and divisive. There was at times little episcopal sensitivity to the currents of domestic English support, and Broomfield had to explain to the bishop of Masasi, in respect of the Governor of Tanganyika's appeal in 1954, that "a Cathedral would [not] go down well in this country." Arguments over the Swahili missal not only displeased Archbishop Fisher but eventually provoked Broomfield to uncommon vehemence: "there is a not inconsiderable feeling of impatience when individual dioceses, for reasons not generally acceptable, make changes which separate them off from the rest of the Anglican Communion. I think a lot of people, if they knew about it, would regard it as quite fantastic. . . . After all, the Mass is the worship of the Church, and that part of the Church with which we are in communion is the world-wide Anglican Communion. What one diocese does about the Mass is therefore the concern of all the rest."[74]

The creation of a new East African Province under its own archbishop was also hotly debated. Designed in part to end the anomalous position of UMCA bishops still directly accountable to Canterbury, this too was delayed by Anglican party politics and Anglo-Catholic resistance.[75] UMCA concern

70. UMCA Papers, SF 15/XIII, Broomfield to William Zanzibar, 16 Jan. 1950, and to UMCA Bishops, 20 Dec. 1949; and SF 15/XIV, to UMCA Bishops, 14 Sept. 1955.

71. *Central Africa*, May 1939, pp. 122-33.

72. Blood, 3:284, 302.

73. Blood, 3:282; UMCA Papers, SF 15/XIII, Broomfield to William Zanzibar, 14 Feb. 1950.

74. UMCA Papers, SF 15/XIII, Broomfield to UMCA Bishops, 8 Sept. 1950, and SF 15/XV, (quotation) 24 Apr. 1958.

75. UMCA Papers, SF 15/XIII, Broomfield to UMCA Bishops, 8 Jan. 1948.

centered on the possibility that control might be lost to the CMS tendency with its enthusiasm for unions and intercommunion. This danger arose in two ways: over ministerial training and constitutional representation. On the one hand UMCA rejected any suggestion that there could be a united training college. Distinctive theological principles had to be protected. On the other, the UMCA bishops' insistence that there were no African candidates fit for consecration as assistant bishops meant the Anglo-Catholic position in a new provincial synod would suffer by their absence. While Broomfield pressed, as he had for some time, for immediate steps to bring on well-trained Africans, the bishops were more disposed to delay the provincial reform, in order to remove altogether the risk of "CMS Africans" taking charge at the highest levels of the church.[76] One of the few ready concessions to African feeling came in the suggestion that the inauguration of the province might take place in Dar es Salaam, thus removing any suggestion that Kenya with its Europeans had any particular ecclesiastical weight.[77] Even this had a partisan slant, however, given the strong CMS association with Mombasa.

VII

Striking by its absence in the sources examined here is any significant attention, by the UMCA, to the changing political scene in eastern and central Africa, the growth of nationalist opinion, or the prospects of decolonization. As the dean of Salisbury (Southern Rhodesia), Gonville ffrench-Beytagh, noted in the late 1950s, "we spent hours and hours working on the canons of the new province [of Central Africa] and things of this kind while the Federation for which the province was created fell apart around us."[78] In Bishop Thorne of Nyasaland, expressions of paternal concern for the position of Africans were allied to political conservatism. He was also disinclined to press for changes in the federal plans, openly disapproved of the criticisms made of them by others such as Michael Scott or Guy Clutton-Brock, and lost African support as a result. Thorne conformed to the general injunctions of the Anglo-Catholic archbishop of Cape Town, Geoffrey Clayton: "It is not your duty to be popular. It is your duty to be faithful. . . . You do not exist to preach

76. UMCA Papers, SF 15/XV, Conference with the Bishops, 14-16 May 1958, Aide Memoire, para. 12, and Broomfield to Bishops of Zanzibar, South-West Tanganyika, and Masasi, 29 Jan. 1959.

77. UMCA Papers, SF 15/XV, Broomfield to UMCA Bishops, 7 Apr. 1960.

78. Adrian Hastings, *A History of African Christianity, 1950-1975* (Cambridge, 1979), p. 98. I am grateful to Deborah Gaitskell for this reference.

the Gospel of the Federation of Central Africa but to preach the Gospel to the Federation." In the view of the most recent historian of the USPG, the UMCA's "support for the nationalist cause was generally very belated, if it occurred at all."[79]

It is therefore hardly surprising that six months before independence one sympathetic colonial official, in close touch with UMCA work in Tanganyika, wrote fearfully about the future:

> Bluntly it [UMCA] is falling behind its environment. . . . In practical terms, U.M.C.A. is still working on the assumption that Africans are unable to take over their own affairs for a long time yet, and still need a very permanent guiding hand on top (e.g. Bishop) especially in such things as finance. . . . British control in Tanganyika ends this September. . . . A Church which retains Europeans in control after that is in danger — not physical, but . . . of being at odds with its people, and hence starved. . . . I wonder if U.M.C.A. has ever seriously settled down to working itself out of Africa, because this is what should be happening.[80]

This was a pertinent comment, and the answer to the final question was negative. However, it was not for want of trying at headquarters in London. Broomfield was not cast in the mold of a Max Warren, and allowed himself to think more of racial problems outside the church than of sclerosis within. But in various ways he had long been knocking at the episcopal door. He pressed home the theme of constitutional episcopacy in the belief that greater openness would produce a "greater degree of orderliness in the Church, a more willing acceptance of authority, a fuller and more integrated corporate life, and a truer witness to the Gospel of Christ."[81] At intervals since the late 1940s he had exhorted them to learn from the practical successes of the CMS. He pointed to the value of fresh thinking, sending them each the new edition of Roland Allen's *The Spontaneous Expansion of the Church* and referring them to Joseph Oldham on political issues.[82] Moreover, his increasing frustration

79. James Tengatenga, "The Good Being the Enemy of the Best: The Politics of Bishop Frank Oswald Thorne in Nyasaland and the Federation, 1936-1961," *Religion in Malawi* 6 (1996): 23-24; Clayton is quoted in Sachs, pp. 315-16; O'Connor et al., p. 128.

80. UMCA Papers, SF 15/XV, Enclosure in Broomfield to Bishops of Tanganyika and Nyasaland, their Archdeacons and Canons, 13 Apr. 1960.

81. Broomfield, *Constitutional Episcopacy*, p. 21.

82. UMCA Papers, SF 15/XIII and XV, Broomfield to UMCA Bishops, 14 Dec. 1947, 24 Nov. 1949, 27 Oct. 1955.

with what seemed to be the dominant episcopal and clerical parochialism, sustained at the expense of the commitment to advance Africans in the church, is palpable. As the mission's centenary approached, he was pressing the bishops of Zanzibar and Nyasaland on their visit to Britain to speak to the General Council on the advances made in diocesan constitutional government for both laity and clergy. Alive to the link between African involvement and African self-support, he observed provocatively in passing that "there has been some talk recently about the dictatorship of Bishops."[83]

As we have seen, that dictatorship was nothing new. As direct successors to the apostles, heads of the mission, builders of the church and protectors of its tradition, and rulers of their dioceses, UMCA bishops were exceedingly and self-consciously powerful figures. When the general secretary wrote to them, as he often did, that neither he nor the council "has, or should have, any authority in such a matter,"[84] there was no iron fist in his velvet glove, only hope that they would take wise advice. When the centenary was celebrated in 1957-58, the exercise of episcopal control was coming to be seen as the chief weakness of the mission, a check on efficient diocesan administration, and as such a danger to the church.

After consulting the president (the Honorable Richard Wood) and the chairman of the council (Bishop Eric Hamilton), Broomfield therefore drafted a memorandum concerning "certain discontents in some of our dioceses in Africa." After discussion at home, it was circulated early in 1958 to the bishops for their views, Broomfield making it plain that "The most important point in the memorandum is . . . the nature and extent of the Bishop's authority, and the nature and extent of the obedience owed to him. . . . It is the system which is at fault."[85] Although the General Council only came firmly to grips with the issue after appointing a special Policy Sub-Committee in July 1960, Broomfield's paper was of immense significance not only in reshaping the UMCA but in preparing the way for its merger with the SPG in 1964.[86]

It is impossible here to follow the complexities of the debate in any detail. The debate itself was couched in the sober terms of financial responsibility, the contractual obligations of missionaries, and ecclesiastical constitutional accountability; it was complicated by Broomfield's retirement and Canon

83. UMCA Papers, SF 15/XV, Broomfield to William Zanzibar, 26 Sept. 1956.

84. See, for example, UMCA Papers, SF 15/XIII, Broomfield to Bishops of Zanzibar, Masasi, and Nyasaland, 20 Dec. 1949.

85. UMCA Papers, SF 102, Broomfield to President, 4 Mar. 1957; marked confidential, the paper, "The Relation between Church and Mission in Africa," was circulated, and followed by further explanation in Broomfield to the Bishops, 19 Mar. 1958.

86. For a brief account, see O'Connor et al., pp. 159-61.

John Kingsnorth's appointment as secretary at the end of 1961. There was no doubt, however, that the real task was the redefinition and replacement of one particular view of episcopal authority with another. As the Policy Sub-Committee took the review into its second phase, one of its members, Canon Edward Maycock, anticipating the bishops' resistance, wrote: "autocracy is not only the result of tropical conditions; it is also I feel closely connected with the Anglo-Catholic view of Episcopacy as it existed before the war."[87] Only if the spirit of Bishop Weston could be exorcised could the UMCA and the Anglo-Catholic tradition it represented retain its significance for the growth of the church in Africa.

In the exchanges that followed, Bishop Thorne of Nyasaland was angered by what he saw as an attack on his personal record in office. Others worried at the unfortunate coincidence of moves to reshape episcopal responsibilities just when political independence and the appointment of African bishops was looming.[88] Some bishops, including the newly appointed Trevor Huddleston at Masasi, urged delay because not all dioceses could move at the same pace and because racial conflicts loomed.[89] Reformers were no less concerned than conservatives to preserve valuable features of the old system. To the bishop of Nyasaland, Broomfield was adamant that the "last thing any of us want is to control the Church in Africa from London." To another correspondent he explained that "It is most desirable . . . that there should continue to be a close relationship between the diocesan bishops and the mission, but . . . it is undesirable that any part of their authority or responsibilities should even appear to derive from that relationship."[90]

In the end, however, despite some practical concessions to episcopal sentiment, Broomfield's essential principles seem to have survived. Having argued that the traditional identification of mission and church in the person of the bishop had hindered the growth of both, Broomfield saw separation as necessary. The dean of Windsor's question, "Have you any fear that with the gradual de-missionization the Church in that part of the world may gradually lose

87. UMCA Papers, SF 102, Canon E. A. Maycock to Broomfield, 1 Oct. 1960.

88. Frank Nyasaland to Broomfield, 2 Apr. 1958; Eric Abbott (Dean of Windsor) to Broomfield, 14 Oct. 1960; Trevor Masasi to Broomfield, 7 Jan. 1961, all in UMCA Papers, SF 102.

89. UMCA Papers, SF 102, Trevor Masasi to Broomfield, 7 and 22 Jan. 1961. For Huddleston's years at Masasi, see Terence Ranger, "From Command to Service: Trevor Huddleston in Masasi 1960-68," in *Trevor Huddleston: Essays on His Life and Work,* ed. Deborah Duncan Honoré (Oxford and New York, 1988), pp. 35-52.

90. UMCA Papers, SF 102, Broomfield to Bishop of Nyasaland, 25 Apr. 1961, and Broomfield to Ven. C. Lacey, 12 Sept. 1961.

the 'glamour' of U.M.C.A. traditions?" did not worry him.[91] If from some points of view a more prosaic system had emerged, it was one that would no longer have to wrestle with arbitrary, inconsiderate, and capricious measures by the bishops that had come to seem endemic under the old system.[92] With the creation of the Province of East Africa in 1961, the UMCA lost its formal role in the appointment of the bishops; the bishops as diocesans lost the title of head of the mission, and with it much of their formal control over the mission and its funds. A closer relationship with its missionaries gave the UMCA a potentially greater freedom in decisions over the distribution of its funds. A clear definition of spheres of responsibility brought protection of both the management of UMCA finances and personnel contributed to individual dioceses against independent episcopal control.

It was left to Broomfield's successor in 1962 to tour the field and present to the Policy Committee a final settlement that was to take effect on 1 January 1963.[93] It was, however, an outcome the UMCA was unable to develop on its own. In 1962 exchanges began between the secretaries of the UMCA and SPG that were soon to lead to a merger of the two bodies. Negotiations represented a direct response not to conditions in Africa, but to circumstances at home: pressure from the Anglican hierarchy for "a more united form of missionary action" and changes in the connections within the Anglican Communion; fears that Anglican missionary activity might be handed over to the church assembly; and the perennial problems of increasing income, sustaining local support, and attracting missionary volunteers.[94]

Conclusion

Many aspects of the UMCA's course in the twentieth century offer familiar parallels with those of other missions: the slowness to anticipate and adjust to new conditions, especially in the forms of nationalism and political independence; the reluctance or failure to advance Africans in the ways that Africans themselves often wanted; the complaints about the weakness of local self-support; and the unwillingness of missionaries to decide that their work was

91. UMCA Papers, SF 102, Eric Abbott to Broomfield, 2 Oct. 1961.

92. A. R. Lewis to Bishop Leslie Stradling, 15 June 1958, in UMCA Papers, SF 102.

93. John Kingsnorth, "Confidential. Memorandum to U.M.C.A. Policy Committee," 30 Oct. 1962, in UMCA Papers, SF 102.

94. UMCA Papers, SF 4/II, John Kingsnorth to Bishop Trapp (SPG Secretary), 22 Apr. 1963, SF 4/I; "Highly Confidential. The Universities Mission to Central Africa. Memorandum on a Proposal to Be Put before the General Council on 18th July 1963."

done. All missions felt the constraints of those wider developments in British society that were reducing their ability to recruit volunteers and increase their income.

There is still much to investigate in the history of the UMCA, and even on its selected ground this chapter has hardly begun to penetrate the thicket of issues surrounding the shift from colonial mission to church in an independent state. Nevertheless, there is sufficient evidence to suggest that the Anglo-Catholics of the UMCA found these problems and challenges peculiarly difficult. From some angles this is surprising. In their openness to the idea that African beliefs, customs, poetry, and music were to be taken seriously, among the generality of missionaries UMCA members were exceptionally responsive to their local world.[95] By the beginning of the 1960s there was a growing preparedness to take urban life for granted and to see the future of the mission in Dar es Salaam and Tanga, just as there was in some places a laxity in the practice of Anglo-Catholic liturgy liable to exasperate even a modern bishop.[96] However, their organic, mystical conception of the church, and regard for the centrality of episcopacy in all matters of faith and order, made reforms hard to contemplate. Those features of African society that they admired, together with Anglo-Catholic conceptions of religious and social order, were equally under threat from modernism and modernity. Treating with the enemy on central issues of spiritual concern and theological principle was difficult to accept.

When reform finally came, generated as in so many cases from London, it nevertheless also focused on the nature of Anglo-Catholic mission and the preservation of Anglo-Catholicism within the church. Questions as to the significance of the end of empire for Christian missions as traditionally conceived, or any sense that the church either would or should be in African hands, were distinctly muted in debate. The UMCA steered clear of the vexed question of the Central African Federation. The relations of bishops, church, and mission were adjusted not to bring about African control, but to counter the fact — in Kingsnorth's words to his Policy Committee — "that the Mission ethos and sense of belonging to a great tradition is at a low ebb." Anglo-Catholic revival was a first priority of the UMCA's reformers; in other respects there was little expectation of immediate change. "Necessarily at this stage missionaries have to be units in the local Church. I would hope that when that Church is fully self-governing and has no more suspicion of the paternalism of missionaries or their desire to run the show, then there could

95. For instance, "Poetry in Central Africa," *Central Africa,* Feb. 1942, pp. 19-20.
96. Information, Dr. Gavin White.

be and should be a closer-knit community of expatriate missionaries serving the local Church as a body in the same way as a Religious Community does in, for example, South Africa."[97]

That the Union of South Africa should have suggested to the general secretary a model for the future is perhaps in itself sufficient sign of the singularity of the UMCA's twentieth-century colonial encounter. For members of the UMCA, wedded to a concept of the religious life and episcopal authority over the mission, a world of struggle offering "naught for your comfort" was one likely to strengthen their sense of community and commitment.[98] Other Protestant missions, less clerical in ethos, more secular in tone, were more at ease in negotiating that new set of relations demanded of the Christian churches in a decolonized world.

97. UMCA Papers, SF 102, Kingsnorth, "Confidential. Memorandum to U.M.C.A. Policy Committee," 30 Oct. 1962.

98. Trevor Huddleston, *Naught for Your Comfort* (London, 1956); this was written by Huddleston, a member of the Community of the Resurrection at Mirfield, as he returned to Britain after thirteen years in Sophiatown, Johannesburg.

PART II

Emergent Christian and National Identities in Asia and Africa

CHAPTER 5

Who Is an Indian? Dilemmas of National Identity at the End of the British Raj in India

JUDITH M. BROWN

The title of this chapter contains no reference to Christian missions. This may seem curious in a volume on missions and the end of empire, but my purpose is to examine issues surrounding the end of British rule in India that were to prove crucial as part of the changing, and often turbulent, environment in which expatriate missionaries and Indian Christians were living, working, and practicing their faith.

There are at least three reasons why the end of the British Raj posed major problems for Christians at the time and demands historical attention now. Firstly, India was the first part of the British Empire in Africa or Asia, outside areas of white settlement, to achieve total political independence. Contemporaries, Indian and British, had never experienced "decolonization" before. Nobody could predict the timescale of political change or the political and cultural outcomes of the demand for independence. In particular, nobody could envisage what this unprecedented political shift might mean for missionaries who had, in a sense, a protected position on the subcontinent since at least 1813, when they were first permitted into the territories controlled by the East India Company. British imperial power had for a century and a half provided a protective shelter for their work; and the sources suggest they faced the unknown in 1947 with considerable disquiet. Even more problematic was the way Indian politics had become entangled with issues of religious identity; and there were strands in Indian nationalism that implied that to be Indian one had to be Hindu. If national identity was tied to a particular religious identity, this raised immense dilemmas for India's minority religious communities: Muslims, Sikhs, Christians, and the many tribal groups that had never been part of Hindu society. Christians on the subcontinent, particularly those of mixed race or Anglo-Indian descent and those converts from the base of Indian society, like other minorities, faced questions about whether they were "really Indian" or not, and what their position would be in a nation predicated on Brahmanical ideals, where the successful nationalist party, the Indian National Congress, was largely composed of higher-caste Hindus. Finally, the particular circumstances and timing of the end of the British Raj posed complex questions for the growing Indian churches, questions relating to leadership and personnel, finance, and the role of church organizations in public and national life and their stance on crucial public issues.

I

These problems have to be placed in a longer time frame, reaching right back into the nineteenth century. From the earliest years of that century "religion" was an intensely debated and sensitive issue in Indian public life. This was partly because India's complex society and culture were rooted in sophisticated religious traditions, particularly those of Hinduism and Islam. These traditions were now being challenged by missionary teaching and the assumptions rooted in evangelical Christianity that the representatives of the imperial regime brought with them from Europe, compared with the "Orientalist" appreciation of Indian religion and culture evident among the British in the eighteenth century.[1] Moreover, there developed on the subcontinent a vibrant "public sphere" of debate about religious issues, among others, as literacy rates rose and increasing numbers of Indians began to discuss publicly in English and in vernacular languages matters relating to the influence of Western ideas and institutions on their lives and identities.[2] Such intra-Indian debates on social, economic, and political issues intensified

1. On attitudes in the eighteenth century, see P. J. Marshall, ed., *The British Discovery of Hinduism in the Eighteenth Century* (Cambridge, 1970); and on later British understanding of India, T. R. Metcalf, *Ideologies of the Raj* (Cambridge, 1994).

2. On the development of a public sphere of debate, see C. A. Bayly, *Empire and Information: Intelligence Gathering and Social Communication in India, 1780-1870* (Cambridge, 1996). For some statistics on the expansion of the Indian-owned press in the later nineteenth century, see Anil Seal, *The Emergence of Indian Nationalism: Competition and Collaboration in the Later Nineteenth Century* (Cambridge, 1968), app. 5.

across the subcontinent in the early twentieth century, as the number of schools and colleges rose and more Indians from many different regions joined the ranks of the literate and educated. Between 1921 and 1941, the date of the last census in imperial India, the percentage of literates in the population aged ten and over jumped from 8.3 percent to 15.1 percent. This total figure was dragged down by the lower educational standards of women; for men alone the figure rose from 14.2 percent to 27.4 percent.[3]

The growth of different Christian communities in India was a significant element in the broader religious background to the questions of identity that became acute in the mid–twentieth century. By the 1920s there were between 5 and 6 million Christians in India out of a total population of well over 300 million. Since the first regular census in 1881, their number had been rising considerably, and by 1921 Christians were the third-largest religious group in India.[4] The "community" was by no means homogeneous. Virtually all Christian denominations were represented, and Roman Catholics probably accounted for about a quarter of Indian Christians, particularly in the south and west of India, reflecting older Catholic missionary activity and the pre-British Portuguese presence on the subcontinent. Christians also came from very different social backgrounds. Expatriate and domiciled Europeans obviously counted for a small percentage of the community. As India was never an area of significant white settlement, the number of Europeans was tiny by contrast with the size of the subcontinent and of the Indian population. In the part of India directly ruled by the British (that is, excluding the third of the subcontinent left under the control of subsidiary Indian princes), Europeans numbered only 156,637 in 1921. Another significant group of Christians were those of mixed-race descent, Eurasians or Anglo-Indians, for whom Christianity was a critical boundary marker, enabling them to distance themselves from ethnic Indians and claim common bonds with the ruling race. (The precise number of this group is difficult to discern, but in 1921 was probably about 113,000.) Indian Christians could be divided into two groups — those "Syrian" Christians in southern India who claimed descent from converts dating from the earliest days of the faith and the claimed missionary work of the apostle Thomas, and later converts, many of whom were drawn mainly from the poorest and most lowly in Indian society. The Syrian Christians had an honored place in their own localities, long accepted and inte-

3. Judith M. Brown, *Modern India: The Origins of an Asian Democracy,* 2nd ed. (Oxford, 1994), tab. E, p. 260.

4. This ranking is accurate if the Buddhists in Burma are excluded: Christians then came third after the vast Hindu majority and the very large Muslim minority.

grated among Hindus and Muslims.[5] Recent converts, however, still bore the stigma of their often untouchable, outcaste origins.[6] Their rapidly growing numbers in areas that witnessed "mass movements" in the late nineteenth and early twentieth centuries caused deep anxiety to Hindus in particular, who feared that their own numbers would decrease, and thus lessen their total influence in society and the emergent public sphere. Some contemporaries viewed the conversion of those at the base of society as heralding a threat to the whole social order. In the words of one vernacular newspaper in 1893: "the Christian Missionaries are doing a great deal of harm to the country by converting sweepers and *chamars*, as after their conversion these people cease to work as sweepers, &c. If the Missionaries think that the progress of their religion depends on the conversion of sweepers, let them continue to convert them, but they should not try to make them civilized, and induce them to give up their occupations."[7] Some reflective contemporaries, however, also recognized that such conversions did indeed reflect major problems in Hinduism that demanded reform.[8]

It was thus hardly surprising that religious questions became topics of intense dispute and discussion in the nineteenth century, and that within all India's religious traditions there developed movements of revival and reform.[9] The debates were at their most sophisticated and articulate among those who represented the "high culture" of Hinduism and Islam, though they soon had repercussions in popular culture and among the lowliest in society. Although among educated Hindus, Muslims, and Sikhs there were very few converts to Christianity, there was certainly a profound awareness that the modern manifestations of Christianity, and missionary work in particular, required a range of responses — theological, organizational, and spiritual. Indians reacted along a broad spectrum of attitudes, drawing on the resources of their own traditions to make sense of and manage this challenge. Some took the line of overt hostility; many misunderstood the Christian message and felt deeply

5. See Susan Bayly, *Saints, Goddesses, and Kings: Muslims and Christians in South Indian Society, 1700-1900* (Cambridge, 1989).

6. An informative study of northern Indian Christians, many of whom were "mass movement" converts, is John C. B. Webster, *The Christian Community and Change in Nineteenth-Century North India* (Delhi, 1976).

7. Quoted in Webster, p. 146.

8. An important study of a Hindu reformist movement in the Punjab, an area of mass Christian conversions, is K. W. Jones, *Arya Dharm: Hindu Consciousness in Nineteenth-Century Punjab* (Berkeley, 1976).

9. A good survey is K. W. Jones, *Socio-Religious Reform Movements in British India* (Cambridge, 1989).

wounded by missionary discourtesy and aggressiveness; while others were deeply attracted to the person of Jesus and to his moral teaching.[10] M. K. Gandhi was ultimately to fall into the last category, but when growing up as a boy in western India in the late nineteenth century he had felt only dislike for what he thought was Christian faith, and for the practices of the Irish missionaries he encountered. As he later noted in his autobiography:

> In those days Christian missionaries used to stand in a corner near the high school and hold forth, pouring abuse on Hindus and their gods. I could not endure this. . . . About the same time, I heard of a well known Hindu having been converted to Christianity. It was the talk of the town that, when he was baptized, he had to eat beef and drink liquor, that he also had to change his clothes, and that thenceforth he began to go about in European costume including a hat. These things got on my nerves. Surely, thought I, a religion that compelled one to eat beef, drink liquor, and change one's own clothes did not deserve the name.[11]

It was only later in London as a law student that he realized that Christians did not have to eat meat or drink alcohol, and on the advice of a courteous Christian friend, he began to read the Bible, finding parts of the New Testament a deep inspiration, despite the soporific effects of the Old Testament![12]

Indian responses to the presence of a new, evangelical Christianity took place not just in the individual mind and heart. They were also manifested publicly in formal debates with missionaries; among Indians in books, pamphlets, and the expanding press; and in the milieu of the growing numbers of religious associations for renewal and reform.[13] Among the central issues discussed were the nature of religious truth and inspiration, and the sources of religious authority: institutions, functionaries, tradition, and scripture. Influential in these debates were also ideas drawn from more secular philosophical

10. For a sensitive examination of some of these issues, see chap. 5, "Transformation of Religious Sensibilities in Nineteenth-Century Bengal," in Tapan Raychaudhuri, *Perceptions, Emotions, Sensibilities: Essays on India's Colonial and Post-colonial Experiences* (New Delhi, 1999).

11. M. K. Gandhi, *An Autobiography: The Story of My Experiments with Truth* (London, 1966; originally published, 1927), pp. 28-29.

12. Gandhi, *An Autobiography,* p. 58.

13. On the conduct of formal religious debate and the development of an ambience of reformist discussions, see Webster, chap. 4; Avril Powell, *Muslims and Missionaries in Pre-Mutiny India* (London, 1993); Jones, *Socio-Religious Reform Movements in British India;* and Rosalind O'Hanlon, *Caste, Conflict, and Ideology: Mahatma Jotirao Phule and Low Caste Protest in Nineteenth-Century Western India* (Cambridge, 1985), chaps. 3 and 4.

debates in the Western world about nature, reason, and knowledge, and Europe's own traditions of religious radicalism. By the end of the century even European academic scholarship on the nature of scripture was impinging on Indian discussions as a wide range of critical ideas reached India through the flowering of modern education.

Many of these "religious" issues were also of urgent practical significance. When Indians discussed the desirability of many social reforms, they inevitably had to weigh issues of religious authority, where social customs were thought to be rooted as much in scripture as in tradition and custom. For example, when colonial rulers, Indian conservatives, and reformers addressed the issue of sati (the rare practice of a widow's self-immolation on her husband's funeral pyre), the debate was often less about women than about the proper sources of tradition and the nature of the Hindu scriptures. Further, the British need to know and understand colonial society led them increasingly to draw on the expertise of Brahmanical specialists, and thus to privilege Brahmanical scriptures in the publicly accepted understanding of "Hinduism," at the expense of earlier diversities of belief and practice.[14] At the end of the century the authority of Hindu scripture was again fiercely debated, this time in relation to the age of consent, when in 1891 the British raised it from ten to twelve years. Indian reformers and conservatives alike drew on different interpretations of the *shastras* to justify their stand, with the former, for example, drawing on an authoritative statement from the pandits of the sacred city of Benares that there was no religious objection to the new law.[15] When educated Muslim men discussed the question of educating their women, similar issues surfaced in their milieu (as elsewhere in the Islamic world) about the authority of tradition and custom, and whether one could be a good Muslim and also a social reformer. Although women's issues were amongst the most contentious in religious terms, for Hindus social and ideological problems relating to caste, and the practice of untouchability in particular, also caused heart searching and deep rifts between conservatives and reformers. Some argued that caste was a sign of India's spirituality and cultural strength, while others considered it testimony to Hindu spiritual and social degeneracy. Most argued that untouchables needed "uplift" and recla-

14. Lara Mani, "Contentious Traditions: The Debate on *Sati* in Colonial India," in *Recasting Women: Essays in Colonial History*, ed. K. Sangari and S. Vaid (New Delhi, 1989), pp. 88-126: and Mani, *Contentious Traditions: The Debate on* Sati *in Colonial India* (Berkeley, Los Angeles, and London, 1998).

15. M. Sinha, chap. 4, "Potent Protests: The Age of Consent Controversy, 1891," in her *Colonial Masculinity: The "Manly Englishman" and the "Effeminate Bengali" in the Late Nineteenth Century* (Manchester and New York, 1995).

mation — ironically defined according to Brahmanical standards of right behavior.[16] Gandhi, radical in his opposition to untouchability but conservative in his understanding of appropriate behavior, even went to the point of declaring that untouchability was such an evil that if it could be proved that it was part of Hinduism he would cease to be a Hindu. Implicitly and explicitly he was questioning the relative significance of scripture, tradition, reason, and conscience as authorities in religious matters.[17]

It was not just those with education and knowledge of the high traditions and scriptural foundations of Hinduism and Islam, however, who were involved in the questioning of religious authorities and identities in the nineteenth and early twentieth centuries. The cultural and religious horizons of those at the base of society were also widening as a result of rising literacy (often the product of mission schooling) and public debate on social and religious matters, efforts at "reform" by their social superiors, and the pressures of urban life where the lowliest moved to town in growing numbers in search of work, and found themselves still poor and degraded. For such people, too, religious identity became to an extent no longer a "given" but a part of their experience that could be challenged and changed. Within Hindu traditions was a reservoir of identities and role models on which the discontented could draw, to make sense of their past history and their present predicaments, and to redefine and reinvent themselves. This was demonstrated in the life of Jotirao Phule, for example, the son of a lower-caste family, who owed his early education to a local missionary and campaigned against the religious authority of Brahmins in western India in the nineteenth century. His developing ideological stance was an example of the way myth and particular versions of regional history could be pressed into service to make a new identity for low castes, that of the Kshatriya, over against the Brahmin, to give the despised and downtrodden a sense of worth and pride, and an ideology to sanction changes in behavior and social relations.[18] Similarly, a generation or more later, poor urban untouchables and low-caste Hindus in the United Provinces sought religious sanction for a changing self-understanding, and redefinition of self and the group. Untouchables drew on the tradition of devotional religion, which gave the worshiper access to the divine, regardless of caste status, and began to ar-

16. Susan Bayly, "Caste and the Modern Nation: Incubus or Essence?" in her *Caste, Society, and Politics in India from the Eighteenth Century to the Modern Age* (Cambridge, 1999), chap. 4.

17. Judith M. Brown, "Mahatmas as Reformers: Some Problems of Religious Authority in the Indian Nationalist Movement," *South Asia Research* 6, no. 1 (May 1986): 15-26; Brown, *Gandhi: Prisoner of Hope* (New Haven and London, 1989).

18. O'Hanlon, *Caste, Conflict, and Ideology.*

gue that they were descendants of the earliest Hindus before society was corrupted by the distinctions imposed by Aryan conquerors; while low-caste Hindus, with a foothold in polite Hindu society, asserted a warrior ancestry and Kshatriya caste status.[19] Similar reworking of myths and traditions to transform social deprivation and degradation and create new religious identities was to be found in the many movements that began to transform the lives of untouchables. Where some took the way of "conversion," to Christianity or later in the twentieth century to Buddhism under the influence of B. R. Ambedkar, many more drew on the multiple resources of Hindu tradition, demonstrating that religious change and choice were possible.[20]

II

By the beginning of the twentieth century there had thus occurred a significant redrawing of the religious map of the subcontinent, and multiple reconsiderations of the meaning of "religion" and the nature of "religious belonging." This was a crucial aspect of the milieu in which ideas of Indian national identity evolved. This section investigates how ideas of nationhood related to religious identity, and how being Indian and Hindu became increasingly intertwined. This came to pose major problems for those who were not caste Hindus, in the immediate context of British devolution of power to Indians and eventual withdrawal from Indian Raj, and in the longer term within the new Indian state.

Nations are not, of course, natural political communities, although protagonists of nationhood assumed and asserted this wherever nationalist movements flourished in the nineteenth and twentieth centuries. Historically nations have to be created at several levels of human experience. At the very least they have to be produced or invented at the level of imagination and feeling, eliciting an ideological and affective response from potential members of the new community. They depend on the development of an organizational reality, through various political and cultural movements and parties. The processes of imagination and organization require leaderships with

19. Nandini Gooptu, "Caste and Labour: Untouchable Social Movements in Urban Uttar Pradesh in the Early Twentieth Century," in *Dalit Movements and the Meanings of Labour in India,* ed. P. Robb (New Delhi, 1993), pp. 277-98; and Gooptu, "The Urban Poor and Militant Hinduism in Early Twentieth-Century Uttar Pradesh," *Modern Asian Studies* 31, no. 4 (1997): 879-918.

20. For a regional study, see M. Juergensmeyer, *Religion as Social Vision: The Movement against Untouchability in Twentieth-Century Punjab* (Berkeley, Los Angeles, and London, 1982).

particular skills. They also derive strength from a range of disposing and enabling factors such as modern communications, literacy, shared language, and shared commonalities of varied kinds, often including culture and religion, and in colonial nationalism a common experience of alien rule.

On the Indian subcontinent the religious identities that had become so disputed in the nineteenth century became in the twentieth deeply problematic aspects of the definition and experience of "Indianness." There was no reason this should have been inevitable, despite British assertions that India was composed of a multiplicity of groups, many of them defined by religion, and could therefore never become a nation.[21] Echoes of this attitude toward Indians as essentially divided on religious lines could be heard even as late as 1930, when the Simon Commission reporting on the workings of the Indian constitution and related matters could justify the nature and presence of the Indian army partly on grounds of "internal security," because, in explicit contrast with Britain, the police "could not be expected in all cases to cope with the sudden and violent outburst of a mob driven frantic by religious frenzy."[22] In contrast to this essentializing view, issues of Indian national identity and its relationship to religious identity have to be understood in the context of unfolding ideas and styles of political organization in the very specific context of British imperial rule.

The first phase in the development of a vision of Indian nationhood and the evolution of a countrywide political organization in the name of a nation occurred between the mid–nineteenth century and the First World War. During this seminal phase a mixture of ideas blended and interacted to create a sense of nationhood among the small numbers of Western educated, the majority of whom were high-caste Hindus, as a result of the geographically and socially uneven spread of the new education. (In the 1880s, for example, nearly 90 percent of college students were Hindus, although they were only just over 73 percent of the population.) Among such people there was little active opposition to British rule, but across the subcontinent they began to share a sense of anxiety and frustration at aspects of that rule that seemed to demean them as an Indian race or deprived them as a particular social group of professional opportunities that they felt to be their right. Aspects of overt racial discrimination, such as the restrictions on Indians bearing arms, or the difficulties Indian boys had in competing for the prestigious Indian Civil Service, were cases in point.[23] Among

21. See Metcalf, *Ideologies of the Raj.*

22. *Report of the Indian Statutory Commission. Vol. 1 — Survey* (Cmd. 3568, 1930), p. 95.

23. For a discussion of episodes where Indian men's senses of racial pride and of masculinity were wounded, see Sinha, *Colonial Masculinity.*

such people there was an implicit assumption that Western ideas of nationhood were philosophically acceptable and desirable, and also applicable to India, and that India needed a nation-state. It was plain for all to see that something was "wrong" with Indian society — and by "Indian" those who participated in these debates meant "Hindu" — for why else should a handful of foreigners have taken control of the country? The remedy for this parlous situation lay partially in varieties of social and religious reform, but primarily in the possession of a strong nation-state.[24] Gandhi was one of the very few Indian thinkers and protagonists of nationalism who did not share this aspect of Indians' selective appropriation of Western ideas and practices. In his extended pamphlet *Hind Swaraj,* published in 1909, he castigated his countrymen for wanting "English rule without the Englishman," "the tiger's nature, but not the tiger." They would thus make India "Englistan" rather than "Hindustan"; whereas he advocated radical reform that would extend from society to create a new form of national polity. True swaraj (self-rule) could not be given by the British to Indians by political handouts: Indians would have to create it by hard work and moral reform.[25]

Alongside these political ideas relating to imperial rule and possible Indian self-governance was an even more powerful sense of cultural pride at being Indian, and a deeply emotive attention to the nature of the Indian race, with particular emphasis on its cultural roots and its spiritual strength. It was visible as educated Hindus debated the reasons for British rule, and evaluated what aspects of European civilization they could adopt and adapt to reinvigorate and enhance their indigenous inheritance. It was also present in concerns about racial stock and strength, and the nature of Indian gender identities, surfacing in such diverse situations as the development of martial arts and bodybuilding, or in concerns for women's health, and the age of marriage and childbirth. However, in these varied discussions about the nature of the nation, there was often a profound unease about the place of Muslims within it; and more particularly, a failure to come to terms with the period of Muslim rule in India and the role Muslims and their culture had played in the development of Indian culture and political forms. Often Hindu writers took refuge in imagery of Muslim rule as a time of destruction and tyranny, echoing the views of early British historians.[26] Of equal significance for the future

24. See chap. 2, "Hindu Responses to British Rule," in Bhiku Parekh, *Colonialism, Tradition, and Reform: An Analysis of Gandhi's Political Discourse,* rev. ed. (New Delhi; Thousand Oaks, Calif.; and London, 1999).

25. A. J. Parel, ed., *M. K. Gandhi: "Hind Swaraj" and Other Writings* (Cambridge, 1997). The metaphor of the tiger is on p. 28.

26. Parekh, pp. 49-51.

identifications of "nation" with Hindu was the ominous absence of Muslims as participants in these discussions. Compared with high-caste Hindus, India's diverse Muslim groups produced proportionately fewer Western-educated men; and they in turn tended at this time to concentrate on issues of post-Mutiny relations with the British, and of internal reform and reconstruction of what it meant to be a good Muslim in a changing world.[27]

At the same time educated Hindus began to imagine the Indian nation, so they also developed new, voluntary, and secular associations out of which the organization of a nationalist movement was to develop. Many of these early gatherings were self-help or discussion groups, addressing social and intellectual as much as political issues. But by the 1880s a critical number of Indians had realized that a pan-Indian voice and organization was crucial if they were to be an effective pressure group in Indian political life and gain credibility in the eyes of the rulers. The resulting Indian National Congress, which first met in 1885, became eventually the major political organization of Indian politicians, and the main mouthpiece of Indian nationalism. In the years before the First World War, however, it was totally "unrepresentative" of the Indian population, its participants who gathered for its annual Christmas meeting being predominantly Hindu and disproportionately high caste. Between 1892 and 1909 the total number attending Congress sessions was nearly 14,000. Of these, 5,500 were Brahmins, and nearly 7,000 non-Brahmin Hindus. Muslim delegates normally numbered well under a hundred at each session. Christians produced just over a hundred delegates through these years, the highest number at any one session being 15 in Calcutta in 1896.[28] Congressmen recognized the fragility of their new unity, and in an attempt to preserve it deliberately excluded from their discussions those issues that might have divided them on ideological, socioeconomic, or religious grounds, for example, by relegating discussions of social reform to a parallel Social Conference.

Hence the problems of Indian diversity — diversity of many kinds, regional, socioeconomic, as well as religious — were masked by deliberate ambivalence within the Congress, and by the fact that a new nation-state was at this time not on the political agenda. Congress demands were for reforms within the system of British rule. To the British rulers notions of Indian independence were virtually unthinkable; those who claimed to speak for an Indian nation were considered unrepresentative townies, unable to speak for

27. See David Lelyveld, *Aligarh's First Generation: Muslim Solidarity in British India* (1978, 1st ed.; Delhi, 1996).

28. P. C. Ghosh, *The Development of the Indian National Congress, 1892-1909*, 2nd rev. ed. (Calcutta, 1985), chart A, p. 23.

the masses of rural India or for the religious minorities of the subcontinent. In 1912 the viceroy, Lord Hardinge, insisted to the secretary of state for India that there could be no question about the permanence of British rule, while the latter agreed that any goal of colonial self-government for India was a hallucination.[29]

World war was, however, to have a decisive impact on Indian politics, on the way Indians perceived themselves, and on the nature and trajectory of British rule. Firstly, self-rule was firmly set on the Indian political agenda during the First World War, and in the course of the Second the British promised independence when it ended. Thus the nation-state became an increasingly imminent reality, and the nature of the nation became an urgent ideological and practical issue. Secondly, the British recognized that they would have to bolster their rule by incorporating into its alliance structures, among others, those they had once decried as unrepresentative, educated upstarts. This they did by a series of constitutional reforms (in 1919 and 1935) that devolved power on provincial matters increasingly into the hands of Indian politicians elected to the provincial legislatures by an expanded electorate. However, in continuation of their view of India as composed of numerous interest groups, including religious groups, who had a rightful place in the polity, they enlarged their strategy of providing separate electorates for significant groups and reserved seats in the provincial and central legislatures. In the construction of such special political provisions, earlier exercises in knowledge gathering about Indian society became politically significant in new ways. In particular, the decennial censuses, during which members of religious groups were counted for each province, began to link religious identity and numerical strength to the political process. Under the electoral rules following the 1919 reforms, members were nominated to the provincial legislatures to represent the untouchables (so-called Depressed Classes), Anglo-Indians, Indian Christians, Labour, and "Others" who included mining and European interests in some areas. Among the elected members there were seats for non-Muslims, Muslims, Sikhs, Anglo-Indians, Indian Christians, Europeans, landholders, universities, and commerce and industry. Indian Christians had five elected seats in Madras and one nominated representative in Bombay, Bengal, United Provinces, Punjab, and Bihar and Orissa.[30] In discussions prior to the 1935 reforms, the government announced the continuation of separate electorates and reserved seats for religious minorities, not least because of minor-

29. Cambridge University Library, Hardinge Mss. (118), Hardinge to Crewe, 4 July 1912, Crewe to Hardinge, 18 July 1912.

30. *Indian Statutory Commission. Vol. 1 — Survey*, pp. 144-45.

ity pressure for this. Indian Christians were to receive twenty-one reserved seats, the largest number (nine) being in Madras.[31] In this new situation of an enlarged franchise and developing electoral politics, the boundaries of religious belonging became increasingly significant. Not only did numbers begin to count toward special representation, politicians had constituencies labeled by religion and it consequently made sense to appeal for support in terms of religious community interests. The debates about religious belonging that had originated in the previous century now impinged on politics, and religious and political identities were increasingly intertwined in India's evolving political culture. The identity that became even more problematic in this situation was that of the nation.

The main ideologues of the Indian nation at this juncture were to be found within the Congress or in Hindu groups on its periphery. Among those who called themselves nationalists was a very wide spectrum of "imaginings" of national identity. At one end were those, comparatively few, who saw the future in secular terms. Jawaharlal Nehru, for example, looked for a radical secular state that would encompass everyone who lived within India's geographical borders, regardless of religious or social status. He believed India's strength lay in its composite culture and what he saw as its tradition of tolerating difference, and for him its national unity lay in its shared geography, history, and culture.[32] Others, less learned in Western philosophy and less philosophical in bent, assumed that India's national identity lay in its deeply rooted culture. But here, of course, the problem was that most such "nationalists" were caste Hindus, who combined Brahmanical ideals of culture and appropriate behavior with trends appropriated from Victorian British culture that included concerns for duty, discipline, education, public service, and civic order. Ironically this meant that many of them shared with their British rulers a deep fear of disorder and mass unrest, and were in their way as paternalist and patronizing toward the poor and ill-educated as the colonial authorities.[33] Gandhi was in some senses part of this broad envisioning of the Indian nation, believing it to be rooted in Indian culture and spirituality and thus superior to Western, materialistic political identities. He claimed — and believed sincerely — that all religious groups participated in this spirituality

31. *East India (Constitutional Reforms). Communal Decision* (Cmd. 4147, 1932).

32. See, for example, J. Nehru, *The Discovery of India* (originally published 1946).

33. See C. A. Watt, "Education for National Efficiency: Constructive Nationalism in North India, 1909-1916," *Modern Asian Studies* 31, no. 2 (1997): 339-74; also Judith M. Brown, "Gandhi — a Victorian Gentleman: An Essay in Imperial Encounter," in *The Statecraft of British Imperialism: Essays in Honour of Wm. Roger Louis*, ed. R. D. King and R. W. Kilson (London and Portland, 1999).

and were equal brothers in the nation, but his imagery and language suggested that deep down it was a Hindu spirituality and culture, however much reformed, on which the nation must be built. At the far end of the spectrum, however, were those who were overtly Hindu nationalists, and argued and worked for the building up of a strong, homogeneous nation founded on a revived Hindu race. Among the most prominent in this group were V. D. Sarvarkar, who wrote *Hindutva: Who Is a Hindu?* (1923), one of the founding texts of this vision of the nation, and M. S. Golwalkar, author of *We, or Our Nationhood Defined* (1939), who argued that those who did not comply with Hindu culture and standards should not even have citizens' rights in an independent India.[34]

Men such as Sarvarkar or Golwalkar gloried in the exclusive nature of their vision of the nation: it was precisely the exclusion of corrupting or diluting influences that would guarantee its purity and strength. However, many more of India's "nationalists" were pragmatically aware of the need to accommodate India's religious minorities who were spread throughout the subcontinent, even if they did not, like Nehru, glory in the notion of a composite nation. Yet none of them were able to understand or assuage the fears of many non-Hindu segments of the population in the new political situation between the wars. Gandhi spoke of "brotherhood" between those of different religions, while a broad spectrum of experienced politicians led by Jawaharlal Nehru's father, Motilal, tried at the end of the 1920s to persuade Muslims that they did not need special political provisions such as separate electorates because their culture would be guaranteed and there would be religious freedom in any new India. The younger Nehru dismissed the growing "communalism" (whether of the Hindu or Muslim variety) as "antinationalism" and mere manipulation of popular religion by socioeconomic elites.[35]

Furthermore, the very tactics and style that served in the 1920s and 1930s to popularize the idea of the nation and to gather support for nationalist protest movements served to alienate many non-Hindus. Gandhi, the Hindu mahatma, was at the heart of this new populism, and his imagery and style were inevitably redolent of his Hindu inheritance. He looked like a Hindu ascetic; miracle stories surrounded his name and reputation in popular culture; he lived in an ashram; and he used the mythical figures of Hinduism to popularize his message of reconstruction. His whole idiom was religious, often to the

34. For an exposition of the Hindu nationalist strand, see Christophe Jaffrelot, *The Hindu Nationalist Movement and Indian Politics, 1925 to the 1990s* (1993, 1st ed.; English ed., London, 1996), chap. 1.

35. J. Nehru, *An Autobiography* (originally published, 1936; London, 1941), pp. 138, 467-68.

embarrassment of colleagues like Nehru, for whom politics was about principles and rationality, not about listening to an "inner voice," and the political gathering was a natural milieu rather than a prayer meeting.

Even more seriously, from the perspective of Indian Christians, was Gandhi's attitude to conversion. He was, of course, by this stage of his life conversant with and sympathetic to much of Christian teaching, venerated the person of Jesus, and was at home with Christian hymns and prayers, which he regularly used in his ashram. Moreover, he had close friends among both Indian Christians (such as Raj Kumari Amrit Kaur) and foreigners, foremost among them C. F. Andrews, who had worked with him since his time in South Africa. For Gandhi, however, religion was the individual's search for truth rather than adherence to a particular creed or membership of a distinctive community of faith and worship. So he believed that truth seekers should stay within their own traditions, and neither leave them nor seek to recruit others into them. As he wrote in 1935:

> I believe that there is no such thing as conversion from one faith to another in the accepted sense of the term. It is a highly personal matter for the individual and his God. . . . It is a conviction daily growing upon me that the great and rich Christian missions will render true service to India, if they can persuade themselves to confine their activities to humanitarian service without the ulterior motive of converting India or at least her unsophisticated villagers to Christianity, and destroying their social superstructure, which notwithstanding its many defects has stood now from time immemorial.[36]

As many Indian Christians were recent converts, particularly through mass movements of low-caste Hindus and untouchables, Gandhi's stance was profoundly disturbing. In the 1930s he engaged in public conflict with missionaries on the subject of work amongst outcastes, particularly accusing them of unfair methods in luring the poor and ignorant into a change of religion.[37] This was, not coincidentally, just at the time when he was immersed in his own campaign to transform high-caste attitudes to untouchables and to urge untouchables to live cleaner and more disciplined lives. Further, it was at the juncture when the number of untouchables and their political position was a

36. *Harijan,* 28 Sept. 1935, in *The Collected Works of Mahatma Gandhi* (New Delhi, 1975), 61:457-58.

37. See Susan Billington Harper, *In the Shadow of the Mahatma: Bishop V. S. Azariah and the Travails of Christianity in British India* (Grand Rapids and Richmond, Surrey, U.K., 2000), chap. 9.

highly sensitive issue within the nationalist movement. On this issue Gandhi had embarked on a fast to death in the wake of British policy to give untouchables separate electorates in 1932. Although a compromise had been effected that saved the Mahatma's life, the mass conversion of untouchables to Christianity (or indeed to Buddhism) was still seen by nationalist Hindus as a threat to the integrity of the nation that would compound the growing problem of Muslim separatism.

It was not, however, just the diverse imaginings of the Indian nation that underlined its Hindu nature. Nationalist organization confirmed the trend. Congress was the dominant mouthpiece of nationalist demand by the later 1930s, and had become not only capable of mounting major anti-imperial movements of civil disobedience under Gandhi's leadership, but was fast becoming an efficient electoral machine. Its status in Indian political life and its increasing power to determine events were clear when it swept to triumph in the elections that followed the 1935 constitutional reforms. Congress won 716 of the 1,585 seats in the newly constituted provincial legislatures, and had clear majorities in five provinces, and eventually formed governments in seven. By this time it had become for many Hindus the natural arena of political activity, the party to join if one was to achieve any position of political authority, or to win a seat in the legislature, with all the patronage and legislative and local influence that implied. The party strategy, however, that achieved this national role for Congress was not that of a simple nationalist appeal, despite the founding national myths of a heroic and popular nationalist movement. As the British devolved power into Indian hands as a method of co-opting new allies to bolster their rule, so a far broader spectrum of Indians began to realize the importance of attending to the elections and the politics of the legislators. Congress in turn adapted to local power structures, welcoming into its ranks substantial rural folk who a generation earlier would have seen little point in Congress politics, and would not have been enfranchised. Such "vernacular politicians" became the backbone of the Congress party, carrying it through to become the party of independence and of government after 1947.

The "price" for this deep-rootedness was twofold in terms of national identity. In the first place, Congress had to permit a broad range of attitudes within it, and could not enforce an ideological commitment to a particular vision of the nation. This meant that pockets of Hindu nationalism could flourish within its ranks, despite the pluralistic tolerance of leaders such as Gandhi and Nehru. Second, it became rooted in the dominant groups in the countryside who received the vote as the franchise was widened, but this in practice meant resting on those Hindu castes that were conservative in attitudes and practices, and were most likely to understand India in terms of the market town and village where Hindu culture molded life and social relations, whatever the reformist or Westernized outlook of the elite all-India leaders. Gandhi and Nehru were both in their own ways aware of the dichotomy between their vision of the nation and that of rank-and-file congressmen. Gandhi saw how even Congress committee members would toss away his plans for grassroots social reconstruction, while Nehru was disturbed by the Hindu temper of congressmen in his own United Provinces.

In this rapidly evolving political situation, it became clear that many Indians felt fearful for their position in a Congress-dominated India, and began to dispute the dominant version of nationalism and to seek ways of protecting themselves as the constitution was reformed and the prospect of independence loomed. For the first time provincial groups of Muslims began to see the importance of a pan-Indian voice and strategy, and like the Sikh minority, began to take up defensive positions through constitutional bargaining, internal organization, and eventually violence. By contrast those who were weaker in numbers and dispersed through the subcontinent, or were poor and with little political clout, became increasingly fearful about their place within a nation increasingly associated with "Hinduness." Among them were tribal people, untouchables, and Christians; and of course, Christians were often drawn from just these social groups on the fringes of Hindu society. There were some prominent Christians who supported the nationalist movement, but they tended to be highly educated and Westernized. Even Christian leaders who saw themselves as staunch nationalists, such as the first Indian Anglican bishop, Azariah, bishop of Dornakal, in whose diocese were many thousands of mass-movement converts, feared that Christians were being categorized as antinational. He explicitly denied that giving up Hinduism meant abandoning Indian nationality, and urged Christians as good citizens to assist in the reformist programs of nationalists (and Congress governments), such as prohibition, and work to reduce rural illiteracy and indebtedness. As wartime politics indicated how near independence might be, however, he sounded a note of warning about what national freedom might mean for Christians.

> Would India's freedom mean a return to the old caste tyranny? From recent experiences [the Indian Christian] is not at all sure it will not. The educated Christian in an academic sort of way desired complete freedom: but would the rural Christian be free when India's freedom comes, to practise his religion, to propagate it to his countrymen and to lift up his head as one made in Christ and raised above the ignominy and dis-

> grace that are attached even to-day to the word *Harijan?* These are [the Indian Christian's] vague fears. Congress leaders have never given the slightest consideration to clearing these doubts.[38]

Azariah voiced these anxieties in 1942. In August 1947 India became independent and was partitioned into a secular Indian state and a Pakistan that was created for a presumptive Muslim nation. The speed of these developments was dramatic and unforeseeable. It was partly because the British recognized they had lost control of the political situation and hoped to achieve a peaceful departure with as much credit as possible. They knew they no longer had the manpower and resources to control a renewal of civil disobedience, because of their reliance on Indian troops, police, and civil servants. Moreover, in some places communal violence was not only a grim reality but seemed likely to infect the army, the bastion of colonial order. As the penultimate viceroy confided to his diary on the last day of 1947:

> the administration has declined, and the machine in the Centre is hardly working at all now, my ministers are too busy with politics. And while the British are legally and morally responsible for what happens in India, we have lost nearly all power to control events; we are simply running on the momentum of our previous prestige. The loyalty of the Police is doubtful in some of the Provinces, they are tinged with communalism; fortunately the Indian Army seems unaffected so far, but it can hardly remain so indefinitely, if communal tension continues.[39]

Indian politicians were as responsible as the British for the partition of their country. This remains one of the most disputed issues in twentieth-century Indian history. But modern scholarship suggests that many Muslims had little sense of national identity even as late as the 1940s, and that the idea of "Pakistan" was a bargaining counter with which to achieve special status for India's diverse Muslim groups in a federal India. Congress leaders, however (apart from Gandhi), wished for a strong state rather than a loose and accommodating federation. Partition was a price they were prepared to pay for this, feeling that the greater good was a nation-state where the government was strong enough to push forward economic and social reconstruction. The result was that partition and the violence that surrounded it in northern India con-

38. Cited in Harper, p. 343. (*Harijan,* meaning "children of god," was Gandhi's name for untouchables, and was disliked by many of them as being patronizing.)

39. Penderel Moon, ed., *Wavell: The Viceroy's Journal* (London, 1973), p. 402.

firmed the understanding of India and Indian in largely Hindu cultural terms. Muslims who left for Pakistan were now seen as violent and aggressive foreigners rather than former neighbors and friends, while the millions of Muslims left behind in India were often considered to be antinational and potential fifth columnists. By the same procedures of envisioning the new India, Anglo-Indians and Indian Christians who were recent converts were thought to be "foreign," though in their case "foreignness" lay in religious and/or ethnic closeness to the former imperial rulers.

III

This analysis of the religious dimensions of emerging Indian national identity concludes with the making of the new Indian state immediately after independence and its implications for Christians. Official policy in Delhi was clear. India was to be a secular state, in contrast to Pakistan, and the presence of significant religious minorities was a symbol of this inclusive identity. The assassination of Gandhi in January 1948 by a Hindu who thought he had betrayed the Hindu nation brought a public revulsion against overtly and exclusively Hindu nationalism, and for a period organizations defined as "communal" — Hindu and Muslim — were banned. In the immediate aftermath of independence and the outpouring of grief at the loss of Gandhi, the politicians in the Constituent Assembly drew up the constitution of the new Indian Republic. The assembly was dominated by congressmen, and among them by the all-India leaders who had taken India to freedom, including Nehru. Among the twenty key individuals in the assembly was one highly educated untouchable, two Muslims, and one Christian (Professor H. C. Mookerjee, a Bengali professor and president of the All-India Council of Indian Christians).[40] The constitution provided for a secular, democratic, and federal republic. Among the fundamental rights guaranteed to all citizens was the right to freedom of religion, and also cultural and educational rights. However, religious minorities were no longer to have entrenched political protection through separate electorates and reserved seats, as these were seen as divisive and a relic of antinational colonial policy. The only group for whom such special protection remained was the untouchables, and that was intended for a limited period only.

Nehru, India's first prime minister until his death in 1964, was deeply committed to the vision of India as a composite nation. In an interview with the London *Catholic Herald* in 1946, he maintained that Christians were an

40. Granville Austin, *The Indian Constitution: Cornerstone of a Nation* (London, 1966).

integral part of India with a long tradition: "They form one of the many enriching elements in the country's cultural and spiritual life. In a country where there are so many creeds we must learn to be tolerant."[41] Some years later he wrote to his chief ministers sensitively of Christian apprehensions about their place in the new India, urging them to see how vital it was to build up a new Indian sense of unity.[42]

In a federal state and in such a vast country, even the commitment of the prime minister could not ensure that secularism would be the dominant ethos. Throughout his premiership he battled with the problems of the minorities and with the persistence of Hindu conservatism in the Congress itself and in the governments of the states that made up the Indian Union. His struggles and his rhetoric on national integration and the need for minorities to feel secure in their position within the nation and to be represented in its public services suggest just how fragile was an inclusive sense of Indian identity and how vulnerable were non-Hindu groups.

Examples from the early 1950s make this plain. For example, in 1950 and 1951 Nehru battled for dominance in the Congress party itself, deeply concerned at the Hindu version of "nationalism" he felt was becoming acceptable within it, as represented by P. D. Tandon, who had become Congress president. Eventually Nehru won what he felt was a battle for the soul of Congress, and forced Tandon out, achieving his own election to the party presidency instead.[43] Even personal supremacy in the all-India Congress from this date did not mean he could control local congressmen, whether in or out of state governments. In 1952 word reached him through his Christian confidant and ministerial colleague Raj Kumari Amrit Kaur, that Christians in central India were facing harassment and discrimination. He faced his chief ministers on the issue, insisting that this should not happen, and clearly showing awareness of the poor and often backward nature of the Christian community, but also a recognition that Christianity was in many senses an indigenous religion and was no longer attached to the coattails of an imperial power.[44] The fol-

41. S. Gopal et al., eds., *Selected Works of Jawaharlal Nehru,* 1st ser., vol. 15 (New Delhi, 1972-82), p. 171.

42. Nehru to Chief Ministers, 20 Sept. 1953, 26 Apr. 1954, in G. Parthasarathi, ed., *Jawaharlal Nehru: Letters to Chief Ministers, 1947-1964. Vol. 3, 1952-1954* (New Delhi, 1985), pp. 376-77, 535-36.

43. On this key episode see Judith M. Brown, *Nehru* (London and New York, 1999), pp. 98-99: key letters showing Nehru's basic fears for Congress are in R. Chalapathi, S. Gopal, et al., eds., *Selected Works of Jawaharlal Nehru,* 2nd ser., 16, ii, pp. 131ff.

44. Nehru to Chief Ministers, 17 Oct. 1952, in G. Parthasarathi, ed., *Letters to Chief Ministers* (1947-1964) (New Delhi and Oxford, 1988-), 3:132-33.

lowing year he also chided his government about alleged harassment of missionaries. Although he disliked proselytism himself, he maintained that missionaries should be welcomed if they served the poor of India, and their activities should only be controlled if, for example, they appeared to threaten national security.[45]

Nehru's dilemmas in the early years when the new state was being fashioned showed how independence had not resolved the religious aspects of Indian identity. Christians and Muslims, however long their families had lived in the subcontinent, were not secure in their Indianness in the eyes of their neighbors, and in their own sense of identity. Moreover, and ironically for Christians, although the end of the Raj had removed one ground for allegations of "otherness," the circumstances of partition had made them, along with Muslims, more suspect in the eyes of the Hindu majority, as being Hindu was confirmed as being bound up with being Indian, whatever the public rhetoric of the prime minister and the constitution.

Independence and the making of a new national state and political culture posed critical problems for Indian Christians, problems that half a century on still remain. How were they to participate in the political life of India, given the ambiguities of their identity and the loss of a special voice in the legislatures, particularly when so many of them lacked the ties of caste and patronage that assisted others in public life? How were they to vote now that even the poorest of them were enfranchised, and with what parties would they throw in their lot? More critically in terms of theological and practical issues, would they be able to build a new sort of church, a mission church in the biblical sense rather than a colonial missionary church, in a situation where foreign leadership and finance were rapidly aspects of the past, and where conversions were deeply contentious in local society? Or would the churches with their existing resources of land, buildings, and money become another set of power structures in India's complex political life, arenas where those with special "community" access would exploit and defend those resources in an insecure environment? Such questions are matters for research by scholars with secular skills, if we are to grasp the complexity of Indian Christians' position in the Indian nation.

45. Nehru to Chief Ministers, 1 Aug. 1953, in Parthasarathi, *Letters to Chief Ministers*, pp. 352-53.

CHAPTER 6

China and Christianity: Perspectives on Missions, Nationalism, and the State in the Republican Period, 1912-1949

KA-CHE YIP

In assessing the state of Christianity in China after 1950, M. Searle Bates maintained that "the decisive change in China about 1950 requires a special effort of understanding," and that a careful evaluation of the Christian efforts in the past would provide useful lessons for the future.[1] It is indeed important for students of Christian missions in China to gain a better appreciation of the political, social, and intellectual forces that had shaped the missionary and church experience in China before the founding of the People's Republic. Critical to the historical development of missions before 1949 were the growth of Chinese nationalism and the process of state building. These two were closely related since nationalism in Republican China contributed to and significantly affected the aims and process of state building in the twentieth century.

Nationalism

Reformers and revolutionaries in the late nineteenth and early twentieth centuries had been concerned with China's survival as a nation in face of continual external encroachment and domestic weakness. The founding of the re-

1. M. Searle Bates, "The Church in China in the Twentieth Century," in *China and Christian Responsibility: A Symposium,* ed. William J. Richardson (New York, 1968), p. 46.

public in 1912 had raised expectations among many of a new beginning in China's struggle for national strengthening and modernization. Instead, the country was soon fragmented by ambitious warlords bent on personal aggrandizement while the foreign powers, supported by their privileges guaranteed in the "unequal treaties," exploited the chaos and instability for their own ends. China's failure in the Versailles Conference to regain control over the German concessions in Shantung (Shandong) compounded the anger and sense of urgency that immediate action had to be taken to achieve national unity and strengthening and assert national sovereignty. Intellectuals called for a thought transformation that would embrace, among other ideals, science, which, with all its perceived potential of promoting technological advances as well as social betterment and progress, was deemed a key to Western power and modernity. At the same time, the surge in national consciousness demanded the end to China's domination by the imperialist powers whose gunboat diplomacy had humiliated China but whose claim to moral superiority had, in the eyes of many Chinese, been exposed as a sham in the First World War. Indeed, for many Chinese Nationalists the acquisition of Western science and technology did not mean the embrace of facets of Western culture deemed morally bankrupt or unscientific. As John Fitzgerald put it, "the Chinese awakening was, in the main, a secular one."[2]

It is ironic that Christian missionary activities had in fact contributed to the rise of nationalism through the introduction of Western ideas, education, social reforms, and other activities that were subversive of the old order. But their very success as stimulus to change also helped open the door to secular ideas that Chinese intellectuals found more relevant and attractive in their search for China's salvation. In the name of science and the emancipation of the individual, many intellectuals of different ideological persuasions in the early republic repudiated religion as irrelevant in a modern society; for anarchists it was a form of autocratic authority, for Marxists the opium of the people, and for liberals an obstacle to individual development.[3] All of them believed, however, that scientific and technological progress was far more vital to China's well-being than any historic or supernatural religion.

Not surprisingly, Christianity came under attack for being irrational and unscientific, and indeed, for being part of the foreign political and economic establishment. Claims or approaches of the Christian missionaries came un-

2. John Fitzgerald, *Awakening China: Politics, Culture, and Class in the Nationalist Revolution* (Stanford, 1996), p. 37.

3. Ka-che Yip, *Religion, Nationalism, and Chinese Students: The Anti-Christian Movement of 1922-1927* (Bellingham, 1980), pp. 19-22.

der close scrutiny and were condemned. To the assertion that Christianity was the religion of the civilized person, Chinese intellectuals rejected the civilizing mission of Christianity and maintained that a civilized person of a modern society did not believe in superstitions or behave with such bigotry and ignorance as foreign missionaries did in China. To the claim that only Christian morality and values could save China, they countered that the morally bankrupt Christian West that had slaughtered its own people in the name of religion and blasted its way into China was in no position to teach the Chinese, and that it was scientism and modern knowledge that could save China. To those missionaries who advocated the social gospel and stressed social and economic reconstruction based on Christian values, they either dismissed the linkage between Christianity and social betterment, arguing that a secular approach to social and economic regeneration could be effective and fruitful without embracing the teachings of Christ, or insisted that nothing short of a class struggle and revolution would bring about social and economic equality.[4]

Chinese nationalism also demanded the building of a strong sovereign and independent state. There were two dimensions to this process: the termination of foreign domination of China and the establishment of a powerful centralized state with strong organizations capable of implementing new agendas of socioeconomic modernization that would save China from backwardness and humiliation. In the context of early Republican China, the first aspect inevitably involved an intense anti-imperialistic movement targeted at the abrogation of the unequal treaties and the elimination of foreign encroachment. Chinese Nationalists pointed to the failure of the Washington Conference in 1922, the killing of unarmed students in Shanghai by the British police on 30 May 1925, or the Shameen incident about a month later when Chinese demonstrators were fired upon by foreign troops as ample evidence of the evils of imperialism. The establishment of a strong centralized state, on the other hand, meant the destruction of the warlords and the unification of China to be followed by the creation of centralized rule and reconstruction. Events late in the decade 1910-19 and in the 1920s convinced many intellectuals that the two movements should be pressed forward in tandem since the imperialist powers were in league with the warlords and China's survival as a nation required immediate action.

Christian missions were particularly vulnerable to anti-imperialist attacks

4. These themes abounded in the writings of Chinese intellectuals late in the decade 1910-19 and in the 1920s. For an example of this, see T'ang Liang-li, *China in Revolt: How a Civilization Became a Nation* (London, 1927), pp. 57-78.

since the right to propagate their faith and claim to protection were yielded by the Chinese in the so-called toleration clause in the unequal treaties. Moreover, the fact that the missionaries and their properties were protected by extraterritorial rights, and that some of the missionaries abused their favored legal position to expand their work or protect native converts, reinforced in the minds of many Chinese the association between missions and imperialism, and the belief that the missionaries were in fact agents aiding and abetting the foreign exploitation of China. This perception was reinforced by the foreign domination of the church in China, in its administration, finances, the interpretation of doctrines, as well as the superior position of the foreign staff. So long as the freedom of the missionaries was guaranteed by treaty rights, the Christian church continued to impinge upon the sovereignty of the Chinese state. Certainly, some missionaries had expressed their willingness to refuse treaty protection, but foreign governments generally rejected such intentions as misguided and impractical in a country torn by civil strife whose government was still incapable of providing legal protection to its own citizens.

To Chinese Nationalists in the 1920s, Christian missions were more than an arm of imperialism; in fact, they labeled Christianity a form of "cultural imperialism," designed to "denationalize" the Chinese so that they would repudiate their own country and become "slaves" and willing accomplices of the imperialist powers. Mission schools at all levels were instruments of denationalization, as charged by one anti-Christian declaration in 1924: "[Cultural invasion] is to use religion to deceive and hold Chinese youths, and to use the power of the principal [of mission schools] to suppress at will any organization and propaganda against the foreign powers carried out by the students; it is to prohibit the social and political movements of the students, to waste the intelligence and time of youths in studying the Bible and attending services. . . . It is to recommend [the students] for work in foreign firms so that they will be dependent on foreigners for their livelihood."[5] Overthrowing imperialism required patriotic Chinese youths, and Christian missions would not be allowed to corrupt their minds and subvert their spirit. It was the state that had the right and responsibility to inculcate the proper values befitting a loyal citizen of the Chinese state.

There was really no centralized Chinese state in the decade 1910-19 and the early 1920s. During his brief tenure as president of the republic, Yuan Shikai did try to bring about national unification and introduced authoritarian reforms aimed at national strengthening and political centralization before the

5. Manifesto of the Fujian Youth Society, in *Zhongguo qingnian* (China's youth), June 1924, pp. 12-13.

collapse of his monarchical restoration ushered in the period of warlordism. It was against this background of political fragmentation that anti-Christians, most of them students, prompted by nationalism and aided in tactics and organization by the Guomindang (GMD) (Kuomintang, KMT) and the Chinese Communist Party, attacked Christianity and mission institutions in wide-ranging movements from 1922 to 1927. The anti-Christian themes discussed above constituted the focal points of attack, but the anti-imperialist line proved the most powerful and popular. The issue of national sovereignty and power remained a major concern for the new nationalist regime after 1928 and exacerbated the tension between the state and the church, even when the nationalists decided to seek the support of the West and the cooperation of the church in state building and national reconstruction.

The State

After the GMD's nationalist government imposed a nominal unity over the country in 1928, it was anxious to implement its own agenda to create a modern state that would fulfill the nationalistic goals of achieving "wealth and power" for China. Inheriting the role of the state as the sole font of authority and expanding on the duties and functions of the state as the shaper of the moral and material world, the GMD party-state went about building a central administrative structure and organizing society based on "modern" ideas that would propel China toward modernity. In this process the issue of religion, and Christianity in particular, posed complicated dilemmas that led to an uneasy accommodation between church and state.

The Nationalist regime under Chiang Kai-shek, who was baptized in 1930, had sought to gain the goodwill of Western imperialist powers after its purge of the Communists. Anti-Christian activities subsided (except in Communist-controlled areas) with the imposition of order and discipline. The government, however, was not giving up its demands for sovereignty, but its attempts to end the extraterritoriality that the powers enjoyed proved unsuccessful. Although many missionaries expressed support for negotiation, the powers remained unconvinced of the new government's ability to protect the rights of foreigners, despite the Nationalist government's guarantee of religious freedom during the period of party tutelage.[6] But increasingly the mis-

6. For an interesting discussion of the debate over religious policy in the GMD, see Zha Shijie, *Minguo Jidujiao shi lunmin ji* (Essays on the history of Christianity in the Republican period) (Taibei, 1994), pp. 492-517.

sions exhibited more restraint and were more conservative in the interpretation of their treaty rights in China.[7] Nonetheless, although missionaries generally declined to invoke the rights in the treaties, the "psychological burden carried by Christians sensitive to the cultural and national aspirations of their society was considerable."[8] And the attempt at accommodation between church and state still did not settle the status of the Christian churches in China. As long as they were not registered with the government, they remained "extra-legal institutions, protected by treaty and the favor of a friendly government."[9] Registration as a civic society, on the other hand, would have placed the church under the "guidance" and control of a party-state that would not tolerate antiparty or antigovernment actions, including any challenge to party doctrines and Sun Yat-sen's *Sanmin zhuyi* (Three principles of the people).[10]

For the GMD, Sun's thought provided the party-state's moral and ideological underpinning, and the state was the final arbiter of ideological orthodoxy and morals. During the period of "tutelage" the party was to inculcate in the people ideology and norms, essentially the party's interpretation of *Sanmin zhuyi,* that would foster unity and patriotism. Ideological oneness, as Chiang made clear, was necessary for state building to succeed.[11] In fact, the party introduced *Sanmin zhuyi* education in the schools so as to induct China's youth into a national political culture congruent with and supportive of the party's ideals of political and socioeconomic construction, and to create a powerful loyalty to the state as exemplified by the GMD government. Secular values of commitment to nationalistic goals, sacrifice, hard work, obedience, self-discipline, as well as the traditional virtues of loyalty, filial piety, propriety, righteousness, integrity, and a sense of shame constituted the core of the new national morality.[12] In this process of political socialization, the party brooked no rivals and found Christian teachings in the schools unacceptable.

7. Arne Sovik, "Church and State in Republican China: A Survey History of the Relations between the Christian Churches and the Chinese Government, 1911-1945" (Ph.D. thesis, Yale University, 1952), pp. 260-65.

8. Bob Whyte, *Unfinished Encounter: China and Christianity* (London, 1988), p. 179.

9. Sovik, p. 271.

10. Sovik, pp. 270-71.

11. Chiang Kaishek, "Zhongguo jianshe ji tujing" (The path of China's reconstruction), in *Geming wenxian* (Documents of the revolution) (Taizhong and Taibei, 1960), 22:290.

12. Ka-che Yip, "Education and Political Socialization in Pre-Communist China: The Goals of San Min Chu-I Education," *Asian Profile* 9, no. 5 (Oct. 1981): 401-13.

Religious education in mission schools was condemned not only because Christianity offered a competing, and unscientific, ideology, but also because the state insisted on its right to educate the nation's youth in a way it deemed appropriate. As a sovereign nation, China should have the right to formulate educational policy for all schools and regulate educational matters. The movement "to restore educational rights" had already been a major part of the anti-Christian campaigns in 1922-27, and the Nationalist government continued to pressure mission schools to register with the government, a step that would require, at least on paper, the transfer of the control of the schools to a Chinese principal or president and a board with a Chinese majority. It would certainly place the schools under increased government supervision and control.[13] It was revealing that in all schools a weekly memorial ceremony to Sun Yat-sen and the teaching of *Sanmin zhuyi* became mandatory.

The enforcement of the regulations on religious education, however, was not consistent. The truth is that the GMD, despite its aspirations to be a modern party-state, was plagued by internal weaknesses and ambiguities in its interpretation of Sun's ideology. Above all, it did not possess the power to force absolute compliance, especially when it actively sought the support of the Western powers for domestic reconstruction and to counter Japanese aggression after 1931. Unlike the imperial state before it or the Communist state after 1949, the Nationalist state was far less successful in imposing absolute control, and the centralized administrative structure needed to extend and consolidate state control over an expanded agenda of responsibilities and functions considered to be within the proper domain of state power was never fully and firmly established. The state and church actually found grounds for compromise and accommodation. In education the government provided grants to Christian colleges that had proved to be among some of the best schools in the country, essential to China's strengthening and modernization.[14] Mission medical schools such as Shantung (Shandong) Christian University and West China Union University helped train modern medical personnel desperately needed for the government's state-medicine plans.[15]

Accommodation existed in other fields. Missionaries had always been active in popular education, public health, and rural and industrial reforms, for

13. Zhang Qinshi, *Guonei jin shinian lai ji zongjiao sichao* (Religious thought movements in China in the last decade) (Beijing, 1927), p. 373; *Chine Moderne* 7 (1926-27), pp. 233-35; and C. S. Miao, "Status of Registration," in *China Christian Yearbook* (1931), pp. 242-43.

14. *China Christian Yearbook* (1934-35), pp. 273-75.

15. Ka-che Yip, *Health and National Reconstruction in Nationalist China: The Development of Modern Health Services, 1928-1937* (Ann Arbor, 1995), pp. 148-50.

instance, and despite the new state's reluctance to allow them to usurp its authority and vastly expanded roles in matters fundamental to the well-being of its citizens, it could countenance cooperating with the church as an organization interested in the social reconstruction of China. Mission groups were active in flood and famine relief, care for refugees, and other social welfare activities. The most prominent example of cooperation was the Jiangxi rural reconstruction program launched in early 1934, in which a nondenominational group was entrusted with the task of establishing socioeconomic reforms in a small county in the southeastern part of the province.[16] Early that same year the New Life Movement was also launched in Nanchang, the capital of Jiangxi. The movement represented Chiang Kai-shek's attempt to provide the basis for the spiritual regeneration of the Chinese people. Its ideology, seen as an alternative to Communism and other undesirable foreign ideas, combined the new morality discussed above with Christian character-building ethics and military ideals.[17] The Reverend George W. Shepherd, a Congregational missionary from New Zealand, became the movement's director in mid-1936. Such cooperation revealed to a significant extent the symbiotic relationship that existed between church and state. Increasingly, Christian groups were attempting to make their message relevant to the transformation of China, and while some missionaries were chary of Chiang's authoritarian regime, they were even more worried about the spread of Communism. Yet at the same time, some liberal Christians were veering away from the gradualist reformism of the Nationalists, especially when they became offended by the corruption and inability of the regime to solve pressing socioeconomic problems. Some of them would eventually move toward Communism, which they believed would end social and economic injustices for the people.

The war against Japan provided even more opportunities for state-church cooperation. In fact, the church and Chinese Christians actively supported anti-Japanese patriotic activities and provided relief to the wounded, sick, and homeless, oftentimes working jointly with government agencies.[18] Before Pearl Harbor, foreign-owned church properties actually became safe havens for many Chinese. Christian educational institutions in the interior welcomed refugee colleges and students, and mission hospitals provided much needed support to the vastly inadequate civilian and military medical sys-

16. Ka-che Yip, *Health and National Reconstruction,* pp. 90-92.

17. Zou Shuwen, *Xin shenghuo yu xiangcun jianshe* (New life and village reconstruction) (Nanjing, 1934), p. 1.

18. *China Handbook, 1937-1943* (New York, 1943), pp. 733-59.

tems.[19] These developments helped erase some of the gulf that existed between Christians and non-Christians as well as the "foreignness" of the Christian church. At the same time, many missionaries became propagandists for China's war efforts and many missions urged their respective governments to work toward abrogating the "unequal treaties." The step was taken in 1943, and the Christian church in China could finally divest of its identity with foreign political and economic coercion. Yet as Timothy Brook points out, despite its independence from the West, at least in terms of treaty protection, the church's autonomy from the state remained unattained.[20]

Missions and the Chinese Church

The surge of Chinese Nationalism with its accompanying critique of Christianity and the missions compelled many missionaries to reevaluate their purposes and roles in a changing China. At the beginning most missionaries probably did not fully understand the nature of the changes that were gripping China nor the intensity of the Nationalist movement. But by the 1920s many missionaries recognized the need for a strategy more suited to the temper of the times. The liberal-conservative divide among the missionary bodies that was already apparent at the turn of the century became more pronounced as advocates of the social gospel placed increasing emphasis on changing the conditions in Chinese society through social service that would, they believed, be particularly relevant to a China suffering from social and economic disintegration. As one missionary explained, "the present social emphasis in the realm of politics, labor, education and religion will inevitably impinge upon and change our missionary message and method. The sooner we reorientate our message and methods in view of this new social emphasis the more fruitful will our work be."[21]

The active involvement of many missionaries and Chinese Christians in the Nationalist period in social welfare activities was a manifestation of this attempt to participate in the social reconstruction of China and demonstrate

19. J. Heng Liu, "National Health Organization," in *China Christian Yearbook, 1936-37* (Glendale, 1937), pp. 352-53; Szeming Sze, *China's Health Problems* (Washington, D.C., 1943), p. 16.

20. Timothy Brook, "Toward Independence: Christianity in China under the Japanese Occupation, 1937-1945," in *Christianity in China: From the Eighteenth Century to the Present*, ed. Daniel H. Bays (Stanford, 1996), pp. 317-37.

21. See A. R. Kepler, "The Need for a Changed Approach to the People in Our Missionary Enterprise," *Chinese Recorder* 51 (Jan. 1920): 21-31.

that Christianity did have a role to play in China's future. Yet as China's conditions deteriorated during and after the war, many Chinese Christians in particular began to despair of the "selfish preaching and selfish enthusiasm for individual salvation" of the evangelists[22] or the efficacy of Christian social activism in dealing with the overwhelming human tragedy in the country. Unable to resolve what Emily S. Rosenberg labels the "contradiction between advocating structural reform and trying to remain true to a liberal-capitalist world order,"[23] some of them actually found in Communism the creed they believed capable of bringing about the fundamental reconstruction of Chinese society. Wu Yaozong (Y. T. Wu) of the Chinese YMCA, a firm believer in the social gospel, concluded in 1943 that "belief in God is not contradictory to materialism." After the Communist victory in 1949, Wu emerged as the leader of the Chinese Protestants and president of the Three-Self Movement in 1951.[24]

The Nationalist movement in the republican period also accelerated the progress toward more independence by Chinese Protestant churches. As early as the mid–nineteenth century, some missionaries had already begun devolution of control through promoting "self-management, self-support, and self-propagation" in the churches. Important milestones in this process included the formation of the National Christian Council in 1922 and the first General Assembly of the *Zhonghua Jidujiaohui* (Church of Christ in China) in 1927. First founded in 1918, the Church of Christ in China combined Presbyterian, Congregational, Methodist, and Baptist elements and represented a significant attempt to overcome denominational division prior to 1949.[25] Yet as Daniel H. Bays has pointed out, before 1937 there was still relatively little movement toward an "authentically autonomous or indigenous Chinese church," and from the 1920s to 1949 "attitudes of paternalism persisted among many foreign missionaries, and the influence of foreign financial subsidy remained a potent, if usually an implicit, factor in most Christian institutions."[26]

The development of this "Sino-Foreign Protestant Establishment," as Bays calls it,[27] did not satisfy some Chinese Christians anxious to create a truly in-

22. T. C. Chao, "The Christian Spirit Tried by War," in *Christian Voices in China*, ed. Chester S. Miao (New York, 1948), p. 17, quoted in Whyte, p. 184.

23. Emily S. Rosenberg, *Spreading the American Dream: American Economic and Cultural Expansion, 1890-1945* (New York, 1982), p. 111.

24. See Gao Wangzhi, "Y. T. Wu: A Christian Leader under Communism," in *Christianity in China*, pp. 338-52.

25. Yang Senfu, *Zhongguo jidujiao shi* (History of Christianity in China) (Taibei, 1968), p. 302.

26. Daniel H. Bays, "The Growth of Independent Christianity in China, 1900-1937," in *Christianity in China*, p. 309.

digenous church, and not merely a Western model controlled by Chinese. They aimed to achieve complete independence from foreign organizations, as well as develop Chinese leadership and an indigenous theology. Although the rising tide of nationalism and anti-Christian activities of the 1920s helped promote and hasten this development, this movement was already in existence earlier in the century. For example, Yu Guozhen's *Zhongguo jilihui* (Chinese Independent Church) was founded in 1906 in Shanghai, and Zhang Lingsheng and Paul Wei's *Zhen Yesu jiaohui* (True Jesus Church) was founded in 1917 in Beijing. By the 1920s the growth in independent Chinese evangelism was marked by the emergence of such groups as the *Jiaohui Juhuisuo* (The Assembly Hall) or Xiaoqun ("Little Flock") under the leadership of Ni Tuosheng (Watchman Nee), or *Yesu jiating* (The Jesus Family) founded by Jing Dianying. Distrusted by some missions, they flourished in varying degrees before 1949, searching for a theology and forms of worship more adapted to the Chinese environment and indigenous tradition unhampered by the institutional standards of Western churches.[28]

On the eve of the founding of the People's Republic of China, the Nationalist state was confronted with massive and overwhelming problems generated by years of political, social, and economic disintegration; foreign pressure; the rise of nationalism; and war. For many Chinese the church's assertions on spirituality or social services could offer no solutions to China's problems. As Ng Lee-ming has concluded: "theologians in China were forced by the peculiar circumstances there into a 'no-win situation.' They were forced to state the case of Christianity in a particular context in which no specific Christian claim could properly be made. In not being able to convince the Chinese people of the social necessity of Christianity, they failed to convince the same people of its religious validity."[29]

For the Nationalists, despite their limited accomplishments, the failure to

27. Bays, "Growth of Independent Christianity," p. 309.

28. The growth of an indigenous church has received increasing attention from scholars in recent years. Daniel H. Bays has done much to develop this field. See, for example, his *Christianity in China* and "Indigenous Protestant Churches in China, 1900-1937: A Pentecostal Case Study," in *Indigenous Responses to Western Christianity,* ed. Steven Kaplan (New York, 1994), pp. 124-43. See also Yang Senfu, pp. 291-303; Ying Fuk-tsang, "Bensehua yu minguo jidujiao jiaohui shi yenjiu" (Indigenization and studies of Chinese church history in the Republican period), *Journal of the History of Christianity in Modern China* 1 (1998): 85-100; and Jonathan T'ien-en Chao, "The Chinese Indigenous Church Movement, 1919-1927: A Protestant Response to the Anti-Christian Movements in Modern China" (Ph.D. thesis, University of Pennsylvania, 1986).

29. Ng Lee-ming, "The Promise and Limitations of Chinese Protestant Theologians, 1920-50," *Ching Feng* 21, no. 4 (1978): 181, quoted in Whyte, p. 183.

create a strong modern centralized state that could bring about national reconstruction with social and economic justice for the people cost them the support of vast segments of the population. The removal of the government from the mainland marked the end of an era for the Christian churches, which were now faced with the uncertain prospect of dealing with a new government. There were continuities in the process of state building before and after 1949, as well as in the religious policies of the Nationalist and Communist states, but unlike the Nationalists, the Communist state was in a much stronger position to enforce its policies and assert what it considered the sovereign rights of a state.

CHAPTER 7

Foreign Missions and Indigenous Protestant Leaders in China, 1920-1955: Identity and Loyalty in an Age of Powerful Nationalism

DANIEL H. BAYS

In the first half of the twentieth century, Chinese Protestant leaders lived and worked in an age of rapid change and considerable ambiguity. The larger context in which they operated was one of a national "awakening" and growth of a modern mass nationalism.[1] For most of the period from 1900 to 1920, Chinese Protestants found themselves fully in sympathy with, and zealous participants in, the rising tide of patriotic sentiment and activism. Many Chinese Christians took a leading role in local and provincial reform movements in the last decade of the Qing, and many were also active in the overthrow of the dynasty in 1911-12 and the organization of provincial legislative assemblies in the early years of the republic.[2]

During these two decades the Chinese church and its leaders became much more visible, albeit on a Protestant stage still in many ways dominated by foreign missions. With well-educated and self-confident Chinese Protestant leaders emerging from the nexus of Christian institutions in China, from 1900 to 1920 there developed what I call the "Sino-Foreign Protestant Establishment." This was a more publicly visible collaboration between foreign missions and Chinese Christians than had existed in the nine-

1. John Fitzgerald, *Awakening China: Politics, Culture, and Class in the Nationalist Revolution* (Stanford, 1996).

2. Ryan F. Dunch, "Piety, Patriotism, Progress: Chinese Protestants in Fuzhou Society and the Making of a Modern China, 1857-1927" (Ph.D. thesis, Yale University, 1996); this work is forthcoming from Yale University Press.

teenth century, and a much more balanced one. It is instructive, for example, simply to note the change in composition of the two great nationwide conferences of 1907 and 1922. At the former, the China Centenary Missionary Conference, over 1,100 delegates attended, but only 6 or 7 were Chinese — although the program had many topics concerning "the Chinese church."[3] At the National Christian (not "missionary") Conference fifteen years later, a majority of delegates were Chinese (although much of the business of the conference was still directed by foreign missionaries).[4] This was the first generation of substantially autonomous Chinese Protestant leaders. Some worked in mission churches or Christian institutions as pastors, evangelists, teachers, medical personnel, or YMCA/YWCA leaders, among other professions directly related to the church. Others were lay Christian leaders, including teachers at government schools, professionals such as doctors or lawyers, bureaucrats in the customs or post office administrations, or businessmen. These constituted the core of maturing Chinese Protestant congregations in many of the coastal cities of China.[5]

Until the early 1920s Christian leaders in China, foreign missionaries and Chinese nationals alike, could reasonably assume that with steadily increasing "progress" in China, by which was meant development on the Western liberal social and political model, Christianity would have an important role in, would indeed be in the vanguard of, that national progress. But then the May Fourth Movement of 1919 reshaped the intellectual and political landscape of urban China. In China the end of empire began soon after this watershed year of 1919. By the early 1920s new currents of intense nationalism had settled into a pattern of implacable hostility both to Chinese warlord politicians, who allegedly kept the nation weak, and to the varied manifestations of Western imperialism in China, which allegedly exploited China and trod Chinese national aspirations underfoot, and therefore must be demolished. These currents fed the growth of China's first modern political parties, the Guomindang and the Chinese Communist Party, and their common platform of antiwarlordism and anti-imperialism. In this period of transition in the early 1920s, which was a momentous one for modern China and in many

3. *China Centenary Missionary Conference Records* (New York, 1907).

4. Frank Rawlinson, Helen Thoburn, and Donald MacGillivray, eds., *The Chinese Church as Revealed in the National Christian Conference* (Shanghai, 1922).

5. See Dunch, "Piety, Patriotism, Progress," and Daniel H. Bays, "A Chinese Christian 'Public Sphere'? Socioeconomic Mobility and the Formation of Urban Middle Class Protestant Communities in the Early Twentieth Century," in *Constructing China: The Interaction of Culture and Economics*, ed. Kenneth Lieberthal, Shuen-fu Lin, and Ernest Young (Ann Arbor, 1997), pp. 101-17.

ways shaped the contours of public discourse for most of the rest of the twentieth century, Christianity was radically relocated on the political map. The upheavals of the 1920s changed Christianity from being seen by many Chinese (including many non-Christians) as progressive, modern, and a desirable part of China's future to being targeted as just another part of the hated foreign imperialist presence in China. Now labeled cultural imperialism, Christianity, including foreign missions and Chinese Christians alike, was denounced by many nationalist spokesmen as an insidious form of cultural deracination.

This turn of events, which took Christianity and Chinese Christians from one pole (positive) of the political spectrum to the other (negative) practically in the blink of an eye, placed Chinese Christians, especially those thoughtful and well-informed Christians who were acutely aware of this transformed national context, under great pressure. Most of them were part of the Sino-Foreign Protestant Establishment, with at least some personal as well as institutional loyalties to foreign missions. Yet they were patriotic Chinese intellectuals as well, and from the standpoint of that identity they sometimes shared the criticisms of foreign missions expressed by radical nationalists. The dilemmas faced by these Chinese Christian men and women — dilemmas of national and religious identity, personal and institutional loyalties, impulses both to dependence and autonomy, and ultimately after 1950 the question of their stance toward a strong secular state — provide much of the drama and fascination of twentieth-century Chinese Protestantism.[6]

Chen Chonggui was one of these Protestant leaders, and the story of his life and career, which is not well known outside of his denominational tradition, manifests clearly many of these dilemmas of modern Chinese Protestantism. Although associated with foreign missionaries for most of his career, Chen had a complex and sometimes stormy relationship with them. He was a lifelong theological evangelical who believed in personal conversion and the

6. This subject is much broader than the individual story I recount here. The most comprehensive work on the nationalistic anti-Christian pressures of the 1920s is Jessie G. Lutz, *Chinese Politics and Christian Missions: The Anti-Christian Movements of 1920-1928* (Notre Dame, 1988). For Chinese church leaders who tried to deal with these pressures from within the Sino-foreign Christian sector in the 1920s, see Jonathan T'ien-en Chao, "The Chinese Indigenous Church Movement, 1919-1927: A Protestant Response to the Anti-Christian Movements in Modern China" (Ph.D. diss., University of Pennsylvania, 1986). Other Chinese Protestants struck out entirely on their own, forming new movements totally separate from foreigners; see Daniel H. Bays, "The Growth of Independent Christianity in China, 1900-1937," in *Christianity in China: From the Eighteenth Century to the Present*, ed. Daniel H. Bays (Stanford, 1996), pp. 307-16.

literal truth of the Scriptures, but he threw his support to the new Communist government after 1949, deeply perplexing and disappointing his missionary friends. Later he forthrightly criticized the government's religious policy implementation in 1957, for which he was vilified and purged. He died in obscurity in 1963, but in recent years he has been posthumously rehabilitated and praised in church circles in China.[7]

Chen Chonggui as Model Convert and Junior Mission Colleague

Chen was born in Hubei Province in central China, close to Wuhan (the Yangzi River tri-city metropolis of Wuchang, the provincial capital; Hankou; and Hanyang). His family was extremely poor, a fact that colored Chen's entire life. His father received some education at a missionary school, and in the mid-1880s, after Chonggui's birth in 1884, the father became a Christian and a member of the American Board of Commissioners for Foreign Missions (Congregational) church in Wuchang. After 1890 Chen himself attended a school in Wuchang operated by the Covenant Mission (Xingdao hui) through the 1890s; thus began his lifelong relationship with the Covenant Mission.[8] He excelled academically at this small school, apparently the equiv-

7. The only complete biographies of Chen of which I am aware are: Zha Shijie (James Cha), *Zhongguo Jidujiao renwu xiaozhuan* (Concise biographies of important Chinese Christians) (Taibei, 1983), pp. 147-58; Chen Renbing, with Chen Meida, "Chen Chonggui mushi xiaozhuan" (A short biography of Rev. Chen Chonggui), in *Huainian Chen Chonggui mushi* (Commemorating Rev. Chen Chonggui), ed. Three-Self Committee (Shanghai, 1991), pp. 68-102 (Chen Renbing is Chen Chonggui's son. Some of Chen Renbing's personal family knowledge is evident in this essay, and is consistent with his oral account when I spoke with him in Shanghai in 1986); and O. Theodore Roberg, "Marcus Ch'eng (c. 1883-1963), Apostle or Apostate? Relations with the Covenant Mission in China" (M.A. thesis, North Park Theological Seminary, Chicago, 1982). Roberg had access to some very interesting materials in the Covenant archives, but used no Chinese sources. Two excellent recent essays by Professor Xing Fuzeng of the Alliance Theological Seminary in Hong Kong analyze important aspects of Chen's theological and political thought spanning several decades: "Jiyaozhuyi yu aiguozhuyi de zhangli — Chen Chonggui sixiang yanjiu" (Tensions between fundamentalism and nationalism — researches into Chen Chonggui's thought) (unpublished paper, n.d.); also "Chen Chonggui yu gongchanzhuyi — sixiangshi de jieshi" (Chen Chonggui and communism — interpretations of ideological history) (unpublished paper, n.d.).

8. I will refer to this missionary organization simply as the Covenant Mission. In Sweden, pietistic and revivalist dissenters from the state Lutheran church formed the Swedish Mission Covenant in 1878. In 1885 the Swedish Evangelical Mission Covenant of America was formed in Chicago by Swedish immigrants in the pietistic, revivalist, and Free

alent of lower middle school, but he was always aware of his family's poverty and the resulting uncertainty of being able to continue his study from year to year. He was baptized in the Covenant Mission in 1900 or 1901.

In 1901, upon graduation from the Covenant school, Chen was without resources to continue his education, but the Covenant Mission sponsored him to enroll at Wesley College, the equivalent of a higher middle school operated by the British Wesleyan Methodist Missionary Society in Wuchang. There again he excelled, especially in English. Chen must have been extremely grateful for this opportunity. However, in an episode not directly addressed by the sources, after two years at Wesley the Covenant Mission, perhaps because of Chen's English facility, fearful that he would forgo future mission work for the sake of more lucrative employment in business, withdrew its support of him. Fortunately an American acquaintance provided funds that, occasionally supplemented by small grants from the president of Wesley College, were sufficient for Chen to finish his last two years at Wesley. Thus despite always being in financial straits during his four years there, Chen succeeded in graduating in 1905, at age twenty-one. At this time in his life he had already had Swedish, British, and American patrons or benefactors.

As a middle school graduate with a Western education and language facility in both English and Swedish, now Chen had considerable leeway in choice of career. As a potential member of that new upwardly mobile urban middle class, Chen could have found a permanent place in the commercial sector. His first choice in fact was to take a job in business, so as to make enough money to support his parents, who still lived in dire poverty, and to be able to afford to marry. Yet he remained an active Christian, with still enough ties to the Covenant Mission to lead him to teach part-time at that mission's small school in Wuchang.[9]

For Chen, now twenty-two, 1906 was a watershed year in many ways. In the spring of the year he married, and was immensely happy in his marriage,

---

Church traditions. Later the North American denomination adopted the name Evangelical Covenant Church of America. Its headquarters, college, and seminary are in North Park, Chicago. The American and Swedish Mission Covenants had overlapping and cooperating mission activities in China, beginning in 1890. For the two Mission Covenants see Frederick Hale, *Trans-Atlantic Conservative Protestantism in the Evangelical Free and Mission Covenant Traditions* (New York, 1979). The most detailed source on Chen's early life is Marcus Ch'eng [Chen Chonggui], *Echoes from China, the Story of My Life and Lectures* (Chicago, 1921).

9. What these ties may have been are only implicit in his account, *Echoes from China.* They were probably a sense of obligation and personal ties to both the Swedish and American members of the Covenant Mission.

but his young wife died after only six months of marriage. Distraught, Chen was then profoundly affected by the message of a visiting evangelist, Li Shuqing. After individual discussions with Pastor Li, Chen underwent an intense personal religious experience in which he received an intensified faith in the resurrected Jesus. This strong personalized faith undergirded his religious commitments for the rest of his life.[10] Forty years afterward, in a brief autobiography, Chen still referred to this experience as "the great crisis of my life."[11] He abandoned his commercial job for the sake of full-time employment in the Covenant Mission school, believing he had been called by God to dedicate himself to Christian education as his ministry. He did this despite the financial hardships such a decision meant for himself and his parents.

Chen, who was bright and outgoing, an articulate speaker and a hard worker, and who had foreign language skills, now found that opportunities for advancement opened for him within the mission itself. When the very next year in 1907 the head of the Swedish branch of the Covenant Mission visited China, Chen's charm and eloquence helped persuade him to return to Sweden and to begin to raise funds for a Covenant seminary in central China (the mission had no seminary at this time). This project drew upon the resources and personnel of both the Swedish and American sectors of the Covenant China mission (the former based in north China, the latter in south China). It resulted in the establishment in 1909 of a denominational seminary with fine new buildings in the small city of Jingzhou, Hubei Province. This seminary, which later had a high school attached, was Chen's base of operations until 1925 and provided his springboard to national prominence.

Chen, despite his lack of formal higher education beyond the middle school level, was a member of the original staff of the Covenant Jingzhou Seminary. For over a decade, from 1909 to 1920, it would seem that he worked long and hard at the seminary, often to the point of exhaustion and with little time off. His 1921 memoir, written when he was still on the staff, does not allude directly to the tremendous effort Chen personally put into the seminary, but his 1947 autobiography indicates strongly that he was the fulcrum of both its academics and its administration. He typically taught thirty-four hours

10. Information on Li Shuqing is scarce. We know from Chen's own accounts that Li was a medical doctor and a native of Suzhou, who conducted several days of revival meetings in Wuchang. Ch'eng, *Echoes from China,* pp. 28-30, and Marcus Cheng [Chen Chonggui], *After Forty Years* (London, 1947), pp. 4-5. In these accounts Chen does not use precise theological language to describe this experience. Considering his four years at Wesley College, a Methodist school, this may have been a Wesleyan "entire sanctification" experience.

11. Cheng, *After Forty Years,* p. 1.

per week, and every conceivable subject over the years. He was first to rise to gather the students for morning drill, and last to retire after locking up. He even supervised the kitchen. At the same time, he strove to make up the deficiencies in his own education, especially in theology but also in foreign languages and Chinese literature, in a determined program of self-study. After all, his own education, ending with Wesley College, which was at that time only middle school level, was barely higher than that of some of the seminary students. His lifelong drive for high achievement, already visible here at the seminary, was undoubtedly further fueled by sensitivity to real or imagined slights to his background of poverty and low level of formal education. In 1947 he wrote that in these early years at Jingzhou his students had despised him for his lack of higher education and poor written Chinese language skills.[12] This lack of respect apparently only drove him to achieve more.

These were years of rapid growth of the Christian enterprise in China, the age of the emerging Sino-Foreign Protestant Establishment. The prominent Chinese participants in this partnership, themselves products of the mission education system, typically were highly trained, many with Ph.D. or Th.D. degrees from abroad, usually from the United States.[13] Chen Chonggui was clearly a potential member of this group, but was handicapped by his lack of higher educational credentials. His own hard work and rising prominence in the Covenant Mission, however, opened further doors for him. By the end of the decade 1910-19, the Swedish mission headquarters were holding him up as a model, "an interpreter . . . between East and West."[14] He was invited to spend a year in Sweden in 1920-21, where apparently his energetic personality and fluent Swedish language ability made him a great hit. His first memoir, *Echoes from China* (1921), was originally written and published in Swedish. In 1921, coming through the United States en route to China, Chen managed to find and seize the opportunity to gain the college-level academic credentials he had always been so conscious of lacking. While being hosted by the Covenant's North American headquarters in North Park, Illinois (just north of downtown Chicago), Chen was accepted as an undergraduate student at Wheaton College, an evangelical liberal arts school in a nearby western suburb. With credit granted for previous work and his professional standing, Chen studied strenuously for one full year and received his B.A. degree in 1922, at the age of thirty-eight.

12. Cheng, *After Forty Years,* pp. 10-11.

13. For example, Ding Limei, Cheng Jingyi, Zhao Zichen, Wang Zhengting, Yu Richang (David Yui), and others.

14. Roberg, p. 17.

By the time Chen returned to China in mid-1922, the nationalistic tides that had begun with the May Fourth Movement in 1919, but whose impact on the church was still unclear when Chen had left two years earlier, were becoming more and more obvious. Chinese Christians, including Chen, were not immune from these currents of thought and emotion. Already in the memoir-lectures he had published in the United States in the fall of 1921, Chen had expressed the opinion that the foreign missionary sector of the Sino-Foreign Protestant Establishment must steadily give way to Chinese Christian leadership and responsibility. He wrote, "The mission history of China has come to [the stage where] the right attitude of the missionaries should be that of John the Baptist, when he said, 'He must increase but I must decrease.' The most important and the greatest need for the present is to call and train the native workers and as many as possible."[15] Now undoubtedly more self-confident than before his two years in Sweden and America, Chen was probably further stimulated in his hopes for rapid devolution of power to Chinese Christian leaders by the stress on the Chinese church of the National Christian Conference of 1922, to which Chen was a Covenant Mission delegate.

Chen's Quest for Autonomy as a Chinese Christian Leader

It was probably difficult for Chen in 1922 to return to the restricted environment of the small Jingzhou Seminary. It may have been especially hard to resume the pattern of doing much of the work but receiving only a fraction of the pay and partial allocation of the living quarters enjoyed by the foreign missionaries at the seminary.[16] Friction over this and over other issues of Chinese versus foreign control of the mission and the seminary was probably inevitable. Such friction did not erupt into overt conflict, but it seems to have been real nonetheless. Chen taught at the seminary in 1922 and 1923, but then for the next two years he spent more and more time traveling around the country as an evangelist and revival speaker, a calling for which he had considerable talent. These were years in which several dynamic Chinese preachers made the rounds of the revival circuit of Protestant churches, and were welcomed by both missionary and native Chinese pastors of most denominations.[17] Chen

15. Ch'eng, *Echoes from China*, p. 71.

16. Oral recollections of Chen's son, Chen Renbing, in 1986 indicated his father's resentment over this disparity of pay and living quarters.

17. Daniel H. Bays, "Christian Revivalism in China, 1900-1937," in *Modern Christian Revivals*, ed. R. Balmer and E. Blumhofer (Urbana, Ill., 1993), pp. 159-77.

joined them, and finally, approaching age forty, his reputation began to go beyond Jingzhou and Covenant Mission circles.

While traveling in north China in 1924, Chen met General Feng Yuxiang, a warlord with evangelical Christian convictions who provided a staff of chaplains for his troops. Feng pressed Chen to enter his employ, and in 1925 Chen did so after the school year at the seminary ended. In his 1947 memoir Chen wrote cryptically, "In the summer of 1925 God wonderfully led me to leave Kingchow [Jingzhou] (this story in itself would make another book!) and to join General Feng."[18] There had apparently occurred some sort of final falling out between Chen and the foreign head of the seminary. It is inherently difficult to extract the details of such a matter when most of the written sources are euphemistic. Chen's son, Chen Renbing, claims his father was forced out: that in spring 1925 his father was removed from the teaching roster for the autumn of 1925 by eliminating his courses and told he would be assigned to research work. Therefore he resigned and joined General Feng.[19] Yet despite his apparent conflict with at least some persons at the local seminary, Chen remained on good terms with many individuals in the Covenant Mission, especially at the headquarters in Sweden. In years to come he would continue to visit many Covenant churches in China as a guest speaker, and as we will see, in 1937 and 1938 he would even offer to return to Jingzhou Seminary but on his own terms.

Chen was General Feng's head chaplain, but being attached to a warlord was risky. In summer 1927 Chen was trapped by the forces of an enemy militarist in Inner Mongolia, and hid for more than three months in the home of a missionary friend. He passed his time studying, praying, and writing dozens of short devotional essays. Later in 1927 Chen escaped and took his family to Shanghai, where he began a new career as a Christian journalist and editor-publisher. Finding that a newly founded Christian magazine *(Budao zazhi; Evangelism)* was looking for material, Chen offered his file of short essays; these daily meditations became immensely popular with readers. He quickly became the leading writer of the magazine, and then its managing editor in 1928. Circulation grew, and with it grew Chen's stature in the Christian community. For the next decade *Evangelism* was probably the most widely read Protestant evangelical periodical in China, and it continued to be published at least through the 1940s.[20]

18. Cheng, *After Forty Years,* p. 11. While in the general's employ, Chen wrote a small English-language volume in praise of him. Marcus Ch'eng, *Marshal Feng: The Man and His Work* (Shanghai, 1926).

19. Chen Renbing with Chen Meida, p. 83.

20. Gustav Carlberg, *China in Revival* (Rock Island, Ill., 1936), pp. 45-46. A late 1930s survey of the religious press in China estimated that the circulation of *Budao zazhi* at that

In 1928 the Covenant Mission headquarters in Sweden invited Chen for a speaking visit, which he gladly accepted. En route he attended the International Missionary Council Conference at Jerusalem. This, the first such ecumenical international gathering since the great Edinburgh Conference of 1910, had a much stronger representation of leaders of the non-Western churches than its predecessor eighteen years earlier. Some of the most prominent Chinese leaders of the Sino-Foreign Protestant Establishment, including Zhao Zichen, Yu Richang, and Zeng Baosun, attended. Chen joined this elite group in a very visible international arena. After Jerusalem Chen had a successful visit in Sweden. Then he returned to China via the United States, where he cooperated with the American Covenant Mission by speaking in several Covenant churches, openly reaffirming his Covenant roots and in general allowing himself to be used as a "trophy."[21] He seemed here to display no resentment over the circumstances of his departure from Jingzhou Seminary three years earlier.

Chen returned to China in late 1928, and now joined the faculty of the Hunan Bible Institute in Changsha, Hunan Province.[22] This was an interdenominational evangelical, even fundamentalist, institution founded several years earlier by Frank Keller. Keller had originally been a member of the China Inland Mission. Even before 1910 he had developed a personal relationship with the wealthy Stewart family of Los Angeles and was able to draw upon their resources in support of his evangelistic activities in Hunan Province. Stewart funds, which also helped found the Bible Institute of Los Angeles (BIOLA) in the United States, flowed directly to Keller for his Hunan operations.[23] Later, after Keller founded the Hunan Bible Institute, it was natural to affiliate with BIOLA. However, the linkage was ambiguous. Keller was head of the institute, with an all-Chinese staff except for the business manager Charles Ròberts, a nonacademic who was also informally the local liaison person of BIOLA. Some funds supporting the institute were raised in China, while some were also directed to it through BIOLA in the United States, which conducted fund-raising activities and publicity in North America on behalf of the Hunan Bible Institute. Keller himself, as founder, was

---

time was 4,500 to 5,000 per issue, which put it among the very top rank of publications in readership. Rudolf Lowenthal et al., *The Religious Periodical Press in China* (Peking, 1940), pt. I, chap. 3, chart III, sheet no. 1.

21. Roberg, pp. 41-42.

22. The archives of Biola University in Los Angeles have considerable material on the Hunan Bible Institute.

23. The Stewart family generously supported many other evangelistic endeavors elsewhere in China and worldwide during these years.

quite autonomous in his actions in China, but as his retirement approached in the mid-1930s, the issue of his successor as president and the nature of future links to BIOLA in the United States loomed larger.

Chen was on the faculty of the Hunan Bible Institute from early 1929 until 1937. During this period of less than a decade, he turned fifty, his father died, and his youngest children reached adulthood. Chen was one of only three teachers appointed as full "professor" *(jiaoshou)* in addition to the Chinese dean, Xiao Muguang. Clearly Chen took a leading role in the instructional program of the institute, and was popular with the students and active in their organizations.[24] At the same time, he continued his successful editorship of *Evangelism,* which reached the height of its national circulation and reputation in the mid-1930s. The institute subsidized the magazine, perhaps to the extent of $2,000 per year, and this subsidy was probably crucial in making its publication viable.[25] Finally, Chen also continued his guest appearances and speaking tours. Among the churches he visited were nearly all the Covenant Mission churches of central China, where of course he was well known and whose pulpits were by now staffed by graduates of Jingzhou Seminary, who had been Chen's students there earlier. He also corresponded cordially with T. W. Anderson, head of the American Covenant Mission in North Park, Illinois.[26] It seems that from the early 1930s on, Chen dealt almost exclusively with the North American Covenant Mission organization; almost nothing was said in the written record about the Swedish end.

Between 1935 and 1937 there occurred a protracted crisis over the succession to Keller as president of the institute, a crisis in which Chen played a central role. The story is complex, though it is well documented in letters and telegrams still preserved in the archives of Biola University in Los Angeles. The roots of the controversy were twofold. One factor was the strong current of Chinese nationalism of the times, to which many allude in the record. Chinese staff and students expected that leadership should devolve to Chinese nationals once Keller retired. In fact, if the Hunan Bible Institute had been a secular institution, it would have been required to have a Chinese president in order to receive government registration (religious institutions could not receive registration regardless of the nationality of the president). In addition to the agitation of staff and students, local and provincial officials also en-

24. See the 1936 student yearbook, *Hunan shengjingxueyuan tongxuelu,* in the Biola University Archives, Los Angeles.

25. Chen himself used the $2,000 figure in a two-part letter to the U.S. denominational newspaper, the *Covenant Weekly,* 27 July and 3 Aug. 1937.

26. Roberg, p. 48.

tered into the dispute on behalf of those Chinese staff vying for power, showing the extent of nationalistic feelings in all quarters.[27]

The other factor was intense dislike and distrust by some staff and students toward Charles Roberts, the business manager, who was rumored as early as 1935 to be slated to succeed Keller. Beginning in March 1935, Dean Xiao, Chen Chonggui, and other staff wrote to the BIOLA board that Roberts was unfit, and some students telegrammed Los Angeles that the institute should be disbanded rather than appoint Roberts as head. Student dislike of Roberts was amply manifested in the student yearbook of the class of 1936, published in May 1936. All the staff, even the janitors, had their pictures and titles included, but the only foreigner so honored was President Keller. Roberts, who as business manager held an important position, was not even mentioned in the yearbook. Nevertheless, Roberts marshaled his influence with the BIOLA board and with local foreign missionaries in Changsha. In a contest for power between two different and hastily assembled local boards of directors, the Chinese group centered on Dean Xiao and Chen Chonggui lost out. Roberts eventually succeeded Keller as president.[28]

Chen's position at the Hunan Bible Institute was now untenable. He was widely viewed as the éminence grise behind the campaign to make Dean Xiao president. Several local foreigners believed Chen would have controlled the institute, and soon would have become president himself after a decent interval during which Dean Xiao would bow out.[29] I cannot tell from the record if any of this is true, but it is a fact that Chen took a leading role in sending the first Chinese letter of protest to the BIOLA board in March 1935. At any rate, Chen maintained a pro forma affiliation with the institute into 1937, and then had to seek another base of operations and income. His task was complicated also by the need to find support for his magazine, which left Changsha with him. And in mid-1937 life was of course further complicated by the beginning of full-scale war between China and Japan, the precursor of the Second World War in the Pacific.

Chen went back to his heritage and earlier roots, perhaps swallowing his pride in so doing. In December 1937 he proposed to the combined American and Swedish Covenant Mission bodies in central China that he reaffiliate

27. Because a collateral issue in the dispute was the absorption of assets of the Changsha school by BIOLA in the United States in order to avert a financial crisis of the latter, this brought the provincial commissioner of finance into the fray as well.

28. Interestingly, Keller's personal inclination seems to have been to pass power to the Chinese nationalistic group. But by 1936 he was desperate to retire, and was happy to accept either group.

29. Correspondence in Biola University Archives.

with them on a half-time basis, spending three months annually with the churches of each. The mission would also provide some support for his magazine. He could thus return on a regular basis to Jingzhou Seminary and do other useful work for the Covenant, and at the same time support his magazine and retain his standing and activities as an autonomous figure during part of each year. Chen received a humiliating rebuff in this attempt to rejoin his old mission. After debating for several months, during which the American mission headquarters in North Park indicated their willingness to strike a deal with Chen, in October 1938, ten months after Chen's proposal, the American Covenant Mission group in China voted 7-6 to reject Chen's offer. The reasons for this were complex, ostensibly involving issues such as principles of self-support and reluctance to subsidize the magazine, but it seems to me that the basic issue was Chen's independence. He would be largely beyond the mission's control.[30] And of course, autonomy was precisely one of the major issues for Chen himself.

Undoubtedly stung by such an egregious insult, of which he would have occasion to remind his former American associates in future years, Chen had to turn elsewhere. With the Japanese advancing westward in late 1938, Chen accepted the invitation of Bishop Frank Houghton, general director of the China Inland Mission (CIM), to come to the far west: the inland province of Sichuan, which was the wartime base area of Chiang Kai-shek's Nationalist government. Chen was close theologically to the CIM and had worked with Keller and other CIM personnel at the Hunan Bible Institute and elsewhere during his career. Yet he must have had mixed feelings about once again serving under a foreign director. Houghton wisely gave Chen considerable leeway, letting him continue to publish *Evangelism* and sending him on evangelistic and revival meeting tours of several provinces in Free China.[31] From the point of view of his past pattern of relationships, perhaps Houghton was Chen's latest patron, though not at all an unsatisfactory one.

In late 1941 Chen went to Singapore for a speaking tour. He arrived in early December, just before the Japanese surprise attack on American and British strongholds in the Pacific, and was interned after the surrender of the British garrison in Singapore. In 1943 Chen was released and made his way back to Chongqing, Sichuan Province, the Chinese Nationalists' wartime capital. There Houghton of the CIM urged him to establish an independent evangelical seminary not under the control of any mission organization, with

30. Roberg, pp. 52-57, discusses this.

31. Cheng, *After Forty Years*, p. 13. Apparently the magazine had to cease publication in late 1939 or 1940. It resumed again sometime after Chen's return from Singapore in 1943.

Chen himself as president. Chen responded with enthusiasm. Although Bishop Houghton stroked Chen's ego by emphasizing the independence of the new seminary, Houghton and the CIM actually were extensively involved in the creation and initial operation of Chungking [Chongqing] Theological Seminary (CTS). Houghton signed, together with Chen, the March 1944 joint Chinese-English announcement of the seminary's opening, though Chen was identified as president.[32] And Houghton invited the rest of the initial staff, the dean and two instructors, who were all foreigners from the CIM. In fact, in 1944 Chen was the only Chinese on the staff. In the late 1940s the staff, as well as having several Chinese members by this time, still included some missionaries "loaned" by the CIM.[33]

The Chongqing seminary was Chen's home and base of operations for almost a decade, from its founding in 1944 until his retirement from the CTS presidency in 1953, at the age of seventy. He seems to have found very much to his liking the situation at CTS, where several of his colleagues were foreigners, but of course here he was in charge, especially of the finances, although the foreign missionaries, who were seconded to the seminary by the CIM, had their salaries paid by the CIM. In this respect the conditions seemed to Chen to be very different than they had been at Jingzhou Seminary and the Hunan Bible Institute. In a 1946 letter to Chicago Covenant headquarters, he claimed that CTS had no staff conflicts "because the missionaries do not hold the mission fund power."[34] Chen obviously enjoyed and excelled at the task of leading the seminary. By 1948, after four years, he had built CTS up to eighty students and ten staff members.[35] Many years later, long after Chen's death, there were more than ten glowing tributes to their old seminary president *(yuanzhang)* by his CTS students among the articles in the 1991 memorial volume to Chen published by the national Three-Self Committee in Shanghai.[36]

In 1946 as the Covenant Mission, like many other foreign missions in China, tried to resume work in its old area of operations in the postwar era, its American mission leaders turned for help to their old protégé Chen Chonggui. They offered Chen the presidency of Jingzhou Seminary, where he had worked from 1909 to 1925. Chen, however, was already fully committed to his seminary in Chongqing, and would not leave. Moreover, he could hardly have been attracted by a situation where despite being president he once

32. Marcus Cheng [Chen Chonggui], *Lamps Aflame* (London, 1949), pp. 69-71.

33. Cheng, *Lamps Aflame*, pp. 69-71, 113.

34. Chicago, North Park College archives, Chen letter of 11 June 1946 to J. W. Jacobson and John Peterson.

35. Cheng, *Lamps Aflame*, p. 67.

36. *Huainian Chen Chonggui mushi.*

again would have been under the authority of a foreign mission board. He pointedly reminded the Chicago headquarters of his spurned 1938 offer to return to the Covenant Mission and the seminary, and he now recommended that instead of reconstituting the old Covenant seminary, it be merged with a nearby Lutheran seminary. One can detect a slight tone of satisfaction in this letter of Chen to his former American colleagues.[37] Chen referred again to his rejected 1938 offer during his last visit to the United States, in 1948.[38] However, as before, Chen did not sever his ties with the Covenant Mission. In June 1949, in a letter to Albert Dwight in Chicago, he referred to himself as a member of the Covenant Mission. And in the fall of 1949 he admitted several Covenant-sponsored students into the Chongqing seminary.[39]

By the late 1940s, after nearly three decades of vicissitudes, Chen had succeeded in achieving a position of considerable autonomy, responsibility, and national stature in Chinese Protestantism. He continued to work with foreign missionaries, but not as a second-class junior associate, as he had been forced to do early in his career. His name was recognized and respected by Chinese Christians as a well-known traveling evangelist and revival speaker, as the longtime editor of *Evangelism,* and as the author of still-popular daily devotional essays.[40] By dint of his talents and hard work, as well as the influence of outside events, Chen was now among those senior Chinese Protestant leaders who hoped to see their church transition from a foreign mission-run church to one operated by Chinese nationals. One factor that had never been a major obstacle to that ambition during the first half of the century was a strong secular Chinese government determined to extend its own system of controls over Christian missions and the Chinese church. The emergence of such a government, and its impact on Chen Chonggui, provided the major motif for the last period of Chen's life and career.

God and Caesar: Chen Chonggui and the New China

In the late 1940s national politics, especially the civil war between the Nationalists and the Communists, intruded into all spheres of life in China. Chen

37. Chicago, North Park College archives, Chen letter of 11 June 1946 to Jacobson and Peterson.

38. Roberg, p. 68.

39. Roberg, pp. 78-80.

40. In 1950 Chen published a new collection of daily devotional essays, *Moxiang zhu Yesu* (Meditations on the Lord Jesus), which he had written while interned in Singapore from late 1941 to 1943. Reprinted by the China Christian Council, Shanghai, 1993.

Chonggui was no exception in being faced with some fateful choices as the civil war wound down with the Communists as clear victors. Chen's own political views, especially on the relative merits of the respective contenders Chiang Kai-shek and Mao Zedong, were not entirely clear in the late 1940s. In his address to incoming seminary students in fall 1945, Chen quoted favorably from Chiang's book *China's Destiny*.[41] But perhaps more telling were the critical comments he made regarding Chiang and his Guomindang party during his visit to the United States in 1948. These remarks aroused considerable indignation among his missionary acquaintances who, of course, were nearly unanimous in their preference for Chiang over Mao.[42] Did Chen's memories of childhood penury and his own lifelong struggle with poverty draw him toward sympathy with the Communist Party at this time? At any rate, Chen chose to return to his seminary presidency in Chongqing rather than remain in safe haven in the United States, as several other Chinese religious and academic leaders did.

During the period from 1950 to 1951 Chen publicly threw in his lot with the new Communist government and with other "progressive" Christian leaders. There must have been many reasons for this: patriotism, idealism, a desire to protect the Chongqing seminary, perhaps naïveté. At any rate, in summer 1950 Chen, ever the journalist, began writing extensively for *Tianfeng* magazine in Shanghai, which had become the organ of the group of Protestant leaders closest to the Communist Party. He was highly critical of the missionary record in China, and praised fulsomely the new regime and its policies.[43] Foreign missionaries' opinion of his behavior was predictable. For example, J. Herbert Kane, a senior CIM missionary in central China, wrote home in September 1950 that Chen, "a CIM protégé . . . has gone for the new regime hook, line, and sinker," and that some items he had written for *Tianfeng* were little short of "blasphemy."[44] At the same time, the last of the foreign teachers at CTS, all from the CIM, were forced to leave China in late 1950. Of course, this was necessary, regardless of what Chen's personal feelings might have been. No foreign

41. Cheng, *Lamps Aflame*, p. 76.

42. Roberg, pp. 68ff.

43. For a thoughtful discussion of Chen's views of Communism at this time in the context of his views of Communism since the 1920s, see Xing Fuzeng, "Chen Chonggui yu gongchanzhuyi." Also see He Weiqiang, "Cong yijiuwuling zhi wuyinian tianfeng zazhi Chen Chonggui de wenzhang kan Chen Chonggui touru sanzi de yuanyin" (Viewing the reasons for Chen Chonggui entering the Three-Self from his 1950-51 articles in *Tianfeng* magazine) (unpublished paper, 1988). An important article of Jan. 1952 has been translated in Francis P. Jones, ed., *Documents of the Three-Self Movement* (New York, 1963), pp. 55-59.

44. Quoted in Roberg, pp. 86-87.

personnel could stay on for long in any institution after the beginnings of Sino-American military conflict in Korea in the autumn of 1950.

During 1951 Chen consummated his commitment to the new political regime. He attended the crucial April meeting in Beijing that created the Protestant Three-Self Patriotic Movement (TSPM), and became one of the four vice-chairpersons of the preparatory committee of the TSPM. The theologically liberal YMCA leader Wu Yaozong (Y. T. Wu) was chairman, and most of the other high-level leaders of the TSPM were also liberals. Thus the participation at such a high and visible level of the evangelical Chen Chonggui, as well as that of another evangelical, Jia Yuming, who was also a vice-chairman, tended to validate the TSPM as a legitimate organization in the eyes of more conservative Chinese Christians. Chen also continued to write for *Tianfeng* magazine, along the lines of the articles he had been contributing since 1950.[45] Chen retired as president of CTS in 1953 and moved to Dalian in the northeast (Manchuria). Not long after this the seminary was closed and merged with others to form a union seminary. Chen, however, remained visible in national-level events; he was present at the important National Christian Conference of Protestants in 1954, and he remained a vice-chairman of the TSPM preparatory committee.[46]

In 1957 Chen was seventy-three years old. He was in effect retired, and might have expected to live out his days in peace, watching younger church leaders carry on. This was not to be. In March 1957 Chen attended as a delegate (due to his TSPM vice-chairman's position) a meeting of the Chinese People's Political Consultative Conference (CPPCC) in Beijing. The CPPCC is a body made up of prominent non-Communist figures from all sectors of life who can, however, be counted on for compliant cooperation with the Communist regime. Its meetings are usually characterized by unstinting praise of the government and Communist Party and undeviating approval of all measures put before it by the regime. This particular meeting, however, was held at the height of the Hundred Flowers Movement, in an atmosphere of candid expression of views actively encouraged by Mao Zedong and a few other party leaders. As a result, this meeting was quite lively; it was the occa-

45. Jones, *Documents of the Three-Self Movement,* has documentation on these early years of the TSPM. For an analytical discussion of the TSPM in the early 1950s, see Philip L. Wickeri, *Seeking the Common Ground: Protestant Christianity, the Three-Self Movement, and China's United Front* (Maryknoll, N.Y., 1988), esp. chap. 5. For discussion of some of Chen's *Tianfeng* articles of this period, see Xing Fuzeng, "Chen Chonggui yu gongchanzhuyi," and He Weiqiang, "Cong yijiuwuling zhi wuyinian tianfeng zazhi Chen Chonggui de wenzhang kan Chen Chonggui touru sanzi de yuanyin."

46. Roberg, pp. 109ff.

sion of some unusually frank public criticisms of many different aspects of the rule of the Communist Party and the government. Religious policy was one issue discussed. At one point Chen had the floor and the limelight. He politely but forthrightly decried the harsh and punitive attitude toward religious believers that had often characterized the first years of Communist rule, despite the seemingly generous official national policy of freedom of religious belief and practice in the constitution of 1954. Chen's speech, given on 19 March, was reported in full in the 25 March issue of the Beijing *People's Daily,* the foremost national newspaper, and later reprinted in the 13 May issue of *Tianfeng* as well.[47] This was unusually wide national circulation for the remarks of a religious figure.

Unfortunately for Chen, the Hundred Flowers Movement was followed within a few weeks by the "Anti-Rightist Campaign" of mid-1957 to 1958, an extended campaign in which most of those individuals who had criticized the government or the Communist Party in the spring of 1957 became targets of vigorous denunciation and lost their positions, some being sent to labor camps. Party members and nonparty members alike fell victim to the purge. Religious leaders who had expressed doubts or open criticism of government policy were among those attacked. Chen Chonggui, because of his remarks at the CPPCC in March, was one of the most prominent targets of denunciation among Protestant leaders during these months. The attack on Chen was led by Wu Yaozong, Chen's close colleague in the TSPM.[48] The denunciation of Chen was harsh and unrelenting. Although perhaps because of his age he escaped the rigors of a labor camp, he lost his position in the TSPM and became a "nonperson." He spent the next few years in obscurity, although he managed to send out of China personal words of greeting to a few old friends in the West, and he died in 1963. Almost thirty years after his death his reputation was officially rehabilitated. This was first marked by the appearance in mid-1990 of a brief biographical sketch in the *Jinling shenxuezhi (Nanjing Theological Review),*[49] and then by the substantial commemorative volume put out in 1991 by the national Three-Self Committee and the 1993 reprint of his daily devotional essays of 1950.[50]

47. A translation is in Jones, pp. 151-56, also in Donald E. MacInnis, *Religious Policy and Practice in Communist China: A Documentary History* (New York, 1972), pp. 201-7.

48. Ironically Wu himself had indirectly but unmistakably criticized implementation of the government's religious policy at the same 1957 CPPCC meeting at which Chen had spoken. In fact, Wu spoke first, which perhaps emboldened Chen in his own remarks.

49. No. 12 (July 1990): 53-56. This journal is published by the premier national Protestant seminary, in Nanjing.

50. See nn. 7 and 40 above.

Conclusion

What are some of the themes of twentieth-century Chinese Protestantism that can be derived from the life and career of Chen Chonggui? One is the reality of social mobility and personal advancement, especially through education, that characterized Chen's life. Until well into the twentieth century, missionary schools provided an important channel of upward mobility for some, like Chen, from the poorest elements of Chinese society. These schools went up through the level of higher middle school in China, and after 1900 were linked to opportunities for postsecondary education abroad for the very brightest of the mission school products.[51] It seems likely that but for mission schools Chen would have been a peasant or a laborer.

Another characteristic of modern Chinese Protestantism visible in Chen is the lack of intense loyalty to a particular denomination, and the predilection for ecumenical or nondenominational Christian work. Some Chinese Protestant leaders had since the early 1900s decried the plague of denominationalism foreign missionaries had brought to China.[52] Although he grew up in the Covenant Mission and taught at its seminary in the early part of his career, he was very comfortable with many varieties of Protestant groups, even with some more liberal than he was theologically. He taught at two independent seminaries, in Changsha and later in Chongqing, and was longtime president of the latter. The alacrity with which Chen and some other Protestant leaders joined the nondenominational TSPM after 1950 indicated the shallow depth of denominational loyalty of many Chinese Christians.[53]

Chen's career also showed the tensions between the quest for autonomy and the practical reality of the necessity of having sponsors or patrons, both individual and institutional, foreign and Chinese. This was visible in his refusal to remain confined by Jingzhou Seminary and his forays into touring evangelism, his mid-1920s experiment in having a Chinese warlord patron, the tenacity with which he held on to his individual editorship of *Evangelism*

51. After about 1920, some mission schools in China, for example Yanjing University and a few others, also developed legitimate college-level standards.

52. For example, in 1910 the young Chinese church leader Cheng Jingyi, a delegate to the 1910 World Missionary Conference in Edinburgh, electrified the delegates to that august assembly by an eloquent speech advocating early independence of the Chinese churches and decrying the pernicious effects of denominationalism. Gerald H. Anderson, ed., *Biographical Dictionary of Christian Missions* (New York, 1998), p. 130.

53. Some of the major opponents of the TSPM in the 1950s were either nondenominational figures, such as Wang Mingdao in Beijing, or leaders not of Western denominations but of independent Chinese ones, such as Ni Tuosheng and his Little Flock.

from 1928 through the 1940s, and his dissatisfaction with seminary life until he could be president of one. Perhaps it was his own personal history of extreme poverty, as well as the constant search for publication subsidies for his beloved magazine for more than two decades, that made him especially sensitive to the financial aspects of autonomy, and to the issue of who held the purse strings. Yet despite his constant pursuit of autonomy, Chen did not forget his personal obligations of gratitude to past patrons, especially to the Covenant Mission, toward which he apparently had benign feelings (mixed with resentment for past slights) through the pre-Communist period.

Chen's quest for personal autonomy, insofar as it inevitably involved confrontation or tension with foreign institutions and individuals at various points in his career, was layered with issues of nationalism as well. I think it is clear that the new nationalistic age of post–May Fourth Movement China, beginning in the early 1920s, influenced Chen as well as many other Protestant leaders in China. He had probably long resented being treated as a second-class colleague at Jingzhou Seminary earlier in his career, but now he did something about it. He resigned and left. A few years later he took a vulnerable public stance on the issue of foreign versus Chinese leadership of the Hunan Bible Institute, a stance that cost him his job. And I believe that after 1949 the nationalistic attraction of China having its own church, one entirely free from foreign influence or manipulation, was a major reason why Chen, as well as others, joined the TSPM despite its clearly visible political subordination to the Communist government. The irony, of course, is that in Chen's personal quest for autonomy, as in the similar quest of the entire Chinese Protestant church, one subordination, that to foreign missions, was exchanged for another, that to a powerful secular state with a deep suspicion of religion. The long-sought-for autonomy has remained elusive, and still remains so.

I would like to conclude with an observation applicable to the present as well as the past. Chen Chonggui demonstrates yet another theme of Chinese Protestantism in the late imperialist and postimperialist age. This is the conflation of evangelical or even fundamentalist theological beliefs with the blurring of lines between church and state.[54] Here I refer to the propensity of some evangelical Christians like Chen readily to accept a degree of state (or Communist Party) control of religious affairs that would be anathema to most Christians in the West. Of course, it is a fact that in recent decades many Chinese Christians have for various reasons resisted the extension of state

54. Xing Fuzeng, "Jiyaozhuyi yu aiguozhuyi de zhangli — Chen Chonggui sixiang yanjiu," has a good discussion of some aspects of this issue.

control over their churches and activities. One of the reasons for this resistance by some Chinese Christians has indeed been a version of the principle of separation of church and state. However, it is also a fact that over the past fifty years many Chinese Protestants, including some evangelicals such as Chen Chonggui who are at least as conservative theologically as those who prefer to remain in the autonomous Christian communities, have been willing to accept and work within the government structures that monitor and control religious affairs. In Chen's case, this may have been his patriotism outweighing an evangelical wariness of state control. Or it may be that Chen, while indisputably an evangelical, simply had very little such innate wariness of state control, and did not see church-and-state issues in anything like the same terms many Western Christians see them. Whatever the reason, the last years of Chen's career remind us that Chinese Protestants were not necessarily duped or coerced into state-imposed structures of religious affairs. Some may have found it quite natural to work within such structures.[55] This is an important point to remember in assessing the church in China today.

55. In discussion of this point at the September 2000 Cambridge conference, more than one participant pointed out that perhaps Chen had also derived his seeming indifference to a major role of the state from his early and long affiliation with the Continental Scandinavian church tradition, which the Mission Covenant, despite its dissenting features, still represented.

CHAPTER 8

The Rhetoric of the Word: Bible Translation and Mau Mau in Colonial Central Kenya

DEREK PETERSON

The relationship between literacy and the making of new political identities has long interested historians and anthropologists.[1] Most recently, Adrian Hastings's *Construction of Nationhood* has revealed important connections between Bible translation and the creation of nationalism.[2] Drawing on evidence from early modern Britain, France, and twentieth-century Africa, Hastings argues that ethnicities turned into nations when their vernacular literature

1. Benedict Anderson, *Imagined Communities: Reflections on the Origins and Spread of Nationalism* (London, 1983). For southern Africa, see Terence Ranger, "Missionaries, Migrants and the Manyika: The Invention of Tribalism in Zimbabwe," in *The Creation of Tribalism in Southern Africa,* ed. Leroy Vail (Berkeley, 1989), pp. 118-50. Most scholarship on literacy and politics has been shaped by Jack Goody's important work on writing and human thought, for which see Goody, *The Domestication of the Savage Mind* (Cambridge, 1977).

2. Adrian Hastings, *The Construction of Nationhood: Ethnicity, Religion, and Nationalism* (Cambridge, 1997).

Research for this project was funded in 1993-94 by a Fulbright (IIE) grant and in 1998 by the Research Enablement Program, a grant program funded by the Pew Charitable Trusts and administered by the Overseas Ministries Study Center. A grant from the Center for Interdisciplinary Studies in Writing at the University of Minnesota in 1999-2000 offered me time to write. An earlier version of this essay was presented at the African Studies Association meeting in Nashville, Tennessee, in November 2000. For their comments, I thank Steve Feierman, John Lonsdale, Allen Isaacman, Jean Allman, and Celia Chazelle.

moved from an oral to a widely used written form.[3] The translation of the Bible played a uniquely important role in this process. A vernacular Bible standardized the constantly shifting words and phrases of oral speech into a common language, imagined a holy people with a common destiny, and created a more conscious community among those who read it.[4] The Bible in the vernacular, argues Hastings, was the textbook of nation making in Africa and in Europe.

Hastings emphasizes how the vernacular Bible fixed words and ideas, inviting readers to imagine themselves, in common with other readers, as sharers of a national identity. This essay takes a somewhat different view. Rather than arguing that the translated Bible fixed vernacular languages, I explore how colonized Gikuyu people in central Kenya rewrote the Word to serve in internally contentious ethnic debates over age, power, and wealth. Bible translation was in colonial Gikuyuland a popular practice, a means by which converts created new grammars of vernacular disputation.

It follows that a history of Bible translation offers insights into the conjoined histories of ethnicity and nationalism. As John Lonsdale has shown, ethnicities in Africa were not simply precursors to nationalism on an evolutionary timescale.[5] As relationships of trust and obligation, moral ethnicities provided the criteria against which new configurations of power and politics were judged. My argument is that Bible translation was one way that Gikuyu argued about the morally challenging implications of economic and political change. For colonialism brought moral tests to bear on Gikuyu social relations. In the decade 1910-19 and the 1920s the advent of formal colonial rule set elders against youth in argument over political authority, and in the 1940s class formation divided landlords from tenants, making Gikuyu debate the moral economy of wealth. Successive generations of converts debated these moral changes by mining the Bible for words. Their investments in Bible translation made the Word into a rhetoric of ethnic debate.

The chapter begins by tracing the first investments that Gikuyu converts, called "readers" in their own language, made in the Bible in the early 1900s. They found in the New Testament grammar of "selfhood" a stock of ideas with which to argue about inheritance and political power with their elders. Their creative translations claimed the future for Christianity, arguing that the knowledge they learned in mission schools entitled them to an inheritance of elders' political power. By the 1940s, however, first-generation converts had be-

3. Hastings, p. 12.

4. Hastings, p. 31.

5. John Lonsdale, "The Moral Economy of Mau Mau," in Bruce Berman and Lonsdale, *Unhappy Valley: Conflict in Kenya and Africa* (London, 1992).

come a class of wealthy landowners. The second part of the chapter sketches how impoverished men and women in the 1940s retranslated the Bible in order to argue about the morality of class formation. Their creative retranslations laid the intellectual groundwork for the moral war called "Mau Mau."

Knowledge and Power in First-Generation Readers' Thought

Formal translation of biblical texts began in the earliest years of missionary work in central Kenya. The first texts to be widely distributed were the Gospels of Luke and Matthew, published separately in 1915 and sold throughout Gikuyuland for 25 cents a copy — a full day's wage for a working man.[6] They were translated by a team of Protestant missionaries and Gikuyu assessors working for weeks at a time in a settler's potato store near Dagoretti.[7] Acts was published in 1920 by American missionaries eager for its heroic evangelistic stories; Genesis followed in 1924.[8] The New Testament as a whole was published in 1926.

The history of "formal" translations of the Bible should not obscure the rich popular history of translation carried out in the day-to-day conversations in which Gikuyu converts made the Christian religion speak. Gikuyu readers worked through their own translations of biblical texts at the same time the formal translation work of missionary linguists was under way. As late as 1918 Arthur Barlow doubted whether missionaries needed to translate evangelistic storybooks, arguing that African evangelists were "skilled in giving gospel narratives in their own words, fitted to the understanding of the villagers."[9] Most of them translated their stories from the Swahili Old Testament, available in central Kenya from 1914.[10] Tumutumu teachers in 1914 went to "great lengths" to learn the Swahili New Testament, despite their difficulty in understanding it.[11] They favored the Epistles, probably finding in Paul's often heated exhortations models for their own rhetoric.

6. Nairobi, Kenya, Presbyterian Church of East Africa archives, St. Andrew's Church (hereafter SA) SA I/Z/4: *Uhoro mwega uria wandikiruo ni Luka* (London, 1915); *Uhoro mwega uria wandikiruo ni Mathayo* (London, 1915). For prices and distribution, SA I/A/20: Leakey to Arthur, 1 Oct. 1915. For wage data, Kenya National Archives (hereafter KNA) KNA/DC/Nyeri/1/1/2: Annual report for Nyeri district, 1916.

7. Barlow, "The Position of Translation Work," *Kikuyu News* 51 (Sept.-Oct. 1915).

8. SA I/Z/19-20: *Mawiko* (Kijabe, n.d. [but 1920]); *Genesis* (Kijabe, 1924).

9. SA I/A/26: Barlow to Arthur, 10 July 1918.

10. SA I/Z/21: *Magano ya Kale* (London, 1914).

11. SA I/A/17: Stevenson at Tumutumu to Arthur, 22 Aug. 1914.

What converts were searching for in their eager reading of the Swahili Bible were new words with which to argue with wealthy elders. Gikuyu had long made intimate connections between speaking, selfhood, property, and politics. They called themselves *mbari ya atiriri,* the "clan of I say to you." Speech made for politics. Wealthy elders always spoke loudest, and best. Their property earned them the right to a hearing: as a common saying put it, "wisdom [or forensic skill] [is] through property."[12] Weighted with the evidence of property, elders' rhetorical skill was called *ûgî. Ûgî* is semantically related to *uga,* the verb "to say," and it was by saying, by arguing vociferously, that elders resolved complicated disputes. Their maxim was *kuuga nagwika,* "say and do" or "doing through speech." Speech was effective, a way of doing things. *Ûgî* demanded "tact," "sense," "skill," "memory," "reason," "acumen," "acuteness," and "eloquence," in the words of an early dictionary.[13] Elders displayed these forensic skills by marshaling stories, allegorical language, aphorisms, and proverbs to convince their colleagues. *Kihooto,* which now has come to mean justice, originally meant something like "the reason that convinces."[14] Gikuyu elders did not argue to determine the truth of matters. They argued in order to convince.

The poor had trouble getting a hearing. Proverbially, their tongues were thin.[15] Men unable to pay entrance fees to elders' courts were dismissed as *ngaria aka,* those who sit with women, or *ngaria nja,* those who stay at home.[16] They were compelled to sit quietly while wealthy elders talked. Their poverty was an ontological problem. Poverty was exhausting, draining: the verb *hungura* meant both "render destitute" and "exhaust, drain of vitality." Sapped of their vigor, poor men were sometimes dismissed as *atereki,* "beggars," but also "timid, silent people."[17] Proverbs enjoined them to keep quiet: a "tenant does not complain," went one.[18] Their lack of property made them immaterial, even forgettable.

The translation of Christian terms opened the range of words in which poor men could make themselves heard. As elsewhere in colonial Africa, early

12. Edinburgh, Scotland, Edinburgh University Library (hereafter EUL), Gen. 1786/6: Barlow, "Proverbs." *Ugi ni indo,* said to be a common proverb.

13. These definitions of *ûgî* are derived from A. W. McGregor, *English-Kikuyu Dictionary* (London, 1904).

14. EUL Gen. 1785/2: Barlow, notes on *ma.*

15. "A poor man's tongue," said a Gikuyu proverb, "is always thin." G. Barra, *1000 Kikuyu Proverbs* (Nairobi, 1994 [1939]), p. 98.

16. EUL Gen. 1785/1: Barlow, notes on *ngariaaka.*

17. EUL Gen. 1786/6: Merlo Pick, notes on *mutereki.*

18. *Muhoi ndairaga,* in EUL Gen. 1786/6: Barlow, "Proverbs."

Gikuyu converts were young men, some of them disinherited by angry fathers, others the junior sons of livestock-poor clans. They could scarcely hope for a hearing from the wealthy, or from God. Christian language offered them words with which to talk. It was as a debating language, a rhetoric, that early converts thought about the gospel. They called the gospel *Uhoro wa Ngai.* Missionaries thought of *uhoro* as Logos, the eternal Word of God.[19] But *uhoro* equally meant "language," "case," "edict," "engagement," "information," "story," "message," or "verdict."[20] The gospel as *Uhoro wa Ngai* was an argument, a polemic, framed to convince listeners out of the back-and-forth of argument. Converts who acceded to this language, who were convinced of the rightness of it, "believed." Like many other languages, Gikuyu did not express the sort of existential "belief" demanded by modern Christianity.[21] The Gikuyu word translated "believe" was *ĩtĩkia,* "assent to."[22] It connoted the approving sounds elders made when listening to others, murmuring "Eeeh" after hearing a convincing argument.[23] To "believe in the gospel," *kuĩtĩkia Uhoro wa Ngai,* thus meant more than the sort of inward, personal faith promised in English. It meant acceding to an argument, converting to a set of premises laid out to form a *kihooto,* a "reason that convinces."

Searching for words with which to argue with their elders, readers in the second and third decades of the century fashioned a purposive Christian language of mind, conscience, and knowledge. To know differently than their elders was the first step to getting a hearing. *Ũgĩ,* the rhetorical wisdom I described above, was an achievement earned through property: being a speaker, a proverb reminded the poor, was not just picked up anywhere. Effective speech took wealth. Young converts lacked the wealth that made claims on knowledge. They found in the Word new ways of talking about knowing, new indices of wisdom with which to prove themselves worthy of hearing.

Readers settled on a way of making themselves knowledgeable in the verb *menya.* The first translations of two Gospels (1915) and Acts (1920) were the context in which they argued out their claims.[24] Jesus' critique of the sophistry of the Pharisees became Gikuyu readers' critique of *ũgĩ,* and the knowledge of God taught by Jesus became the knowledge, *umenyo,* acquired by the readers at the

19. Nairobi, Kenya, Africa Inland Mission Kenya office archives (hereafter AIM) Committees, misc., 1930s to 1970s file: UKLC meeting, 13-14 Aug. 1913.

20. Definitions for *uhoro* culled from McGregor, *English-Kikuyu Dictionary,* and Fr. A. Hemery, *Handbook of the Kikuyu Language* (Nairobi, 1903).

21. Cf. Rodney Needham, *Belief, Language, and Experience* (Oxford, 1972).

22. KNA MSS (BS) 1/2: Barlow to Garriock, 1 Jan. 1914.

23. EUL 1785/9: Barlow, notes on *ĩtĩkia.*

24. SA I/Z/4: *Luka* and *Mathayo;* SA I/Z/19 and 20: *Mawiko.*

missions. The children of this world, admitted converts in 1915, have a knowledge *(ûgî)* that surpasses the children of the light (Luke 16:8). But this wisdom was craftiness, the sort of knowledge the Greeks called sophistry. Readers, the inheritors of Christ's Great Commission, were given *ûgî* so that they could understand, *menya,* the good matters of God (Luke 24:45). Christ throughout the 1915 version of Luke called for his disciples to understand, to *menya,* his teaching. True knowledge, *umenyo,* rightly belonged to those called just (*athingu,* a name applied to converts) by *Ngai,* the Christian God (Luke 1:17).

By 1926, when the New Testament was printed in full, converts had worked out a claim to know better, and more fully, than the elders. We hear them proudly reading to their elders the text of 1 Corinthians 1:27, which claimed that God chose the affairs of children to shame those who had wisdom, *ûgî.*[25] Readers were frequently dismissed as "children" by suspicious elders, who refused to pray to the undiscerning God of youth. Paul's letter allowed them to turn their foolish childlikeness into favor with God. People of today, claimed readers in 1 Corinthians 13:12, see through the glass darkly; they know, *ûûî,* in part, but under the reign of Christ they shall know, *menya,* in full. The verb *menya* allowed readers to position themselves, and their elders, on a continuum of knowledge: *ûgî* belonged to the old dispensation, the craftiness of the past age. Changed times demanded learning, teaching, true knowledge, expressed as *menya.*

By writing themselves into the New Testament critique of the sophistry of the Pharisees, readers claimed an inheritance of familial and political power from their elders. *Menya,* the knowledge they gained in mission schools, suited them for changed times and made them better leaders, better spokesmen, than elders. But if readers were to know better than the elders, they needed a definition of the "knower," a mind from which to *menya.* A conference of Gikuyu readers from the Southern Baptist station in Kambui "strongly recommended" in 1909 a list of terms, translations that reveal readers' investment in their own selves.[26] For "mind" the Kambui readers offered *kiriku, kuirao, guathika,* and *ninderika nindaigua.* The first term is a derivative of the verb *îra,* to tell or to say.[27] In the irregular form *kîrîko,* the verb *îra* becomes the noun describing a condition of being able to say, being able to articulate. This pairing of thinking and speech as "mind" was highly polemical: *kîrîko* as "mind" was a call to discourse, a claim that Christian conversion entitled readers to speak to their elders. The point was driven home in the other

25. In SA II/Z/4: *Kirikaniro kiria kieru kiaJesu Kristo* (London, 1926; reprint, 1931).

26. AIM Kikuyu Language file: "Conference of Kambui Christians," 24 Aug. 1909.

27. SA I/Z/26: Beecher, *A Kikuyu-English Dictionary* (Nairobi, 1938), p. 74.

words the Kambui converts used to translate "mind." *Kuirao,* an irregular noun, was similarly derived from the verb *-îra.* The fourth term, *ninderika nindaigua,* was a compound of *îra,* to say or tell, and *igua,* a term that meant something like "comprehend," "feel," "hear," or "imagine."[28] Mind as *ninderika nindaigua* argued that "I have said I have heard." Thought, for readers no less than for elders, was best expressed publicly, orally. What young converts hoped to prove was that they were entitled to a hearing.

Christian words were good to talk with, enabling impoverished readers to convert their schooling into a claim on Gikuyu wealth and power. We can hear them putting words to their demands for political power in the first translation of Matthew 5, the Beatitudes. In Gikuyu the Beatitudes become promises to readers, prophesying that the skills they learned in school would be rewarded with political power. They began by promising "those without honor," *matari namwîgatho,* the "kingdom of heaven" (Matt. 5:3).[29] Readers knew that honor, like power, belonged to those who had accumulated land and livestock. But their poverty made them the subject of the prophecy. Readers contrasted themselves to the loudly wealthy and called themselves *ahoreri,* "gentle," "meek," and "quiet" in verse 4, promising they would divide, *gaya,* the earth. This was an upstart claim on their inheritance: elders did not divide their possessions until they were ready to die.[30] But readers felt themselves ready for adulthood: some had stolen a march on their age-mates by getting circumcised early in mission hospitals; others married female readers and paid a bride-price of cash to fathers-in-law. Doubted by elders, readers looked for their reward, their *mucara,* by reason of their good work (v. 12). The verse asked them to wait until heaven: but the term they used for "reward," *mucara,* was the term used for the cash they received in earthly wage labor. Elders counted their rewards for hard work in land and property. Readers claimed that wealth, and with it public reputation, could be earned through the wages they received as compensation for their schooling. Many of them acted out this claim by investing their wage earnings in land, and by saving up for the bride-price they owed the elders.[31] Their investments translated wage earning into virtue.

28. Hemery, *Handbook of the Kikuyu Language.*

29. SA I/Z/4: *Mathayo.*

30. Cf. T. G. Benson, *Kikuyu-English Dictionary* (Oxford, 1964), p. 104, who defines *gaya* as "share out," "inherit," "receive a legacy by inheritance."

31. For readers purchasing stock with the wages they earned at the mission and on settler farms, see Barlow, "Mburi," *Kikuyu News* 26 (Mar. 1911). See also Bruce Berman's reading of the 1912 Labour Commission report, in *Control and Crisis in Colonial Kenya: The Dialectic of Domination* (London, 1990), p. 60, which argues that young men entered into wage labor in order to initiate a domestic cycle of family formation.

The Beatitudes helped readers convert their speechless lack of honor and property into a prophetic claim on political leadership and a plea for a hearing from the elders. Christian vocabulary offered subalterns and young readers who had no voice in ethnic debate a language with which to speak. Their translations of "knowledge," "conscience," and "mind" claimed for Christianity a new form of wisdom. And in the Beatitudes and elsewhere in the New Testament, converts translated this new form of knowledge into a claim on Gikuyu wealth. Their creative investments in Bible translation made the Word into a rhetoric of debate over identity and public power.

Translating Mau Mau

Forty years after the Kambui readers had translated themselves into the inheritors of elders' wisdom and wealth, Christian converts had themselves become a powerful class of stock owners and landholders. The commodity boom of the late 1930s had inspired first-generation converts to put more and more land under cultivation, increasing their profits but limiting the land available for tenants and junior family members. Converts built permanent stone houses and planted long-maturing crops like wattle, further pushing up land prices. By 1948 the average landholder in Nyeri district owned 4.45 acres, well below the minimum needed to produce a sustaining diet. Wealthy converts steadily disassociated themselves from the poor; where well-off men had once lent out land to tenants and family juniors in exchange for political support, land in the 1940s increasingly came to be property under private ownership. Tenants and junior clan members found themselves trapped on eroded hillside plots, unable to get access to cultivable land. For Gikuyu landless and land-poor, fearful of becoming proletarians, years of hard labor no longer seemed to earn anything, least of all public power. Many tried to mix farming with wage employment, but their unskilled work failed to earn them enough even to meet minimum standards of diet.[32] Their children suffered from malnutrition. Class formation was a deadly problem.

Terrified at the unrelenting private property of the rich, some Gikuyu poor translated their injury into imaginative politics. We can see this translative practice in action in the life and thought of Bildad Kaggia, the Pentecostal prophet and radical trade union leader who officered the Nairobi branch of the Kenya African Union until his detention by the British in 1952.

32. See Greet Kershaw, *Mau Mau from Below* (London, 1996), pp. 289-91, for a statistical analysis of the shortfall between wage labor and the costs of minimum standards of diet.

Kaggia has long been recognized as one of the intellectuals of what came to be called Mau Mau,[33] but his thought, like that of other Gikuyu politicians, has received little attention.[34] I suggest below that Kaggia's creative retranslations of the Bible may take us close to the language in which the Gikuyu poor argued about class formation in the 1940s. Faced in the late 1940s with evidence that wealthy readers were empty shells, that their Christian selves were corrupt tombs sucking the life out of the poor, Kaggia retranslated the Word into a call for productive unity. Condemning the wealthy for their refusal to enable others, calling for cooperative work among those who would rebuild moral order, Kaggia rewrote the Christian self into a selfless grammar of a Gikuyu common wealth. His radical retranslations help illuminate the language with which Mau Mau obligated Gikuyu to do their moral duty.

In Kaggia's thinking the need for a critical retranslation of Christian language arose from the avarice of the new Gikuyu elite, the readers. Their fences, paddocked land, and fat cattle made other Gikuyu poor; Kaggia's own father was rendered landless when his greedy relatives sold his land and left him to work as a wage earner in Nairobi (pp. 8-9). Kaggia worked his way out of poverty by learning to read English, joining the British army and traveling to England as a military clerk in 1945. His experiences led him to formulate a critique of established British missions in Kenya, a critique sharpened by his interaction with nonconformist Pentecostals in Newcastle (pp. 45-46). Gikuyu literati, Kaggia thought, "had so much faith in the *mzungu's* (European's) continued political dominance and in his intellectual power and capability that they simply abdicated from politics" (p. 63). The avarice of mission readers made them the pawns of the missionaries, who worked in league with officials to extract wealth from the Gikuyu poor. How, Kaggia wondered, could he liberate his people's minds?[35]

Kaggia's answer to the problem of readers' wealth was a kind of lived translation. Kaggia worked for a "clean church," a church purged of the "Eu-

33. Frank Füredi, *The Mau Mau War in Historical Perspective* (London, 1989), p. 139; Marshall Clough, *Fighting Two Sides: Kenyan Chiefs and Politicians, 1918-1940* (Niwott, 1990), pp. 180-82; David Throup, *Economic and Social Origins of Mau Mau* (London, 1988), pp. 243, 271. Kaggia has written his own autobiography in *Roots of Freedom, 1921-1963: The Autobiography of Bildad Kaggia* (Nairobi, 1975). Parenthetical page numbers in the following text are to Kaggia's autobiography.

34. I refer here to Jomo Kenyatta; cf. John Lonsdale, "Jomo Kenyatta, God and the Modern World," in *African Modernities: Entangled Meanings in Current Debate,* eds. J.-G. Deutsch, H. Schmidt, and P. Probst (Oxford, 2002), pp. 31-66.

35. The title of chap. 6 of Kaggia's autobiography is "How Could I Liberate Their Minds?"

ropean customs" imposed by the mission churches. Kaggia's followers abjured English baptismal names: mission church members who joined Kaggia were rebaptized using their Gikuyu names (p. 74). Their marriage ceremonies involved none of the tea and fried food that marked readers' weddings; Kaggia himself made certain that at his own wedding only Gikuyu food was served (p. 75). These were marks of a kind of separatism. Yet Kaggia's concern with cleanliness equally evoked Gikuyu concerns over sorcery and pollution. Readers' material theology, for "prophets" like Kaggia, was dangerously acquisitive: Christians' wealth sucked the life out of the poor. Kaggia's followers' ways of dressing and naming were an attempt to cleanse Christian life of the dangerous greed of the readers, an effort to translate Christian theology to speak in the register of poor men and women's fears.

Kaggia's political project demanded vocal and sustained arguing if this contentious politics of translation was to take hold. Kaggia knew that "God had to be brought to our side" (p. 56). He sought to dislodge God from the mute congregations of the mission churches by making him speak loudly, in public debates with mission supporters. Throughout 1947 and 1948 Kaggia engaged in public arguments with mission church leaders, culminating in 1948 when he and three of his followers debated Obadiah Kariuki, a leading Anglican cleric, and two others for three full days at a church in Fort Hall. Kaggia relished the opportunity to "drive my message straight into the heart of the Pharisees." We can get some sense of the ways he argued in the following: "Besides converting people to my kind of Christianity, the objective of myself and my followers was to destroy the hypocritical 'synagogue Christianity' of the establishment Church. We compared the clergy and the whole hierarchy of the 'mzungu church' to the Pharisees of old, those who outwardly professed godliness but were ungodly inside. Like Jesus, I changed the emphasis from 'converting the heathen' to 'demolishing the citadel of ungodly formalism and hypocrisy'" (p. 70).

Readers of a generation before had similarly translated Matthew 5 into a rhetoric of condemnation. They found in the woes that Jesus announced to the Pharisees ways of condemning wealthy elders. Driven by the evidence of readers' wealth in the 1940s, Kaggia retranslated Matthew into a critique of hypocrisy, a critique also of readers' sorcery. Their sleekly fat bodies disguised their emptiness, their barrenness. Kaggia called them the "devil's congregation" (p. 71). It was more than Christian name-calling. It was judo by translation. Kaggia upended readers' claims that salvation came through property. As we shall see, his criticism opened space for a new form of Christian commonwealth.

Kaggia's cutting reversal of readers' material theology required new Christian languages of politics. As I showed above, readers in the 1920s translated the Christian vocabulary of "soul," "mind," and "conscience" into a grammar with which to claim wealth and power from elders. Their Gikuyu Bible preached that salvation made for wealth, that public power rewarded Christian knowledge. Kaggia thought readers' rhetoric amounted to theft. He knew readers' selves were morally barren, that the conscience they so lovingly fabricated was a disguise for sorcery. Faced with evidence of readers' sorcery, Kaggia looked for words with which to imagine new Christian politics. We can hear him casting about for words in his correspondence with Arthur Barlow, the Scots missionary who was by the late 1940s engaged in translating the last portions of the Old Testament. Kaggia wrote to Barlow on two occasions: once in 1946, while he was resident in England in war service, and again in 1949, as a trade unionist and a member of the Mau Mau central committee in Nairobi (p. 108). Working for the renewal of Gikuyu morality through Mau Mau, Kaggia found in Christian language useful ways of talking about unity of purpose, words with which also to criticize the greedily wealthy.

His argument began with Galatians 6:6, the first translation he advocated to Barlow.[36] The passage reads in English, "Let him that is taught in the word communicate unto him that teacheth in all good things." In the 1926 Gikuyu translation, complained Kaggia, the passage had become a demand that a student "give unto his teacher all his good things," all his property. The crux of the problem was the verb *-gaya,* which the earlier translators had used for "communicate." *Gaya* was "to divide," a verb by which readers of the 1920s had made claims on their elders' property. Kaggia complained in 1949 that this translation compelled the Gikuyu poor to part with all their livestock, their *indo.* The poor, he wrote, "had interpreted it to mean they were to give all their good things to the church, because God had commanded them to do so."[37] The reality of Gikuyu poverty demanded a new translation. Kaggia settled on *Reke mundu . . . magiage ngwataniro na mumuruti maunduini mothemega* — "let him . . . always have *ngwataniro* with his teacher in all good matters."[38] The key word in this phrase was *ngwataniro,* the cooperative labor by which nineteenth-century Gikuyu had cleared the forest of its stubborn trees and rendered it up for agriculture. In the late 1940s *ngwataniro* was a powerful metaphor for Gikuyu unity: the "Mau Mau" oath was often called the *muuma wa ngwataniro. Ngwataniro* made morally instructive connec-

36. KNA MSS (BS) 1/3: Bildad Kaggia, "Amendment of Mistranslations of the Kikuyu New Testament" ([Jan. 1949]).

37. Kaggia, *Roots of Freedom,* p. 49.

38. KNA MSS (BS) 1/3: Kaggia, "Amendment of Mistranslations of the Kikuyu New Testament."

tions between cooperation and civilization, between united human work and advancement. Kaggia's translation invoked this moral lesson in calling for *ngwataniro* among readers. The work of moral and political renewal, he knew, demanded unity, working together, in order to free Gikuyu land of the "stumps" of those who persistently stood apart, the wealthy loyalists.

Kaggia's plea for cooperative unity was accompanied by a series of translations that denigrated the wealthy, those whose property inclined them to resist *ngwataniro.* Another of Kaggia's suggestions to Barlow concerned 1 Peter 2:7: "Unto you who believe he is precious, but unto them who be disobedient, 'the stone which the builders disallowed, the same is made the head of the corner.'" In Gikuyu, Kaggia's translation becomes a compelling critique of Gikuyu stubbornness, and a promise of deliverance to those who assent or believe. The key term is "disobedient," referring to those false builders who had rejected Christ. The 1926 translation had used the verb *-ihoka,* to "have faith" or to "hope in," both for "you who believe" and "the disobedient."[39] Kaggia wanted to translate the passage using *aria aremu* for "the disobedient" and *aria mwitikitie* for "you who believe." *Aremu* was a contentious translation: it was derived from the verb *-rema,* which in 1938 meant "be unmanageable by; 'stump'; be too difficult for; obstinate; too big; undisciplined; disobedient; make stuck; cannot move."[40] *Rema* equated unbelievers with stumps, which held up productive cultivation and took sweat to dig out. For forest-clearing Gikuyu, stumps meant hard work. Without machinery it had taken Gikuyu up to two man-days to fell a single tree and up to fifty days to clear an acre.[41] By calling unbelievers "stumps," Kaggia claimed that the uncooperative were unproductive obstacles to the civilizing laborers of Mau Mau. Mau Mau units that fought in the Gikuyu reserves were named the Kenya Levellation Army: their job was to uproot loyalists.[42] The *andu aremu* of 1 Peter were not simply "unbelievers," they were hindrances to the moral unity that Mau Mau sought to cultivate among Gikuyu.

Kaggia's Christian translations of unbelief and cooperation criticized the wealthy for their sorcerous greed, their lusting after private gain. First-generation converts had translated the Christian vocabulary of selfhood and knowledge into a platform for effective speech, a claim also on familial power and wealth. Intellectuals like Kaggia knew that a politics of cooperation de-

39. Missionaries had decided to use *-ihoka* for "believe on" or "hope in" from 1907. AIM Kikuyu Language file: Minutes of language meeting, 17 June 1907.

40. SA I/Z/26: Beecher, p. 177.

41. Kershaw, pp. 31-32.

42. Karari Njama, *Mau Mau from Within* (New York, 1966), p. 247; Lonsdale, "Moral Economy," p. 332.

manded a selfless vocabulary of sacrifice and common commitment. They worked out this new language by retranslating the Word, making it speak to the morally imperative need for cooperation.

It seems that Kaggia also found in his retranslations a language to think through the meanings of oath taking, the cultivating practice that rendered the wilderness of Gikuyu class formation into productive unity of purpose. Kaggia seems to have thought about oath taking as speaking in tongues. His translation of 1 Corinthians 14 bears evidence of this fusion between tongues and oaths. Translators in 1926 had rendered the phrase "speaking in tongues" in 1 Corinthians 14:6 as "speak matters which could not be known *(menya).*" This translation had placed charisma outside the ken of readers' knowledge: tongues were simply an unknowable matter, and probably not interesting for 1920s readers intent on making themselves heard by their elders. Kaggia in 1949 wanted "speaking in tongues" as *kwaria thiani,* "'ground up' speech."[43] *Thîani* was a noun that evoked pulverizing, pulping, the sort of work done by women in grinding millet.[44] The term was a metaphor for the kind of coded speech used by "Mau Mau" when talking of oath-taking. One of my informants described this way of talking thus:

> People knew each other and messages were disseminated using interpersonal contacts. Those who had not taken [oaths] were called fleas *(thua).* The greetings between those who had taken were distinct. If you have not taken and entered a house of among those who had taken, they would say "Hey, there are fleas here!", meaning there is someone among them who had not taken. The owner of the house would retort — "its the wife who did not sweep well," and the case would rest there and the life of the one who had not taken would be there. . . . This ground-up *(thîani)* language was taught amongst those who took the oath.[45]

In an environment where vernacular speech had to be guarded, where ill-directed words could bring detention at British hands, Kaggia found in biblical injunctions regarding charisma a powerful way of thinking about strategic communication. Mau Mau words, like the charismatic gifts described by Paul, had to be carefully regulated. Open speech was dangerous. *Kwaria thiani* protected Gikuyu words from irresponsible ears. Mau Mau supporters in the

43. KNA MSS (BS) 1/3: Kaggia, "Amendment of Mistranslations of the Kikuyu New Testament."

44. Benson, *Kikuyu-English Dictionary.*

45. Oral interview, Macharia Gachanu, Kagere location, Othaya division, 15 Sept. 1998.

reserves, nervous about betrayal by neighbors, relied on coded language to distinguish friend and foe. Loyalists were fleas, *thua,* whose insidious biting irritated the Gikuyu body. Mau Mau supporters greeted one another by shaking hands and scratching simultaneously.[46] Careful words put off ill-intentioned listeners and defined languages of trust and obligation. Mau Mau exchanged letters with each other written in a kind of code that brought together native speakers and excluded outsiders.[47] Mau Mau demanded a language of trust that allowed its believers to talk to each other.

Kaggia's Bible translations evoke precisely this language of trust. In the biblical language of charismatic speech, and in the vocabulary of unbelief and cooperation, Kaggia found a richly evocative stock of metaphors with which he and others similarly committed to the building of Gikuyu unity could criticize the stubbornly wealthy, a way also to call Gikuyu to moral duty.

Kaggia's tendentious translations never made their way into authorized missionary texts. But Mau Mau continued to imagine new politics in Bible translation. In 1953 James Karanja was told by Mau Mau oath administrators to stop reading his Bible "because the missions were cheating people with the Bible — they were the ones who wrote those lies for the people."[48] Biblical criticism led to anticolonial politics. Early on in the war, missionaries found that students in Presbyterian schools had rubbed out the name Jesus Christ in church hymnbooks and penciled in the name Jomo Kenyatta.[49] Forest fighters marched to the tune of "Onward, Christian Soldiers." Other fighters set Lamentations 5 to music, and sang it "when we were praying, when being chased, and when we were killing."[50] Mau Mau general Karari Njama used Peter's vision in Acts to explain to illiterate fighters why it was proper to eat wild game captured in traps.[51] Kahinga Wachanga had the chief native commissioner read the Ten Commandments out loud during peace negotiations, to illustrate the many sins the British had committed.[52]

This translative practice, this speculation on languages of politics, orga-

46. Oral interview, Paul Thuku Njembwe, Gitugi location, Othaya division, 18 June and 19 July 1998.

47. Cf. Ian Henderson, *Manhunt in Kenya* (New York, 1958), for a description of one series of written exchanges.

48. SA II/G/4: James Karanja to church elders at Thogoto, 22 Dec. 1954.

49. Katarina, Nyeri, Kenya, Tumutumu church archives; Minutes of DSC file: District School Committee, letter to teachers, 12 Feb. 1953. (Transcripts of oral interviews are held at Tumutumu church in Nyeri and in the Kenya National Archives.)

50. Interview, Njembwe.

51. Njama, p. 420.

52. Kahinga Wachanga, *The Swords of Kirinyaga* (Nairobi, 1991), p. 118.

nized Mau Mau as a political community. For Mau Mau was, among other things, a war of words. Well before Richard Rorty, Kaggia knew that new politics always demand new vocabularies, new ways of talking about the self and others.[53] Confronted with evidence of standoffish readers' greedy wealth, Mau Mau invested in Gikuyu words. Control over words gave shape to Mau Mau's political vision. By reworking the Word, Gikuyu, like Kaggia, imagined a new moral order, an order shaped by ethnic lessons about cooperation and unity.

All of which amply bears out many of Professor Hastings's observations about the relationship between Bible translation and the creation of nationalism. Gikuyu readers of standardized missionary grammars and Bibles imagined themselves the subjects of biblical stories, read their own history into the history of Israel, and in so doing imagined new, broader political configurations. But here, in distinction from Hastings's work, there was no tribal or national future naturally forecast in standardized vernacular texts. By highlighting the changing content of the Bible, I am also complicating the rather linear view of nationalism that Hastings offers. For Gikuyu at least, the vernacular Bible did not itself create new political configurations. Rather, Gikuyu applied their internally divisive social thought to retranslate the Word, mining the Bible for words with which to conduct interior arguments among themselves over questions of generational power and class formation. Translating the Bible was one way the Gikuyu argued about their divisive, shared past in order to come to terms with the moral and social challenges of colonialism.

53. Richard Rorty, *Contingency, Irony, and Solidarity* (Cambridge, 1989), p. 13.

PART III

Christian Responses to Crises at the End of Empire

CHAPTER 9

"Speaking for the Unvoiced"? British Missionaries and Aspects of African Nationalism, 1949-1959

JOHN STUART

This chapter examines the ways in which British Protestant missionaries attempted to interpret and come to terms with certain aspects of African nationalism during the 1950s. Nationalism was but one of a variety of challenges, or threats, as some saw it, to the church and to the missionary movement itself; others included communism, Islam, and Roman Catholicism. Given the ostensible missionary ambition of (eventually) creating national churches, nationalism was a phenomenon that seemed to necessitate particular attention. It was what one prominent missionary described as "an additional complication" to be considered when responding to, or indeed when attempting to influence the initiation of, social, political, and economic changes.[1] As such it tended to be intimately and awkwardly bound up with everyday missionary concerns; it could not readily be considered abstractly or in isolation. And seeking as they were to "realign" themselves to the changed circumstances of the postwar colonial world, British missionaries were aware, to varying degrees, of the need to formulate a response (or a set of responses) to nationalism. The Church Missionary Society's (CMS) own Realignment Commission concluded as much in 1949, noting that "this nationalist empha-

1. University of Birmingham Library, Church Missionary Society Archives (hereafter CMS), G/AP 11, Policy, 1946-47 file, Canon M. A. C. Warren to Rev. F. H. West, confidential, 13 Feb. 1946.

sis will not be seriously diminished in the next ten years; it may well increase."[2]

Any response to nationalism in the settler colonies of British East and central Africa — Kenya, the Rhodesias, and also Nyasaland — was complicated by the history of these territories. Missionary intervention on behalf of Africans was hardly unprecedented, but such intervention had always previously taken place within the context, and the certainty, of ongoing colonial rule. In an Africa, after 1945 "increasingly in revolt against dependent status," British missionaries had to give careful thought as to the best means of engagement with nationalism and nationalists.[3] As this chapter attempts to show, some British missionaries, Anglo-Catholics, chose in the main to tread warily; some, almost invariably Scottish, trod one might say more rashly; while some others, Anglican evangelicals, acted with more than a degree of calculation. Of course, their responses varied, as the societies themselves varied and as conditions differed within the territories where they operated, but missionary attempts to respond to the changing nature of African nationalism also had to take account of the nature of official British and colonial responses to that nationalism.

* * *

In 1959 there existed in central Africa what one British Anglican missionary, Rev. John V. Taylor of the CMS, described as "a widespread and dangerous disillusionment with the Church." This he attributed to the postwar failure of many British missionaries to speak up for what he chose to call "unvoiced" African interests.[4] Although it is debatable to what extent African interests were indeed "unvoiced," given the extent of the clamor for nationalism since 1945, it was evident that some British missionaries, such as Taylor, regarded as misguided and mistaken the apparent unwillingness of the church to allow itself to be identified with African nationalist aspiration. It had been a long time, almost exactly sixteen years, to the day, earlier, that the general secretary of the International Missionary Council had noted in 1943 the "growth of national feeling in the countries of the East and [the] increasing sense of racial self-consciousness in Africa. . . . We must," he had said, "marshal our total

2. CMS G/C 2/3, General/Executive Committee, 1949 file, Report of the Commission on the Realignment of the Foreign Work of the Society, Oct. 1949, p. 4.

3. CMS G/C 2/3, Report of the Commission on the Realignment of the Foreign Work of the Society, p. 4.

4. Rhodes House Library, Oxford, Universities' Mission to Central Africa Archives (hereafter UMCA), SF 139, Rev. J. V. Taylor to Canon G. W. Broomfield, 20 Apr. 1959.

Christian forces round the centre of an increasingly self-governed indigenous Church."[5] But while moves toward "devolution" or "integration" of church and mission were indeed afoot by the late 1950s, nationalism in its African incarnation would continue to present problems of acceptability to British Protestant missionaries.

In the immediate postwar period, many British missionaries shared the "official" view of African nationalism, a view that Frank Füredi has noted as being characterized by a mixture of apprehension and suspicion.[6] There were exceptions of course, but Africans were in the main viewed as unprepared for responsible political leadership and all too ready to resort to unacceptable methods of protest. The belief that the road to self-government would be long and gradual (just as the road to the indigenous church was expected to be) encouraged missionaries to support government ideas of "partnership" and "multiracialism" in the settler colonies of eastern and central Africa. Such support found typically cautious expression in British church and missionary pronouncements during 1952 and 1953 on plans for political federation in central Africa. By allying themselves, even implicitly, with official colonial policy, however, British missionaries were unwittingly denying themselves the likelihood of future African support in the settler colonies, support that typically would appear to increase in value the scarcer it became.

For all that, British Protestant missionary attitudes to African nationalism changed a good deal during the 1950s. At the beginning of this period it was possible for optimistic public pronouncements to be made in the belief that "moderate" and "reasonable" African Christian political leadership could be encouraged, and ultimately that African colonies ostensibly built, at least to some extent, on Christian principles might be devolved in similar fashion. By the end of this period — within about ten years — British missionaries were grappling with the dilemma of whether it could indeed be right and Christian to disavow, and even disobey, the will of the imperial and colonial state in the interest of that same African nationalism.

* * *

The postwar period was one of uncertainty in colonial affairs. British missionaries saw the need to make as plain as possible their attitude to issues of

5. School of Oriental and African Studies (hereafter SOAS), London, Council for World Mission Archives (hereafter CWM), BM/1, W. Paton, address to the directors of the London Missionary Society, 21 Apr. 1943.

6. Frank Füredi, *Colonial Wars and the Politics of Third World Nationalism* (London, 1994), p. 111.

race and nationalism. A 1945 public statement, "The Colour Bar and Race," was duly followed in 1949 by a statement on African national movements. As articulated by their corporate body, the Conference of British Missionary Societies (CBMS), missionary responsibility would encompass the highlighting of injustices and the development of goodwill between the races "in order that the emergence of African nationhood may be peaceful, orderly and secure."[7] In these respects a commitment to lawfulness and orderliness in the political sphere mirrored the envisaged transition from mission to church, itself a process that, even by 1953, was regarded in some missionary circles as "extremely slow," and similar in that very respect to wider developments in colonial affairs.[8]

Missionaries were not in any sense about to attempt to dictate the pace of political and constitutional change. Their role was, wherever possible, to ensure that such change might be informed by Christian principles. In the past, and particularly during the interwar years, such principles might well have been expressed as an aspect of belief in "trusteeship." Postwar African ideas of self-determination could not, however, be encompassed within a concept increasingly regarded as outdated in its paternalism. Missionaries would need to reconsider how they might continue to engage in meaningful political terms with Africans. The urgency of this need was revealed to many British missionaries, both on the spot and at their head offices, by the February 1949 conference at Victoria Falls in Southern Rhodesia, at which settler interests agreed upon a policy of territorial consolidation in the region.

While it appeared that the interests of Africans might be threatened by such a development, it became equally clear that British missionaries were uncertain as to how they should respond. The general secretary of the Universities' Mission to Central Africa (UMCA) sought to emphasize the interracial nature of the church itself and to distance the society, in corporate terms at least, from involvement in political affairs. Such a stance, with its seemingly implicit acceptance of the status quo, had to be reconciled with the contrary views of the Anglican bishop of Nyasaland, Frank Thorne, who was suspicious of plans for federation.[9] Officials in the London Missionary Society, also active in the region, sought unavailingly to evoke a more questioning attitude from church and missionary leaders in Britain toward developments in

7. SOAS, London, Conference of British Missionary Societies Archives, Box 257, African National Movements file.

8. CMS AF59 G3 A7/1, Uganda Mission, 1950-54, subfile 2, unsigned letter — probably Warren — to Ven. Archdeacon R. C. Palin, 16 Jan. 1953.

9. UMCA SF 139, Broomfield to Bishops of Nyasaland and Northern Rhodesia, 30 June 1952, and to Archbishop of Canterbury, 17 Nov. 1952.

central Africa.[10] Federation was in any case supposed to bestow economic benefits upon African and European alike, providing in the process a framework for the growth of "partnership"; missionaries were unable to provide sufficient justification for official amendment to or delay of the scheme.

The imposition of federation during 1952 and 1953 would sow the seeds of future discord. Some missionaries sensed this, though there was a general reluctance to say so in public. Events in Kenya developed differently and drew a rather different missionary response. If Rhodesian settlers were deemed worthy recipients of devolved political power, the same could not be said of their counterparts in East Africa. The declaration of a state of emergency in October 1952 was an admission that the colonial administration there lacked the ability to counteract the effects of Mau Mau activity. The situation in the colony appeared uncertain and potentially dangerous, a perception reflected and enhanced by lurid press headlines in Britain. Rather than engage in any attempt to instigate a British missionary consensus on the matter, officials at the CMS head office in London determined at once to assess the situation and promote what was described as some "straight talking" amongst the locals in Kenya. To these ends the society dispatched its Africa secretary, Canon Cecil Bewes, to Nairobi.[11]

Bewes's visit to Kenya reflected the view of the general secretary of the CMS, Canon Max Warren, that the best hope for the society's future in its African fields lay in its ability to, amongst other things, engage strategically with political issues and with the representatives of government, settlers, and Africans. Warren was taking the long view, certain that a church that would one day be reliant upon African leadership could not afford to alienate its African supporters at the present time. He was also careful, however, while encouraging attention to be drawn to incidents of police brutality, to avoid appearing unduly antigovernment or antisettler. As he observed in June 1953, following representations to the Colonial Office, "we've made our negative criticisms. I think the time calls for a constructive approach as well."[12] The difficulty for the CMS, or indeed for any missionary society attempting to involve itself in colonial affairs during the 1950s, lay in its being able to continue to work with and on behalf of government without becoming too closely identified with the policies of that government. One representative of the nationalist Kenyan African Union visiting Britain in 1952 had warned the society of the danger of

10. CWM AF40/80A and AF34/37A-F, correspondence, Feb. 1949–Apr. 1953.

11. CMS AF59 G3 A5/6/1, Mau Mau, Aug. 1952–Feb. 1953 file, B. D. Nicholls to Canon T. F. C. Bewes, 18 Dec. 1952.

12. CMS AF59 G3 A5/6/1, Mau Mau, 1953 file, Warren to Bewes, 7 June 1953.

just such an eventuality, drawing the comment from Bewes that "it is inevitable that we should try and do our utmost to remove any such misunderstandings among our African friends."[13] The involvement of the CMS in the Kenyan government's program of "rehabilitation" of Mau Mau suspects made it particularly important that the society maintain a flexible approach to its affairs in the region, constantly reviewing and reassessing perceptions of its involvement with government, settlers, and Africans.

The political activities of the CMS extended even to attempts to initiate public discussion on the ineffectiveness of the governor of Kenya, Sir Evelyn Baring, in early 1955. Officials in the society shared the perception of many Kenyan Africans that the "Lyttelton Constitution" of the previous year had made insufficient concession to nationalist needs. The assertion by the Kenyan trade union and political activist Tom Mboya that Britain remained committed to a policy of white domination struck a particular chord within the CMS, one official observing that "to the African, 'multi-racialism' and 'partnership' are concepts just about as congenial as 'communism' or 'nazism' are to us." More worryingly, not least to Warren, was the same individual's assessment that "the significance and the contribution of the Churches and Missions in Kenya seemed to be peripheral — if in the picture at all."[14] The general secretary's anxiety about the consequences for the society of growing African dissatisfaction was palpable. He wrote, "there is the most grave danger that the Church will be not so much neutral over political issues as hopelessly compromised by being tied to the Government's chairot [*sic*] wheels."[15]

Warren was only too aware of the strong passions and reactions that nationalism was engendering. Events in Kenya had demonstrated this tendency only too clearly. The church, he increasingly felt, could and should be doing more, particularly through the encouragement of its African members and clergy. He was particularly concerned, in 1955, with what he also perceived as a lingering Christian and European resentment of the nationalist impulse. This, he believed, might take the form of a growth in conservatism and reaction amongst Western Christianity more generally, developments that could only have an adverse effect upon the work of missionary societies. While nationalism appeared to have the potential to become what he described as an "international asset," the opposite might increasingly be said to hold for colonialism.[16]

13. CMS AFg O16/1, Bewes to L. B. Greaves, 21 Feb. 1952. The Kenyan African Union representative was Achieng' Oneko.

14. CMS AFg O1, Nicholls, notes on Africa Bureau Conference, London, 12 May 1956.

15. CMS AFg O1, Warren to Bewes, n.d., but ca. May 1956.

16. Max Warren, "Nationalism as an International Asset," *International Review of Missions* 176 (Oct. 1955): 385-93.

* * *

Limited as the granting of concessions to Kenyan Africans may have appeared, they marked an improvement compared with developments in central Africa. There the much-vaunted economic benefits of federation had proved insufficient recompense for lack of African political advancement. Conversely, settler self-confidence and aggrandizement had grown sufficiently by the mid-1950s for the possibility of dominion status to be openly considered, a move that shook the confidence of Canon Gerald Broomfield, the UMCA's general secretary, in federation. He wrote to Warren in October 1956, urging that "something must be done."[17] And indeed, officials in the British Council of Churches (which included representatives from the missionary societies) were now keeping the archbishop of Canterbury informed of developments. There was a growing realization amongst Christian groups in London that faith in federation had been misplaced and that perhaps more heed might have been paid to African reservations about its implementation at an earlier stage. It was within central Africa itself rather than in London, however, that the implications of the churches' uncritical stance were now beginning to manifest themselves.

In 1958 Roland Oliver of the School of Oriental and African Studies in London (who had become a member of the CMS Africa Committee in 1955) visited eastern and central Africa. On his return he conveyed his impressions, and his concerns, to the Africa Committee of the CBMS. Noting regional and territorial differences in lay and religious Christian opinion, he remarked that "even 'moderate' Christian opinion was so moderate that it commanded the assent of perhaps 10% of Europeans and 1% of Africans . . . though the vast majority of Church members in east and central Africa were Africans, the voice of the Church was still largely European."[18] Oliver's prognosis served to confirm existing reports from the field of growing polarization of political views within and between racial groups. Far from providing the capacity for uniting the races in Christian fellowship, as had been hoped by Broomfield and others in 1952 and 1953, the churches of central Africa appeared to have, as another visitor to the region in 1958 noted, "signally failed their ecumenical responsibility to hold together the Christian community across the lines of political bitterness."[19] To an increasing number of British missionaries on the

17. UMCA SF 139, Broomfield to Warren, private and confidential, 31 Oct. 1956.

18. CMS AFg O16/1, CBMS Africa Committee minutes excerpts, 28 Nov. 1958.

19. London, British Council of Churches Archives at the Church of England Records Centre, 5/2/2/xiv, A. R. Booth, "Rhodesia and Nyasaland Diary," n.d., but ca. 1958, p. 19. Booth was secretary of the Commission of the Churches on International Affairs.

spot, this bitterness appeared the result not merely of the policies of the federal government in Salisbury, but of those of the Colonial and Commonwealth Relations Offices in London.

* * *

Events in Kenya continued to preoccupy officials of the CMS, but the society's general secretary was by now ready to acknowledge the increasingly influential effect of developments within the Federation on colonial and indeed Commonwealth affairs. In correspondence with Warren, his counterpart on the Foreign Missions Committee of the Church of Scotland, Rev. James Dougall described how Africans were increasingly "being driven to extremes of opposition and non-cooperation" by the enactment of legislation on the franchise and amendment of the constitution. The possibility that Her Majesty's government might also be prepared to consider the issue of dominion status for the Federation at the Constitutional Review Conference scheduled for 1960 was also causing considerable unease amongst Africans. Missionaries too were increasingly uneasy; the idea of federation with its ostensible commitment to the ideals of "partnership" was proving less than easy to excuse, much less support. Scottish missionaries in Northern Rhodesia and Nyasaland were finding themselves in an increasingly politicized situation. As Dougall admitted to Warren, even ministers previously considered cautious and conservative in their outlook were preparing to ally themselves with nationalist movements.[20] Such a development had not necessarily been a foregone conclusion despite the supposedly radical inclination of certain Scottish missionaries.

Missionaries of the Church of Scotland had, with their colleagues in the wider British missionary movement, given tentative support to the idea of central African federation, although they had also made clear their reservations. The energetic opposition of some missionaries in Nyasaland during 1952 and 1953 had, however, resulted in the church's activities (and the activities of what was to become its successor, the Church of Central Africa Presbyterian) being viewed with suspicion in official circles in London and Salisbury. Indeed, the years since then had been marked by a gradually growing antipathy between the church and the federal state in particular. By late 1958 anxiety in Edinburgh had developed so much that Dougall expressed it thus, again to Warren: "What worries us . . . is that any statement

20. Edinburgh, National Library of Scotland (hereafter NLS), 7548/A140, Rev. J. W. C. Dougall to Warren, 19 Nov. 1958.

of the facts or criticism of Government is taken to be something approaching high treason."[21]

Scottish missionaries were viewed as a breed apart, and not merely by civil servants and government officials. Amongst some African nationalists at least there was the expectation that Scots, merely by being Scots, would tend to oppose the policies of a government based in London. Members of a local branch of the Northern Rhodesian African National Congress had taken issue in 1952 with one Scottish minister, assuming him to be by birth as "a Scotchman" an advocate of Scottish devolution: "You are unbuilding your own federation," they protested, "but are eager to build one for us — what a plan."[22] Scottish missionaries in Kenya might also be regarded in official circles as "troublemakers," but there they were Protestant troublemakers, drawing attention, with their Protestant colleagues of other denominations, to official malpractice.[23] They were not burdened to the extent of their compatriots in Nyasaland by expectations engendered by a radical heritage. By early 1959, however, it appeared that only a "radical" response to events in central Africa would prove sufficient to draw attention to the continuing iniquity of federation.

The rioting that broke out in Nyasaland in February 1959 demonstrated the extent of African disaffection and gave justification to Scottish expressions of grievance. The governor responded by declaring a state of emergency, a similar declaration having also been made in Southern Rhodesia. Once it had been established that its missionaries were safe, the Foreign Missions Committee of the Church of Scotland was able to make a remarkably sanguine assessment of events. Its Africa secretary, Rev. John Watt, noted in a circular to colleagues: "They [Africans] have for long urged the reality of partnership to be shown, and no one has paid any attention to them. Since constitutional representatives are not listened to, violence is the only way to draw attention to the situation, it appears!" Even Canon Broomfield of the UMCA would ultimately be forced reluctantly to a similar conclusion.[24] In the aftermath of this violence the appointment of the Devlin Commission of Enquiry would ensure, or so it was hoped by British missionaries, Scottish and others, that African voices might have an opportunity not so much to speak as, finally, to be heard.

21. Dougall to Warren, 19 Nov. 1958.

22. NLS 7548/B313, Executive Committee, Northern Rhodesian African National Congress, Chinsali, to Rev. F. Macpherson, 25 Mar. 1952.

23. NLS 7548/B271, Rev. R. Macpherson, confidential memo, "The Church of Scotland Mission and the Emergency," Apr. 1954.

24. NLS 7548/B400, Rev. J. A. R. Watt, circular letter, 6 May 1959; Broomfield, *1960: Last Chance in the Federation,* UMCA pamphlet, Mar. 1960, p. 17.

The previous summer the Federal Assembly member for Nyasaland, the Reverend Andrew Doig, also a Scottish missionary, had personally come to realize the futility of any attempt to instigate change in central Africa from within the existing political system. Not only were he and his colleagues on the assembly failing to make headway with government, their very membership in the assembly was causing them to be branded as untrustworthy by Africans. Doig would later recount how the realization that he must abandon the assembly had come to him extremely late, but that he was still able to retain at least some credibility by resigning in July 1958. An African colleague, Manoah Chirwah, who had delayed his resignation until 1959, had found himself consigned, in contrast, to what Doig described as "the political wilderness."[25] That, it seemed, was the inevitable fate of political moderates in central Africa in 1959.

Regrettable as African protest might have appeared to British missionaries, it was the apparent resolve of the Nyasaland administration to resist calls for the release of detainees that now, in contrast, began to seem unreasonable. The credibility of British colonial policy in general suffered a further blow with the deaths of detainees at Hola Camp in Kenya. In June 1959 a British Council of Churches delegation to the Secretaries of State for Colonies and Commonwealth requested a statement from government on the possible right of federation territories to secede. It was a belated acknowledgment of church and mission disenchantment with the aims and objectives of British colonial policy and a tacit admission of belief in the African right to self-determination, by whatever means Africans deemed best.

* * *

In 1949 British missionaries were well aware of the existence of African nationalist movements in British colonial territories. They believed African self-determination to be a worthwhile aspiration, and they had hopes of being participants in a process, or a series of processes, in which that aspiration would eventually be fulfilled. But nationalism "is seldom an independent variable," it is rather "a form through which a variety of responses, aspirations and interests are expressed."[26] And in 1949 African nationalism was typically characterized by the negativity of its stance against colonial rule, a stance typified by the response of Hastings Banda of Nyasaland and Harry Nkumbula of Northern Rhodesia to the Victoria Falls conference of February

25. NLS 7548/B418, Rev. A. B. Doig, circular letter, 2 Feb. 1961.
26. Füredi, p. 21.

1949. This negative approach was not the kind of politics with which British missionaries, by instinct or by background, found it particularly easy to engage. The apparent reasonableness of official British colonial policy appeared a safer bet (as it had proved so often in the past), and every effort could still be put into the activity that would define missionary policy toward eastern and central Africa during the mid-1950s — that of "winning the confidence" of Africans in the ways of government, church, and mission alike.

It took some time after 1952 for the shortcomings of British colonial policy to become apparent to British missionaries, first in Kenya, then in central Africa; only then, and in contrast to those shortcomings, did the essential legitimacy of African nationalist movements become truly apparent. And African nationalism had, of necessity, to develop an increasingly radical voice, if for no other reason than to make itself heard. It is by no means certain, despite the assertion of Rev. John V. Taylor, that the corporate voice of British churches and missionary societies would necessarily have been welcomed by nationalists in eastern and central Africa in any attempt to speak for the "unvoiced." By the late 1950s, as Roland Oliver had observed, the religion of Europeans, of whatever denomination, was becoming the object of African "suspicion and contempt." "Possibly," he noted, "the Anglican Church came off worst, as being most closely associated with the ruling power; but it would be no good for Presbyterians to plead that they were Scottish nationalists, or Methodists that they abhorred the Establishment — in African eyes all alike were identified with those who bore rule."[27]

27. CMS AFg O16/1, CBMS Africa Committee minutes excerpts, 28 Nov. 1958.

CHAPTER 10

Church and State in Crisis: The Deposition of the Kabaka of Buganda, 1953-1955

CAROLINE HOWELL

> Someday, when the historians tackle our files, they will find the evidence for just how hard we have worked in the interests of black and white relationships . . . in general over this whole issue and of the Baganda people in particular.[1]

The issue to which Max Warren, general secretary of the Church Missionary Society (CMS) from 1942 to 1963,[2] was referring in our epigraph was one of the most notorious episodes in the decolonization of East Africa. Kabaka Mutesa II was the hereditary ruler of Buganda, the central, southern kingdom of the Uganda Protectorate. Fearing Buganda's absorption and loss of status within an independent Uganda or, worse still, within an east African federation, the Kabaka refused to cooperate with British constitutional plans. The

N.B. Language note: When referring to the kingdom of Buganda, "Baganda" (singular, "Muganda") are the people, "Luganda" is the language, and "Kiganda" is the adjective for things that are done by or belong to the Baganda. Customary usage retains the prefixes "ba-," "mu-," "bu-," and "lu-," but drops "ki-" in the adjectival form.

1. Church of Uganda, Namirembe Archives (hereafter NA), 02 Bp 110/9 (CMS London — General Secretary vol. I): Warren to Brown, 8 Nov. 1954. I am grateful to the Church of Uganda for allowing me access to their archival holdings.

2. See F. W. Dillistone, *Into All the World: A Biography of Max Warren* (London, 1980).

I am grateful for comments received on an earlier draft, particularly those from Professor Ian Phimister and Professor Andrew Porter.

governor, Sir Andrew Cohen, however, was determined to push ahead with the development of Uganda as a unitary state. Cohen saw no alternative but to remove the Kabaka from power, and on 30 November 1953 he deported him to Britain.[3]

The relationship between the Anglican Church and the colonial state in Uganda was historically very close. It was, after all, the CMS that had clamored so loudly for the establishment of a British protectorate back in the 1890s.[4] Hence the Kabaka's deposition provoked a crisis of legitimacy not only for the state but also for the church in Uganda. Church and state were forced to consider afresh the nature of their relationship with one another, their plans for devolving power, and their response to racial and ethnic divides. In the event, the deposition proved untenable, and within two years the British were compelled to restore Mutesa to his throne.

Max Warren, as quoted above, was confident that the CMS played a positive, progressive role in bringing about a peaceful resolution to the crisis. The historian "tackling the files" cannot fail to be impressed by the extraordinary effort the church made to secure a just and workable settlement.[5] Kevin Ward has recently outlined how the crisis reopened the debate about the place of established religion within the Buganda kingdom, and how the continued identification of the Kabakaship with Anglicanism had grave repercussions for the church. While acknowledging that the church was deeply shaken by the whole affair, Ward has suggested that the intervention of Anglican leaders, in Uganda and in Britain, was decisive, pointing to "the vital role played by the Anglican Church in securing the return of the Kabaka."[6]

3. For an account of the crisis, see D. A. Low and R. C. Pratt, *Buganda and British Overrule, 1900-1955* (London, 1960), pp. 317-49, and D. A. Low, "The Buganda Mission, 1954," *Historical Studies* 13, no. 51 (1968): 353-80. For autobiographical records of the affair, see Mutesa II, *The Desecration of My Kingdom* (London, 1967), pp. 117-48; P. Kavuma, *Crisis in Buganda, 1953-55: The Story of the Exile and Return of the Kabaka, Mutesa II* (London, 1979); L. Brown, *Three Worlds: One Word — Account of a Mission* (London, 1981), pp. 99-107; O. Lyttelton, *The Memoirs of Lord Chandos* (London, 1962), pp. 417-24; and W. K. Hancock, *Professing History* (Sydney, 1976), pp. 90-109.

4. For an outline of the interaction between religion and politics in early colonial Buganda, see D. A. Low, *Religion and Society in Buganda, 1875-1900* (Kampala, 1957).

5. P. M. Mutibwa, "The Church of Uganda and the Movements for Political Independence 1952-1962," in *A Century of Christianity in Uganda, 1877-1977*, ed. T. Tuma and P. Mutibwa (Nairobi, 1978), pp. 131-41, briefly discusses the Kabaka crisis and stresses the positive role of the church. Edward Carpenter, *Archbishop Fisher — His Life and Times* (Norwich, 1991), pp. 524-40, emphasizes the importance of Fisher's intervention, but is a rather inadequate account of this complex episode.

6. Kevin Ward, "The Church of Uganda and the Exile of Kabaka Muteesa II, 1953-55," *Journal of Religion in Africa* 28, no. 4 (1998): 411-49.

This chapter seeks to clarify the extent to which the Anglican Church was in fact influential in bringing about the Kabaka's return, why the church acted as it did, and what consequences its actions had. While supporting a number of Ward's findings, a preliminary look at a wider range of sources than those consulted by Ward suggests that the church had rather less leverage on the colonial state. In addition, there are other important aspects of the crisis requiring fuller exploration. The Anglican Church emerged from the Kabaka's deposition closely associated not only with the Buganda monarchy, but also with the colonial state at a critical time in the protectorate's history. More broadly, the role of the church in the Kabaka incident sheds light on a number of key historiographical themes, not least the relationship between missions and imperialism and theories of decolonization. The final years of colonial rule have been characterized as a period when church and state in Africa drew closer together than ever before, though tensions and imbalances simmered beneath the surface.[7] The role of the church in the Kabaka's deposition sheds significant new light on this emerging picture of confusion and ambiguity in church and mission responses to colonial politics in the late imperial era.[8]

Church and State in Buganda

The Native Anglican Church in Buganda occupied a quasi-established position, both within the indigenous structures of the kingdom and in the broader framework of colonial rule. The late nineteenth century had seen a series of wars between rival Protestant, Catholic, and Muslim converts, finally won for the Protestants by the intervention of British forces. British treaty makers tended to favor the Protestant cause, using religious adherence to determine grants of land and public office. Bishop Tucker and Archdeacon Walker of the CMS helped to negotiate, and were themselves official signatories to, the Uganda Agreement of 1900, which granted Buganda a significant degree of autonomy within the wider protectorate and by which Protestant hegemony in the kingdom was officially institutionalized.[9]

The Anglican Church, colonial state, and indigenous administration in

7. Adrian Hastings, *A History of African Christianity, 1950-1975* (Cambridge, 1979), pp. 94-107.

8. See, for example, John Stuart, "'A Measure of Disquiet': British Missionary Responses to African Colonial Issues, 1945-53," *NAMP/CWC Position Paper* (Cambridge, 2000).

9. Low, *Religion and Society in Buganda, 1875-1900*.

Buganda were thus linked together in a dynamic, tripartite relationship, but the dynamics between them altered over time. By the interwar years, while the state had less need for the church's supportive, legitimizing function, the church had become much more reliant, politically and economically, on the colonial state.[10]

It was the philosophy of Bishop Stuart, bishop of Uganda from 1934 to 1953, that "when you have governors and others who are out and out Christians it is the job of the Church to work with them." As a result, with the stirrings of Ganda nationalism, Stuart became very unpopular and was accused of being a "British spy"[11] and a "servant of the . . . State."[12] Max Warren, arguably the most forward-thinking and insightful missionary leader of his day, had warned that such close associations between church and state might cause more trouble in the future,[13] fears that were soon realized in a most acute form.

Stuart's successor, Leslie Brown, a theological teacher from South India, was a very different type of bishop. Governor Cohen considered Brown "able and saintly,"[14] but also "politically naïve," an opinion shared by Brown himself. As Brown later reflected, "I was not trained in political insight and had no experience of politics."[15] Visiting Uganda in 1949, Warren had pondered the need to modify the "prince-bishop" tradition that Stuart had inherited. "But," he wrote, "it would be a blunder if it was modified too rapidly and its rapid modification would be misunderstood by the Africans."[16] Four years on, the Kabaka's deposition revealed just how extensive and damaging such a misunderstanding could be.

10. H. B. Hansen, *Mission, Church, and State in a Colonial Setting: Uganda, 1890-1925* (London, 1984). See also Hansen, "Church and State in Early Colonial Uganda," *African Affairs* 85, no. 338 (1986): 55-74, and "Church and State in a Colonial Context," in *Imperialism, the State, and the Third World*, ed. M. Twaddle (London and New York, 1992), pp. 95-123.

11. London, Lambeth Palace Library (hereafter LP), MS 3983, Memoirs of Cyril Edgar Stuart, pp. 35-37. For an overview of church-state controversies in the time of Bishop Stuart, see Ward, "The Church of Uganda," pp. 418-24.

12. *Report of the Commission of Inquiry into the Disturbances in Uganda during April, 1949* (Entebbe, 1950), p. 88.

13. LP, Fisher Papers, vol. 150, fo. 65: Stuart to Fisher, 18 Jan. 1954.

14. LP, Fisher Papers, vol. 164, fo. 18: note on meeting with the governor of Uganda, 23 Mar. 1955.

15. Brown, *Three Worlds*, pp. 111-12.

16. University of Birmingham Library, Church Missionary Society Archives (CMS), Max Warren Travel Diaries, "Forty Thousand Miles," III, 19 Dec. 1949, p. 569.

The Native Anglican Church and the Kabaka's Deposition

Sir Andrew Cohen seriously underestimated the depth of anger that the deportation would provoke. He had assumed that Buganda would soon settle down and elect a new Kabaka so that constitutional progress could resume. In the event, Mutesa was transformed into a national hero and the deposition became, to quote Brown, "a *causus belli contra episcopum* in almost every parish."[17] Church attendance dropped dramatically and pagan ceremonies were revived. Things perceived to be European, including the church, were reviled as racial tensions increased.

Given the legacy of Bishop Stuart and his predecessors, it was widely presumed that Cohen must have consulted Brown prior to the deposition, and though Brown tried continually to clear his name, he met with little success. The bishop's position was made even more difficult by the widespread assumption that if only the church would speak out, Mutesa would be allowed to return. The church was held to have a special responsibility because of its role in the 1900 agreement, under whose terms the Kabaka was deposed. Moreover, it was argued that the heavy-handed manner of Mutesa's deportation raised a moral issue that the church had a duty to address.[18] Mutesa himself was "dismayed at Bishop Brown's vagueness . . . [and] apparent neutrality."[19]

Brown knew he was evading taking sides, but he did not see what else he could do and remain loyal to the truth. Though he was deeply sorry for the Baganda, he felt their campaign was so full of lies that he could not publicly express his sympathy. Governor Cohen, by contrast, Brown considered "entirely honourable," and he sought to be of use to him as a pastor.[20] Cohen, conversely, considered himself on "extremely friendly terms" with Bishop Brown. He was careful to keep in close contact with him to ensure that Brown did "everything possible to be helpful to us."[21] He insisted on Brown's presence in the Lukiko, the parliament of Buganda, when key constitutional decisions were announced, and sought to gain his support for his statements.[22]

17. CMS, AF AL 1950-59 BRJ-COG (Annual letters): L. W. Brown, 3 Aug. 1954.

18. CMS, AF 59 G3 A7/8 (Kabaka deposed): Warren to Brown, 16 Dec. 1953.

19. NA, 02 Bp 110/9 (CMS London — General Secretary vol. I): Mutesa to Warren, 22 Jan. 1954.

20. LP, Fisher Papers, 150, fo. 58: Brown to Fisher, 16 Jan. 1954; NA, 02 Bp 110/9 (CMS London — General Secretary vol. I): Brown to Warren, 16 Feb. and 21 Apr. 1954.

21. London, Public Record Office (hereafter PRO), CO 822/569 (Withdrawal of recognition from the Kabaka of Buganda), fo. 167: Cohen to Barnes, 31 Dec. 1953.

22. Brown, *Three Worlds*, p. 105; LP, Fisher Papers, vol. 150, fo. 147: Cohen to Fisher, 4 Mar. 1954.

As the crisis progressed, the bishop often found himself in a mediatory role. A discussion group of young Africans and Europeans continued to meet at his house and served as an important forum for interracial contact.[23] Any action Brown did agree to undertake was modest and limited in scope. At the request of the Baganda Regents, for instance, Brown asked Cohen to delay calling for the election of a new Kabaka, but he felt unable to commit the church to more.[24] Though the rural deans of Buganda, and later the Diocesan Council and Synod, passed resolutions calling for the Kabaka's return, they did so in what Cohen termed "very moderate language." Brown did eventually ask both Cohen and the colonial secretary to allow the Kabaka back, but at no stage did he press publicly for Mutesa's reinstatement.[25] Instead, he urged that the 1900 agreement be revised, to prevent similar misunderstandings in the future.[26]

Though there were exceptions, most notably Brown's assistant bishop Lutaya, the majority of Baganda churchmen, lay and clerical, pressed Brown to take a much firmer stand. On a tour of twenty churches in Kyagwe County, for example, in every case except one Brown was tackled about the Kabaka issue. At a clergy retreat, when Brown suggested that Cohen's actions might have been legitimate in terms of the 1900 agreement and his duty to keep the peace, senior churchmen begged him not to speak so openly again.[27] Hence the Anglican Church in Buganda was by no means a united body, with a positive, coherent policy of working for the Kabaka's return. On the contrary, in a dispute charged with racial tension, Bishop Brown, a European, came under fierce attack by many in his African flock. If the Native Anglican Church did play a vital role in the return of the Kabaka, its contribution was far more subtle and ambiguous than many of the Baganda would have liked.

23. LP, MS 3779, L. W. Brown Diaries, Mar. 1953–May 1954, fo. 137: 24 Mar. 1954.

24. CMS, AF 59 G3 A7/8 (Kabaka deposed): Brown to Warren, 26 Dec. 1953.

25. PRO, CO 822/569 (Withdrawal of recognition from the Kabaka of Buganda), fo. 167: Cohen to Barnes, 31 Dec. 1953; CO 822/751 (Situation in Buganda: the Future of Kabaka Mutesa II), fo. 4: Cohen to Lennox-Boyd, 8 Aug. 1954, and fo. 44: Summary of discussions with the Secretary of State on the Buganda situation, 8-12 Oct. 1954.

26. NA, 02 Bp 219/27 (Rulers 1953-1961): Bishop to Diocesan Council, 15 Jan. 1954; LP, MS 3815, L. W. Brown Papers, 1953-55, fo. 24: Charge to Synod, 5 May 1954.

27. Institute of Commonwealth Studies (ICS), W. K. Hancock Buganda Papers, HANC/1-11, fo. 5: The Bishop's impressions during a tour, 11-21 July 1954, in Kyagwe County; NA, 02 Bp 110/9 (CMS London — General Secretary vol. I): Brown to Warren, 4 May 1954.

The Response of the Church in Britain

Churchmen in Buganda were not alone in their unease at Bishop Brown's handling of the crisis. Some clerical figures in Britain also expressed their concern. Soon after the deportation, Brown's predecessor, Stuart, sent a widely publicized telegram to Uganda, asking the church to protest against the "monstrous and mad decision of Lyttelton," the colonial secretary. He sent an even more outspoken letter to the *Observer* and the Ugandan press, predicting that "there will be bloodshed in the whole of Africa and Mr Lyttelton will be responsible."[28]

Michael Scott of the Africa Bureau was another Anglican figure prepared to campaign publicly on the Kabaka's behalf.[29] In a letter to the *Spectator,* Canon H. M. Grace, former Africa secretary of the Conference of British Missionary Societies, termed the deposition the most "short-sighted and provocative action in . . . recent colonial history," describing Cohen as "a governor unfitted to work with the African."[30] Yet the established missionary leaders were careful to distance themselves from such outbursts. Grace's successor, L. B. Greaves, at once wrote to Cohen to assure him that Grace's comments were by no means representative of official missionary opinion.[31]

Though he was appalled at the indiscretion of Stuart and Grace, Max Warren was concerned at the extent of Brown's sympathy with the governor. Warren was frustrated by Cohen's "unimaginative, *non-possumus* attitude" and wanted Brown to impress on him the psychological and emotional impact of his decisions.[32] Indeed, while feeling able to rely on Bishop Brown, Cohen realized that the church in Britain might prove more troublesome and asked the Colonial Office to ensure its "careful handling." He was furious about Stuart's letter to the press and threatened to prosecute the church for sedition.[33]

When a delegation of Baganda arrived in London, the CMS was at once

28. LP, Fisher Papers, vol. 150, fo. 53: Hopkinson to Fisher, 15 Jan. 1954 and fo. 67: Warren to Fisher, 19 Jan. 1954.

29. Rhodes House Library (hereafter RHO), MSS Afr. s. 1681, Africa Bureau, Box 295/File 1: Uganda — Deposition of the Kabaka, correspondence and statements, 1953-54.

30. *Spectator,* 11 June 1954.

31. School of Oriental and African Studies (hereafter SOAS), Conference of British Missionary Societies (CBMS), Box 281, Kabaka's dismissal 1954: Greaves to Trowell, 29 June 1954.

32. NA, 02 Bp 110/9 (CMS London — General Secretary vol. I): Warren to Brown, 4 Feb. 1954.

33. PRO, CO 822/569 (Withdrawal of recognition from the Kabaka of Buganda), fo. 167: Cohen to Barnes, 31 Dec. 1953; LP, MS 3801, L. W. Brown Letters 1954, fo. 2: 13 Jan. 1954.

concerned to offer them Christian counsel. The archbishop of Canterbury, Geoffrey Fisher, who took an active interest in Ugandan affairs and had previously given Mutesa marital advice, was also intimately involved.[34] Warren and Fisher were anxious to understand the different perspectives of all those involved in the dispute, speaking with and writing to members of the Baganda delegation, the Colonial Office, and the Native Anglican Church. Their task was complicated by the fact that the Baganda were, as Max Warren put it, so "badly at sea on . . . the relations of Church and State. They seemed to have imagined that, things having gone wrong from their point of view, all that was needed was for the Church to say something."[35] Though he tried to explain that the church no longer exercised a decisive influence in matters of state, the Baganda still made a public appeal for the church to intervene. Since the Kabaka was "completely a product of the Christian heritage," the Baganda were "sure that the Christian conscience of Britain will not allow its leaders to remain silent on this issue."[36]

The CMS felt a strong sense of responsibility not only to the Baganda, but also to the British public, wanting to provide a Christian interpretation of events. Max Warren was especially concerned to address the racial issue. On 15 January 1954, in a perceptive attempt to explain the root causes of the crisis, Warren published a lengthy article in the *Church of England Newspaper,* setting the Kabaka crisis in the context of events elsewhere on the continent.[37] A CMS press release a week later also aimed to put on record the Society's "growing concern . . . at the rapid deterioration in relationships between black and white in Africa." Yet the CMS did not, significantly, call for Mutesa's return. Instead, following the line taken by Bishop Brown, it suggested that the 1900 agreement might be in need of revision. Though the statement did criticize some aspects of the government's handling of the Kabaka case, it held that all sides were partly to blame.[38] Mutesa complained to Warren that "I have found little consolation as to whether the Church would be glad to see me back in my country or not, both in your article and the resolution."[39]

Warren devoted two of his monthly newsletters, with their worldwide

34. For a biography of Fisher, see Carpenter, *Archbishop Fisher — His Life and Times.* For the details of Mutesa's marriage, see Ward, "The Church of Uganda," pp. 423-24.

35. CMS, AF 59 G3 A7/8 (Kabaka deposed): Warren to Palin, 6 Jan. 1954.

36. *Times,* 24 Dec. 1953.

37. *Church of England Newspaper,* 15 Jan. 1954.

38. NA, 02 Bp 110/9 (CMS London — General Secretary vol. I): Brown to Cohen, 21 Jan. 1954; CMS, AF 59 G3 A7/8 (Kabaka deposed): CMS Press Release, 22 Jan. 1954.

39. NA, 02 Bp 110/9 (CMS London — General Secretary vol. I): Mutesa to Warren, 22 Jan. 1954.

Christian readership, to a discussion of Ugandan matters, taking a similarly measured and moderate line. He warmly applauded the recent constitutional pledges of both the colonial secretary and Governor Cohen, wanting "informed Christian opinion . . . [to] realise just how deeply committed Britain is to the people of Uganda."[40] Despite his private reservations, Warren's public attitude toward Cohen was remarkably sympathetic, and Cohen himself was very grateful for Warren's favorable reporting of his constitutional plans.[41]

Archbishop Fisher was also very guarded in his public declarations on the Kabaka affair. To the Church Assembly in London, for example, he stated that no clear question of Christian principles had arisen.[42] Privately, behind the scenes, however, Fisher took a far more proactive role. The Baganda delegation saw the archbishop before they had even met the colonial secretary, and Fisher sent a long memorandum to Lyttelton outlining their talks. He explained that, in his opinion, the Baganda's primary fear was for the future of their kingdom in a possible multiracial state. Hence Fisher put considerable pressure on the Colonial Office to clarify Lyttelton's pledge that Uganda would develop as "primarily an African country, with proper safeguards for minorities." He told Thornley, chief secretary of Uganda, that unless an announcement was made before Epiphany, he himself would speak out on the matter.[43]

Yet publicly at least, despite the outspokenness of some other Anglican voices, in their concern not to alienate any side in the dispute, ecclesiastical leaders in Britain gave only very qualified support to what was, for the Baganda, the crucial issue at stake: the return of their Kabaka. Church dignitaries like Warren, Fisher, and Greaves kept in close contact with Cohen, respecting his request that they refrain from public comment on Mutesa's future, at least until the results of constitutional talks with the Baganda were made known.[44] It was in ensuring the success of these talks that the Anglican Church played its most crucial role in resolving the Kabaka crisis, talks that for the first time in the history of eastern and central Africa mapped out the concept of the "primarily African state."[45]

40. RHO, MSS Afr. s. 1681, Africa Bureau, Box 295/File 1, fo. 2: CMS Newsletter, no. 160, Apr. 1954. For information on Warren's newsletters, see Dillistone, pp. 88-94.

41. LP, Fisher Papers, vol. 150, fo. 238: Cohen to Warren, 25 May 1954.

42. *East African and Rhodesian,* 22 Feb. 1954.

43. LP, Fisher Papers, vol. 133, fo. 99: Memorandum by Fisher on meeting with the Baganda delegation, 12 Dec. 1953, and fo. 125: Note on meeting with the Chief Secretary of Uganda, 22 Dec. 1953.

44. SOAS, CBMS, Box 281, Kabaka's dismissal 1954: Cohen to Greaves, 22 Sept. 1954.

45. For an assessment of the significance of this settlement, see Low, "The Buganda Mission, 1954."

The Role of the Church in the Constitutional Settlement

In March 1954, in an attempt to regain the initiative, Cohen asked the Lukiko to set up a committee, led by Sir Keith Hancock, to consider constitutional reform. After three months of intensive discussion during the summer of 1954, Hancock's conference recommended the internal reconstruction of the government of Buganda and substantial changes, with active African participation, in the protectorate's central institutions. The Kabakaship was to be transformed into a "constitutional monarchy," and it was only on this basis that Mutesa was allowed to return home in October 1955. It is very significant, therefore, that church figures, in Uganda and in Britain, helped to ensure Baganda cooperation with this scheme.[46]

Soon after the deportation, Archbishop Fisher told the Baganda delegation that the Christian attitude was, for the moment, to leave aside the question of Mutesa as one on which no agreement could be reached and to turn instead to other issues. Two key members of the delegation, Mulira and Makumbi, later appointed to Hancock's committee, were active Protestant communicants, ready to listen to the counsel of their Anglican leaders. In addition to the archbishop, Max Warren; John Lawrence, the chairman of the CMS Executive; and Roland Oliver, then best known as a historian of the East African church, all gave them the same advice.[47] The crisis had become a "morally tortuous dispute," and Warren recommended "taking the spotlight as much as possible off the Kabaka." Warren suspected the Colonial Office of using Mutesa's marital problems, even rumors of incest and homosexuality, to discredit him.[48]

The Anglican authorities realized they were largely responsible for the Baganda's readiness to pursue a constitutional line, so they felt obliged to do all they could to make Hancock's work succeed. When Mulira and Makumbi resigned from the constitutional committee over a dispute with Cohen about the scope of the inquiry and the composition of the team, both Fisher in London and Brown in Uganda attempted to intervene. Fisher wrote to Cohen urging him to compromise, while Brown wrote to Mulira to explain Cohen's posi-

46. Low, "The Buganda Mission, 1954," is a detailed analysis of the constitutional settlement, but it does not discuss the role of the church. Ward, "The Church of Uganda," devotes only limited space to the constitutional conference and does not draw on the evidence provided by Hancock's personal papers.

47. LP, Fisher Papers, vol. 150, fo. 89: Fisher to Hopkinson, 2 Feb. 1954 and fo. 200-201: Warren to Fisher, 30 Apr. 1954.

48. NA, 02 Bp 110/9 (CMS London — General Secretary vol. I): Warren to Brown, 8 Nov. 1954; CMS, AF 59 G3 A7/8 (Kabaka deposed): Warren to Palin, 6 Jan. 1954; LP, Fisher Papers, vol. 150, fo. 71: Warren to Fisher, 21 Jan. 1954.

tion.[49] A fellow academic informed Hancock that Max Warren had "sent out the warmest and most whole-hearted commendation of you and your mission and has urged on all concerned the maximum degree of co-operation."[50]

In the months before Hancock started work, he inquired of "church opinion" on the constitutional matters he was to address. His relationship with Warren became especially close, and he spent over two hours with him before deciding to accept the post.[51] In Buganda itself, Hancock stayed in Bishop Brown's guest house on Namirembe Hill and held his meetings in the cathedral grounds. That Namirembe was the delegation's preference aptly symbolized the role of the Anglican Church in the whole constitutional process.[52] Hancock's contact with local Christians helped inform his eventual recommendation that Mutesa should return, since "the Christian tradition among the masses is deep and carries with it a deep fund of . . . loyalty to Britain." Hancock later told the CMS that "Christian belief in Uganda more than anything else has averted catastrophe and made possible a peaceful solution."[53]

That the church played a vital role in the conclusion of a new, highly significant constitutional settlement is incontestable. The settlement helped pave the way for Mutesa's reinstatement and helped the government save face, since it could argue that it created a "new situation" in which its former ruling no longer applied.[54] The deciding factor in the Kabaka case was nevertheless a rather different issue, over which the church had rather less influence.

The Influence of the Church on the State

Historians have often found it difficult to assess the impact of domestic influences on colonial decisions in the decolonization process.[55] The state, like the church, was itself divided, and the different elements within it did not neces-

49. LP, Fisher Papers, vol. 150, fo. 200-201: Warren to Fisher, 30 Apr. 1954, and fo. 217-18: Fisher to Cohen, 15 May 1954; ICS, HANC/1-1, fo. 15a: Cohen to Hancock, 22 Apr. 1954.

50. ICS, HANC/1-3, fo. 42: Philips to Hancock, 24 Mar. 1954.

51. ICS, HANC/1-3, fo. 24: Hancock to Stuart, 11 Mar. 1954; NA, 02 Bp 110/9 (CMS London — General Secretary vol. I): Warren to Brown, 25 Feb. 1954.

52. ICS, HANC/1-1, fo. 1: Hancock to Cohen, 25 Feb. 1954.

53. ICS, HANC/1-28, fo. 6: Hancock to Lennox-Boyd, 28 Oct. 1954, and HANC/1-29, fo. 88: Hancock to Price, 18 Nov. 1955.

54. *Hansard,* 16 Nov. 1954.

55. For example, J. G. Darwin, *The End of the British Empire: The Historical Debate* (Oxford, 1991), chap. 2. For an interesting analysis of left-wing pressure groups and decolonization, see Stephen Howe, *Anticolonialism in British Politics: The Left and the End of Empire, 1918-1964* (Oxford, 1993).

sarily share the same outlook or succumb to the same pressures. Governor Cohen, a Labour appointee, was distrusted by many in the Colonial Office, not least by successive Conservative secretaries of state, Lyttelton and Lennox-Boyd. On a number of issues, most notably the development of Uganda as an African state, Cohen struggled against an attempt by London to limit the pace and scope of change.[56] While Cohen felt concerned about "liberal opinion" in Britain, including the church, the Colonial Office was far less worried about its potential power.

By August 1954 Cohen was beginning to reconsider his view that the Kabaka's deposition could never be reversed. The constitutional committee had agreed to the principle of Uganda as a unitary state, with Buganda participating fully in the protectorate government. Restoring Mutesa to his throne might guarantee acceptance of the new proposals, while his status as a "constitutional monarch" would make him less of a threat than before. Bishop Brown was among those who now advised him that for the sake of political expediency, he should allow the Kabaka back. Cohen was, moreover, becoming increasingly fearful of a campaign by the British public on the Kabaka's behalf. Hancock had told him privately that he felt the Kabaka should return, and Cohen feared the impact this would have, not least in missionary circles, once it was known at home. He warned the Colonial Office that moderate elements of public opinion, namely, the church, the *Times,* some Labour MPs, and certain academics, were likely to exercise a powerful influence if they all took the same line.[57]

Archbishop Fisher, for his part, wrote a very long and strongly worded letter to Lennox-Boyd urging that the Kabaka be restored. Fisher argued that his continued exclusion would "antagonise Africans all over the continent" and that "the great bulk of Christian opinion here at home would deplore it."[58] Representatives of the Conference of Missionary Societies and the International Missionary Council gave similar warnings that if Mutesa's exile were not revoked, they might press publicly for his reinstatement.[59] Eventually, on

56. For an outline of the dispute, see D. Goldsworthy, ed., *The Conservative Government and the End of Empire, 1951-57,* British Documents on the End of Empire Project, vol. 3, part 2 (London, 1994), pp. 254-57. See also P. N. Kakembo, "Colonial Office Policy and the Origins of Decolonisation in Uganda, 1940-1956" (D.Phil. thesis, University of Dalhousie, 1989), chap. 3.

57. PRO, CO 822/751 (Situation in Buganda: The Future of Kabaka Mutesa II), fo. 4: Cohen to Lennox-Boyd, 8 Aug. 1954, and fo. 43: Cohen, "The Buganda Situation," 29 Sept. 1954.

58. PRO, CO 822/751 (Situation in Buganda: The Future of Kabaka Mutesa II), fo. 50A: Fisher to Lennox-Boyd, 23 Oct. 1954.

59. PRO, CO 822/751 (Situation in Buganda: The Future of Kabaka Mutesa II), fo. 49: Gorell Barnes to Lennox-Boyd, 22 Oct. 1954.

6 November 1954, Max Warren, Bishop Stuart, Roland Oliver, and Arthur Creech Jones of the Africa Bureau published a joint letter in the *Times,* calling for "a major measure of reconciliation."[60] By then, however, the state's hand had already been forced by pressures quite external to the church.

The Colonial Office was, from the start, very skeptical about the irresistibility of a Kabaka crusade in Britain. Assistant Undersecretary Gorell Barnes, for instance, did not think it would assume "anything like the proportions of the campaign against Central African Federation, which had been very successfully lived through." Though initially in favor of allowing Mutesa to go back, Lennox-Boyd agreed that public opinion was "not a factor to which excessive importance should be attached."[61] After a series of intense discussions in London and Entebbe, Lennox-Boyd concluded that Mutesa's reinstatement would not, after all, be in the best interests of Uganda or of the British position in Africa as a whole, and that only an unfavorable court judgment would necessitate his return.[62]

The legality of the deposition was challenged by the Baganda in the Ugandan High Court, and judgment was finally issued on 4 November 1954. The government had always justified its action over Mutesa by reference to the Uganda Agreement of 1900, yet the court ruled that it had invoked the wrong article when doing so. Mutesa's deportation would have been fully justified under Article 20, but not under Article 6, as was maintained. Hence the state had, technically speaking, acted in breach of the agreement. Given the importance attached to observing the strict letter of agreements between Britain and her protected states, Lennox-Boyd told the cabinet that "we have no option in the light of these circumstances but to permit Mutesa's return on certain conditions," the implementation of the Namirembe proposals.[63]

Max Warren was summoned to Whitehall to be told the news in person. On hearing of this, Bishop Brown joked that "the next logical step would be to give the General Secretary a seat in the Cabinet!"[64] The church clearly per-

60. *Times,* 6 Nov. 1954.

61. PRO, CO 822/751 (Situation in Buganda: The Future of Kabaka Mutesa II), fo. 6: Discussion on the question of Mutesa's return, 16 Aug. 1954.

62. PRO, Cab 129/71, C(54) 317: Memorandum by the Secretary of State for the Colonies, 20 Oct. 1954. For an account of Lennox-Boyd's attitude to the Kabaka question, see P. Murphy, *Alan Lennox-Boyd: A Biography* (London, 1999), pp. 142-48. For the attitudes of the colonial administration, see D. Brown and M. V. Brown, eds., *Looking Back at the Uganda Protectorate: Recollections of District Officers* (Dalkeith, 1996).

63. PRO, Cab 129/71, C(54) 336: Memorandum by the Secretary of State for the Colonies, 9 Nov. 1954.

64. NA, 02 Bp 110/9 (CMS London — General Secretary vol. I): Warren to Brown, 16 Nov. 1954, and Brown to Warren, 23 Nov. 1954.

ceived that it had been instrumental in persuading the government to allow the Kabaka back. In reality, however, though Cohen, on the ground, was acutely aware of his reliance on church support and took church opinion very seriously indeed, the Colonial Office, where the power really lay, had been quite prepared, if necessary, to ignore it altogether.

The Church's Role in Retrospect

A number of factors informed the church's action over the Kabaka affair, not least its own sense of historic responsibility. As the crisis developed, moreover, the church became greatly impressed by the determination of the Baganda to secure the reinstatement of their king. Bishop Brown informed Fisher that "almost all the Baganda can think of nothing else . . . better relations and progress in understanding will be impossible until he [Mutesa] has returned."[65] The Native Anglican Church had been aware of its gradual decline over a long period, and the Kabaka crisis highlighted just how weak it had become. To the Church Synod of 1954, Bishop Brown declared that the church was probably weaker than it had been at any time in the previous thirty years.[66] There was a marked resurgence of "traditional" religious belief, as groups of diviners announced that the powers of their fetishes and of the old hero gods would restore their king. A man claiming to be possessed by the spirit of Kibuka, the god of war, drew huge crowds to hear him in the outskirts of Kampala, and a "Mutesa Psalm" was published in the local press.[67]

There was also the issue of Anglican rivalry with the Catholic Church. Protestant-Catholic tensions had a long history in Buganda, and Warren had "no doubt whatever that the Roman Catholics are jockeying for position . . . seeking to exploit the situation in their own favour." The Anglican authorities feared that if a new Kabaka were chosen, he might convert to Roman Catholicism. Alternatively, the Catholics might lobby the Colonial Office on Mutesa's behalf and then take the credit for his return.[68] The Anglican Church was

65. LP, Fisher Papers, vol. 150, fo. 268: Brown to Fisher, 18 July 1954.

66. LP, MS 3815, L. W. Brown Papers, 1953-55, fo. 24: Charge to Synod, 5 May 1954. For a detailed analysis of the church's growth and decline, see J. V. Taylor, *The Growth of the Church in Buganda: An Attempt at Understanding* (London, 1958).

67. For an overview of traditional religious activity in the period, see F. B. Welbourn, *Religion and Politics in Uganda, 1952-1962* (Nairobi, 1965), pp. 42-43. See also PRO, CO 822/1191 (Neo-Paganism in Uganda).

68. LP, Fisher Papers, vol. 150, fo. 196: Warren to Fisher, 30 Apr. 1954, and fo. 207: Warren to Fisher, 6 May 1954.

most concerned to retain the initiative, hence its commitment to bringing about a satisfactory end to the dispute.

As Ward has discussed, constitutional change in Buganda, especially the participation of Catholics in Hancock's discussions, appeared finally to offer real opportunities for Catholic advance. In the event, however, the Kabaka used his powers in the new settlement to ensure that the old Protestant elite continued to dominate Buganda's political scene. Ward has shown how this appeal by the Kabaka to a traditional Protestant establishment was hardly what the church needed. The Kabaka was more of a liability to the Protestant cause, given the public scandal surrounding his private life.[69] Bishop Brown even considered Mutesa "one of the main foci militating against real religion and Christianity among the Baganda."[70]

Hence the Anglican Church in Buganda remained intimately associated with a regime that was "Christian" in name only, promoting values and practices of which it profoundly disapproved. Mutesa soon ousted from power any chiefs who had not proved sufficiently loyal, including many who had remained faithful to the church.[71] Key Protestant leaders like Mulira also lost official favor. From the initial announcement of the Hancock proposals and the decision that Mutesa could return if they were accepted, it took eleven months of constitutional wrangling before the Kabaka finally flew back home. As Mulira later complained, because of all the delays "the extremists jumped at us and threw us out . . . they emerged heroes at the expense of what we had done."[72]

By the time Mutesa arrived in October 1955, a new government of Buganda was in power, with a far less sympathetic attitude toward the Anglican Church. There were not, significantly, any ecclesiastical witnesses to the new Buganda Agreement. Cohen left the matter for the Baganda to decide, and was told by Kintu, their new chief minister, that it would "not be appropriate" for the bishop to sign.[73] Brown felt this was "all for the best," though his archdeacon feared that "our clergy and others will find it hard to understand."[74] The church's intervention in the Kabaka crisis, motivated at least in

69. Ward, "The Church of Uganda," pp. 436-43.

70. PRO, CO 822/751 (Situation in Buganda: The Future of Kabaka Mutesa II), fo. 4: Cohen to Lennox-Boyd, 8 Aug. 1954.

71. LP, Fisher Papers, vol. 182, fo. 78-82: Brown to Warren, 27 Dec. 1955.

72. D. W. Nabudere, *Imperialism and Revolution in Uganda* (London, 1980), p. 162.

73. PRO, CO 822/909 (Inauguration of the 1955 Buganda Agreement), fo. 101A: Cohen to Lennox-Boyd, 19 Oct. 1955.

74. LP, MS 3781, L. W. Brown Diaries, Oct. 1955–May 1957, fo. 1: 18 Oct. 1954; CMS, AF 59 G3 A7/8 (Kabaka deposed): Palin to Bewes, 19 Oct. 1955.

part by a desire to improve its own position, seemed to have backfired. The Anglican Church appeared in a weaker position than ever, not only compromised by the Buganda regime but also, crucially, identified even more closely with the colonial state.

Conclusion

Soon after the crisis broke, Bishop Brown thought it "likely that we shall be able to make the whole position of the Church in relation to the State much clearer as a result of these events." Four years later, however, Brown was still complaining that the myth of his political influence had not yet been exploded.[75] When the Kabaka returned home, the links between Namirembe and Government House had seemed stronger than ever. Incidents like the holding of Hancock's discussions at Namirembe had done little to dispel the notion that Anglicanism was the "established church."

The Anglican Church's primary contribution to the resolution of the Kabaka crisis was in pushing for a constitutional settlement and in securing Baganda support for it. Thus the church played a significant, if indirect, role in defining what it meant for Uganda to be a "primarily African country," and in providing the constitutional context for Mutesa's reinstatement once the court case had made it inevitable. However, though some sectors of the Baganda were profoundly grateful to the church and mission leaders who had advised them to act constitutionally, the settlement, with its conditions and restrictions, was never popular among the Baganda at large.[76] For most Baganda, Mutesa's return had remained the crucial issue, an issue on which the church authorities, in their desire to steer a middle course and mediate between all sides involved in the dispute, had failed to take a strong public stand.

The Namirembe settlement was, moreover, gradually discredited, proving unable to offer a lasting formula for the development of Uganda as a unitary state. The problems of defining Buganda's position within a wider national framework were soon to resurface, and the church, once again, found itself deeply implicated in the struggle.[77] Nor was the church immune from the rise

75. NA, 02 Bp 110/9 (CMS London — General Secretary vol. I): Brown to Warren, 22 Dec. 1953; CMS, AF AL 1950-59 BRJ-COG (Annual letters): L. W. Brown, 27 Aug. 1957.

76. LP, Fisher Papers, vol. 164, fo. 15-17: Note on meeting with the Kabaka, 24 Feb. 1955.

77. See, for example, G. N. Uzoigwe, ed., *Uganda: The Dilemma of Nationhood* (New York and London, 1982), and Dan M. Mudoola, *Religion, Ethnicity, and Politics in Uganda* (Kampala, 1992).

in racial tensions, and it had to contend with its own black-white divides, as suspicions of its protectorate links continued. Baganda delegates to the Church Synod of 1956, for example, refused to allow Uganda to join a regional conference on Christian literature, fearing it was "a ruse to get the Church behind the government's secret plan for . . . federation."[78]

Quite apart from attracting African hostility, the Anglican Church's identification with the state was damaging in other, more subtle ways. Bishop Brown was very concerned about the secular, materialistic tone of most expressions of government policy. As he put it to the chief secretary, "every appearance of self-sufficiency on government's part confirms the people's drift from God and appears to seal it with government approval."[79] There seemed to be little reciprocity in the church-state relationship. Though the state had benefited greatly from the church's restraint over the deportation, the church appeared to be progressively sidelined by the colonial regime. This ambiguity in church-state relations, with the church remaining closely identified, though growing increasingly uneasy, with the state, was to prove a dangerous legacy in the postcolonial era.[80]

That the church was not the "handmaiden of colonization" is now widely accepted.[81] Nor, it seems, was it the "handmaiden of decolonization." Previous accounts of the church's response to the deportation have stressed the extent of its support for the Baganda people, and assumed that its intervention played a vital role in securing the return of their king.[82] Though future research may bring new evidence to light, the material studied so far suggests that this picture needs some modification. In fact, in this highly complicated crisis of the end of empire, British church and mission leaders felt able to give only qualified support to the cause of their colonial followers. Even when they did intervene on their behalf, they could exercise only limited influence on

78. LP, Fisher Papers, vol. 182, fo. 107: Brown to Fisher, 23 May 1956.

79. NA, 02 Bp 148/16 (Governor and Governor-General 1953-60): Brown to Thornley, 22 Oct. 1954.

80. For the problems of the postindependence church, see Kevin Ward, "The Church of Uganda amidst Conflict," in *Religion and Politics in East Africa: The Period since Independence,* ed. H. B. Hansen and M. Twaddle (London, 1995), pp. 72-105. For parallels elsewhere in Africa, see E. Fasholé-Luke et al., eds., *Christianity in Independent Africa* (London, 1978), pt. I, "Religious and Secular Structures."

81. See, for example, A. Porter, "Religion and Empire: British Expansion in the Long Nineteenth Century 1780-1914," *Journal of Imperial and Commonwealth History* 20 (1992): 370-90.

82. Mutibwa, "The Church of Uganda and the Movements for Political Independence 1952-1962"; Carpenter, *Archbishop Fisher — His Life and Times;* and Ward, "The Church of Uganda."

the colonial state. Though the Kabaka was finally allowed back to his kingdom, the church was not, ultimately, responsible for the decision. Nor were the repercussions favorable for the church. George Grimshaw, regional secretary for the CMS in East Africa, had feared that his society's intervention might "put the Church right back into that place of inextricable muddle in its relationships, both political and social, with government and the Kabaka."[83] Mutesa's return did, in the event, have precisely that effect.

83. CMS, AF 59 AFE AM1/1 (Regional Administration in East Africa): Grimshaw to Warren, 22 May 1954.

CHAPTER 11

Moral Re-Armament in Africa in the Era of Decolonization

PHILIP BOOBBYER

In exploring how Christian missions adapted to the end of empire, it is important to consider the experience of the Moral Re-Armament (MRA) movement. Growing from Christian evangelical roots, MRA evolved into a movement that, while retaining an underlying Christian vision, also embraced people of all faiths and sometimes none: a fact that evidently set it apart from most Christian missions. In spite of this, MRA's work deserves inclusion in a modern history of missions.

MRA was launched in 1938 as the program of the Oxford Group, an influential interwar movement of Christian renewal led by an American pastor, Frank Buchman (1878-1961). Its work was permeated by practices that reflected a particular tradition of Christian spirituality, and was in the postwar era generally led by people who interpreted their work in Christian terms. Although MRA did not seek to spread Christianity through the framework of the church, it took seriously the idea that God's will might "be done on earth," and sought to make moral and spiritual values central in national and international life.

Buchman admired the Scottish scientist and religious writer Henry Drummond (1851-97), and MRA's work can be interpreted as a practical expression of his vision. Drummond had called for a class of mission work that was "not wholly absorbed with specific charges, or ecclesiastical progress, or

---

The author wishes to thank James Baynard-Smith, David Birmingham, Peter Everington, Alisa Hamilton, Charles Piguet, Brian Stanley, and Charis Waddy for their comments on drafts of this article.

the inculcation of Western creeds, but whose outlook goes forth to the nation as a whole." He envisaged a kind of missionary who would place the accent not on a church "but on the coming of the Kingdom of God."[1] Buchman and his followers sought to foster a new kind of spiritually inspired leadership. Much of their work involved trying to introduce a dynamic of repentance and forgiveness into international affairs. Recent scholarship has highlighted MRA's contribution to the process of reconciliation between France and Germany after the Second World War and in Rhodesia-Zimbabwe in 1975-80.[2] MRA was active in several African countries after 1945. It contributed to the transitions to independence of Tunisia and Morocco, and to tribal reconciliation in the Congo in 1960. In Kenya it was involved in seeking to offer a Christian response to the Mau Mau rebellion and encouraging national reconciliation in the run-up to the country's first free elections. The purpose of this chapter is to outline the key features of the "dialogue of decolonisation"[3] which MRA promoted in these African countries, and thereby to illustrate some of the characteristic features of its mission.

MRA's Christian Origins

Buchanan's ideas grew out of the evangelical tradition from which he came. He owed a lot to the spirituality of the YMCA and the Keswick Convention. He believed that Christians could receive "luminous thoughts and leadings from the Holy Spirit," which he called "guidance."[4] He also challenged people to measure their lives against four absolute moral standards: honesty, purity, unselfishness, and love.

Buchman's work in Oxford after 1921 was initially known as the First Century Christian Fellowship, and after 1928 as the Oxford Group.[5] The move-

1. Henry Drummond, "The Problem of Foreign Missions," in *The New Evangelism and other Papers* (London, 1899), pp. 121-22, 130.

2. Edward Luttwak, "Franco-German Reconciliation: The Overlooked Role of the Moral Re-Armament Movement," and Ron Kraybill, "Transition from Rhodesia to Zimbabwe: The Role of Religious Actors," both in *Religion: The Missing Dimension of Statecraft*, ed. Douglas Johnston and Cynthia Sampson (New York, 1994), pp. 37-63, 222-33.

3. "Dialogue of decolonisation" was a phrase coined by French political journalist Jean Rous to describe MRA's work; see Michael Henderson, *The Forgiveness Factor* (Salem, Oreg., 1996), pp. 38-39.

4. MRA (Initiatives of Change) UK archive, Dial House, Whitbourne, UK (hereafter MRA archive), File "Frank Buchman — Personal Work 1917-1928," Buchman to Sam Shoemaker, 26 Apr. 1920, p. 2.

5. Garth Lean, *Frank Buchman: A Life* (London, 1985), p. 138.

ment spread through house parties, conferences, and personal contact. Humphrey Milford's *What Is the Oxford Group?* (1933) included chapters entitled "Sin," "Sharing for Confession and Witness," "Surrender," "Restitution," "Guidance," and "The Four Absolutes,"[6] and these same elements passed on into MRA.

Buchman was not a typical evangelical, and he came to appreciate non-Christian religious traditions. He met Gandhi in India in 1915 and corresponded with him for years, and kept in touch with him through mutual friends, such as the missionary C. F. Andrews and the Anglican metropolitan of India, Foss Wescott, both of whom had good links with the Oxford Group.[7] Buchman remarked on Gandhi's qualities of "sainthood"[8] and seems to have felt that some missionary activity was too Western in orientation. On a visit to China in 1917-18 he clashed with the foreign missionary community over what he saw as its isolation from the Chinese leadership.[9] He hoped to influence the country through the nationalist Chinese, and he got to know Sun Yat-sen quite well.

Buchman's early involvement in social and political issues is manifest in a 1929 Oxford Group visit to South Africa. The team of thirty, including Buchman, arranged a series of house parties at which the bitterness between English- and Dutch-speaking South Africans, following the Boer War, was the big issue. The visit had a considerable effect on political scientist Edgar Brookes, a professor at Pretoria University, who had an interest in the "native question" and became an early pioneer of racial reconciliation.[10]

Buchman was always "consciously shaping his movement so that it resonated with the currents of the time,"[11] and the Oxford Group emphasized that "modernity" and Christianity need not be incompatible.[12] It offered a "relational spirituality" where distinctions between clergy and laity were to a large extent broken down.[13] The group had substantial support from some within the church. In 1933 the bishop of London formally commissioned five hundred "life-changers" for mission work in London.[14] Amongst Oxford

6. The Layman with a Notebook, *What Is the Oxford Group?* (London, 1933).

7. Lean, pp. 115, 143, 150, 408.

8. Lean, pp. 45, 120, 408.

9. Lean, pp. 50, 57-58.

10. Lean, p. 142.

11. Ian Randall, "'We All Need Constant Change': The Oxford Group and Mission in Europe in the 1930s," *European Journal of Theology* 9, no. 2 (2000): 179.

12. *What Is the Oxford Group?* p. 130.

13. Ian Randall, *Evangelical Experiences* (Carlisle, 1999), pp. 245-46.

14. Randall, "Constant Change," p. 181.

theologians, L. W. Grensted, Oriel Professor of the Philosophy of Religion, and the prominent New Testament scholar B. H. Streeter were much involved.

MRA as an Ideology

Buchman dared people to "think for continents" or to think on a large scale.[15] His 1930s speeches indicate a man searching for a Christian concept of national and international life. In 1935 he declared that he could see Switzerland "a prophet among the nations, and a peacemaker in the international family," and suggested that "vital Christianity" might become the controlling force of the state in Switzerland through "individual responsibility to God." The reference to Switzerland's potential role reflected Buchman's growing interest and vision for international life. In the same speech he spoke of "God-controlled supernationalism," suggesting an emerging belief that international society itself might be guided by the wisdom of the Holy Spirit.[16] Elsewhere he suggested that the League of Nations was failing because it was not "God-arched."[17] He evidently saw the Oxford Group as trying to model "supernationalism," and he described those who attended the Oxford house party of 1935 as a "family of many nations."[18]

MRA was launched in May 1938. Speaking in Visby, Sweden, that year, Buchman called for a "spiritual revolution" in the life of every nation.[19] At the first World Assembly for MRA in Switzerland in September 1938, he stated that nations were sometimes given new spiritual direction by prophetic individuals. He asked: "If this is true of one man, what can happen if a group of people in every nation carry through the illumination and give a whole new public opinion?" A new kind of leadership was needed: "inspired statesmen, guided not alone by human wisdom, but by that added help that sees and recognises the Supreme Plan."[20] Clearly, Buchman saw a role for MRA. He envisaged small groups working to encourage new leadership and spiritual revolution in their countries and, as part of the wider MRA fellowship, to foster a new international society.

15. Theophil Spoerri, *Dynamic Out of Silence: Frank Buchman's Relevance Today* (London, 1976), p. 32.

16. Frank Buchman, *Remaking the World* (London, 1961), p. 18.

17. Lean, p. 244.

18. Buchman, *Remaking the World,* p. 13.

19. Buchman, *Remaking the World,* p. 55.

20. Buchman, *Remaking the World,* pp. 60-61.

They were to be what one of Buchman's biographers called "teams as formative cells of history."[21]

Buchman's emphasis on "revolution" was an example of the way he sought to inject the language of the day with Christian meaning. He called extremists of right and left to turn to a spiritual revolution, and at the same time he used their fervor as a challenge to Christians. Another word he sought to give a new content to was "ideology." After initially using the word in a negative context, Buchman concluded that Christianity, to the extent that it was an all-embracing worldview, was also an ideology.[22] From July 1943 he began to describe MRA as an ideology, suggesting that whereas communism and fascism were essentially negatives forces, built on "divisive materialism and confusion," MRA had the positive message of restoring God's leadership to national life.[23] In June 1945, while in San Francisco during the United Nations Conference on International Organisation, he declared: "Today we see three ideologies battling for control. There is Fascism, and Communism, and then there is that great other ideology which is the centre of Christian democracy — Moral Re-Armament."[24] MRA thus emerged from the war, in Buchman's mind, as a kind of Christian ideology.

At the center of this ideology was an emphasis on the cross. In April 1946 Buchman called for a "revolution under the Cross of Christ that can transform the world."[25] MRA can partly be seen as Buchman's attempt to universalize a personal spiritual experience of the cross, and to show its relevance to international as well as personal life. Speaking to colleagues at Garmisch-Partenkirchen in Germany, he stated that at Keswick, England (in 1908), he had been stirred by a sermon on the cross by the evangelist Jessie Penn-Lewis. He had experienced the "recuperative and restorative processes of God." Moreover, he declared that MRA's future lay "in such moments occurring in the future in different lives, in different countries, the outcome sometimes being illustrated in national circumstances."[26]

Buchman's emphasis on "experience" is also evident in his understanding of the kingdom of God: "The Kingdom of God as symbolic of a definiteness of experience directly observable by somebody else, but not easily described. What is observable is a peace, a confidence, a recovery of freedom, and spontaneity of thought, of will and of nerve. It is not joinable. You have to experi-

21. Spoerri, p. 175.
22. Lean, p. 320.
23. Lean, p. 141.
24. Buchman, *Remaking the World,* p. 146.
25. Buchman, *Remaking the World,* pp. 57, 148.
26. Lean, p. 406.

ence it for yourself."[27] This emphasis on experience rather than doctrine was probably what allowed him to see his work as essentially Christian. On the basis of a shared experience, Christians could work closely with people of other faiths. Gabriel Marcel, the French philosopher who much admired MRA, suggested that "what we are dealing with here is not a theology . . . and still less a philosophy; it is an experience."[28]

The fact that MRA included people of different faiths and that in its public expression Christian terminology was in some countries played down, meant it ran the risk of being interpreted as offering a kind of "natural" religion that was simply a common denominator of all the major faiths, or as one historian suggests, "undoctrinal moralism."[29] Such perspectives, however, miss the spiritual agenda of MRA and the implicit, and sometimes explicit, emphasis that Buchman always placed on the cross. Peter Howard, MRA's leader following Buchman's death, was no different. In a play he co-wrote on African nationalism, *The Hurricane* (1960), the character who represented the authors' opinions stated that what Africa most needed was the blood of Jesus Christ: "It cleanses us from all sin. Nothing short of that experience can touch the root of evil in your country or in mine."[30] It was assumed that Christians, while working alongside people of other traditions, would remain true to their own.

An African Strategy

In its postwar strategy MRA focused on healing the wounds of war. There was a systematic attempt to build bridges between France and Germany. In 1946 members of Buchman's team in Switzerland established a large conference center at Caux-sur-Montreux, and between 1946 and 1950 many French and German citizens, including large numbers of politicians, industrialists, and trades unionists, attended the conferences there. French and German visitors to Caux were encouraged to share their fears and resentments. It was hoped that a conversation involving expressions of forgiveness and repentance would emerge.[31]

Many features of MRA's Franco-German initiative were replicated in its

27. Lean, pp. 406-7.

28. Gabriel Marcel, ed., *Fresh Hope for the World* (London, 1960), pp. 6-8.

29. Adrian Hastings, *A History of English Christianity, 1920-1985* (London, 1986), p. 201.

30. Peter Howard and Alan Thornhill, *The Hurricane* (London, 1960), pp. 42-43.

31. Luttwak, pp. 47-50.

African work. From the late 1940s onward, efforts were made to bring African leaders and students to Caux in order to draw them into a conversation designed to encourage reconciliation between Europeans and Africans. At the same time, MRA's thinking about Africa was specific to the region and the context of the cold war. It saw itself as competing with communism for the minds of the future leadership of Africa. F. S. McEwen, the national secretary of the National Council of Nigeria and the Cameroons, visiting Caux in the mid-1950s, stated: "There is today a new scramble for Africa. The old scramble was for nations to own parts of Africa. The new scramble is for the minds of men. The world is asking which way Africa will go." In *The World Rebuilt* (1951), Peter Howard wrote that Africans were enthusiastic about what MRA offered: "When Africans see an ideology at work which fights for both East and West, an ideology based on change for the white people as well as for every other race, they accept it wholeheartedly."[32]

The MRA work in Africa was designed to answer the Western arrogance, African bitterness, and general moral weakness on which, it was believed, communism thrived, and to offer an ideology in which the ideas of God's guidance, absolute moral standards, and national reconciliation were central. Caux conferences sought to develop a "dialogue of repentance." Speaking there in 1950, Hugh Elliott, a member of the British Colonial Service in Nigeria, repented of a long-standing demand for gratitude from Africans for what colonialists like him had contributed in Africa: "I begin to see the wrongs white people have done to coloured people in many parts of the world and I am sorry for them."[33] Similarly, at Caux in the summer of 1952, John Seroney, a Kenyan, stated: "I must take this opportunity to apologise to you who come from the countries of Europe for the bitterness I have felt towards you."[34] Taken out of context, such statements appear artificial; however, fifty years later Elliott recalled that his public expression of sorrow was very genuine: "Most of us had to go through quite a big change from our paternalistic good intent to living to make [Africans] great."[35]

MRA's approach to fostering a new African leadership is illustrated by the way it developed a friendship with Nnamdi Azikiwe, president of the National Council of Nigeria and the Cameroons, and later the first president of independent Nigeria. Azikiwe visited London in 1949 for talks with the Colonial Office at a time of considerable unrest in Nigeria. The talks did not go

32. Peter Howard, *The World Rebuilt* (London, 1951), pp. 101-2.

33. Hugh Elliott, quoted in Howard, *The World Rebuilt,* pp. 109-10.

34. MRA archive, "Africa" file, John Seroney, quoted in "The World Assembly for Moral Re-Armament, 1st Aug.–6th Oct., Africa and Caux 1952."

35. Interview with Hugh Elliott, London, 26 Oct. 2000.

well, and he was courted by the communists and given a visa to attend the International Conference on Civil Rights in Prague. At that point he was contacted by Nigerians involved in MRA, and accepted an invitation to Caux. Azikiwe was impressed with Caux, and on his return to London adopted a much more conciliatory attitude to the British government.[36] According to an MRA report, he apologized to British ministers for his previously hostile attitude, and turned down further approaches from communists.[37] He did not visit Prague, and he stayed in contact with MRA in subsequent years. He later said MRA had led him to seek rapprochement with one of his main political opponents,[38] and in February 1959 he showed the MRA film *Freedom* to Ghanaian Prime Minister Nkrumah while he was on a state visit to Nigeria.[39]

Azikiwe was a Christian, but many non-Christians visited Caux, and there was no attempt to convert them. The aim was rather to encourage a change of heart. The Tolon Na, the Muslim president of the Northern Territories Council of Ghana, was profoundly changed by a visit to Caux in 1954. A meeting with Buchman prompted the Tolon Na to return to his schools all the textbooks he had stolen and make a series of apologies for wrongs he had committed.[40] In effect, the Tolon Na became a better Muslim. MRA attracted the interest of a number of prominent Muslims. Following an MRA meeting with King Mohammed V of Morocco after independence, the king cabled Buchman: "Morocco is a fertile ground for the ideas of Moral Re-Armament, which are in perfect harmony with the ideas of Islam."[41]

In general, Christian MRA workers, while viewing their work in Christian terms, did not make conversion a priority. They seem to have viewed some missionary work as flawed. The black heroine of *The Hurricane* complained of Westerners who had brought their Bible to her country and tried to force it upon her people,[42] and there was a reference to the hypocrisy of Western Christians in another MRA play, *Freedom*.[43] This did not mean that Buchman and his colleagues lacked a Christian vision for Africa. In a Christmas mes-

36. *Daily Worker,* 8 Dec. 1949; *Times,* 9 Dec. 1949, p. 2; see also *Church Times,* 2 Dec. 1949, p. 803.

37. MRA archive, "Azikiwe" file, unsigned confidential memorandum.

38. *Zik: A Selection from the Speeches of Nnamdi Azikiwe* (Cambridge, 1961), pp. 257-58.

39. *MRA Information Service, News Report,* 3 Feb. 1959; for a summary of some of MRA's work in Nigeria, see "Moral Re-Armament in West Africa," *Times British Colonies Review,* spring 1955, p. 42.

40. Marcel, *Fresh Hope,* pp. 7, 174; Lean, p. 457.

41. Simon Scott Plummer, *MRA Information Service* 16, no. 18 (13 Jan. 1968): 5.

42. Howard and Thornhill, p. 30.

43. *Freedom* (New York, 1956), p. 11.

sage of 1956 Buchman observed that "a Moor came to worship the Babe; Egypt sheltered the Child Jesus and an African carried the Cross to Calvary," and suggested that the "voice of this Africa can speak to every humble heart everywhere."[44] Yet there was clearly an attempt to challenge subtle assumptions of Christian or Western superiority, and to give Africans of all religious traditions a vision of what they could contribute to the world. It was suggested that Africa might have an "answer" for the world,[45] and that there were "great reserves of spiritual power in Africa."[46]

It is hard to generalize about how Christians in MRA viewed what they were doing. The desire to avoid paternalism was clear. Peter Everington, a British Anglican who spent nine years with the Sudan Ministry of Education before deciding to work full-time for MRA, was very impressed by the unconditional religious commitment in many of his Muslim friends. He wished to avoid an "us to them" relationship, where only the Christians had something to give. Part of his work, he believed, was to look for "evidence of the living Christ" in the non-Christian traditions.[47]

Cecil Rose, an Anglican clergyman involved in MRA, suggested that MRA was pioneering a new kind of Christian mission. In the face of the challenge of materialist ideology, it was not sufficient to think solely in terms of the Christianization of non-Christian lands, since this was bound to be a long-term process. The church's immediate task was to help the emerging states "lay the true foundations of freedom on absolute moral standards and change in people." "The Mission of the Christian Church today is to be a true servant of the nations, offering inspired leadership in their hour of decision. This is the Mission that MRA is pioneering. We believe that this is the leading of the Holy Spirit."[48] On the same theme, the French Catholic Michel Sentis, who worked with MRA in Tunisia, suggests that the work there was influenced by the French White Fathers, whose concept of missionary work emphasized "service" rather than "conversion." Sentis argues that, in the 1950s, MRA was searching for a way toward a missionary concept that emphasized service.[49]

44. Buchman, *Remaking the World,* p. 233.

45. *Report on Moral Re-Armament* (London, 1955), p. 91; Peter Howard, *Frank Buchman's Secret* (London, 1961), p. 51.

46. Stephen Foot, *Africa — Choice for a Continent* (London, 1954), p. 25.

47. Interview between Peter Everington and Philip Boobbyer, Tirley Garth, 6 Oct. 2000.

48. Rev. C. H. Rose, "MRA in Non-Christian Lands," two-page document, n.d., in possession of Peter Everington.

49. Letter from Michel Sentis to author, 13 Nov. 2000.

Freedom

Before 1939 the Oxford Group began to use sketches and plays, and this continued in Britain after the war with the purchase and use of the Westminster Theatre in London.[50] In fact, plays and musicals became central to MRA's whole global strategy after 1945; the MRA team was fortunate to have some gifted writers and musicians in its fellowship. In general, MRA productions had an easily discernible moral or religious message. The idea was that audiences might be awakened by drama in a way that direct preaching could not achieve.

In the summer of 1955 an MRA World Mission, the Statesmen's Mission, visited eighteen countries on four continents, including Africa, and was the guest of governments in eleven of the countries.[51] Its central instrument was a play, *The Vanishing Island,* a musical satire on the cold war. The cast of 244 from twenty-eight countries included Africans from Ghana, Nigeria, Rhodesia, Kenya, South Africa, Egypt, and Tunisia.[52] That same summer a delegation of Africans, including members of Parliament, students, and trades union leaders, visited Caux. Buchman suggested they write a play that would "speak to the world."[53] The result was *Freedom,* written mainly by Mannaseh Moerane, vice-president of the African Teachers of South Africa; John Amata, a student leader from Ibadan University in Nigeria; and the Honorable Karbo, a member of Parliament from Ghana.[54]

Freedom takes place in an imaginary African state, Bokondo, at a time when colonial rule is threatened by rising nationalism. At the end of the play the most powerful nationalist leader of Bokondo, Mutanda, apologizes to the colonial administrator, Roland, for his hatred. Roland, in turn, asks forgiveness for thinking he knew best, and decides not to introduce an unpopular tax. The king (Obong) of Bokondo acclaims the new spiritual revolution brought into the country by his chief minister, Adamu, and calls for a "revolution of the heart":

> MUTANDA: This is a day to right all that is wrong. Mr Roland, I certainly have been a thorn in your flesh.
>
> ROLAND: *(Coming forward)* I expect there have been faults on both sides.
>
> MUTANDA: All these years I have hated you and called you the enemy of

50. D. W. Bebbington, *Evangelicalism in Modern Britain* (London, 1989), p. 238; Lean, p. 340.

51. Lean, pp. 478-80; Buchman, *Remaking the World,* p. 219.

52. Agnes Leakey Hofmeyr, *Beyond Violence* (Johannesburg, 1990), p. 77.

53. MRA archive, "Africa" file; Buchman, *Remaking the World,* p. 238; John Amata, 18 Aug. 1956 Afternoon Meeting.

54. Eva Rickets, *Light on the Horizon* (Upton-on-Severn, 1995), pp. 66-67.

my people. I do not forget the wounds of my people, but hatred and bitterness can not heal those wounds. Please, will you forgive me?

ROLAND: But, Mutanda, I can assure you that there has been nothing personal about our relationship. . . .

ADAMU: Mr Roland, is that not where the trouble lies? We have been so blinded by our own politics and points of view that we have not been able to see one another as people at all.

MUTANDA: Mr Roland, you've always regarded me as a revolutionary, and you're right. Today I'm more of a revolutionary than ever. But if we miss that bigger revolution that changes the hearts of men, we miss everything. We need a revolution that is far wider, in which you and I can stand together and change the world — starting with ourselves.

ROLAND: Starting with ourselves? Your honesty and courage have made me very much ashamed, and I have been thinking of what you said to me two days ago. I and my people have handed out material benefits. We have reaped power and possessions for ourselves, but we have lost men's hearts because we have always been so sure we knew best. Forgive me. I and my country need to change. And we will change. I am sorry, Your Majesty.

MRS PALAVER: What is to happen about this tax?

ROLAND: Yes, I would like to say something about that. Do you know, one of the reasons that I pushed that plan so much was because it was a brain child of my own. Your Majesty, may I leave it in your hands and those of your ministers and Mr Mutanda here and Mr Palaver to draw up a plan together that you feel to be in the best interests of the country? And may I have your permission to withdraw my own proposals. . . .

OBONG: My dear sons and daughters. God never planned a divided world for us. We brought division into our family life, our national life, when we stopped listening to Him. The chick that is nearest the feet of the hen eats the fattest worms. We are like chicks that have strayed from the mother hen. We have refused to listen to the Voice of God.

Now I see a new age planned on God's guidance. Empty hands will be filled with work, empty stomachs with food and empty hearts with an idea that really satisfies. This is the revolution that Adamu has brought us. To be a part of this great uniting force of our age should be the crowning experience of our lives.[55]

55. *Freedom,* pp. 37-38.

Freedom tried to model the kind of reconciliation that MRA wished to encourage. Through watching the play, people would learn how to listen to God, how to apologize, and how to relate their inner struggles to the future of their country. To the extent that it reflected the thinking of Buchman and his team, *Freedom's* message was not specifically "African." On the other hand, the play, and the subsequent film that was shot in Nigeria in 1956-57, captured the rhythm of African life very effectively. It was written with considerable humor, and Africans undoubtedly identified with it.

Freedom was designed to speak to people of different religious traditions. According to Charles Piguet, a Swiss who worked with MRA in the Congo, the film contained an implicitly "evangelical" message, in that spiritual forces were at work throughout the film; yet it was also deliberately designed to be accessible to African animists as well as Christians and Muslims: "This universal message emerged from countries in the process of transformation, situated on the frontier of Islamic and Christian influence, at a time when the natural inclination of their people towards God might easily degenerate into confrontations between extremists."[56] Although the content of *Freedom* was not specifically Christian, Peter Everington recalls that seeing the play in London in 1956 gave him a "deeper Christian experience," and consequently suggests that its use outside Africa "could be regarded as missionary work by Africans in Europe and other continents."[57]

Freedom was shown widely in Africa and other parts of the world, including Little Rock, Arkansas, where racial unrest was attracting worldwide publicity. In January 1958 another MRA film that addressed racial conflict, *The Crowning Experience,* opened in Atlanta, Georgia. It was the first film to play to desegregated audiences there.[58]

Kenya

MRA was much involved in Kenya in the decade before independence in 1963, both in trying to offer a Christian response to the challenge of Mau Mau and in using *Freedom* to try to articulate a vision of national unity.

In early 1953 a retired British RAF group captain, Patrick Foss, who was involved in MRA, proposed to the head of Kenya Prisons Service that an MRA

56. Charles Piguet, *Freedom for Africa,* Caux edition (Caux-sur-Montreux, 1996), pp. 34-35.

57. E-mail letter from Peter Everington to Philip Boobbyer, 23 Nov. 2000.

58. Lean, pp. 499-500.

group could offer an effective rehabilitation program for Mau Mau prisoners. Foss believed the Mau Mau rebellion was inspired by "communist sources" that had sought to exploit feelings of nationalism and inferiority, spread division, and draw on superstition.[59] He thought some missionary activity amongst the dominant Kikuyu people, in which the Mau Mau was most influential, had been too denominational and inward-looking, and had failed to prepare the Kikuyu for the challenge of communism: "When a divisive and materialist ideology is brought among them and clothed with their local colours and tradition, they cannot discriminate. Indeed, many try to embrace both personal Christianity and the Mau Mau." According to Foss, "Christianity as a powerful force, undenominational, and as Democracy's inspired ideology" was what was needed.[60]

Foss's proposal was accepted. A British colonel, Alan Knight, a Kenyan settler who had first encountered the Oxford Group in 1931, became commandant of the Mau Mau camp at Athi River, twenty-three miles from Nairobi, in March 1953. The MRA program began on 1 July.[61] Howard Church, from the Church Missionary Society and also part of the MRA group, was made one of the chaplains, and a prominent African District officer and Kikuyu, David Waruhiu, was also involved.

After a time the MRA group had to rethink some of its underlying assumptions. For the first six months the detainees were very resistant to the intensive reorientation program that had been devised for them. In despair Alan Knight asked God for guidance. He recalled that God said to him: "You are to blame for the hatred because of your arrogance and superior attitude and your selfishness as a white man all these years in this country; apologise to the men in your camp for the way you have lived in their land." Although fearful of what his white friends would think, Knight lined the Mau Mau prisoners up and publicly apologized. It had an extraordinary effect. Some men broke ranks and rushed up to him with enthusiasm.[62] This seems to have led

59. P. S. Foss, "Confidential Memorandum on a Visit to Kajiado," n.d. [early 1953], Patrick Foss Papers (c/o James Baynard-Smith), p. 2; see also MRA archive, "Kenya" file, p. 3, Foss to Buchman, 31 Mar. 1953.

60. MRA archive, "Kenya" file, pp. 1, 5, P. S. Foss, "An Appreciation of Ideological Methods of Tackling the Mau Mau," 14 Apr. 1953.

61. Patrick Foss Papers, p. 1, P. S. Foss. "Memorandum on the Detainees' Rehabilitation Scheme and the Influence of Moral Re-Armament" (9 July 1953); interview between Drs. Joanna Lewis and John Lonsdale with Colonel Alan Knight, 15 Mar. 1994 (in possession of James Baynard-Smith).

62. Alan Knight, quoted in documentary film, Alan Channer, director, *Now, I Call Him Brother,* MRA Productions (London, 1997).

to a change of attitude in a number of Mau Mau prisoners. In July 1954 the *Times* quoted a report that 270 hard-core prisoners had broken their vows to the Mau Mau,[63] and apparently 500 detainees eventually renounced theirs.[64]

While many detainees broke their vows, probably far fewer embraced MRA's Christian ideology. One who did was a former general secretary of a Mau Mau district council, Nahashon Ngare, who went on to work with MRA. In London in 1960, Ngare paid particular tribute to the effect of Knight's apology: "I believed that no white man could change and for that reason I gave my life to fight for the Mau Mau to see that every white man left Africa. . . . When I heard this white man apologise for his superiority towards us Africans I began to think. . . . I changed and lost my hatred and decided to fight with clean hands and a pure heart."[65]

The group at Athi River made use of plays. In August 1955 there were five performances of *The Vanishing Island* at the Kenya National Theatre. Amongst those who attended were the governor, Sir Evelyn Baring, two cabinet ministers, and a number of African chiefs, including Chief Kirito, founder of the loyalist Kikuyu group the Torch Bearers. There was a full presentation of MRA to the 1,400 personnel at the Athi River camp by the cast of the play, with speeches and songs, followed by four former Mau Mau leaders speaking about the change MRA had wrought in them. Two meetings were arranged for Mission leaders to speak to Kikuyu audiences: one at Githunguri, where the MRA group spoke and the chorus sang in the Kikuyu language, was apparently attended by over 7,000 people.[66] Subsequently, in the autumn of 1955, some of the Mau Mau detainees wrote and performed their play *The Answer,* which, like *Freedom,* presented certain easily recognizable character types and their struggle to let go of prejudice and hatred and embrace God's vision for the country.[67]

Not all were convinced by the MRA approach. While a few Athi River detainees clearly changed, some camp administrators believed the Mau Mau converts were simply looking for a way out of the camp.[68] The government

63. See "Christian Attack on Mau Mau," *Times,* 14 July 1954, p. 7.

64. Stephen Foot, "Godless Materialism or Moral Revolution?" *Methodist Recorder,* 27 Jan. 1955, p. 1; Hofmeyr, p. 82.

65. MRA archive, "Kenya" file, Nahashon Ngare, 3 Nov. 1960.

66. MRA archive, "Kenya" file, "MRA World Mission Report no. 14: Visit to Kenya," 24 Aug. 1955; see also MRA archive, "Kenya" file, "MRA World Mission (Document with Report with no. 14): Moral Re-Armament and Mau Mau," 24 Aug. 1955, p. 1.

67. MRA archive, "Kenya" file, *The Answer,* Athi River, Oct. 1955; also see P. S. Foss to Peter Howard and Bremer Hofmeyr, 1 Dec. 1955, in MRA archive, "Kenya" file, p. 1.

68. Robert Egerton, *Mau Mau* (London, 1990), p. 189.

became concerned that MRA had an anti-imperial bias, and Thomas Askwith, African municipal affairs officer for Nairobi, launched an investigation into the camp. The investigators were distressed to discover that Mau Mau detainees had been told that the government's confiscation of Kikuyu land was partly to blame for the crisis.[69] At a camp entertainment some Nairobi officials were shocked to see a sketch written by detainees in which Howard Church's wife played the part of a pompous white woman.[70] Furthermore, Knight's vision that the rehabilitated detainees should eventually become involved in the public life of the country jarred with the colonial government's desire to work with loyalists who had fought against the Mau Mau.[71] These differences with Knight were among the reasons the government closed the Athi River camp in 1956.[72]

The colonial government initially withheld permission for *Freedom* to be shown in Kenya, apparently because it objected to mob scenes, but it was eventually released.[73] Two former Mau Mau detainees were among a group of Africans who obtained official permission to show *Freedom* to Jomo Kenyatta (who had already seen an MRA play, *The Forgotten Factor*)[74] while he was under house arrest.[75] While in prison Kenyatta had been much affected by a meeting with the Anglican Kikuyu bishop, Obadiah Kariuki, and was open to a message of reconciliation.[76] He liked *Freedom* and suggested that a Swahili version be made. There were subsequently mass showings of the film in Nairobi Stadium, and it seems that up to a million people saw it in the run-up to Kenya's first free elections in March 1961.[77] In regard to Kenyatta himself, an MRA full-page advertisement in the *East African Standard* in December 1963 suggested that the Kenyan leader's emphasis on national unity and forgiveness made him an African "prophet voice," and called for a Kenya "governed by men governed by God."[78]

The effect of the film and of MRA work seems to have been considerable.

69. Egerton, p. 190.

70. Patrick Foss, *Climbing Turns* (Yeovil, 1990), pp. 239-40.

71. A point by Harvard University researcher Caroline Elkins in e-mail letter to Philip Boobbyer, 1 Nov. 2000.

72. For details on the government's hostility to Alan Knight's work, see MRA archive, "Kenya" file, Alan Knight to Roly Wilson, 7 Mar. 1956.

73. Rickets, p. 67; see also *East Africa Standard,* 5 Dec. 1960, p. 4.

74. MRA archive, "Kenya" file, *The Forgotten Factor in East Africa,* pamphlet (n.d.), p. 3; "Kenya" file, *The Bremer Hofmeyr Story* (privately printed, n.d.), p. 37.

75. Hofmeyr, p. 82; Foss, *Climbing Turns,* p. 241.

76. Jeremy Murray-Brown, *Kenyatta* (London, 1972), pp. 291-92.

77. Lean, p. 456.

78. *East African Standard,* 11 Dec. 1963, p. 14.

In spring 1961 the *Reporter* of Nairobi declared that MRA had done much to stabilize the recent election campaign,[79] and when Peter Howard died in February 1965, twelve senior Kenyans, including ministers and former government ministers, cabled Howard's wife, Doë, that "the philosophy and practice of MRA applied on a national scale have contributed decisively to our stability and progress."[80]

Congo

Freedom was used widely in the Congo at the time of independence. In early 1960 it was shown to a number of the Congolese delegates to the Belgian-Congolese Round Table in Brussels, which had opened in January and paved the way for formal independence on 30 June.[81] The film made a strong impression on Albert Kalonji, a representative of the Baluba people in Kasai Province, who subsequently visited Britain to learn more about MRA. He was accompanied by François Lwakabwanga of the Luluas, who were at that time involved in a bloody conflict with the Balubas for which previous Belgian attempts at mediation had failed. On the visit to Britain the two men committed themselves to work for peace. It is possible that this spirit of cooperation had a "hidden influence" on a new Lulua-Baluba Convention, which was signed in late February and which effectively allowed Balubas to live in Lulua territory.[82]

Lwakabwanga then accompanied Paramount Lulua Chief Kalamba to Caux. Kalamba met Buchman and invited an MRA delegation to go Kasai Province to contribute to the reconciliation process. The MRA group of about twenty arrived in Congo on 1 May. It included two of the actors from *Freedom*, two former Mau Mau activists now working with MRA, Bremer and Agnes Hofmyer from South Africa, Charles Piguet, and a trio of young American singers, the Colwell Brothers. The group visited Luluaburg (capital of Kasai) and other places in Lulua and Baluba territory, before touring the main provincial capitals, everywhere showing *Freedom*. There were regular showings in the townships of Léopoldville, and on 26 June, just before the formal independence celebrations, the newly elected prime minister Patrice Lumumba

79. Quoted in Lean, pp. 456-57.

80. See bound collection of cables received after Peter Howard's death, in possession of Mr. Peter Howard.

81. MRA archive, "Zaire" file, A. S. G. Hoar, "The Congo," 6 Aug. 1960, p. 1.

82. E-mail letter from Charles Piguet to author, 14 Nov. 2000; Charles Piguet, pp. 28-29, 36.

saw the film with seventeen of his ministers.[83] Their chauffeurs also attended.[84] The entire MRA group attended the official Independence Dinner on 30 June, and the program of celebrations included "Hymn to the Congo" by the Colwell Brothers.[85] Other MRA films were shown, including *The Crowning Experience,* to Joseph Kasavubu, the Congo's first president, on 28 July.[86]

In mid-July Lumumba's minister of information, Aniset Kashamura, invited the MRA group to present regular radio programs.[87] The programs were broadcast twice daily. They often presented personal testimony, articulating the message that people might abandon their hatred and personal ambition and listen to God. The stories told by the Nigerian, Kenyan, and South African members of the MRA group were particularly appreciated. One broadcast, on 13 July, introduced by Kashamura himself and entitled "There Is an Answer," provoked more than three thousand letters of support.[88] The Colwell Brothers eventually made some 400 broadcasts, using songs and stories in French and indigenous languages.[89]

A few weeks later the government suspended the MRA broadcasts. According to Charles Piguet, this was caused by a communist faction in the Congolese cabinet associated with the government's then head of protocol, Mme. Andrée Blouin, that was hostile to MRA. It was at a time when Lumumba was threatening to turn to Moscow for military aid. Piguet also states that the head of the CIA in the Congo, Ted Devlin, made an attempt to influence the MRA team and observes: "We found ourselves involved in the war of ideas and struggle for dominance between the great powers."[90]

The MRA team, while emphasizing national reconciliation, sought to avoid taking sides over the question of the future organization of the Congo — whether there would be a unitary state, as Lumumba wanted, or a federal system, as Kasavubu and others wished. Piguet observes that they were "conscious of the danger of imposed solutions from the former colonial power, the UN, or anybody," although he also notes that the idea of avoiding political issues could encourage laziness in studying the deeper issues in the country.[91]

83. *MRA Information Service,* 2 July 1960; *Bremer Hofmeyr Story,* p. 49.

84. Charles Piguet, pp. 45-46.

85. Charles Piguet, p. 53.

86. MRA archive, "Zaire" file, MRA press release, Léopoldville, 29 July 1960.

87. MRA archive, "Zaire" file, MRA press release, Léopoldville, 13 July 1960; Charles Piguet, p. 53.

88. Jacqueline Piguet, *For the Love of Tomorrow* (London, 1985), p. 95.

89. Lean, pp. 459-60.

90. Charles Piguet, pp. 59, 42. The broadcast ban lasted until November.

91. E-mail letter from Charles Piguet to author, 20 Nov. 2000.

At this time the MRA group was in touch with Moïse Tshombe, the leader of Katanga Province. Furthermore, it subsequently established a link with Major General Sese Mobutu, partly through an American member of the MRA team, William Close, who was for a time Mobutu's doctor.[92] In March 1965, following discussions with a group of senior Congolese army officers who had been to Caux, two Swiss representatives of MRA, Paul-Emile Dentan and Eric Junod, who were based in the Congo, proposed that MRA offer a systematic program of moral and spiritual training in the country. The first objective of the program was to make of the Congo an example of a "morally rearmed country"; this, it was suggested, would guarantee peace and prosperity for the Congo on the basis of the "solid character" of the country's leaders and the "global perspective of their thought and action." The work was to be done through the agency of the army, which was at that time the one stable institution in the country. Visits to Caux for representatives of the Congo were planned; the widespread use of MRA films in the country was envisaged. In separate conversations with Dentan and Junod, both Tshombe, who was now prime minister, and Mobutu endorsed the proposal. The initiative, however, came to nothing after Mobutu took power in November 1965 and Tshombe was isolated and exiled.[93]

MRA's speed of response to the opportunity that opened up in the Congo was impressive. To gain access to the main political leadership in just a few months was testimony to this, as well as the evident attractiveness of its message. MRA's achievement in Kasai Province, in particular, was considerable. There is substantial evidence that MRA's influence on Paramount Chief Kalamba helped prevent a massacre of forty-three Baluba villagers by Luluas in May,[94] and it seems clear that MRA contributed to the process leading to the peace treaty between the Luluas and Balubas that was signed before President Kasavubu in August 1961.[95] Piguet is ambivalent about the longer-term impact, mentioning the agonies he felt at the subsequent tragedies that enveloped the country,[96] but he notes that MRA did not seek to be a "fireman in an emergency," and that the longer-term objective was for

92. For some of Close's perspectives, see MRA archive, "Zaire" file, William Close, *Struggle for a Continent,* pamphlet (1964).

93. Proposal by Paul-Emile Dentan and Eric Junod, signed by Tshombe (15 Mar. 1965) and Mobutu (undated), document in possession of Dentan (Geneva); telephone interview between Dentan and Philip Boobbyer, 14 Sept. 2001.

94. MRA archive, "Zaire" file, *Service de presse et d'information, Réarmament Morale,* "Massacre Averted in Congo"; Charles Piguet, p. 38.

95. Lean, p. 460; Charles Piguet, p. 39.

96. Charles Piguet, p. 62.

"change in the conduct of individuals with influence in their own spheres of activity."[97]

Tunisia and Morocco

MRA was much involved in Tunisia, Morocco, and Algeria, and had some influence in the first two through its contacts with certain nationalist figures.

In 1953 the most senior member of the Tunisian nationalist independence movement (Néo-Destour) still at liberty, Mohamed Masmoudi, visited Caux. Masmoudi was full of hatred of the French and was considering an armed struggle in Tunisia directed from Switzerland.[98] The story of Franco-German reconciliation was a feature at the Caux conference, and Masmoudi was struck by the story of Irène Laure, a former French resistance activist who had publicly apologised to Germans in Caux for her hatred. He recalled a French colonialist he had once tried to kill. After some inner struggle, he told the conference that he would be willing to meet any representative of the French state, even one who still wanted to retain control of Tunisia. Masmoudi returned to Tunisia determined to press for a negotiated solution to his country's problems.

Through MRA connections in Paris, Masmoudi began to meet some of the French leaders, including Foreign Minister Robert Schuman. In July 1954 the MRA group in Paris organized a dinner at which Masmoudi met Jean Basdevant, the civil servant responsible for Tunisian and Moroccan affairs at the Quai d'Orsay. The atmosphere was such that Masmoudi felt able to explain to those present how he had lost his hatred of the French. Subsequently he met the French prime minister, Pierre Mendès-France, who was at the same time trying to deal with the problems in Indo-China. They agreed to prepare for internal autonomy in Tunisia. Masmoudi was one of the Tunisian delegation sent to negotiate autonomy, and Tunisia was eventually granted full independence in 1956.[99]

In Morocco MRA had a discreet influence on one of the country's nationalists. The French had been able to retain their control in Morocco because of divisions in the Moroccan leadership. In August 1953 the French deposed the sultan of Morocco, Sidi Mohammed Ben Youssef, because of his support for the independence movement, and exiled him to Madagascar. They were

97. Charles Piguet, p. 63.

98. Henderson, p. 41.

99. Henderson, pp. 41-42; Diane de Watteville-Berkheim, *Le Fil Conducteur,* Caux edition (Caux-sur-Montreux, 1973), pp. 174-78.

backed in this by the pasha of Marrakesh, El Glaoui, who wanted a slower move toward independence. In 1955 Ahmed Guessous, one of the underground leaders of the nationalist movement, Istiqlal, visited Caux. Guessous hated El Glaoui for what he perceived to be his betrayal of the Moroccan independence movement. While at Caux, somebody remarked to Guessous: "I am no closer to God than I am to the person from whom I feel most divided."[100] The comment prompted Guessous to rethink his attitude to El Glaoui. On his return to Morocco, where the political situation was deteriorating, Guessous was one of an Istiqlal delegation to El Glaoui, who was himself anxious for a reconciliation with the sultan. Some of the tension of the meeting was defused, Guessous stated later, when he expressed his desire to let go of his past feelings toward El Glaoui and his hope that they could work together for the good of the country.[101] When the sultan returned from exile in Madagascar, El Glaoui went to pay him homage, and begged mercy for having gone astray. The Moroccan leadership reestablished its unity, and the French were left isolated and then forced to withdraw.

Reconciliation in the Moroccan leadership might well have happened without Guessous's attitude toward El Glaoui. The political impact of a change of heart is difficult to measure, and in this sense MRA's influence both in Morocco and Tunisia remains to some extent obscure. Yet contemporary observers evaluated it highly. Robert Schuman observed that "there can be no doubt that the history of Morocco and Tunisia would have been different if it had not been for Moral Re-Armament."[102] Apparently the first president of independent Tunisia, Habib Bourguiba, who was in prison when Masmoudi first visited Caux, told Buchman that MRA had created the atmosphere where peace negotiations were successful, and Masmoudi himself said that if it had not been for Caux, and what he learned there about reconciliation, his country would have been involved in a war "without mercy" with the French.[103] He also said: "I was but one of the instruments for disentangling the events. But at a given moment I had the chance to push forward violence or stop the diabolical rhythm."[104] Guessous also stated later

100. Paul Campbell, *A Dose of My Own Medicine* (London, 1992), p. 54.

101. Frederic Chavanne, "Où aimerais-tu que je change? Présence du Réarmement moral au Maroc au moment de l'accession à l'indépendance," notes gathered, 1995, p. 25; see also Simon Scott Plummer, *MRA Information Service* 16, no. 18 (13 Jan. 1968): 5.

102. Lean, p. 454.

103. Henderson, p. 43.

104. Mohamed Masmoudi, "Plus radical que la violence," *Courrier d'Information* (Paris), no. 26 (28 Dec. 1968): 6; Henderson, p. 43; see also Mohamed Masmoudi, "Risquer La Paix," in Gabriel Marcel, ed., *Plus Décisif Que La Violence* (Paris, 1971), pp. 63-75.

that without his change of heart, he would not have been ready for dialogue.[105]

Rhodesia-Zimbabwe

MRA's activity in Rhodesia-Zimbabwe in the 1970s and early 1980s exhibited many of the features of its work elsewhere in Africa. A key figure in the MRA work was Alec Smith, son of the prime minister, Ian Smith. While at university in South Africa he had drifted into a hippy lifestyle, before a religious experience turned him to Christianity. He then became involved in MRA, attracted by the idea of relating his faith to the situation in the country: "I discovered that there was a difference between giving my life to God so that He could sort me out and giving my life to God to work towards establishing His authority in the power structure of the country."[106]

In June 1975 Smith helped organize a multiracial MRA conference in Salisbury. Here he publicly expressed regret for his past behavior, apologized to the white South Africans present for his hatred of them, and expressed his commitment to the reconciliation of black and white under God.[107] Smith's statement prompted the Methodist minister and black nationalist Arthur Kanodereka to see the universal appeal of Christ: "I saw Christ, the suffering Christ, not just for whites, not just for blacks, but for all people."[108] He decided "to try the experiment of listening to God's guidance every morning," and invited Alec Smith to come and speak at his church.[109] Smith and Kanodereka became central figures in an MRA "mobile force" that traveled widely in and outside the country, presenting a message of reconciliation.[110] On their tours they met many black nationalists for whom Christianity was associated with hypocrisy and colonial attitudes, and it was part of their message to argue that true Christianity was something very different. As Kanodereka stated: "Preachers like me have preached a long time and never lived as Christ expected us to."[111]

105. Chavanne, p. 25.

106. Peter Hannon, *Southern Africa, What Kind of Change?* (Johannesburg, 1977), p. 25.

107. Alec Smith, *Now I Call Him Brother* (Basingstoke, 1984), p. 63; MRA archive, "Zimbabwe" file, Report "MRA International Assembly, Salisbury, Rhodesia — June 1975."

108. Alec Smith, pp. 63-64.

109. Hugh Elliott, *Darkness and Dawn in Zimbabwe* (London, 1978), pp. 9-10.

110. Alec Smith, pp. 75-79.

111. Alec Smith, p. 79.

The Salisbury conference of 1975 had other ramifications. After attending the final sessions of the conference, Desmond Reader, a senior academic at the University of Rhodesia, felt he should apologize to an African colleague for underestimating him as a "lightweight." The colleague, Gordon Chavanduka, at the time secretary-general of the African National Congress (ANC), responded warmly, and the two men subsequently arranged a series of dinner parties to try to encourage racial dialogue. A dozen dinners were held between 1975 and 1976. Guests included several members of Ian Smith's cabinet and prominent ANC leaders.[112]

In the next few years Smith, Kanodereka (until his assassination in 1978), Reader, and Chavanduka were part of a small MRA group that came to be known as the Cabinet of Conscience.[113] It met as many as eight or ten times a year to seek God's will and support one another spiritually. A key figure, Henry Macnicol, was a Scotsman who first met the Oxford Group while a student at Edinburgh in the 1930s. The group's members were well connected with people on different sides of the political spectrum, thus putting the group in a position to review what it considered to be the wider moral and spiritual needs of the country. According to Hugh Elliott, who was working in Zimbabwe at the time, the Cabinet of Conscience was united around a belief that Rhodesia's politicians should consider the needs of the "whole country" rather than sectional interests, and it sought "wisdom from the Almighty" as to how God's plan might unfold.[114]

In the years 1975-79, delegations of about ten to twenty Rhodesians visited Caux every year, and in 1979 the delegation went on to the Lancaster House talks in London. During these talks an eight-person MRA group, including Macnicol and Elliott, met many of the delegates and sought to play a reconciling role behind the scenes, as well as offering spiritual support and friendship. MRA's connections were generally closer to the Rhodesian government and the more moderate United African National Congress headed by Bishop Abel Muzorewa than to the more radical parties.[115]

MRA played a critical role in 1980 in defusing tension following the February elections. It was known that General Peter Walls of the Security Forces was ready to stage a coup if Robert Mugabe's ZANU party won. At a Cabinet of Conscience meeting a few days before the election result, one of its members with connections to ZANU, Joram Kucherera, suggested that Smith and

112. Elliott, pp. 19-20; Kraybill, p. 227.
113. Elliott, p. 42; Kraybill, p. 226.
114. Elliott, p. 42.
115. As described in Kraybill, p. 230.

Mugabe should meet. Through Kucherera and Alec Smith, a meeting took place on 3 March, just twenty-four hours before the election results were announced, and when both men knew that Mugabe had won. Mugabe's attitude and proposals led Smith to trust him,[116] and following the announcement of the election results Smith called on whites to stay on in the country. Mugabe's first speech on 4 March also emphasized the importance of reconciliation, although how far the meeting with Smith contributed to its tone is less clear, since the ZANU leadership had been working on the theme of unity for some months.[117]

As in North Africa, since its work was devoted to an often-invisible "change of heart," MRA's influence in Zimbabwe is not easy to quantify. Nevertheless, according to the scholar Ron Kraybill, the Mugabe-Smith meeting "altered the history of the nation,"[118] and at the personal level MRA was clearly very effective at promoting honesty and reconciliation.

Conclusion

David Bebbington suggests that the work of the Oxford Group was "an exercise in maximum inculturation"; that is, it sought to reexpress traditional Christian truths in contemporary language.[119] Similarly, the German theologian Klaus Bockmuehl stated that the genius of Moral Re-Armament was "to bring the central spiritual substance of Christianity . . . in a secular and accessible form."[120] These comments sum up the nature of MRA's work in Africa. MRA sought to introduce certain traditional Christian insights into the secular debate about decolonization. It aimed to foster an African leadership that was obedient to God and absolute moral standards, and thereby to contribute to the consolidation of these newly independent nation-states. The concern to bring the spirit of the kingdom of God into national life was a distinctive feature of MRA's way of "doing mission."

The concept of MRA was a response to an emerging global society and the accompanying ideological war. A Russian religious philosopher, Semyon Frank, wrote in 1946 that in the face of aggression from "anti-Christian" forces, Christians should ally with anyone in whose hearts the "force of love"

116. Alec Smith, p. 119.

117. Kraybill, pp. 223-24, 252 n. 84.

118. Kraybill, p. 232.

119. Bebbington, p. 235.

120. Lean, p. 513; for Bockmuehl's views on the Christian nature of MRA, see his *Frank Buchmans Botschaft und ihre Bedeutung für die protestantischen kirchen* (Bern, 1963).

was actually present, including non-Christians and nominal unbelievers.[121] This was, in a sense, realized in MRA work. In Africa, in its struggle with Moscow for the minds of the new leaders, MRA sought to bypass dogmatic disputes and foster teamwork with any who sought to live by absolute moral standards or were open to the idea of God's guidance. Whether or not a person in practice sought to live by absolute moral standards was a kind of universal litmus test of his or her potential openness to the Holy Spirit.

The multinational dimension of MRA was used to great effect. MRA traveling groups involved people from many countries. Representatives of different cultures would speak from the same platform. Sometimes the combinations of people were very striking: for example, white South Africans and former Mau Mau detainees were deployed together in the Congo. The Caux conferences led to a kind of spiritual pan-Africanism in that Africans met people from African countries whom they would not otherwise have met.[122] As well as meeting Westerners and other Africans in Caux, Africans would encounter visitors from Asia, Latin America, and the Pacific, some of whom were in similar situations to their own. In addressing the end of empire, British and French colleagues could exchange experiences and contacts, and members of different Christian denominations worked together. The multinational and interreligious element was another of MRA's distinctive features. The Caux conferences evidently came to function as a kind of spiritual United Nations.

The fact that in MRA people of different faiths often worked together raises some important issues for the historian of Christian missions. For example, the fact that in Africa Muslims found a new dimension to their faith through MRA raises the question of how to define "conversion." By acknowledging the depth of the Muslim faith in Africa, and encouraging moral and spiritual change in Muslims without seeking their conversion to Christianity, Buchman was in a way saying that the spread of the Spirit of Christ is not always synonymous with the spread of Christianity. It was an implicit challenge to certain aspects of the traditional missionary project.

In adapting to the modern world, MRA ran the risk that the spirituality that had originally informed it would be altered, and that it would itself be remolded by the world it sought to change. Although that doubtless happened to some extent, the insights and practices that Buchman drew from the evangelical tradition remained present in MRA, even if sometimes implicitly rather than explicitly. MRA was instrumental in helping many people find or

121. S. L. Frank, *God with Us,* trans. N. Duddington (London, 1946). p. 287.

122. A point made by Dr. Charis Waddy in conversation with author, 27 Oct. 2000.

deepen their Christian faith. Its readiness to adapt was the very thing that made possible its outreach; furthermore, it enabled it to offer a spiritual message that was specifically tailored for people who were involved in decolonization. How effective the strategy was is difficult to measure, partly because the "change of heart" it encouraged is hard to quantify, and also because the evidence cited to suggest its influence is often of an anecdotal nature. Nevertheless, it is clear that MRA changed many lives and that it was a major force for reconciliation in a number of African states as they moved toward independence.

CHAPTER 12

Apartheid, Mission, and Independent Africa: From Pretoria to Kampala with Hannah Stanton

DEBORAH GAITSKELL

This chapter is constructed around a comparison of two texts written by Hannah Stanton in the early years of the era of African independence. One was published with a degree of acclaim at the beginning of the 1960s; the other failed to find a publisher. *Go Well. Stay Well* (1961) is an engaging account of Hannah Stanton's four years in South Africa working for the Anglican Church with the advantage of culminating in the tale of her unexpected detention, during the security crackdown after the Sharpeville shootings of March 1960, and brief experience of imprisonment.[1] Sometime in 1973 Stanton completed another manuscript, "Back to Africa: A Picture of Uganda in the 1960s." It describes her eight years in Uganda as warden of Mary Stuart Hall, the women's residence at Makerere University in Kampala. It remains unpublished despite approaches to at least three publishers and a literary agent in the period 1978-79.[2] Yet this account goes beyond a tale of personal

1. H. Stanton, *Go Well. Stay Well. South Africa, August 1956 to May 1960* (London, 1961). References to this work are annotated in the text as *Go Well.*

2. London, School of Oriental and African Studies, Special Collections (hereafter SOAS), PP MS 54, Hannah Stanton Papers, Box 7, No. 33, unpublished manuscript "Back to Africa: A Picture of Uganda in the 1960s." (References to this work are annotated in the text as "Back to Africa," followed by the chapter number, a hyphen, and the page reference, as each chapter in the manuscript is paginated individually.) The same folder contains a small batch of letters from publishers. The manuscript amounts to 295 pages and seems to have been further revised in the 1970s. The original is held at Rhodes House Library, Ox-

missionary growth to signal the possibility of an insightful, and sympathetic, encounter between Western Christians and independent Africa.

The contrasts in content, stance, and tone between "Back to Africa" and *Go Well* suggest a wider significance for the unpublished manuscript beyond a mere biographical vignette, or even the story of one British woman's evolving engagement with Christian mission in the era of decolonization. A comparison between the two texts helps chart missionary recognition of the claims of African nationalism and points to the importance of enduring links, especially between women, forged through education and Christianity at the end of empire.

So who was the author of these works, and how had she come to be in Africa? Hannah Stanton (1913-93) found herself, in her early forties, and somewhat to her own surprise, living in the African freehold township of Lady Selborne in Pretoria, running a female mission center and providing theological training for black women. Previously a hospital social worker in Liverpool in the 1930s (after an English degree from University College, London, and some social studies at the London School of Economics), she had worked with the Friends' Relief Service in 1947-48 at refugee camps in Austria, and then took a theology degree from Oxford. Her lighthearted holiday visit to South Africa in 1956 to see her brother, a priest in the Community of the Resurrection, turned into a longer sojourn working for the black urban church. Detained under the State of Emergency on 30 March 1960, she was released seven and a half weeks later on condition that she left the country.

For her university job in Uganda from 1962 to 1970 she joined a band of unusually progressive white women working with Ugandan women for female advancement in education and employment. Nor was it with Ugandan women only, for in the early years at Makerere students came from Kenya and Tanzania too. The high degree of interracial cooperation of African, Asian, and European women in Uganda from the 1940s to the 1960s has been seen as a vital foundation of female organizational strength in the 1980s and 1990s.[3] Later in retirement in England, the anti-apartheid movement was among her many commitments, along with the World Conference of Religions for Peace, for which cause she traveled widely to raise money.

---

ford. It is listed there as "Education; A picture of Uganda in the 1960s. A tribute to Makerere University College and to African women by Hannah Stanton," Mss. Afr. s. 2285 (information supplied by Aili Tripp).

3. See Aili Mari Tripp, "A Foot in the Door: Historical Dimensions of the Women's Movement in Uganda," chap. 2 in Tripp, *Women and Politics in Uganda* (Oxford; Madison, Wis.; and Kampala, 2000); Tripp, "A New Look at European Women in Colonial Africa: British Teachers and Women's Rights Activists in Uganda (1898-1962)" (unpublished paper, 2000).

How representative of female mission in the 1950s and 1960s was Hannah Stanton? Does her sensitivity to African political, ecclesiastical, and intellectual advance make her distinctive? She seems to have regarded her geographical relocation to independent Africa as crucial in her journey to "enlightenment," but surely her "wake-up call" to the realities of African nationalism and political autonomy was not unique. Her personal story also raises the wider question of the destiny of missionaries after the end of empire. The female trajectory seems to have been rather different from the male, not least because women missionaries were negotiating a new role in relation to a church and an Africa in which they had not held clerical or overt political power. How large was the cohort of former women missionaries, such as Drs. Louise Pirouet and Jocelyn Murray, who turned academics and activists on their relocation to Britain? Such women facilitated new links between Britain and Africa through their historical research or social campaigns around issues such as the expulsion of Ugandan Asians or, latterly, asylum seekers. Their personal relationships and political actions continued to reverberate, in however modest a way, with significance for the church's survival in Africa in the era of independence.

I have chosen three points of comparison between the two Stanton works: the Christian nature of Hannah's work in both South Africa and Uganda, her relationships with indigenous women, and her understanding of the political contexts in which she found herself.[4] The chapter concludes with suggestions as to the broader missiological and political significance of Stanton's individual path.

From Missionary Work to Christian Vocation

Hannah arrived in South Africa still stalling for time about the bishop of Pretoria's offer of the post of warden at Tumelong Mission ("The Place of Faith"). "I felt that I wanted gaiety and laughter and a good time. I wasn't at all sure that I wanted to be a missionary" (*Go Well*, p. 17). Ready to find fault, she felt out of tune with the "impression of piousness" about the mission, which "appeared in a way remote from the stresses and strains of the lives of the people around it" (p. 26). Its standard repertoire of church- and community-building

4. For comparisons between Hannah and four of her predecessors on these three issues, see Deborah Gaitskell, "Female Faith and the Politics of the Personal: Five Mission Encounters in Twentieth-Century South Africa," in "Reconstructing Feminities: Colonial Intersections of Gender, Race, Religion and Class," ed. M. Kosambi and J. Haggis, special issue of *Feminist Review* 65 (summer 2000).

activities by the mid-1950s, echoing strongly its Sophiatown (Johannesburg) predecessor, the Ekutuleni of the late 1930s,[5] was at odds with her considerable professional training and employment history. "I had never taught a Confirmation class, and I had very little experience in Sunday School work. My experience as a Girl Guide was twenty years out of date, and I certainly wasn't a trained Nursery School teacher" (p. 29).[6]

The idea of "identification" through actual living conditions was an important motivating factor in drawing her to the job, however: "possibly it would be as near as a white person could get to Non-European neighbours in South Africa at the present time." She recognized she did not share the poverty of many: "I was already thinking of buying my own car. . . . I enjoyed my comforts" — but she would be sharing not only in the "dust, heat, flies, and bucket sanitation, but some of the insecurity of the future." "I was convinced one could not really help unless one was prepared to share, and get to know people as friends, and to suffer too if required, although I hoped nothing of that sort would come my way" (pp. 31-32). There was admittedly much at the mission in the nature of "good works," relief for the old and infirm caught up in ghastly poverty; "but there might also be an opportunity of working *with* the African people" (p. 35).

Stanton saw in herself an attitude of pride and superiority that had to go; she had much to learn from African worship and prayer; the freehold township offered chances to promote meetings and reconciliation between members of all races. Accepting the job, Hannah noted her aim for the mission: "I wanted it to continue as a place where there was love and welcome and understanding, and where there was no feeling of 'apartheid' or separation. . . . I prayed also that I might be shown the opportunity of spreading the gospel — the aim of missionary work" (p. 36). Hannah Stanton's theological training was soon put to good use as she took a farsighted initiative and started giving a handful of African women intensive residential theological training. She took them for Old Testament, while some of the male clergy taught New Tes-

5. On which, see Audrey Ashley, *Peace-Making in South Africa: The Life and Work of Dorothy Maud* (Bognor Regis, 1980), and Alan Paton, *Apartheid and the Archbishop: The Life and Times of Geoffrey Clayton Archbishop of Cape Town* (Cape Town, 1973), chap. 16.

6. Hannah's hiring seems to have been somewhat ad hoc, via personal contacts — unlike many earlier Anglican women missionaries to South Africa, she was not recruited through the Society for the Propagation of the Gospel or listed in their reports. (Similar informal networking had recruited an earlier generation of helpers at the two Johannesburg women's missions started by Dorothy Maud.) Nevertheless, Hannah was undoubtedly a missionary — see her reflections on her dilemma in chap. 3 of *Go Well,* "To Be a Missionary?"

tament, church history, and doctrine, and Tumelong female colleagues covered liturgy and appreciation of the arts. For practical training they went on expeditions to various welfare projects, attended the subcommittee on African affairs of the National Council of African Women, and went to open-air meetings of interest in Pretoria. The spiritual demands were rigorous: daily attendance at six religious offices from matins at 6:20 A.M. to compline at 8:30 P.M., plus twenty minutes private prayer and meditation daily (pp. 96, 103-5)!

Later in Kampala, Hannah's work was much less explicitly religious. She was running a busy university residence and trying to give pastoral care and educational encouragement to a hundred — by 1970, more like five hundred — young women students. She obviously relished the socializing and partying involved, which are enthusiastically recalled in the unpublished manuscript, but she also tutored in the Religious Studies Department, again using her theological training. Hers was not a missionary appointment as such, but she and some of her Christian colleagues saw their university responsibilities as a religious calling. She quotes the ebullient Noel King, head of the Religious Studies Department, who commented when he had to act as principal of Makerere and was tackling his in-tray: "Ah, Hannah, this is the new missionary work" ("Back to Africa," 12-8).[7]

Her erstwhile colleague Louise Pirouet asserted recently: "I am sure Hannah did not think of herself as a *missionary* in Uganda; what mattered was being a *Christian*, and that meant living one's faith. . . . Everyone knew she was a Christian, a strong supporter of the chapel and a very regular worshipper, as well as being a deeply caring Warden and a delightful and fun-loving person who commanded great respect."[8] Of course, many of the students were graduates of premier mission schools, and her manuscript pays tribute to the churches' role in female education. In that sense at least, Hannah was very aware of the East African missions — and they would have respected her pastoral role with their old girls who had moved on to higher education.

The university chapel, having to cater to people of diverse Anglican backgrounds, including areas served by the Universities' Mission to Central Africa

7. See also Louise Pirouet to author, 27 March 2001: "There were a considerable number of very dedicated Christian staff at Makerere, both Roman Catholic and Protestant, who saw it as their Christian calling to give of their best to the people who would be leaders in a country just becoming independent, and to their students as individuals. Many still have links with people they helped to train. I do not think the Protestant missionaries always understood this Christian vocation." I am greatly indebted to Dr. Pirouet for her detailed letter responding to my queries.

8. Pirouet to author, 27 March 2001.

in Tanzania, was relatively High Church, with its main service on Sunday being a sung Eucharist. This Makerere chapel was not altogether in sympathy with the Church Missionary Society (CMS) Anglican missions in Uganda (especially the powerful Balokole revival movement). The CMS headquarters' leadership itself was deemed by some to "deeply" distrust the university, especially its eccentric chaplain (vividly portrayed in Hannah's memoir), the Reverend Fred Welbourn, greatly loved and trusted by Africans but a cutting critic on occasion of missionary paternalism. Makerere "had gone further than many of the missions," which were "too often still paternalistic," in working on an equal footing with Africans. But Hannah's High Church sympathies need not preclude great friendship with those of other CMS origins — as Pirouet commented, "whether I belonged to CMS or not made no difference at all."[9] Uganda also brought striking encounters for Hannah with the wider African church and universal Christianity. She met the interesting delegates at the 1963 All Africa Conference of Churches, and was present in 1969 when the pope visited for the beatification of the Uganda martyrs ("Back to Africa," chap. 14).

From Selective Egalitarianism to Female Empowerment through Education

Even before reading Stanton's unpublished manuscript, I had found the way Hannah wrote about Africans, church women, colleagues, and students in 1950s Pretoria warmer, more informed, and personal than the manner of many of her predecessors. Women's individual qualities are recalled with respect and affection. Hannah paid brief tributes to African women on the staff, the "talented and imaginative" Grace Kekana and Lilian Tau, who ran the nursery school; Johanna Maditse, pillar of the Mothers' Union, who had been running church classes for over forty years; her daughter, Beatrice Mtetwa, "our loved and treasured Thabi," who had great spiritual insight and "a delightful way with children"; Josephine Mokou, gay and friendly, with a genius for visiting, but also "solidly sensible, reasonable and ready to undertake anything in her power" (*Go Well*, pp. 63-71, 117).

Understandably, Stanton's reflections on the Pretoria theology students were fuller and more considered. Eva Ramoaka, "a brilliant individualist" and very good at getting the best out of young girls, was "very stimulated by the intellectual side of the training and always had tricky questions ready for the

9. Pirouet to author, 27 March 2001.

lecturers" (p. 106). Mary Molatedi, mother of eight and keen to make up for the fact that she had not been able to afford high school, had been active for years in the National Council of African Women and ran the local Sunday school. The greatest evangelist of all the students, in Stanton's opinion, she had charm, fluency, tireless energy in visiting, as well as organizational skills. After the course she went on to work for the Mothers' Union. Two other students had junior certificates: Johanna Mbelle, who became a court interpreter in Johannesburg, and Lydia Bogacu: "we loved her for her ready wit and highly developed sense of humour . . . she could and did pose most difficult questions. She was, we hoped, the forerunner of many who would come to Tumelong Mission from outside our own Diocese. Already we were putting our feelers all over the Union. We wanted . . . to be a centre for the training of African women missionary workers for the whole of the Church of the Province" (p. 111). "In these women I put much faith and trust," Hannah commented, for the training gave "great point to the rest of our life in Lady Selborne." Though the mission would die (because of the imminent forced relocation of the black population), "we would as quickly as possible pass on our experience and our life to these promising African women who, in their own rich African ways, would make Tumelong live again in their African missions and parishes" (pp. 112-13).[10]

One must acknowledge, however, that the personal relationship that *really* sets the book alight with unrestrained warmth is the one struck up in prison with Helen Joseph, the rare white supporter of the African National Congress (ANC), with whom Hannah was allowed to share a cell. Shared exercise, gossip about other detainees, a mutual enthusiasm for Jane Austen — all provided an exciting end to the demoralizing isolation of prison. And a great time they had together, well supplied with flowers and chocolates, a thermos for nightly hot drinks, and the company of Matron van Onselen's cat, whom they dubbed Horace.

The Uganda manuscript, by contrast with the book, although it has glowing references to British colleagues such as Louise Pirouet, packs full two or three chapters with personal details on Hannah's myriad women students, mostly African, in all their huge variety. Stanton clearly kept amazingly good track of what they did in their Makerere studies, where they went afterward, whether overseas or in local professional work, whom they married and so on

10. The female theological empowerment that was Hannah's distinctive missionary contribution is discussed in Deborah Gaitskell, "Beyond 'Devout Domesticity': Five Female Mission Strategies in South Africa, 1907-1960," *Transformation* 16, no. 4 (Oct./Dec. 1999): 127-35.

(see esp. "Back to Africa," chaps. 10 and 13).[11] Affection, pride, and ongoing links are all evident. Much of the manuscript, in fact, after conveying Hannah's initial experiences of Uganda, is a study of women's education at the university and its precursors and foundations, in both mission schools and girls' cultural background (chaps. 4 and 5). This gives the manuscript a much greater gender awareness and focus on *women* than is present in *Go Well. Stay Well.*

From Resisting Apartheid to Welcoming African Independence

As far as political understanding is concerned, Hannah in the 1950s appeared much more in tune with changing times than many of her European Christian contemporaries. She was keen to identify, as far as possible, with African life by living in a black area. She was also shrewdly aware of the inappropriateness of much of that white South African charitable spirit that Dorothy Maud (Ekutuleni's founder) and her like had sought to foster a generation earlier, but which could so easily degenerate into a condescending generosity. The Pretoria schoolgirls knitting for the poor, commented Hannah:

> will soon be adults, conscientiously carrying out charitable efforts. They will not understand when at last it is an unescapable [*sic*] reality that the Africans are no longer content with being "kept in their place." Then the cry will be, "Oh, but we have been so kind to them. Oh, we have been so good to our servants. Oh, we knitted jerseys for their children. Oh, what ingratitude." They will not understand that the Africans haven't really wanted "to be done good to." . . . Many of these dear white South Africans are back in the nineteenth century, doing a little slumming as our grandmothers used to do in the 1890s. They must realise that modern Africa is knocking at the door. (*Go Well*, p. 140)[12]

Stanton expressed some bafflement about her detention, asserting that she had not been an extremist in any way. She had merely shown solidarity with local white activists, made a couple of public protests in the press, and helped collect affidavits after police brutality against black political demonstrators

11. Pirouet to author, 27 March 2001, notes that she, and others, had advised against publication of the later manuscript in part *because* they felt this naming of individuals was inappropriate and — under Amin — potentially unsafe.

12. For white women's charitable efforts in general in Johannesburg, see p. 24.

(pp. 155-58). Though she joined the Liberal Party in South Africa, she rarely managed to get to meetings. She allowed the local ANC to meet once in the Tumelong club room but had not attended herself (pp. 38-40, 147, 203-4). It was during imprisonment with Helen Joseph that Hannah's "political education started": "I was ashamed at how little I knew of African politics; I had really not had time to study the past history of the ANC. I was extremely ignorant about the Treason Trial and had, to my shame, rather lost interest in it. Now the whole story of the ANC came to life for me" (p. 217). When other women detainees came to their prison, Hannah, realizing they did not share her belief in God, wished the church had taken a stronger political stand (p. 234).

By contrast with her book, the unpublished manuscript shows how much *more* of a learning experience Uganda was. Hannah conceded honestly at the start that she came out of South Africa "with a bit of a condescending attitude" and needed another set of experiences "to put me on the right road to respect on a basis of equality and to realize the further richness of what there was to be learnt in Africa" ("Back to Africa," 1-6). Thinking she was "the cat's whiskers with my experience of protest and gaol in the South," she was brought up short as to her ignorance of the rest of the continent, especially its educated elite and university community, when Professor Idowu of Nigeria put her "kindly and firmly" in her place by asking "How is your Hebrew?" in response to her query about teaching vacancies in his theology department at Ibadan (1-7). She had to some extent, she realized, become a victim of South African propaganda, writing off the rest of black Africa, falling into a white liberal or missionary paternalist self-congratulatory trap, saying, "'Look at what we are doing,' and not to look at free Africa and to see what Africans are doing for themselves" (1-6, 7, 10).

This realization was reinforced for her by a watershed trip south through Zambia to Ian Smith's Rhodesia in 1965. Afterward it was a relief to be back in Uganda, where Africans were *really* free and adult, and taking responsibility, free of the distortions of a settler presence (chap. 9). Uganda became independent a few months after Stanton's arrival, and she describes the excitement of processions, flag raising, and fireworks, also of hearing an inspiring sermon series at Makerere on African independence and Christian freedom (3-10ff.). By 1964, as part of the African takeover in every sphere, an African principal and secretary-registrar were together running Makerere with admirable competence, "in complete contrast with the reluctance, even in church circles, to give responsibility to Africans in South Africa" (3-28). All the expatriate staff at Makerere knew they were meant to be working themselves out of their jobs, and "preparation and training all had to aim at this" (3-34). Her reaction had itself been conditioned by prior residence in apartheid South Africa:

> I suppose delighted surprise was my dominating reaction to this new situation.
>
> Although I had come out of South Africa belligerently on the side of the African, I don't think I had really believed that Africans were capable of taking on the most responsible jobs involved in running a modern state with all its intricacies, and also running a large university.
>
> In a way my excited pride wasn't a normal reaction; it was born out of my South Africa experiences. I needed to get through to a frame of mind when I took these competent efficient Africans, doing things in their own ways, entirely for granted. (3-38)

On the whole, Stanton provides a positive picture of happy relations on campus and the way a lively student population "made the Hall vibrate." So many of the girls were "vivid and entertaining personalities," it was a pleasure to nurse them, share their problems, teach them, meet their boyfriends and families, give endless lifts, help sort out their finances, work on committees with them. "To my proud eyes, all talented, all going out from Makerere to prove that east African women can make a great impression" (10-20, 23). When conceding the growing student resentment of authority in the late 1960s and occasional scribbles on her pinned-up notices, however, she expressed her frustration candidly (but subsequently crossed out this sentence): "And so when the comment went up on the notice board 'We are tired of this regime' I said 'fine, over to you chum.' I had done all I could and it was time to go" (10-26). She portrayed timely departure as rational, and the African wish for autonomy as to be expected: "the black people have in the last ten years developed self confidence at a tremendous speed, and they speak out now aggressively. They are more educated, more experienced, more vocal, more powerful than they were. They are demanding equality; they will learn and learn quickly. They are not going to sit down under instruction, and smile and be polite and agree with everything, as white people expected them to do years ago, and doubtless in South Africa are still expecting" (10-25).

Conclusion

The very aspects of Hannah Stanton's manuscript that show how much she had moved on from apartheid South Africa to independent Africa contribute to its failure to find a publisher. It is *not* a book primarily about herself, which *Go Well. Stay Well* largely is, and she incorporated the historical findings of others rather awkwardly into her Ugandan text. Hence, with some justice, one publisher in 1978 commented that it did not "add up to a book, only a number of interesting themes concerning African education," while another, regretting that it lacked the inbuilt drama of her earlier prison narrative, considered the manuscript "both leisurely and anecdotal." Implicitly it was too tame, without "any particular topicality," as Hannah had been in Uganda "prior to Idi Amin's spectacular reign."[13]

The manuscript was also really aimed in large part at the white conscience (echoing the closing tenor of Alan Paton's *Cry the Beloved Country*, published a generation earlier in 1948). It appears as though she intended at first to end the book with an upbeat comment on African independence: "In freedom and independence mistakes are always made, but there is also the freedom to look into the future and plan calmly, wisely and responsibly" ("Back to Africa," 18-5). In fact, however, the final appeal looks farther south, from whence she had come:

> And part of the object of this book is to re-assure . . . the white readers in Southern Africa that it is possible, and indeed a most stimulating experience to live in a free African environment and to help to make a contribution towards the future. To the countries where there are larger white populations, I would say, as I said in "Go Well Stay Well," realise the richness of the African contribution round you, step out into the last half of the 20th century, and realise that in a good deal of the world colour is now irrelevant. If you step forward with generosity it is still not too late to be met with generosity. (18-6)

Perhaps these closing remarks suggest Hannah Stanton was stuck in something of a time warp at the end of the 1970s. It is more likely that her anti-apartheid solidarity work in London as she was writing turned her thoughts again to South Africa, "where black people were still not trusted, and she was back to having to beat an old drum."[14]

Hannah Stanton in South Africa in the late 1950s was probably *not* "repre-

13. SOAS PP MS 54, Box 7, No. 33, publishers' letters: Robin Denniston (Oxford University Press), 4 Dec. 1978; Juliet Burton, 16 May 1979.

14. Pirouet to author, 27 March 2001, where she notes that this "theme of comparing her attitude in Uganda to earlier South African attitudes" was another reason why friends advised Hannah against publication: "this didn't do her justice because in Uganda there was no trace of those former attitudes in her manner."

sentative" of Anglican women missionaries of her time and place. There does not seem to have been some larger, independent-minded, female mission group similarly aware that "modern Africa [was] knocking at the door," and of whom Hannah might constitute a "typical" example. Rather, Hannah's education, social class, confidence, personal contacts, and Christian conscience combined to ensure that she, unusually, was not cowed by authoritarian heavy-handedness as the political crackdown came. Perhaps the timing of her arrival in South Africa helped: after having read Trevor Huddleston's *Naught for Your Comfort* and heard him speak, she was especially aware that the church was facing a moment of crisis under apartheid. Her outspokenness and openness to the urgent need for change in South Africa make her exceptional for women of her mission milieu.

Louise Pirouet's remarks suggest, however, that Hannah was far from exceptional in the Uganda of the 1960s as regards Makerere staff with a Christian vocation.[15] Interestingly, this set her apart from actual *missionaries*, who may not have quite caught up with the support and welcome the university expatriates were giving to independent Africa. The classic missionary era was coming to an end. The All Africa Conference of Churches meeting confirmed how "the mission" had become "the church," and its leadership was African. Politically, too, the colonial rulers were leaving tropical Africa. These major ecclesiastical and political changes evoked a changed response from Hannah and others. Africa was to be served now by educational empowerment, especially for women, rather than direct evangelism (which had already made its mark) or even the theological and ecclesiastical empowerment in which Hannah had been involved in Pretoria. Hannah Stanton exemplifies an encounter with, and acceptance of, the end of empire and of a necessary repositioning of British Christians that was not unique, even though it may not have been widespread.

Finally, an important part of the story relates to what former missionaries do when they leave Africa. As the little Anglican periodical *Partners* shows, there are still networks of retired clergy and committed lay workers active today in spreading information, offering publicity and hospitality, and raising funds for dioceses in Zimbabwe, Botswana, and the former Transvaal. One of the projects they report on is Tumelong Mission, Pretoria, which has reinvented itself as a multifaceted church welfare body. Hannah Stanton was not alone in continuing to care about African people and issues after leaving the continent. From London she maintained astonishingly wide and long-lasting connections with individuals over more than two decades. The personal was

15. Pirouet to author, 27 March 2001, see esp. comment in n. 7.

also political, as seen in her solidarity work through the anti-apartheid movement in the 1970s and 1980s.

Women, so often marginalized in ecclesiastical and organizational decision making, appear to have invested even more than men in the "politics of the personal." These webs of personal relationships should not be discounted entirely in the analysis of broad social trends. Shula Marks, reflecting on how the relatively harmonious transition to democracy in South Africa in the 1990s is to be explained, suggests that the myriad "small gestures and personal connections" between women of different races played their part. Encountering one another through education, missions, and social welfare projects, they forged links that helped to keep alive "some sense of a single society," a counterweight to "the oppressive 'separations' and brutalities of twentieth-century South Africa."[16] The process of building and maintaining an international church across the divides of race, empire, and nationalism has operated, like the dismantling of apartheid, at both a macro and a micro level. Hannah Stanton's series of amazingly well filled visitors' books attest to her ongoing affectionate and material links with Africa and Africans, which are part of the wider personal and institutional web (built up by many individuals) that has helped sustain a world church in the postimperial age.

16. Shula Marks, "Changing History, Changing Histories: Separations and Connections in the Lives of Three South African Women," *Journal of African Cultural Studies* 13, no. 1 (June 2000): 99.

CHAPTER 13

Passive Revolution and Its Saboteurs: African Christian Initiative in the Era of Decolonization, 1955-1975

OGBU U. KALU

Historiographical Undertone

This chapter is situated within a genre of African historiography that emphasizes the religious experience, practices, and initiatives of Africans as the starting point of the story of the encounter with Christianity. From this perspective the process of decolonization is imaged as a passive revolution, a concept borrowed from political scientists to understand the power relations in the missionary enterprise, especially the fact that decolonization took the missionaries unprepared, unwilling to give up power, unable to halt the trend, and anxious to create a condition that would enable them still to influence the policy from behind the curtains of the vestry or boardrooms of their metropoles.

The chapter will, therefore, paint the historiographical undertone in bold strokes and examine both the nature of missionary presence in the colonial project and the decolonization process to indicate that both the colonial governments and the missionaries, often operating as intimate enemies, still suffered from disheveled responses to decolonization and fought rearguard battles to turn a rout into a passive revolution. The matter of periodization is crucial here because the declaration of political independence is not the same as the decolonization of the churches in Africa. The reluctance of the missions to devolve control, in spite of premonitions of the future, meant that for the churches the crisis and response spanned the broad period 1955 to 1975.

After this period, "new dimensions" or the maturity process of the modern church in Africa became rather obvious and the vestiges of missionary Christianity were duly contested and reformulated. It could also be argued that new challenges arose for the church in the public space and overawed old discourse. As pressure mounted from the outside to retool, the internal turmoil took two directions: from the center the indigenization debate was a catalyst for change, and from the fringes youthful charisma sabotaged passive revolution. A case study of the Scripture Union in Eastern Nigeria, 1966-75, will illustrate the sabotage, which is akin to the case study of young puritan preachers of Malawi.[1] With the missionary agenda embattled from outside and inside, from the center and fringes, the face and size of African Christianity changed dramatically from the middle of the 1970s through the 1980s.

An excursus on Africanist church historiography is germane because the interpretation of decolonization is fraught with deep ideological biases relating to two issues: how one understands the gospel-culture encounter in Africa and the role of the missionary in the colonial enterprise. Some lay emphasis on the good intentions and achievements of the missionary, while others see the controlling, dehumanizing character. Still others take to the philosophical high road to argue that the nature of culture encounter would make it impossible for the few missionaries to have controlled so many people without their consent. These deep-level biases determine the interpretation of the decolonization era precisely because the problems in decolonization were inextricably linked with the character of Christian presence in colonial times.

Four strands of interpretation have prevailed. In spite of robust opposition, the "domination and hegemony" model has continued in various guises with its binary lens and emphasis on control, collusion, and conflict scenarios in the gospel-culture encounter. A plurality of voices has challenged the model by emphasizing "African agency" in the missionary enterprise and the resultant "Christianities."[2] Deeper than agency is the mode of appropriating the gospel. "Translation" as a conceptual scheme enables the historian to plumb indigenous spirituality and initiative, refashioning the image of passive receptors. Some historians employ biography to underscore that Christianity is a lived religion and that "faithing" leads to practices that do not

1. R. van Dijk, "Young Born Again Preachers in Independent Malawi," in *New Dimensions in African Christianity,* ed. Paul Gifford (Nairobi, 1992); see also Klaus Fielder, "The Charismatic and Pentecostal Movements in Malawi in Cultural Perspective" (paper presented at the Theology Conference, Chancellor College, Blantyre, 1998).

2. John Lonsdale, "Kikuyu Christianities," *Journal of Religion in Africa* (hereafter *JRA*) 29, no. 2 (1999): 206-29.

yield easily to simple characterization. The scenario has been further confused by the fragmentary nature of mission history, as if the historian is a Shakespearean equivocator who can swear on either side of the balance.

To elaborate briefly: Adrian Hastings remarkably sang for the unsung African heroes or "native agents" and employed an Africanist periodization in the reconstruction of the missionary past in Africa. As he argued, "The pace was very clearly being set by African demand rather than by missionary hard work. . . . What was happening in place after place was a spiritual revolution sparked off by native evangelists in conditions created by the unsettlement of early colonial rule."[3] Peel called it the "contest between rival narratives"[4] because Christianity merely catalyzed changes that indigenous movements had initiated.[5] Other historians highlighted the creative "rebel"[6] factor of Bantu prophets, Zulu Zions, or Ethiopianism.[7] Meanwhile, social scientists turned the searchlight on how the common person responds to the gospel with "hidden transcripts" in the "infra-political" zone[8] away from the rulers and priestly agents; or, as the Comaroffs would say, how Christian values permeate the community in the long conversation and epic of everyday life.[9] They argued that when cultures meet, each devises various forms of "universe maintenance" that determine the patterns of vertical and horizontal expansion of the gospel.[10] Therefore, urged T. O. Ranger, emphasis should be on the interior of Christianity or varieties of African spirituality.[11]

Some historians have employed the resources of the biographies of a wide

3. Adrian Hastings, *The Church in Africa, 1450-1950* (Oxford, 1994), pp. 452-53.

4. J. D. Y. Peel, "For Who Hath Despised the Day of Small Things? Missionary Narratives and Historical Anthropology," *Comparative Studies in Society and History* 37, no. 3 (1995): 581-607, esp. 589.

5. Robin Horton, "African Conversion," *Africa* 41, no. 2 (1971): 87-108.

6. F. B. Welbourn, *East African Rebels* (London, 1961).

7. B. G. M. Sundkler, *Bantu Prophets in South Africa*, 2nd ed. (London, 1961); Sundkler, *Zulu Zion and Some Swazi Zionists* (London, 1976); Jehu Hanciles, "Ethiopianism: Rough Diamond of African Christianity," *Studia Historiae Ecclesiasticae* 23, no. 2 (1997): 75-104. See also C. G. Baëta, *Prophetism in Ghana* (London, 1962); H. W. Mobley, *The Ghanaian's Image of the Missionary* (Leiden, 1971); O. E. Uya, "Alexander Crummell: Apostle of African Redemption through Religion," *West African Journal of Religion* 16, no. 2 (1975): 1-12.

8. See J. C. Scott, *Domination and Arts of Resistance: Hidden Transcripts* (New Haven, 1990); R. Fatton, "Africa in the Age of Democratization," *African Studies Review* (hereafter *ASR*) 38, no. 2 (1995): 67-99.

9. J. Comaroff and J. Comaroff, *Of Revelation and Revolution*, Volume 1: *Christianity, Colonialism, and Consciousness in South Africa* (Chicago, 1991), p. 3.

10. P. Berger and T. Luckman, *The Social Construction of Reality* (London, 1976).

11. Terence Ranger, "'Taking on the Missionary's Task': African Spirituality and the Mission Churches in Manicaland in the 1930's," *JRA* 29, no. 2 (1999): 175-206.

range of individuals such as Nxele, Ntsikane, Tiyo Soga, Kenyatta, and Father Tansi to demonstrate the varieties of conversion experiences and to compel a shift from a Eurocentric to an Afrocentric focus so as to illustrate the ambiguities of colonial evangelism.[12] At the core were the projects of overrule: the creation of satellite mission communities insulated from African life and at the same time the introduction and practice of Christianity in the mother tongue. Lamin Sanneh argues that it was the third phase that "struck deep roots in the culture, roots that outlived the ephemeral nature of alien rule and of marginal mission enclaves."[13] Translation as an indigenization project soon became the staple of African church historiography of the 1990s, especially with the theological concern about the role of the Bible in emergent African Christianity. John Draper's account of Magema Fuze's career and Birgit Meyer's study of the making of the Ewe Bible attempted to counter the image of passive proselytes and underscore the fact that there was often a divide between missionary intentions, accounts, and indigenous Christianity at the grass roots.[14] The exigencies of the mission field continually transformed the hardware of missionary goals as both the subjects and objects were transformed in the power encounter. The cloud of witnesses reinforces the fact that the *divide* played a major role in determining how both parties responded to the gospel-culture interface in the colonial period and to the anticolonial nationalist movement, and how they perceived decolonization. African Christian initiative appeared quite early in the encounter, had an identifiable character, and could not be totally suppressed by missionary control. Obviously both parties would perceive decolonization differently.

Paul Gifford argues strongly that externality remains the enduring quality

12. J. B. Pieres, *The House of Phalo: A History of the Xhosa People in the Days of Their Independence* (Johannesburg, 1981); David Chidester, *Religions of South Africa* (London, 1992); D. Atwell, "The Transculturation of English: The Exemplary Case of Tiyo Soga, African Nationalist" (inaugural lecture, University of Natal, Pietermaritzburg, 1994); Elizabeth Isichei, *Entirely for God: The Life of Michael Iwene Tansi* (London, 1980); John Lonsdale and Bruce Berman, *The House of Custom: Jomo Kenyatta, Louis Leakey, and the Making of the Modern Kikuyu* (forthcoming).

13. Lamin Sanneh, "World Christianity and the New Historiography," in *Enlarging the Story: Perspectives on Writing World Christian History,* ed. Wilbert R. Shenk (Maryknoll, N.Y., 2002), pp. 94-114; Sanneh, *Translating the Message: The Missionary Impact on Culture* (Maryknoll, N.Y., 1989).

14. J. A. Draper, "Magema Fuze and the Insertion of Subjugated Historical Subjects into the Discourse of Hegemony," *Bulletin for Contextual Theology* 5, no. 2 (1998): 16-26; Birgit Meyer, "Beyond Syncretism: Translation and Diabolization in the Appropriation of Protestantism in Africa," in *Syncretism /Anti-Syncretism: The Politics of Religious Synthesis,* ed. Charles Stewart and Rosalind Shaw (London, 1994), pp. 45-68.

of African Christianity, whether in the colonial past or in its new dimensions, compelled by "the shocking inequality of cultural forces." He maintains that in the gospel-culture encounter, Africans merely and "consciously turned western links to their own ends and purposes." Was there more to it, or was adaptation the only pattern of initiative? Gifford asserts that neither in the past nor in the present salience of Pentecostalism has the force of "extraversion" diminished; the creativity in African Christianity has not overawed the consequences of the control installed in the colonial past.[15] So what was achieved in the decolonization process? At the root of this debate are the values, presuppositions, and basic orientations that have consciously or unconsciously shaped the prevalent methods of doing African church history, especially the level of sensitivity to how the colonized perceive and reflect on their past.

Three caveats could be added. Using religion as a discourse, A. F. Walls views African Christianity as an extension of the religious quest from African primal religion into the domain of Christianity, forcing the latter into unfamiliar, vulnerable terrain with new possibilities as people demanded that Christianity fulfill the same needs as primal religion or do better.[16] From a theological perspective, the word and spirit empowered for change, following the lines of predominant charismatic religiosity of primal religion. Gifford ignored the limits of social scientific study of religion that, as Rodney Stark alleged, originated in atheism and retains much of its militant antireligious roots and assumptions.[17]

It would appear that two scholarly positions have emerged: one that emphasizes African initiative as liberation from the control and dehumanizing missionary tutelage, and one that does not ignore some measure of African creativity but would depict a softer image of missionary presence whose imprint on the African sacred landscape was nonetheless indelible. As Brian Stanley put it in a helpful personal correspondence, "institutions which had invested decades' worth of dollars and personnel in the missionary enterprise wanted to ensure that the central goals of the enterprise were as far as possible preserved amidst the rapid and tumultuous political changes of decolonization. These people had Christian humanitarian ideals; although we may judge that they did not live up to them (who does?). . . . The sincerity of

15. Paul Gifford, *African Christianity: Its Public Role* (Bloomington, Ind., 1998), p. 332.

16. Andrew F. Walls, "Africa in Christian History: Retrospect and Prospect," *Journal of African Christian Thought* 1, no. 1 (1998): 2-15.

17. Rodney Stark, "Atheism, Faith, and the Social Scientific Study of Religion," *Journal of Contemporary Religion* 14, no. 1 (1998): 41-62.

the vision that lay behind the preoccupation with 'control' deserves a bit more recognition." Further rejecting the hegemonic image, Andrew Porter, in a perceptive essay, stressed that in culture-contact there is tremendous freedom, inspiration, opportunity, capacity, and initiative for cultures to respond to change agents and to assimilate, adapt, tolerate, re-create, transform, and reconstitute them. The missionary presence elicited the compliance, collaboration, and freedom to choose from indigenous receivers. Furthermore, in an atmosphere of tolerance, bargaining, restraint, and stark reality, it was evident that imperialism could not be sustained by force. The salient contributions in medicine, education, and translation could not be ignored.[18]

The danger of such interpretation is to blunt the sharp edge of missionary presence that created the adjustment problems for the modern churches in Africa. Some scholars have nuanced the so-called benefits of language policy and education. Indigenous entrepreneurial contributions illustrate the fact that the content was not "fundamentally determined by what the colonial peoples wanted to take from them."[19] The Eric Ashby Report in 1960 and the controversy with Roman Catholics in eastern Nigeria thereafter indicate the Achilles' heels of missionary education.[20]

A balanced perspective will not deny the humanitarian roots of the missionary movement but will recognize that the terrain changed over time. Using the relationship with chiefs as an index, missionaries began with much caution and a sense of vulnerability and attention to what Africans wanted. A shift occurred in the 1880s for a number of reasons: the enlargement of scale of missionary activities, the presence of the colonial security system, and involvement with the "civilization project." Missionaries abandoned Henry Venn's ideology of euthanasia, dismantled indigenous leadership of churches, and installed a control system. This collusion of Maxim guns and the godly cause explains the reluctance of missionaries to devolve power, the stigma of foreignness that dogged the heels of the postcolonial churches and essayed to

18. A. Porter, "Cultural Imperialism and Protestant Missionary Enterprise, 1780-1914," *Journal of Imperial and Commonwealth History* (hereafter *JICH*) 25, no. 3 (Sept. 1997): 367-91.

19. Porter, p. 381.

20. P. E. H. Hair, *The Early Study of Nigerian Languages* (Cambridge, 1967), p. 88; A. Hastings, *The Construction of Nationhood* (Cambridge, 1997), chap. 6; Nicholas I. Omenka, *The School in the Service of Evangelization* (Leiden, 1989); C. Cook, "Church, State and Education: The Eastern Nigerian Experience, 1950-1967," in *Christianity in Independent Africa*, ed. E. Fasholé-Luke et al. (London, 1978), pp. 193-206; M. Beti, *Poor Christ of Bomba* (London, 1956), discusses the Ashby Report.

drive them from the public space, and the apparent weakness in manpower and theology. Though missionaries anticipated the end of colonial rule, they did little to prepare for it, perhaps in the belief that they could survive better than the colonial rulers. This is the point of the incredible conversation between the French colonial officer Monsieur Vidal and the priest in Mongo Beti's *Poor Christ of Bomba.*

Decolonization as Passive Revolution

Beside the character of the missionary presence in the colonial enterprise are the nature, process, and consequences of decolonization. Was it planned or compelled and pursued hastily? Was it a transposition, a passive revolution, or a transformation? How did the missionaries respond? One impression is that they were uneasy about the prospects. For instance, in 1967 T. A. Beetham, secretary of the Conference of Missionary Societies of Great Britain and Ireland, reflected on the anxieties of member churches in the face of decolonization. Uppermost was the resilience of primal religion in the midst of cultural revival and resurgent nationalism and the side effects of years of missionary control. White control, he argued, bequeathed weak churches characterized by disunity, a dependency syndrome, and poor manpower development.[21] Commentators have pointed to the unprophetic silence and passivity of postindependence churches. In 1939 a delegation from the Paris headquarters of the Holy Ghost Christians visited Nigeria to evaluate the missionary activities of Bishop Shanahan. In their report they expressed concern that the concentration on the education apostolate had diminished the imperative to preach the Word.[22]

Beetham's disquiet was partially because decolonization exposed the differing agendas of the colonial government and missionaries. Colonial rule, while it manifestly produced significant changes, both intended and unintended, was in many respects deeply suspicious and hostile toward anything other than highly instrumental and very tightly controlled modernization. Its centralized, authoritarian administration and great concern for order were designed to achieve this singular goal. Were missionaries bedfellows? Noll has pointed to "the Evangelical roots of Enlightenment and modernity," but he

21. T. A. Beetham, *Christianity and the New Africa* (London, 1967), p. vii.

22. J. W. de Gruchy, *Christianity and Democracy* (Cambridge, 1995), p. 183; A. Hastings, *A History of African Christianity, 1950-1975* (Cambridge, 1979), pp. 187ff.; O. U. Kalu, "Peter Pan Syndrome: Church Aid and Selfhood in Africa," *Missiology* 3, no. 1 (Jan. 1975): 15-29; Desmond Forristal, *The Second Burial of Bishop Shanahan* (Dublin, 1990).

also drew attention to significant shifts.[23] A debate has ensued as to whether missions used education "to plug into" modernity. Beidelman and Strayer would argue that the missionaries met modernity halfway, opposing the full agenda to the chagrin of Africans and frustration of the colonial officers who threatened to withdraw their grants-in-aid to missionary schools. As Beidelman observed, the Church Missionary Society (CMS) missionaries at Kaguru, Uganda, bitterly regretted changes that secular education brought, "replacing the bad old things with all the bad new things." In Strayer's view, the goal was not to create a highly educated elite.[24] This explains the virulent disdain for the "black Englishman" caricatured in Joyce Carey's *Mister Johnson* and Wole Soyinka's *Interpreters.* It explains the colonial French policy that cordoned off North Africa from missionary incursion and, as A. E. Barnes shows, the constraint on missionary presence and protection of Islam in northern Nigeria.[25]

Differences in the goals and curricula of education and cultural policies betrayed the ideological cleavages and competing visions between missions and colonial governments. As the missionaries pursued their goals with consummate passion, Africans became increasingly resistant and critical of the "intimate enemies" (church and state). Africans were against the colonial enterprise for racism and for barring entrance to the decision-making echelon of white power. Similarly, they were reluctant to accept fully a mission demand for cultural transformation, and they demonstrated a desire for freer access to a wider range of modern cultural, educational, and economic opportunities than missionaries were prepared to grant. Africans were sensitive to missionary unwillingness to afford them higher training, ordain an adequate number of indigenous priests, devolve power, or overtly support nationalism. Among the Roman Catholics, priestly formation was riddled with humiliation, racism, abuse of privacy, rejection of African values, and other forms of intolerance. For a long time Irish seminaries refused to admit African candidates.[26] Mean-

23. Mark A. Noll, "Evangelical Identity, Power and Culture in the Great Nineteenth Century," CWC Position Paper 107 (Cambridge, 1999), p. 7; see also Brian Stanley, *The Bible and the Flag* (Leicester, 1990), p. 16.

24. T. O. Beidelman, *Colonial Evangelism: A Socio-Historical Study of an East African Mission at the Grassroots* (Bloomington, Ind., 1982), chap. 7; R. W. Strayer, *The Making of Mission Communities in East Africa* (London, 1978).

25. A. E. Barnes, "Evangelization Where It Is Not Wanted: Colonial Administrators and Missionaries in Northern Nigeria during the First Third of the Twentieth Century," *JRA* 25, no. 4 (1995): 412-41.

26. I. R. A. Ozigboh, *Igbo Catholicism* (Onitsha, 1985); A. N. O. Ekwunife, "Integration of African Values in Priestly Formation," *African Ecclesiastical Review* 39, no. 4 (1997): 194-213.

while virulent rivalry suffused the missionary enterprise. Each denomination sought to imprint its own version of the shared agenda and thereby engendered immense social and political divides that would hinder the mobilization of the community in the modernity project. These factors fueled the antimissionary sentiments that underpinned African understanding of decolonization. Obviously, black Christians and white missionaries perceived the process differently.

There were many warning signs that missionary power could not be exercised in the same way for much longer. For instance, at the heels of the antiforeign movements in China, the Jerusalem Conference of 1928 pressed the case for an indigenous church and a reappraisal of attitude toward other faiths. On the home front attacks appeared from fundamentalists and in academic circles in the 1930s. Other alerts sapped missionary confidence as geopolitical events such as the Great Depression and the toll of rapid expansion combined to diminish the manpower and financial capacities of the enterprise. In a case study of British missionary responses to African colonial issues, 1945 to 1953, John Stuart has shown the increasing strain in the relationship, policies, and power arrangements between missionaries and the British government on the one hand, and Africans on the other. The latter tended to jettison the middleman role of the missionaries so as to deal directly with the secular authorities.[27] By the end of the Second World War the Anglicans considered massive restructuring. Many missionaries, however, were heedless to change; others talked about the situation, wrote wise memos on salient political ethics and reorganization of social services, but remained cautious. Then experiences in the Second World War and knowledge of events in India and Ceylon stimulated and inspired the nationalist challenge.

The missions were rudely awakened by the speed of decolonization. As Basil Davidson concluded, "it could accordingly be said that the colonial powers stumbled out of Africa as best they could, keeping their own interest always in view and at no time applying initiatives that were not, in one way or another imposed or provoked by African pressures for anti-colonial challenge."[28] The British stumbled out of the colonies, the French and Belgians abandoned theirs, while the Portuguese had theirs snatched violently from them. Between 1952 and 1956 most of the Maghrib became politically inde-

27. John Stuart, "'A Measure of Disquiet': British Missionary Responses to African Colonial Issues, 1945-53," CWC Position Paper 109 (Cambridge, 2002); Charles Weber, "Christianity and West African Decolonisation," *NAMP Position Paper 80* (Cambridge, 1997).

28. In Prosser Gifford and Wm. R. Louis, eds., *Decolonization and African Independence: The Transfers of Power, 1960-1980* (New Haven and London, 1988), p. 509; see J. D. Hargreaves, *The End of Colonial Rule in West Africa* (London, 1979).

pendent, West Africa followed from 1957 through 1960, and the rest joined after protracted struggles. Four reasons have been adduced for decolonization. While some may query the concept of nationalism in the African context, many hold that the nationalism of the elite who chafed about their exclusion from power was central to igniting the process. Here cultural nationalism was replaced by political nationalism. The rise of the United States and its foreign policy goals loomed large in the new dispensation. Along with this was the economic factor as Europe sought to rebuild after the Second World War. The role of the "official mind" leaves the impression of a deliberate calculation of British interests that were to be protected with constitutions, and of a conscious initiative to liquidate the empire. This perception of calculation has been vigorously challenged. Another argument is that in the politics of cold war containment, decolonization was an opportunistic response in crisis management. The colonial government abandoned its intimate enemy: "it is no longer Christianity, Civilization and Commerce but social engineering, technical assistance and capital investment which are expected to harmonize the interests of Africa and Europe."[29]

The inescapable conclusion is that decolonization did not imply a radical change of socioeconomic structure. The gap between ideal and reality is explained by Gramsci as "passive revolution," describing the way a dominant sociopolitical group may have to change its way of wielding power if it wants to maintain it.[30] The goal of decolonization was to return to informal empire where former rulers would retain sufficient economic and technological resources to exercise powerful influence upon future development. A limited transfer of power bequeathed ossified state apparatus, institutions, and extensions of colonial policies, which burdened the nations with artificial boundaries, incomprehensible constitutions, and parasitic elites. Passive revolution has fueled the modernization and dependency theories in political analysis of contemporary African pathology. It is the root of the divinity of the market and cooperation between a predatory elite and multinational companies.

29. Hargreaves, p. xii; see also T. O. Ranger, "Connexions between 'Primary Resistance' Movements and Modern Mass Nationalism in East and Central Africa," *Journal of African History* 9, no. 3 (1968), and "Religious Movements and Politics in Subsaharan Africa," *ASR* 29, no. 2 (1986): 1-69; R. Pearce, "The Colonial Office and Planned Decolonization in Africa," *African Affairs* 83 (1984): 77-93; J. E. Flint, "The Failure of Planned Decolonization in British Africa," *African Affairs* 82 (1983): 389-411; see J. F. Ade Ajayi and A. E. Ekoko, "Transfer of Power in Nigeria: Its Origins and Consequences," in Gifford and Louis, eds., *Decolonization and African Independence*, pp. 245-69.

30. See Jeff Haynes, *Religion and Politics in Africa* (London and Nairobi, 1996).

The perspective here is that missionaries shared with the official mind a similar tactical response to decolonization, however at a great cost. They exhibited much resilience and change of tack. For instance, they abandoned their opposition to modernity, embraced it, and sought to channel it toward the hallmarks of liberal theology, reflecting the shift in European culture in the economic boom years, 1960-70, and under the shivers of the cold war. The responses of the missionaries to nationalist insurgence at the twilight of colonialism, 1945-59, however, differed in quality from the retooling strategies in the immediate aftermath, 1960-75. Major developments in the political climate of the decade 1966-75 forced enormous changes in the sacred landscape.

The story goes back to the late 1940s when African nationalist activities rose in crescendo as political parties were established in country after country. One explanation is that a younger breed with sharper focus came to the fore, sidelining both traditional rulers and moderates, to bask in the fiery sun of mass adulation. Some appeasers such as Albert Luthuli, in 1952, abandoned the ideal of racial cooperation disillusioned by the racism in the church. Undoubtedly missionary responses to nationalism varied during the first decade, 1945-54, according to individual whims, official or denominational/institutional policies, and regional contexts. A certain shift followed as missionaries felt powerless to halt the process and betrayed by both government and protégés. Some in the field tried to use available facilities to stem the tide by positing a dichotomy between Christianity and politics. Drama, public debates, and lectures were pressed into the effort to warn Christians to eschew politics and seek first the kingdom of God; that colonialism, when properly reined in, was for the good of Africans. Acting like an anti-masque, the Moral Re-Armament group networked through West Africa to inculcate salient political ethics.[31] Some missionaries, such as Walter Carey, formerly bishop of Bloemfontein, were indiscreetly hostile, while others, such as the irrepressible Michael Scott, the voice of the Herero people, represented those sympathetic to the African cause. Generally, institutional attitudes varied: those at the home base espoused idealistic positions that showed some sympathy for Africans but were so cautious that they amounted to little. In the field some were alarmed at the prospects of Marxism or the resurgence of paganism, angry at the ingratitude of the African elite, and resolved to contain the damage. Nationalism was imaged as irreligious, and the nationalists were portrayed as too immature to lead nations to a democratic vision. N. M. Bowman, in a Church of Scotland journal in 1947, put it succinctly: "a nation does not learn overnight to think of power as servant and not the master of justice. People do not acquire in a sin-

31. See chap. 11 in this volume.

gle generation that sense of responsibility, that sense of stewardship, that integrity without which corruption and greed will speedily threaten all attempts to run their own affairs."[32] The period of tutelage had been too short to produce the right moral environment for independence. The cautious mood can be traced in ecumenical political thought from the concern on the place of the state in God's design at the Life and Work conference at Oxford in 1937, through the interest in "the responsible society" at the inaugural assembly of the World Council of Churches (WCC) at Amsterdam in 1948, to the Willingen meeting of the International Missionary Council in 1952, when, for once, a strong social concern provided a shift.

Regional differences abound. West Africa had plenty of mosquitoes and no white settler community; therefore, indigenization policy predominated in the mid-1950s. It had three prongs: to waltz with nationalists, to utilize the services of indigenous personnel, and to seek to adapt Christianity to African culture in the belief that the African need was to "baptize" ingredients of their culture. Many of the priests trained in the early 1950s were in the vanguard. This limited perception of African Christian initiative in religion would be exposed later. Meanwhile, it formed a part of the arsenal for a passive revolution. The Belgians in central Africa sought to legitimize their rule with Catholicism. Salazar's Concordat of 1940 recognized and funded the Catholic Church as the official instrument to promote national colonial aims of the state in Angola and Mozambique. In the Congo, the career of Bishop Jean de Hemptinne, vicar apostolic of Katanga, buttressed the loyalist support while the nationalist flavor in Simon Kimbangu's imagery of the "baton" earned him imprisonment. Similarly, the church's manipulation of religion in Rwanda has become the subject of indictment.[33] In Ethiopia Emperor Haile Selassie used a revised constitution to rope the Orthodox Church into state structures as the *Abuna* sat in the Council of Regency and Crown Council. In eastern Africa "waltzing" with nationalists in Uganda forced the church into the public sphere, and in the first elections a Catholic Kiwanuka jostled with a Protestant Obote, celebrating the fruits of years of virulent rivalry and thereby dividing the society. Liberia offered an unenviable model where the state stood on the tripod of Christianity, Masonic lodge, and True Whig Party as the rulers bowed to the three power nodes.[34]

32. N. M. Bowman, "Democracy without Religion," *Life and Work*, Oct. 1947, p. 111.

33. Tim Longman, "Empowering the Weak and Protecting the Powerful," *ASR* 41 (Apr. 1998): 49-72.

34. O. U. Kalu, "Tools of Hope: Stagnation and Political Theology in Africa, 1960-95," in *A Global Faith: Essays in Evangelicalism and Globalization*, ed. M. Hutchinson and O. Kalu (Sydney, 1998), pp. 181-213.

The impact of decolonization on church groups varied depending on certain indices: the size of the group and its ecclesiastical organization, the vertical spread and social quality of adherents, the inherited pattern of colonial relationship, the theological emphasis, and international relations. It also depended on the manner of disengagement, the weave of neocolonial fabric, and the dosage of Marxism in the political mix. Any of these could aid well-being or woe depending on the context. For instance, in the Congo, Mobutu perceived the Roman Catholics as a danger to be demolished because gods do not brook competition. The core of godly passive revolution depended on the rearguard actions to retool, so as to maintain influence, using indigenous personnel and resources. This was the main thrust of the missionary policy of indigenization. There were many measures: manpower development, internal restructuring through church unity and ecumenism, balancing aid and selfhood in funding so as to cure dependency and nurture stewardship, revisiting cultural policy through adaptation and thereby catalyzing a controlled initiative in art and liturgy, realigning the church-state relationship by involving more Christians in politics, encouraging theological reflection, installing a new model of relationship that uses the idiom of partnership to camouflage paternalism and thus essaying to maintain social services along the old lines. These cumulatively would remedy the aftereffects of the excessive control of the past and preserve the core of missionary structures while broadening African participation to respond to the challenges created by the insurgent nationalism of the new states.

This counterinsurgence was aided by a paradigm shift in the ecumenical movement that became visible at Uppsala in 1968. Konrad Raiser termed it "the expansion of the ecumenical perspective universally to all humanity."[35] The new ecumenical paradigm raised a new understanding of mission, defined in relation to the challenges of modernity, science, and technology; dialogue with other faiths; and issues of justice and race. The support for freedom fighters stirred an internal debate that only began to subside at the WCC assembly in Nairobi in 1975. Similarly, Vatican II (1962-65), which had only 61 Africans out of 2,500 bishops, was a watershed in redesigning the Catholic Church's policy in mission and social service. It released African energy in the church, as a number of papal pronouncements appeared to speak to Africans in a new voice. In 1969 Pope Paul VI made the famous declaration that "you

35. Konrad Raiser, *Ecumenism in Transition: A Paradigm Shift in the Ecumenical Movement* (Geneva, 1991), p. 54; see also Lesslie Newbigin, "Ecumenical Amnesia," *International Bulletin of Missionary Research* 18, no. 1 (Jan. 1994): 1-5; Charles West, *The Power to Be Human* (New York, 1971).

must have an African Christianity. Indeed you possess human values and characteristic forms of culture which can rise up to perfection so as to find in Christianity, and for Christianity, a true superior fullness and prove to be capable of a richness of expression all its own, and genuinely African."[36] Pope John Paul II's call for inculturation and enrichment released much hope before people realized that curial control and liturgy within Roman rites shortened the ropes. Nonetheless, the renaissance of Christian art left an enduring mark as Father Kevin Carroll in Nigeria, Ethelbert Mveng in Cameroon, John Groeber in southern Africa mentored a number of young artists.[37] Equally impressive was the depth of liturgical renewal in music, dance, use of native languages, and formation of associations around new liturgical practices as vigils, retreat centers, and suchlike sprung up to the consternation of missionaries. Block rosaries that served as catechetical occasions became vibrant charismatic events.

The details of these strategies will not bear repetition. Suffice it to say that the level of ministerial formation galloped from the 1960s. Theological education had an enormous boost with the formation of regional and continental associations that encouraged theological reflection and revision of curricula in Bible schools. Many experimented with theological education by extension, while the genesis of Ecumenical Association of Third World Theologians (EATWOT) brought together many from those regions of the world where the pressing question was, "*Eat what?*" In the rainy season of 1973, the WCC met at Ibadan to explore how to readjust the funding of African churches so as to encourage them to learn the art of giving. When the Board of Faith and Order of the WCC met at Accra in August 1974, there were more union talks going on in Africa than in other continents. The leaders of the Church of South India and those from Ceylon toured Africa to provide advice. Except for the case of Zambia, all others collapsed.

In Nigeria theological and nontheological reasons colluded to thwart the dream. The scions of the faith churches dismissed the Constitution of the Union as lacking adequate spirituality. Other minor doctrinal matters caused concern, but the real weighty issues were personality clashes and rivalries, denominational hostilities that had not healed, competition for the bishoprics, and ethnicity. Finally some Methodist congregations took the

36. *Gaba Pastoral Letter*, 7, pp. 50-51; see also J. Mullen, *The Catholic Church in Modern Africa* (Dublin, 1965); E. E. Uzoukwu, *Liturgy: Truly Christian, Truly African* (Eldoret, 1982); F. K. Lumbala, *Celebrating Jesus in Africa: Liturgy and Inculturation* (Maryknoll, N.Y., 1998).

37. Kevin Carroll, *Yoruba Religious Carving* (London, 1967); Rosalind I. J. Hackett, *Art and Religion in Africa* (London, 1996).

Union Committee to court while the civil war (1967-70) scattered the litigants.[38] Studies from eastern Africa have confirmed how the same factors that destabilized African nation-states wreaked havoc in Christian circles.[39] Admittedly many of these could occur in any context beyond Africa, but the key difference was that it was felt that church unity was imposed from the outside.

Could the retooling strategies be interpreted as passive revolution? Two insiders who served the home base of missionary organizations supply different answers. T. A. Beetham raised the question of ulterior motives behind these salvage operations, but only to dismiss the possibility: "Are the thinking and experiment and action . . . merely a fumbling attempt to retain influence, to gain some new position of authority to compensate for privileges now being rapidly lost? Or has it [the African church] a significant future?"[40] In a more acerbic vein, J. V. Taylor, who served as general secretary of the CMS in the heady 1960s, gave a very ungarnished evaluation of the indigenization process. He observed that it had become fashionable for white men of his generation to join "in the chorus of disparagement against the Gothic churches and pietistic hymn tunes that have everywhere stamped the church as a foreign import" in Africa.[41] Worse, indigenization had failed because the indigenous people believe that "we are playing at it" while holding to orthodoxy, fearing the dangers of syncretism, acting with "mixed motives" and unduly moralistic ethics. "Instead of waiting humbly to discover what kind of leadership the Lord was raising up for his church in Africa or Asia, missionaries have been busily engaged in grooming successors to themselves . . . reproducing their stereotyped kind of leadership."[42] In a way this was a truism, having been the goal of missionary education and elite formation. The strategy was sharpened for new ends. But Taylor reveals that decolonization caused much soul-searching about the meaning and goal of mission. Attention turned briefly from the abilities of Africans to keep away from the warm embrace of witch doctors. Lars Thunberg called it "the redemption for the

38. O. U. Kalu, *Divided People of God: Church Union Movement in Nigeria, 1867-1967* (New York, 1978); Kalu, "Church Unity and Religious Change in Africa," in *Christianity in Independent Africa*, pp. 164-75.

39. J. Mugambi, J. Mutiso-Mbinda, and J. Vollbrecht, *Ecumenical Initiatives in Eastern Africa* (Nairobi, 1992).

40. Beetham, p. 151.

41. J. V. Taylor, "Selfhood: Presence or Persona?" in *The Church Crossing Frontiers: Essays on the Nature of Mission: In Honour of Bengt Sundkler*, ed. P. Beyerhaus and C. F. Hallencreutz (Uppsala, 1969), p. 171.

42. Taylor, p. 172.

wrongs of history."[43] Lesslie Newbigin imagined a context where sending churches would become "bridge-builders" serving at "mission points."[44] The Lutheran World Federation experimented with "reverse flow," in which African ministers were posted to German congregations where everybody treated them with cold civility.

The African story, in the decade 1965-75, is that people increasingly found the missionary version of indigenization to be unsatisfactory and restrictive. Yet Christianity was attractive and grew tremendously as the charismatic spirituality of the Aladura or African Independent Churches (AICs) was absorbed into the mission churches. Liturgical experimentation caused disquiet in many places as "traditionalism" impeded progress. There was also an increasing laicization of the church. Many reasons are adduced: increased use of the Bible and vernacular as Vatican II released people from earlier restrictions, so enabling the Africanization of the liturgy; government takeover of schools and hospitals that jolted the ascendancy of the churches, compelling them to turn to their true calling; the growing competition from the Christian left wing or AICs; the deliberate policy to encapsulate the elite and the impact of a new crop of trained clergy and theologians. The laicization of the church was particularly significant because the churches wanted their people to use their powers and good offices to act as *defensores fidei.* Knighthood orders were designed to attract. These, in turn, found the church members as assured voters. Soon their social and financial influence became more important in church affairs and decision making than anticipated. The "nationalism" of the new theologians harped on the vestiges of missionary structures and the predicaments of an unindigenized church. New terminologies were canvassed, such as contextualization, traditionalization, incarnation, and inculturation, as Africans wanted a new type of church or renewed body of Christ and a new relationship with the West. Celibacy was challenged in the Roman Catholic Church. Some Protestants wanted to celebrate the commensality of the Eucharist with palm wine or kola nut. The Bible supplied precedents proffering the possibility that the spirituality of primal religion did not always conflict with the canon. There was much ferment in the churches and efforts to sabotage the limited indigenization project from the inside.

Outside the church, the growth of the state in Africa in this period was

43. Lars Thunberg, "Redemption for the Wrongs of History," in *The Church Crossing Frontiers,* pp. 209-25.

44. Lesslie Newbigin, "The Call to Mission — a Call to Unity?" in *The Church Crossing Frontiers,* pp. 254-65.

significant by causing political instability, human rights abuse, environmental degradation, and economic collapse. New states imaged their goals in Christian garb in obvious attempts to bowdlerize — national redemption, economic salvation, political justification, national regeneration, sanctity of the state, and so on. Many became one-party states, others praetorian; some took to Marxism. The churches became alarmed. The Catholics assigned the Jesuit veteran missionary J. C. McKenna to study the problem. Of forty-four sub-Saharan nations, fifteen leaned in this direction soon after independence. On a closer look, none advocated pure Marxism, as the cold war attracted a variety of leftist ideologies from the USSR, China, Cuba, America, and Europe. Africans responded with the homegrown breeds of conscientism, African socialism, humanism, centralized democracy, and others. In spite of Ratsiraka's *Red Book* in Madagascar, the churches thrived. The hostility in former Iberian enclaves soon diminished. Renamo flirted with Pentecostals in Mozambique, FNLA with Baptists in Angola, even as peace was brokered in the civil war by lay Catholics of the Communita di Sant'Egidio in Italy. In Angola and Zambia political rhetoric did not hurt the churches as much as the bad economic policies and disease.[45] On the whole, the power adventurism of the states forced major changes on the pattern of Christian presence in Africa.

All these chickens came to roost in the moratorium debate, 1971-75. "Moratorium" was a more strident and different form of indigenization project. It reflected African impatience with the nature, pace, and results of mission-initiated indigenization. Africans suspected a hidden agenda to embroil them in cosmetics while the same people retained real power. John Gatu, the secretary-general of the Presbyterian Church in Kenya, initiated the call during a visit to the United States in 1971. He embarrassed his hosts by declaring that he had not come to beg for money or personnel but to request that missionary aid in money and personnel cease for at least five years so that the short man could learn how to hang his knapsack within reach. Earlier he led his church to produce a document stating what they believed. This raised the issue of doctrine. Burgess Carr, the secretary of the All Africa Conference of Churches (AACC), Nairobi, was equally enamored of the idea, proposed it at Lusaka, and invited African churches symbolically to Alexandria to draft an African Confession of Faith. By 1974 E. B. Idowu, the new leader of the Methodist Church in Nigeria, who for the last decade had spoken about the predicaments of an unindigenized African church, moved the boundaries to mat-

45. J. C. McKenna, *Finding a Social Voice: The Church and Marxism in Africa* (New York, 1997).

ters of polity by proposing a patriarchal polity in consonance with the early church in North Africa. Were these romantic moves or sabotage?

Many Western mission bodies saw red and responded in a number of telling ways as a debate ensued in seminars, conferences, and pages of journals. It was argued that *theologically* moratorium was unacceptable because of the Pauline imagery of soma, that we are one body, and one part cannot prevent the other from performing a mandatory task. Mission was the raison d'être of the church, a command from the Lord. *Ecclesiastically,* it was dangerous to become a national church. This threatened catholicity; the pilgrim and the indigenous principles must be held in tension. *Logistically,* it would be impossible to dismantle the mission structures that had been built for over a century. Then there was the *gut* reaction of those who presumed that the Africans had proved ungrateful after years of sacrifices by missionaries. Eliott Kendall, who served the same Methodist constituency as Beetham, has documented the overt and subtle pressures mounted on African church leaders.[46] Dissent was punished with denial and low-intensity operations to foment local rebellion as moratorium was perceived as sabotage. It did not take long for ranks to break: some leaders preferred aid rather than to suffer as freedom fighters. Burgess Carr lost his job while Idowu became embroiled in schism; the AACC languished until everyone forgot the spelling of "moratorium." Avoiding the cardinal sin of monocausality, we must attribute more to the fates of these men than this one cause, but the debate was crucial. Moratorium exposed the character of African relationship with the West: extraversion was inbuilt in the pattern of African relationship with the West as an essential ingredient to maintain "eternal juniority." Even the support among white liberals proved ambiguous as some Protestant missions took the opportunity to abandon missionary engagement. They have found, however, that the collapse of their missionary involvement diminished both the volume of local funds received and the sense of importance in their churches, so they are now forced to create new network patterns. Moratorium and African liberation struggles influenced the shifts in the strategy for decolonizing the African churches. When the WCC General Assembly met in Nairobi in 1975, the themes indicated a new mood that accepted African Christian maturity in ways hardly planned by the missionaries.

46. Elliott Kendall, *The End of an Era* (London, 1978), p. 85; See also O. U. Kalu, "Church, Mission and Moratorium," in *The History of Christianity in West Africa,* ed. O. U. Kalu (London, 1980), pp. 365-74; Kalu, "Not Just New Relationships but a Renewed Body," *International Review of Mission* 64 (Apr. 1975): 143-48.

From the Mouths of Babes: Saboteurs on the Fringe

If moratorium encapsulated sabotage from the center of the historic mission churches, plenty more operated from the fringes and gradually infected those in the center more than they could have dreamed. Change usually occurs from the fringes of any system. The last part of the chapter, therefore, examines the patterns of Christian life and ministry that emerged at the fringes of mission churches as Africans further responded to the power of the gospel. The weight of the historiographical excursus at the beginning testified that African religious genius has struggled for long to burst from the boundaries set by the initial gospel bearers. The conversation between David George and the young governor of Sierra Leone at the inception of the colony indicated that right from the beginning of the encounter, Africans had a certain view of the role of the gospel in responding to the challenges of the young colony. They wanted a certain type of biblical religion, tapping the full pneumatic resources provided in the canon, responding to an environment with a predominantly religious cosmology, breaking down the wall between the sacred and profane and thereby bringing the resources of the Spirit world to bear on existential problems and social experience and applying scriptural ethics to family and communal relationships. They wanted music, celebration, and dance. They wanted their own share of the richness of modernity. The story of African initiative in Christianity is one of variations on these themes with certain elements becoming more urgent in particular times. It may be that they wanted the gospel to outperform what their own religion had always done. As Andrew Walls has said, "the effectiveness of Christian faith or of any particular manifestation of it, is accordingly open to the test whether it gives access to power or prosperity or protection against natural or spiritual enemies, purposes to which much traditional practice was directed, and satisfactorily enforces familial and social duty."[47] Thus the Ethiopianism of the nineteenth century was beyond cultural nationalism. It demanded that missions recognize the continuity of Christianity in primal religion. It was a Bible study group led by an indigene, William de Graft, that invited the Methodists to the Gold Coast in 1835. Many missionary groups came by invitation to inherit existent gatherings: the Assemblies of God, Faith Tabernacle, Apostolic Church, and others. The rise of early charismatic leaders betrayed the character of the Christianity Africans desired. When Wadé Harris

47. Christopher Fyfe and Andrew Walls, eds., *Christianity in Africa in the 1990s* (Edinburgh, 1996), p. 5.

reached Axim, the conversion rate was such that the Methodist church did not provide enough staff to handle the situation.[48] When Garrick Braide started healing, his pastor, H. A. Kemmer, rejoiced that so many people flocked to his church, just as the Qua Iboe Church praised God when the Ibibio Revival broke among teachers attending a weekend meeting in 1927. Just about that time, Samson Oppong unleashed a similar response in the Brong-Ahafo region of the Gold Coast. Many other such revivals occurred in various parts of West Africa during the colonial era, pointing to the type of Christianity the Africans wanted.

Between the mission churches and the colonial governments charges were trumped up to douse the flares, before the full-blown challenge from the AICs, which has received much scholarly attention. Some interpretations border on the romantic because they ignore a typology for analysis that H. W. Turner recognized.[49] W. J. Hollenweger has summarized the subversive challenge the Aladura posed to the agenda of the mission churches: instead of missionary racism, emphasis on literacy, abstract concepts, and reliance on the anonymity of bureaucratic organization, medical technology, and Western psychoanalytical techniques, the Aladura emphasized orality, narrativity, family and personal relationships, a holistic understanding of health and sickness, and family therapy.[50] The challenge of the Aladura was to point to the neglect of the pneumatic dimension to Christianity in missionary practice and its resonance in the African worldview. Cultural contestation followed apace. In the era of decolonization, there was an attempt to bring the Aladura under the canopy by the WCC. Some were admitted based on a clean bill of health issued by Christian scholars (black and white).

The quest for powerful religiosity went beyond the Christian bounds in the colonial period as West Africans imbibed Eastern religions, and ordered from India amulets, charms, potions, and decor for Mami Wata shrines. Along the Atlantic coast membership in Freemasonry lodges and the Ancient Masonic Order of the Rose Crucis (Rosicrucians) (AMORC) became important for social mobility and contact with the colonial rulers. As an example of invention of culture, a powerful indigenous cult, Ogboni, was "reformed" for the modern public space by an archdeacon of the Anglican Church. Religious creativity continually drew on the local to transform the extravenous in both cult and Christianity. Perhaps this is why, having proclaimed African Chris-

48. D. Kimble, *A Political History of Ghana* (Oxford, 1967).

49. H. W. Turner, "A Typology for African Religious Movements," *JRA* 1, no. 1 (1967): 1-32.

50. W. J. Hollenweger, "After Twenty Years' Research on Pentecostalism," *International Review of Mission* 75, no. 297 (1986): 3-12.

tianity, the Roman curia sought to alter the direction of change. T. A. Beetham's anxieties become clearer: the mission churches created a new religious space between 1966 and 1968 and, because of a hidden agenda, hedged it with old rules. Africans saw decolonization as the opportunity to install that deep religious structure that undergirds all the varieties of African traditional religion, a religion with power. Thus the proponents of moratorium showed their frustration just when the young people opened a new battlefront by weaving a new mode of sabotage from the fringes.

This will be illustrated with a brief sketch of the rise of charismatic movements in Nigeria between 1967 and 1975. It is argued that this form of pneumatic response to the gospel was a "setting to work" of missionary preaching, a recovery of the old evangelical spirit that had catalyzed mission, a seepage to the surface of the type of Christianity that Africans wanted, and their perception of the opportunities unleashed by decolonization. A spiritual revival swept through Nigeria from 1970 and created a phenomenon that is now known as the Pentecostal movement. It has acquired various hues and become complex, but its origin was a wave of charismatic movements among the youth of various denominations that occurred in different parts of the country and eddied into churches, challenging the parent groups for power failure. The charismatic goals were both to reevangelize the mainline churches as well as to win new souls for the kingdom. Evangelism and passion for the kingdom remained central to whatever followed.

To put matters in perspective, Nigeria witnessed a number of charismatic stirrings between 1914 and 1975. The scattered flares of 1914-39, which were not part of the Aladura movement, ended with the Christ Apostolic Church, the specifically Aladura movements that later flowered into various types, and the 1970 phenomenon. It is possible to weave connections between the three. It is equally useful to show the differences, especially between the others and the Aladura, whose impact predominated for much longer. Another key issue is: To what extent were these indigenous movements? Their cumulative effects changed the face of Christianity in Nigeria and derailed the path of decolonization of the churches.

This chapter will now concentrate on the new phenomenon that became more significant after political independence and during the process of decolonization. There were seven components to this phenomenon: the Hour of Redemption ministry, which operated in Lagos before the civil war; the Benson Idahosa ministry, which was just gathering momentum in Benin when the civil war began; the radicalization of the Scripture Union in eastern Nigeria, between 1967 and 1975; the Hour of Freedom ministry, which started during the civil war in 1969 and held sway in the east in the immediate aftermath; the charismatism of the Christian Union in the universities of southwestern Nigeria; the phenomenon of "Corpers as Preachers," as the Christian university students invaded northern Nigeria while serving in the National Youth Service Corps (NYSC); and the special case of charismatism in the Roman Catholic Church. All these soon meshed together before divisions emerged when many shifted from operating as fellowships to establish churches. Perhaps we can use the Scripture Union as the "mascot" or signifier to reconstruct the spiritual temper of the times and to demonstrate how the various groups cooperated in the heat of charismatism.

Scripture Union, SU as it is called, was introduced from Britain into Protestant secondary schools in the 1950s. It was one of those interdenominational groups that focused on Bible study, prayers, choruses, and hospital visits, and served as the character-formation component of mission education. Occasionally the senior friend, a missionary teacher, would invite the young students for tea and biscuits. While he tried to make conversation, the students would be more concerned with drinking the tea "properly." It was an innocuous body until the civil war broke out in 1967. Schools closed. A new traveling secretary, Bill Roberts, had just arrived from Britain. Instead of heading home, he decided to hold systematic Bible classes for the students around SU House in Umuahia. It soon turned into a prayer group, engaging in deep conversion, deliverance, evangelism, and relief work.[51] It spread like wildfire as young people formed prayer and evangelistic bands in their villages. By 1969 the character of the SU had changed tremendously as people gave their lives to Christ in large numbers and healing occurred during many hospital visits. To illustrate the temper, Roberts tells the story about young men in a village outside Umuahia who refused to participate in a communal oath taking. Threats from parents, elders, traditional priests, and even some church members failed. Instead they retreated to pray against the deity. On the day of the oath, a quarrel broke out among the elders and the ceremony could not hold. The gauntlet to the compromising ethics of the mission church was obvious as the village was enveloped by a new spirituality. A number of university students also participated in the charismatic activities.

The religious dimension to the war is an important backdrop. It took many directions: there was a cultural renaissance, and with scarcity of money, native doctors and the old ways of resolving problems resurfaced. Occult groups also flourished because dire times needed quick solutions. The Aladura, which had not been very successful in Igboland because of the strength of mission churches, now proliferated as prayer houses in the hinter-

51. Bill Roberts, *Life and Death among the Ibos* (London, 1970).

land at the heels of fleeing refugees. The mission churches met stiff competition because their organized structures could not be maintained. Priests and nuns ran for safety, having lost their congregations. British support for Nigeria surprised and angered many who thought "Christian England" would know that the easterners were the most Christianized in Nigeria. Many turned to the prayer houses to deal with the inner and physical needs of the war. So the cutting edge of Christianity shifted to the prayer houses and young radicalized SU boys and girls, ranging in age from seventeen to twenty-five.

Just before Roberts left Biafra he encountered three lads who had been members of the Cherubim and Seraphim movement and later joined a more potent prayer house at Ufuma. They had risen to high offices variously as visioner, cross bearer, and clairaudient (those who had ability to hear from the unseen world). They were groomed in the Book of Mars, Sixth and Seventh Books of Moses, Springfield Books, and other mystic books. Through Roberts they became converted, renounced their dealings in candles and the occult, and went back to preach Christ to other votaries of prayer houses. Of course, the prophetess at Ufuma chased them out of town. Penniless, Stephen Okafor, Raphael Okafor, and Arthur Orizu formed the Hour of Freedom Evangelistic Association (coined from the core message). The civil war ended in 1970. Based in Onitsha, the three itinerated all over the east with a vibrant evangelical fervor. They built a support network of prayer groups as many young people flocked to the outreach programs. Some SU students joined them; others opposed them for preaching against prayer houses, because many SU young people patronized prayer houses for power and thought they could combine the two. During 1970 and 1971 it was as if a revival hit Igboland; the "Freedom Hour" became famous as healings and mass conversions occurred in town after town. Other groups formed in many towns such as Enugu, Owerri, and Aba. Many of these seventeen- and eighteen-year-old boys and girls boldly took their mission to their own villages. Their ministry caused splits in many AICs over means used; for instance, the Christ Ascension Church splintered. Mike Okonkwo led a wing into a charismatic body, the True Redeemed Evangelical Mission. As schools reopened, these young people returned to their secondary schools to form vibrant SU branches. Those who went to universities built fundamentalist Christian Union camps as formidable interdenominational evangelistic groups.

Just at this time Benson Idahosa, who was converted in the early 1960s by an Igbo leader of an evangelistic ministry in Benin, built up a vibrant ministry with the aid of his former pastor and a Welsh missionary, Pa G. Elton, who had come to Nigeria in 1954 under the British Apostolic Church. Elton had retired but stayed on to minister in the country. He put Idahosa in touch with

Gordon and Freda Lindsay, who sponsored him to attend Christ for the Nations Bible Institute, Dallas. That was after the Lindsays saw how the new ministry had grown and the intense energy of the young man who had "fire in his bones" for soul winning.[52] He later formed the Church of God Mission. By 1970 his theology was developing some themes from T. L. Osborn's teaching, as he waxed strong with prosperity motifs that sounded like music in the ears of those who had just come out from the war and witnessed the growth of his huge miracle center, television ministry, All Nations for Christ Bible School, and the effective musical group called Redemption Voices. The leaders of Hour of Deliverance (Oye, Muyiwa, J. M. J. Emesin) from Lagos; Elton of the Apostolic Church; Emma Harris, a Baptist missionary; and a few other older charismatics provided advice and encouragement as a youth-led religious revival enveloped Nigeria. These soon networked with a different insurgence that occurred in western Nigeria among the students of universities of Ibadan and Ife when members of the Christian Union started to speak in tongues during their Tuesday prayer meetings and later organized national conventions to arouse other universities. The CU, as it is known, broke away in 1962 from the Student Christian Movement (SCM), accusing it of being spiritually and ethically tepid. As this was happening, Elton, who lived at Ilesha, turned his attention to fostering charismatism in the universities and to curing the disunity among the SU boys who hurried to found their individual ministries. He urged them to lay down their signboards and partake in retreats. At one such retreat they jointly formed the Grace of God Mission, saying it was by the grace of God that they could detect the sinfulness of their rivalry.

These young people graduated just when the National Youth Service Corps was made compulsory. As they dispersed through the nation, they formed charismatic groups. Those who traveled abroad for foreign language courses in neighboring French-speaking countries took their spirituality with them. Through their attendance at the conferences of the Pan-African Fellowship of Evangelical Students (PAFES), founded in 1962, the message spread to Kenya and the Fellowship of Christian Unions (FOCUS) in East Africa. In northern Nigeria they not only formed branches in Ahmadu Bello University, Kaduna Polytechnic, and many teachers colleges, but they took over the traveling secretary jobs in such organizations as the Fellowship of Christian Students, New Life for All, and the Nigerian Fellowship of Evangelical Students. A central body, Christian Youth Corpers, was constituted in 1973 to mobilize the heady evangelical enterprises. Some of the southern youths

52. Ruthanne Garlock, *Benson Idahosa: Fire in His Bones* (Tulsa, 1981).

who were not university graduates but had "drunk" their charismatism in secondary school surged through northern Nigeria founding ministries just when many southerners were returning to the north after the civil war. About ten ministries blossomed in Jos, Kaduna, Kano, and Zaria between 1973 and 1976. Northern indigenes have since joined the affray.[53]

Raphael Okafor meticulously kept a diary of his and his companions' activities. One entry is intriguing: "28th March 1971: Enu Onitsha campaign continues. Emmanuel Church authorities refused their church compound again. We moved to the Anglican Girls School, Inland town, Onitsha and began around 5.00 pm. People still attended despite the disruptions. Michaelson gave his testimony. Brother Stephen preached while brother Arthur interpreted. Emmanuel Ekpunobi who said the opening prayers also prayed for the converts and later gave them additional instructions . . . TO GOD BE THE GLORY."[54]

Diary entries are often cryptic, and so some comment is warranted on the impact on mission churches and their responses; the gender factor; the impact on the entire sacred landscape, including occult groups; the relationship of literacy, Bible, and revival; and the further radicalization of the SU as they worked with the Hour of Freedom. There are other ironies: mission schools that were created as means of evangelization now fulfilled the goal to the chagrin of proprietors; schoolchildren, on the fringes of mission power structures, created a challenge that was more radical than anything the missionaries anticipated. The youth, in secondary and tertiary institutions, created a new situation where the leadership would be educated, unlike that in the earlier pneumatic challenges of the Zionists and Aladura. The key point is that Pentecostalism started as a charismatic movement within the mission churches. At one level it was the old evangelicalism writ large. On a closer look, it was something new because of the response to the problems raised in African cosmology. This spirituality has created what Peter Wagner called "the third wave" in American evangelicalism. As he argued, "our worldview influences our hermeneutics or how we interpret the Bible."[55] The renewed interest in worldview and mission and in spiritual warfare or the deliverance motif in evangelical theology emerged from a sympathetic understanding of African charismatism.

53. M. A. Ojo, "Charismatic Movements in Africa," in *Christianity in Africa in the 1990s,* pp. 92-110.

54. Okafor lives in Enugu and has the diary intact. Some extracts have been included in F. Bolton, *And We Beheld His Glory* (London, 1992).

55. C. P. Wagner, *Confronting the Powers* (Ventura, Calif., 1996); *Engaging the Enemy* (Ventura, Calif., 1991).

The responses of the missions varied. The Roman Catholic Church was initially hostile, defrocking two priests who succored the charismatic spirituality in the hurry to rebuild after the war. The gale of the wind proved irresistible, and as they were already concerned about the impact of the prayer houses, which intensified during the war, Dr. Arinze, the archbishop of Onitsha, appointed Fr. Ikeobi to start a charismatic service in Onitsha using Catholic liturgy that included healing and exorcism. Later Fr. Edeh returned from the United States to begin a healing center at Elele near Port Harcourt. In 1974 the Dominicans at Ibadan sponsored a tour of Nigeria by a charismatic team from the United States led by Fr. Francis F. MacNutt. MacNutt claims much success.[56] Though Archbishop Arinze allowed them to operate in his domain, and it was rumored that his mother was healed, the priests treated the team with much suspicion because of the received pattern of ministerial formation, but the laity welcomed the opportunity, and the import of the challenge was not lost on the leaders of the synagogue, who had to ensure that their flock would not drift away. These are aspects of the origin of the Catholic charismatic movement.

While the Anglicans were accommodating and the Catholics intent on finding a viable alternative, some churches were downright hostile. For instance, at Enugu the Presbyterian minister denied the SU further use of St. Andrew's Church Hall. In Ohafia the Central Presbyterian Church drove the SU away; they formed Evangel Church, which now competes with the Presbyterian church, which started in Ohafia in 1910. By 1975 a new realism took over as mission churches embraced charismatic spirituality in the form of prayer vigils, fasting, tithing, choruses, evangelistic tours, and land deliverance. These have now become regular features of mission churches.

The second issue is gender, raised by the patronage of the school principal, Madam Erinne, at Onitsha. Many girls flocked to the SU and Hour of Freedom, and parents felt content that their girls were engaged in safe activities. Conflict occurred in cases where the parents' churches opposed the new spirituality. Older women patronized the youthful healing ministries and served as "Mothers in Israel." Another diary entry by Okafor spells this out: "17th May 1971 Three of us, Arthur, Stephen and I, as well as Mrs. D. Erinne, met bishop L. M. Uzodike and we had a very good discussion for about one hour and later he prayed for us, Lawjua and others on 'Wisdom, Love and Power.'" This Anglican bishop remained a patron for many decades. The girl,

56. F. F. McNutt, "Report from Nigeria," *New Covenant Magazine* 4, no. 11 (1975): 10. See Hilary Achunike, "Roman Catholic Charismatic Movement in Igboland" (Ph.D. thesis, University of Nigeria, 2000).

Lawjua, was eighteen and in secondary school. Her maternal grandfather had brought Anglicanism to Obosi; Lawjua and her siblings were fully involved in radicalizing the church their grandfather brought and drawing on their mother's support and resources. She is typical of the activism of girls who led in the music ministry and preaching. The enlarged role of women became increasingly significant.[57]

The third case is that of Michaelson, a professional who rose to high degrees of initiation in AMORC before his conversion. He burnt his regalia and books as the young people witnessed Christ to him. The boldness of the youth against the dreaded Rosicrucians and Masonic lodges is significant. Michaelson became their patron and had the courage to testify in public.

Emmanuel Ekpunobi was a student at Dennis Memorial Grammar School (the first Anglican grammar school in Igboland) and one of the SU leaders who had opposed the Hour of Freedom because many SU boys had become entangled with prayer houses during the civil war. The SU and the Freedom Hour were now reconciled and soon worked with the university students. As the revival gathered momentum, the young people bonded more and were able to face persecution. Many moved into either full-time ministry after secondary school or, like Ekpunobi, went to university and continued until today as active evangelists. Many Pentecostal ministries in Africa were and are founded by former university teachers and professionals. The potent combination of Bible and literacy explains the wide appeal to the upwardly mobile in modern society.

This cryptic account does little justice to what happened but highlights how the youth posed a subversion to the mission churches within the era of decolonization. Around northeast Igboland alone, over fifty charismatic groups were formed between 1974 and 1989.[58] These young people evangelized Africa with a homegrown spirituality that went beyond mere adaptation.

These events challenged the mission churches either to allow the young people more roles in their activities and to permit charismatic activities or to risk the exodus of young men and women to Pentecostal fellowships. Initially these young evangelists stayed in their churches and met to share fellowship, but later some founded churches specializing in evangelism or deliverance or intercession; a few churches remained as ecumenical fellowships. Most secondary schools and all universities have charismatic fellowships comprising young people in various denominations. Finally, it is intriguing that in re-

57. Bolton, *And We Beheld His Glory.*

58. Ogbu Kalu, *Embattled Gods: Christianization of Igboland, 1841-1991* (Lagos, 1996), p. 278.

sponse to the passive revolution in the era of decolonization, Africans changed the face of the churches that became charismatic and fitted into the deep structure that undergirds all African traditional religions in spite of varieties of names and symbols. Charismatism has been the strongest instrument of church growth in Africa since the 1970s.

Outside the case study area, youths were most prominent in creating this form of challenge in Zambia, Malawi, Ghana, Tanzania, Liberia, Kenya, Ivory Coast, Uganda, and elsewhere. This cameo also provides a glimpse into the origin of "born-again" people who are at the cutting edge in transforming the face of Christianity in Africa. Statistics from Ghana indicate that the AICs may be in decline because the mission churches are now operating from the interior of African maps of the universe and serving the same needs.[59]

In summary, the passive revolution designed by the missions as a response in the era of decolonization was sabotaged from a combined force of the implosion of the "theological" state, the creative ferment from the center, and the pneumatic challenge from the mouths of babes on the fringes of the power structure.

59. E. K. Larbi, "The Development of Ghanaian Pentecostalism" (Ph.D. thesis, University of Edinburgh, 1995).

Bibliography of Principal Secondary Sources

Achunike, Hilary. "Roman Catholic Charismatic Movement in Igboland." Ph.D. thesis, University of Nigeria, 2000.

Adonis, J. C. *Die afgebreekte skeidsmuur weer opgebou: Die verstrengeling van die sendingbeleid van die Nederduitse Gereformeerde Kerk in Suid-Afrika met die praktyk en ideologie van die Apartheid in historiese perspektief.* Amsterdam, 1982.

Ajayi, J. F. Ade, and Ekoko, A. E. "Transfer of Power in Nigeria: Its Origins and Consequences." In *Decolonization and African Independence: The Transfers of Power, 1960-1980,* edited by Prosser Gifford and William R. Louis, 245-69. New Haven and London, 1988.

Anderson, Benedict. *Imagined Communities: Reflections on the Origins and Spread of Nationalism.* London, 1983.

Anderson, Gerald H., ed. *Biographical Dictionary of Christian Missions.* New York, 1998.

Anderson-Morshead, A. E. M. *The History of the Universities' Mission to Central Africa 1859-1909.* New revised ed. London, 1909.

Ashley, Audrey. *Peace-Making in South Africa: The Life and Work of Dorothy Maud.* Bognor Regis, 1980.

Atwell, D. "The Transculturation of English: The Exemplary Case of Tiyo Soga, African Nationalist." Inaugural Lecture, University of Natal, Pietermaritzburg, 1994.

Austin, Granville. *The Indian Constitution: Cornerstone of a Nation.* London, 1966.

Azikiwe, Nnamdi. *Zik: A Selection from the Speeches of Nnamdi Azikiwe.* Cambridge, 1961.

Baëta, C. G. *Prophetism in Ghana.* London, 1962.

Barnes, A. E. "Evangelization Where It Is Not Wanted: Colonial Administrators and Missionaries in Northern Nigeria During the First Third of the Twentieth Century." *Journal of Religion in Africa* 25:4 (1995): 412-41.

Barra, G. *1000 Kikuyu Proverbs.* 1st ed. 1939. Nairobi, 1994.

Bates, M. Searle. "The Church in China in the Twentieth Century." In *China and Christian Responsibility: A Symposium,* edited by William J. Richardson. New York, 1968.

Bayly, C. A. *Empire and Information: Intelligence Gathering and Social Communication in India, 1780-1870.* Cambridge, 1996.

Bayly, Susan. *Saints, Goddesses and Kings: Muslims and Christians in South Indian Society, 1700-1900.* Cambridge, 1989.

———. *Caste, Society and Politics in India from the Eighteenth Century to the Modern Age.* Cambridge, 1999.

Bays, Daniel H. "Christian Revivalism in China, 1900-1937." In *Modern Christian Revivals,* edited by R. Balmer and E. Blumhofer, 159-77. Urbana, Ill., 1993.

———. "Indigenous Protestant Churches in China, 1900-1937: A Pentecostal Case Study." In *Indigenous Responses to Western Christianity,* edited by Steven Kaplan, 124-43. New York, 1994.

———, ed. *Christianity in China: From the Eighteenth Century to the Present.* Stanford, 1996.

———. "A Chinese Christian 'Public Sphere'? Socioeconomic Mobility and the Formation of Urban Middle Class Protestant Communities in the Early Twentieth Century." In *Constructing China: The Interaction of Culture and Economics,* edited by Kenneth Lieberthal, Shuen-fu Lin, and Ernest Young, 101-17. Ann Arbor, 1997.

Bebbington, David. *Evangelicalism in Modern Britain: A History from the 1730s to the 1980s.* London, 1989.

Beetham, T. A. *Christianity and the New Africa.* London, 1967.

Belden, David. "The Origins and Development of the Oxford Group (Moral Re-Armament)." D.Phil. thesis, University of Oxford, 1976.

Bell, G. K. A. *Randall Davidson Archbishop of Canterbury.* 3rd ed. London, 1952.

Beidelman, T. O. *Colonial Evangelism: A Socio-historical Study of an East African Mission at the Grassroots.* Bloomington, Ind., 1982.

Benoist, Joseph-Roger. *Église et pouvoir coloniale au Soudan Français.* Paris, 1987.

Bergen, Doris. *Twisted Cross: The German Christian Movement in the Third Reich.* Chapel Hill, N.C., 1996.

———. "'What God Has Put Asunder Let No Man Join Together': Overseas Missions and the German Christian View of Race." In *Remembrance, Repentance, Reconciliation: The 25th Anniversary Volume of the Annual Scholars' Conference on the Holocaust and the Churches,* edited by Douglas F. Tobler, 5-17. Lanham, Md., 1998.

Berger, Elena L. *Labour Race and Colonial Rule: The Copperbelt from 1924 to Independence.* Oxford, 1974.

Berger, Peter L., and Luckman, Thomas. *The Social Construction of Reality.* London, 1976.

Berman, Bruce. *Control and Crisis in Colonial Kenya: The Dialectic of Domination.* London, 1990.

Beti, M. *Poor Christ of Bomba.* London, 1956.

Blood, A. G. *The History of the Universities' Mission to Central Africa,* vol. 2 (1910-32), vol. 3 (1933-57). London, 1957, 1962.

Bloomberg, Charles. *Christian-Nationalism and the Rise of the Afrikaner Broederbond in South Africa, 1918-48,* edited by Saul Dubow. Bloomington and Indianapolis, 1989.

Bockmuehl, Klaus. *Frank Buchmans Botschaft und ihre Bedeutung für die protestantischen kirchen.* Bern, 1963.

Bosch, David J. "Johannes du Plessis as sendingkundige." *Theologia Evangelica* 19:1 (March 1986).

Botha, Andries Johannes. *Die evolusie van'n volksteologie.* Bellville, 1986.

Breslin, Thomas A. *China, American Catholicism, and the Missionary.* University Park, Pa., and London, 1980.

Brouwer, Steve, Gifford, Paul, and Rose, Susan D., eds. *Exporting the American Gospel: Global Christian Fundamentalism.* London, 1996.

Brown, D., and Brown, M. V., eds. *Looking Back at the Uganda Protectorate: Recollections of District Officers.* Dalkeith, 1996.

Brown, Judith M. "Mahatmas as Reformers: Some Problems of Religious Authority in the Indian Nationalist Movement." *South Asia Research* 6:1 (May 1986): 15-26.

———. *Gandhi: Prisoner of Hope.* New Haven and London, 1989.

———. *Modern India: The Origins of an Asian Democracy.* 2nd ed. Oxford, 1994.

———. "Gandhi — A Victorian Gentleman: An Essay in Imperial Encounter." In *The Statecraft of British Imperialism. Essays in Honour of William Roger Louis,* edited by R. D. King and R. W. Kilson, 68-85. London and Portland, 1999.

———. *Nehru.* London and New York, 1999.

Brown, Judith M., and Louis, William Roger, eds. *The Oxford History of the British Empire, Volume IV: The Twentieth Century.* Oxford and New York, 1999.

Brown, Leslie. *Three Worlds: One Word — Account of a Mission.* London, 1981.

Bruls, Jean. "From Missions to 'Young Churches'." In *The Church in a Secularised Society,* edited by Roger Aubert, 385-437. London, 1978.

Carpenter, Edward. *Archbishop Fisher — His Life and Times.* Norwich, 1991.

Carroll, Kevin. *Yoruba Religious Carving: Pagan and Christian Sculpture in Nigeria and Dahomey.* London, 1967.

Chadwick, Owen. *Mackenzie's Grave.* London, 1959.

Chao, Jonathan T'ien-en. "The Chinese Indigenous Church Movement, 1919-1927: A Protestant Response to the Anti-Christian Movements in Modern China." Ph.D. thesis, University of Pennsylvania, 1986.

Chen Renbing, with Chen Meida. "Chen Chonggui mushi xiaozhuan" (A short biography of Rev. Chen Chonggui). In *Huainian Chen Chonggui mushi* (Commemorating Rev. Chen Chonggui), edited by the Three-Self Committee, 68-102. Shanghai, 1991.

Chidester, David. *Religions of South Africa.* London, 1992.

Clements, Keith. *Faith on the Frontier: A Life of J. H. Oldham.* Edinburgh, 1999.

Clough, Marshall. *Fighting Two Sides: Kenyan Chiefs and Politicians, 1918-1940.* Niwott, 1990.

Comaroff, J. and J. *Of Revelation and Revolution, Volume 1: Christianity, Colonialism and Consciousness in South Africa.* Chicago, 1991.

Cook, C. "Church, State and Education: The Eastern Nigerian Experience, 1950-1967." In *Christianity in Independent Africa,* edited by E. Fasholé-Luke et al., 193-206. London, 1978.

Crafford, D. *Aan God die dank: Geskiedenis van die sending van die Ned. Geref. Kerk binne die Republiek van Suid-Afrika en enkele aangrensende buurstate.* Pretoria, 1982.

Damman, Ernst. "Ausblick: Die deutsche Mission in den ehemaligen deutschen Kolonien zwischen den Weltkriegen." In *Imperialismus und Kolonialmission. Kaiserliches Deutschland und koloniales Imperium,* edited by Klaus J. Bade, 289-305. Wiesbaden, 1982.

Darwin, John. *Britain and Decolonisation: The Retreat from Empire in the Post-War World.* Basingstoke, 1988.

———. *The End of the British Empire: The Historical Debate.* Oxford, 1991.

———. "Diplomacy and Decolonization." *Journal of Imperial and Commonwealth History* 28:3 (Sept. 2000): 5-24.

De Gruchy, John W. *Christianity and Democracy: A Theology for a Just World Order.* Cambridge, 1995.

Digre, Brian. *Imperialism's New Clothes: The Repartition of Tropical Africa 1914-1919.* New York, 1990.

Dijk, Richard van. "Young Born Again Preachers in Independent Malawi." In *New Dimensions in African Christianity,* edited by Paul Gifford, 66-96. Nairobi, 1992.

Dillistone, F. W. *Into All The World: A Biography of Max Warren.* London, 1980.

Draper, J. A. "Magema Fuze and the Insertion of Subjugated Historical Subjects into the Discourse of Hegemony." *Bulletin for Contextual Theology* 5:2 (1998): 16-26.

Dreher, Martin N. *Kirche und Deutschtum in der Entwicklung der Evangelischen Kirche lutherischen Bekenntnisses in Brasilien.* Göttingen, 1978.

Dunch, Ryan F. "Piety, Patriotism, Progress: Chinese Protestants in Fuzhou Society and the Making of a Modern China, 1857-1927." Ph.D. thesis, Yale University, 1996.

Du Toit, André. "No Chosen People: The Myth of the Calvinist Origins of Afrikaner Nationalism and Racial Ideology." *American Historical Review* 88:4 (Oct. 1983): 920-52.

———. "Captive to the Nationalist Paradigm: Prof. F. A. van Jaarsveld and the Historical Evidence for the Afrikaner's Ideas on His Calling and Mission." *South African Historical Journal* 16 (1984): 49-80.

———. "Puritans in Africa? Afrikaner 'Calvinism' and Kuyperian Neo-Calvinism in Late Nineteenth-Century South Africa." *Comparative Studies in Society and History* 27:2 (1985): 209-40.

Egerton, Robert. *Mau Mau.* London, 1990.

Ekwunife, A. N. O. "Integration of African Values in Priestly Formation." *African Ecclesiastical Review* 39:4 (1997): 194-213.

Elliott, Hugh. *Darkness and Dawn in Zimbabwe.* London, 1978.

Elphick, Richard. "Mission Christianity and Interwar Liberalism." In *Democratic Liberalism in South Africa: Its History and Prospect,* edited by R. Elphick, J. Butler, and D. Welsh, 64-80. Middletown, Conn., Cape Town, and Johannesburg, 1987.

Fasholé-Luke, E., et al., eds. *Christianity in Independent Africa.* London, 1978.

Fatton, R. "Africa in the Age of Democratization." *African Studies Review* 38:2 (1995): 67-99.

Fiedler, Klaus. *Christentum und afrikanische Kultur. Konservative deutsche Missionare in Tanzania 1900-1940.* Gütersloh, 1983.

———. 'The Charismatic and Pentecostal Movements in Malawi in Cultural Perspective', paper presented at the Theology Conference, Chancellor College, Blantyre, 1998.

Fitzgerald, John. *Awakening China: Politics, Culture, and Class in the Nationalist Revolution.* Stanford, 1996.

Fleisch, Paul. *Hundert Jahre lutherischer Mission.* Leipzig, 1936.

Flint, J. E. "The Failure of Planned Decolonization in British Africa." *African Affairs* 82 (1983): 389-411.

Forristal, Desmond. *The Second Burial of Bishop Shanahan.* Dublin, 1990.

Foss, Patrick. *Climbing Turns.* Yeovil, 1990.

Füredi, Frank. *The Mau Mau War in Historical Perspective.* London, 1989.

———. *Colonial Wars and the Politics of Third World Nationalism.* London, 1994.

Fyfe, Christopher, and Walls, Andrew, eds. *Christianity in Africa in the 1990s.* Edinburgh, 1996.

Gaitskell, Deborah. "Beyond Devout Domesticity: Five Female Mission Strategies in South Africa, 1907-1960." *Transformation* 16:4 (Oct./Dec. 1999): 127-35.

———. "Female Faith and the Politics of the Personal: Five Mission Encounters in Twentieth-Century South Africa." In "Reconstructing Feminities: Colonial Intersections of Gender, Race, Religion and Class," edited by M. Kosambi and J. Haggis, 68-91. Special Issue, *Feminist Review* 65 (Summer 2000).

Gandhi, M. K. *An Autobiography: The Story of My Experiments with Truth.* London 1966; originally published, 1927.

Garlock, Ruthanne. *Benson Idahosa: Fire in His Bones.* Tulsa, 1981.

Geldenhuys, F. E. O'Brien. *In die stroomversnellings: Vyftig jaar van die NG Kerk.* Cape Town, 1982.

Gensichen, Hans-Werner. "German Protestant Missions." In *Missionary Ideologies in the Imperialist Era, 1880-1920,* edited by Torben Christensen and William R. Hutchison, 181-90. Aarhus, 1982.

Gerdener, G. B. A. "Du Plessis, Johannes." In *Dictionary of South African Biography,* edited by W. J. De Kock, 4 vols., 1:263. Cape Town, 1968-81.

Gerstner, Jonathan Neil. *The Thousand Generation Covenant: Dutch Reformed Covenant Theology and Group Identity in Colonial South Africa, 1652-1814.* Leiden, New York, Copenhagen, Cologne, 1991.

Ghosh, P. C. *The Development of the Indian National Congress 1892-1909.* 2nd rev. ed. Calcutta, 1985.

Gifford, Paul. *African Christianity: Its Public Role.* Bloomington, 1998.

Gifford, Paul and Louis, William R., eds. *Decolonization and African Independence: The Transfer of Powers, 1960-1980.* New Haven and London, 1988.

Goldsworthy, D., ed. *The Conservative Government and the End of Empire, 1951-57.* British Documents on the End of Empire Project, Series A, II. London, 1994.

Goody, Jack. *The Domestication of the Savage Mind.* Cambridge, 1977.

Gooptu, Nandini. "Caste and Labour: Untouchable Social Movements in Urban Uttar Pradesh in the Early Twentieth Century." In *Dalit Movements and the Meanings of Labour in India,* edited by P. Robb, 277-98. New Delhi, 1993.

———. "The Urban Poor and Militant Hinduism in Early Twentieth-Century Uttar Pradesh." *Modern Asian Studies* 31:4 (1997): 879-918.

Hackett, Rosalind I. J. *Art and Religion in Africa.* London, 1996.

Hair, P. E. H. *The Early Study of Nigerian Languages.* Cambridge, 1967.

Hale, Frederick. *Trans-Atlantic Conservative Protestantism in the Evangelical Free and Mission Covenant Traditions.* New York, 1979.

Hanciles, Jehu. "Ethiopianism: Rough Diamond of African Christianity." *Studia Historiae Ecclesiasticae* 23:2 (1997): 75-104.

Hancock, W. K. *Professing History.* Sydney, 1976.

Hannon, Peter. *Southern Africa: What Kind of Change?* Johannesburg, 1977.

Hansen, H. B. *Mission, Church and State in a Colonial Setting: Uganda 1890-1925.* London, 1984.

———. "Church and State in Early Colonial Uganda." *African Affairs* 85:338 (1986): 55-74.

———. "Church and State in a Colonial Context." In *Imperialism, the State and the Third World,* edited by M. Twaddle, 95-123. London and New York, 1992.

Hargreaves, J. D. *The End of Colonial Rule in West Africa.* London, 1979.

Harper, S. Billington. *In the Shadow of the Mahatma: Bishop V. S. Azariah and the*

Travails of Christianity in British India. Grand Rapids and Richmond, Surrey, U.K., 2000.

Hastings, Adrian. "Africa's Many Nationalisms." *Worldmission* 6:3 (1955): 343-54.

———, ed. *The Church and the Nations*. London and New York, 1959.

———. *Wiriyamu*. London, 1974.

———. *A History of African Christianity 1950-1975*. Cambridge, 1979.

———. *A History of English Christianity 1920-1985*. London, 1986.

———. *The Church in Africa 1450-1950*. Oxford, 1994.

———. *The Construction of Nationhood: Ethnicity, Religion and Nationalism*. Cambridge, 1997.

———. "The Legacy of Pierre Jean de Menasce." *International Bulletin of Missionary Research* 21:4 (1999): 168-72.

Haynes, Jeff. *Religion and Politics in Africa*. London and Nairobi, 1996.

Hempton, David. *Religion and Political Culture in Britain and Ireland: From the Glorious Revolution to the Decline of Empire*. Cambridge, 1996.

Henderson, Ian. *Manhunt in Kenya*. New York, 1958.

Henderson, Michael. *The Forgiveness Factor*. Salem, Oreg., 1996.

Hewitt, Gordon. *The Problems of Success: A History of the Church Missionary Society 1910-1942*. 2 vols. London, 1971.

Hoekendijk, Johannes Christian. *Kirche und Volk in der deutschen Missionswissenschaft*. Munich, 1967; Dutch original, Amsterdam, 1948.

Hofmeyr, Agnes Leakey. *Beyond Violence*. Johannesburg, 1990.

Holland, R. F. *European Decolonization 1918-1981: An Introductory Survey*. Basingstoke, 1985.

Hollenweger, W. J. "After Twenty Years' Research on Pentecostalism." *International Review of Mission* 75:297 (1986): 3-12.

Hood, George. *Neither Bang nor Whimper: The End of a Missionary Era in China*. Singapore, 1991.

Horton, Robin. "African Conversion." *Africa* 41:2 (1971): 87-108.

Howe, Stephen. *Anticolonialism in British Politics: The Left and the End of Empire, 1918-1964*. Oxford, 1993.

Hurn, David Abner. *Archbishop Roberts, SJ: His Life and Writings*. London, 1966.

Isichei, Elizabeth. *Entirely for God: The Life of Michael Iwene Tansi*. London, 1980.

Jaeschke, Ernst. *Bruno Gutmann: His Life, His Thoughts, and His Work*. Erlangen, 1985.

Jaffrelot, Christophe. *The Hindu Nationalist Movement and Indian Politics 1925 to the 1990s*. 1st ed. 1993; English ed., London, 1996.

Jenkins, Paul. "The Church Missionary Society and the Basel Mission: An Early Experiment in Inter-European Cooperation." In *The Church Mission Society and World Christianity 1799-1999*, edited by Kevin Ward and Brian Stanley, 43-65. Grand Rapids and Richmond, 2000.

Jones, K. W. *Arya Dharm: Hindu Consciousness in 19th-century Punjab*. Berkeley, 1976.

———. *Socio-Religious Reform Movements in British India.* Cambridge, 1989.

Jones, Francis P., ed. *Documents of the Three-Self Movement.* New York, 1963.

Juergensmeyer, M. *Religion as Social Vision: The Movement against Untouchability in Twentieth-Century Punjab.* Berkeley, Los Angeles, and London, 1982.

Kaggia, Bildad. *Roots of Freedom, 1921-1963: The Autobiography of Bildad Kaggia.* Nairobi, 1975.

Kakembo, P. N. "Colonial Office Policy and the Origins of Decolonisation in Uganda, 1940-1956." University of Dalhousie, D.Phil. thesis, 1989.

Kalu, O. U. "Peter Pan Syndrome: Church Aid and Selfhood in Africa." *Missiology* 3:1 (Jan. 1975): 15-29.

———. "Not Just New Relationships But a Renewed Body." *International Review of Mission* 64 (April 1975): 143-48.

———. *Divided People of God: Church Union Movement in Nigeria, 1867-1967.* New York, 1978.

———. "Church Unity and Religious Change in Africa." In *Christianity in Independent Africa,* edited by E. Fasholé-Luke et al., 164-75. London, 1978.

———. "Church, Mission and Moratorium." In *The History of Christianity in West Africa,* edited by O. U. Kalu, 365-74. London, 1980.

———. *Embattled Gods: Christianization of Igboland, 1841-1991.* Lagos, 1996.

———. "Tools of Hope: Stagnation and Political Theology in Africa, 1960-95." In *A Global Faith: Essays in Evangelicalism and Globalization,* edited by M. Hutchinson and O. Kalu, 181-213. Sydney, 1998.

Kavuma, Paulo. *Crisis in Buganda 1953-55: The Story of the Exile and Return of the Kabaka, Mutesa II.* London, 1979.

Kendall, Elliott. *The End of an Era: Africa and the Missionary.* London, 1978.

Kershaw, Greet. *Mau Mau from Below.* London, 1996.

Kimble, D. *A Political History of Ghana.* Oxford, 1967.

Kinghorn, Johann, ed. *Die NG Kerk en apartheid.* Johannesburg, 1986.

Kingsolver, Barbara. *The Poisonwood Bible.* New York, 1998.

Kistner, Wolfram. "The 16th of December in the Context of Nationalistic Thinking." In *Church and Nationalism in South Africa,* edited by T. Sundermeier, 73-90. Johannesburg, 1975.

Kraybill, Ron. "Transition from Rhodesia to Zimbabwe: The Role of Religious Actors." In *Religion: The Missing Dimension of Statecraft,* edited by Douglas Johnston and Cynthia Sampson, 222-33. New York, 1994.

Kriel, H. J. *Die geskiedenis van die Nederduitse Gereformeerde Sendingkerk in Suid-Afrika, 1881-1956.* Paarl, 1963.

Kriele, Eduard. *Geschichte der Rheinischen Mission,* I: *Die Rheinische Mission in der Heimat.* Barmen, 1928.

Krüger, D. W., ed. *South African Parties and Policies, 1910-1960: A Select Source Book.* London, 1960.

Larbi, E. K. "The Development of Ghanaian Pentecostalism." Ph.D. thesis, University of Edinburgh, 1995.

Lazar, John. "Conformity and Conflict: Afrikaner Nationalist Politics in South Africa, 1948-1961." D.Phil thesis, Oxford University, 1987.

Lean, Garth. *Frank Buchman: A Life*. London, 1985.

Lehmann, Arno. "Der deutsche Beitrag." In *Weltmission in Ökumenischer Zeit*, edited by Gerhard Brennecke, 153-65. Stuttgart, 1961.

———. "Die deutsche evangelische Mission in der Zeit des Kirchenkampfes." *Evangelische Missionszeitschrift* 31 (1974): 105-10.

Lehmann, Hartmut. "Hitler's evangelische Wähler." In Hartmut Lehmann, *Protestantische Weltsichten. Transformationen seit dem 17. Jahrhundert*, 130-52. Göttingen, 1998.

Lelyveld, David. *Aligarh's First Generation: Muslim Solidarity in British India*. 1978, 1st ed.; Delhi, 1996.

Lombard, Johan Andries. "Ontwikkeling in die sendingbeleid en -praktyk van die Nederduitse Gereformeerde Kerk gedurende die tydperk 1932 tot 1962." D. Th. thesis, University of the North, 1985.

Lombard, R. T. J. *Die Nederduitse Gereformeerde Kerke en rassepolitiek: Met speciale verwysing na die jare 1948-1961*. Silverton, 1981.

Longman, Tim. "Empowering the Weak and Protecting the Powerful." *African Studies Review* 41 (April 1998): 49-72.

Lonsdale, John. "The Moral Economy of Mau Mau." In Bruce Berman and Lonsdale, *Unhappy Valley: Conflict in Kenya and Africa*, 265-314. London, 1992.

———. "Kikuyu Christianities." *Journal of Religion in Africa* 29:2 (1999): 206-29.

———. "Jomo Kenyatta, God and the Modern World." In *African Modernities: Entangled Meanings in Current Debate*, edited by J.-G. Deutsch, H. Schmidt, and P. Probst, 31-66. Oxford, 2002.

Lonsdale, John and Berman, Bruce. *The House of Custom: Jomo Kenyatta, Louis Leakey and the Making of the Modern Kikuyu* (forthcoming).

Loubser, J. A. *The Apartheid Bible: A Critical Review of Racial Theology in South Africa*. Cape Town, 1987.

Louis, William Roger. *Great Britain and Germany's Lost Colonies 1914-1919*. Oxford, 1967.

Louw, Louis, ed. *Dawie, 1946-1964: 'n Bloemlesing uit die geskrifte van Die Burger se politieke kommentator*. Cape Town, 1965.

Low, D. A. *Religion and Society in Buganda 1875-1900*. Kampala, 1957.

———. "The Buganda Mission, 1954." *Historical Studies* 13:51 (1968): 353-80.

Low, D. A., and Pratt, R. C. *Buganda and British Overrule 1900-1955*. London, 1960.

Lückhoff, A. H. *Cottesloe*. Cape Town, 1978.

Lumbala, F. K. *Celebrating Jesus in Africa: Liturgy and Inculturation*. Maryknoll, N.Y., 1998.

Luttwak, Edward. "Franco-German Reconciliation: The Overlooked Role of the Moral Re-Armament Movement." In *Religion: The Missing Dimension of*

Statecraft, edited by Douglas Johnston and Cynthia Sampson, 37-63. New York, 1994.

Lutz, Jessie G. *Chinese Politics and Christian Missions: The Anti-Christian Movements of 1920-1928.* Notre Dame, 1988.

Lyttelton, O. *The Memoirs of Lord Chandos.* London, 1962.

MacInnis, Donald E. *Religious Policy and Practice in Communist China: A Documentary History.* New York, 1972.

McKenna, J. C. *Finding a Social Voice: The Church and Marxism in Africa.* New York, 1997.

Mani, Lata. "Contentious Traditions: The Debate on *Sati* in Colonial India." In *Recasting Women: Essays in Colonial History,* edited by K. Sangari and S. Vaid, 88-126. New Delhi, 1989.

———. *Contentious Traditions: The Debate on* Sati *in Colonial India.* Berkeley, Los Angeles, and London, 1998.

Marcel, Gabriel, ed. *Plus Décisif que la Violence.* Paris, 1971.

Marks, Shula. "Changing History, Changing Histories: Separations and Connections in the Lives of Three South African Women." *Journal of African Cultural Studies* 13:1 (June 2000): 94-106.

Marshall, P. J., ed. *The British Discovery of Hinduism in the Eighteenth Century.* Cambridge, 1970.

Menasce, P. Jean de. "Nationalisme en pays de mission," *Neue Zeitschrift für Missionswissenschaft* 3:1 (1947), trans. into English as "Nationalism in Missionary Countries." *Worldmission* 5 (1954): 267-78.

Mews, Stuart P. "Kikuyu and Edinburgh: The Interaction of Attitudes to Two Conferences." In *Councils and Assemblies. Studies in Church History 7,* edited by G. J. Cuming and Derek Baker, 345-59. Cambridge, 1971.

Metcalf, T. R. *Ideologies of the Raj.* Cambridge, 1994.

Meyer, Birgit. "Beyond Syncretism: Translation and Diabolization in the Appropriation of Protestantism in Africa." In *Syncretism/Anti-Syncretism: The Politics of Religious Synthesis,* edited by Charles Stewart and Rosalind Shaw, 45-68. London, 1994.

Millington, Constance. M. *Whether We Be Many or Few: A History of the Cambridge Delhi Brotherhood.* Bangalore, 1999.

Mobley, H. W. *The Ghanaian's Image of the Missionary.* Leiden, 1971.

Moodie, T. Dunbar. *The Rise of Afrikanerdom: Power, Apartheid, and the Afrikaner Civil Religion.* Berkeley, Los Angeles, and London, 1975.

Moon, Penderel., ed. *Wavell: The Viceroy's Journal.* London, 1973.

Moriyama, Jerome T. "The Evolution of an African Ministry in the Work of the Universities' Mission to Central Africa in Tanzania, 1864-1909." Ph.D. thesis, University of London, 1984.

———. "Building a Home-Grown Church," in Daniel O'Connor et al., *Three Centuries of Mission: The United Society for the Propagation of the Gospel 1701-2000,* 330-42. London, 2000.

Mudoola, Dan M. *Religion, Ethnicity and Politics in Uganda.* Kampala, 1992.

Mugambi, J., Mutiso-Mbinda, J., and Vollbrecht, J. *Ecumenical Initiatives in Eastern Africa.* Nairobi, 1992.

Mullen, J. *The Catholic Church in Modern Africa.* Dublin, 1965.

Murphy, Philip. *Alan Lennox-Boyd: A Biography.* London, 1999.

Murray-Brown, Jeremy. *Kenyatta.* London, 1972.

Mutesa II. *The Desecration of My Kingdom.* London, 1967.

Mutibwa, P. M. "The Church of Uganda and the Movements for Political Independence 1952-1962." In *A Century of Christianity in Uganda 1877-1977,* edited by T. Tuma and P. Mutibwa, 131-41. Nairobi, 1978.

Nabudere, D. W. *Imperialism and Revolution in Uganda.* London, 1980.

Neave, D. R. J. "Aspects of the History of the Universities' Mission to Central Africa, 1858-1900." M.Phil. thesis, University of York, 1974.

Needham, Rodney. *Belief, Language, and Experience.* Oxford, 1972.

Nehru, Jawaharlal. *An Autobiography.* London, 1941; originally published, 1936.

Newbigin, Lesslie. "The Call of Mission — A Call to Unity?" In *The Church Crossing Frontiers: Essays on the Nature of Mission. In Honour of Bengt Sundkler,* edited by P. Beyerhaus and C. F. Hallencreutz, 254-65. Uppsala, 1969.

———. "Ecumenical Amnesia." *International Bulletin of Missionary Research* 18:1 (Jan. 1994): 1-5.

Ng Lee-ming. "The Promise and Limitations of Chinese Protestant Theologians, 1920-50." *Ching Feng* 21:4 (1978).

Njama, Karari. *Mau Mau from Within.* New York, 1966.

Noll, Mark A. "Evangelical Identity, Power and Culture in the Great Nineteenth Century." Currents in World Christianity Position Paper 107. Cambridge, 1999.

O'Connor, Daniel, and others. *Three Centuries of Mission: The United Society for the Propagation of the Gospel 1701-2000.* London, 2000.

Oehler, Wilhelm. *Geschichte der deutschen evangelischen Mission, vol. II: Reife und Bewährung der deutschen evangelischen Mission 1885-1950.* Baden-Baden, 1951.

O'Hanlon, Rosalind. *Caste, Conflict, and Ideology: Mahatma Jotirao Phule and Low Caste Protest in Nineteenth-Century Western India.* Cambridge, 1985.

Ojo, M. A. "Charismatic Movements in Africa." In *Christianity in Africa in the 1990s,* edited by Christopher Fyfe and Andrew Walls, 92-110. Edinburgh, 1996.

Omenka, Nicholas I. *The School in the Service of Evangelization: The Catholic Educational Impact in Eastern Nigeria, 1886-1950.* Leiden, 1989.

Ozigboh, I. R. A. *Igbo Catholicism.* Onitsha, 1985.

Parekh, Bhiku. *Colonialism, Tradition and Reform: An Analysis of Gandhi's Political Discourse.* Rev. ed., New Delhi; Thousand Oaks, Calif.; and London, 1999.

Parel, A. J., ed. *M. K. Gandhi: Hind Swaraj and Other Writings.* Cambridge, 1997.

Paton, Alan. *Apartheid and the Archbishop: The Life and Times of Geoffrey Clayton, Archbishop of Cape Town.* Cape Town, 1973.

Paton, David Macdonald. *Christian Missions and the Judgement of God.* 1953; 2nd ed., Grand Rapids, 1996.

Pearce, R. "The Colonial Office and Planned Decolonization in Africa." *African Affairs* 83 (1984): 77-93.

Peel, J. D. Y. "For Who Hath Despised the Day of Small Things? Missionary Narratives and Historical Anthropology." *Comparative Studies in Society and History* 37:3 (1995): 581-607.

Pickering, W. S. F. "Anglo-Catholicism: Some Sociological Observations." In *Tradition Renewed: The Oxford Movement Conference Papers,* edited by Geoffrey Rowell, 153-72. London, 1986.

Pierard, Richard V. "John R. Mott and the Rift in the Ecumenical Movement during World War I." *Journal of Ecumenical Studies* 23 (1986): 601-19.

———. "Volkisch Thought and Christian Missions in the Early Twentieth Century." In *Essays in Religious Studies for Andrew Walls,* edited by James Thrower, 136-54. Aberdeen, 1986.

———. "Allied Treatment of Protestant Missionaries in German East Africa in World War I." *Africa Journal of Evangelical Theology* 12 (1993): 4-17.

———. "Shaking the Foundations: World War I, the Western Allies, and German Protestant Missions." *International Bulletin of Missionary Research* (1998): 13-19.

Pieres, J. B. *The House of Phalo: A History of the Xhosa People in the Days of Their Independence.* Johannesburg, 1981.

Piguet, Charles. *Freedom for Africa.* Caux edition. Caux-sur-Montreux, 1996.

Piguet, Jacqueline. *For the Love of Tomorrow.* London, 1985.

Porter, Andrew N. "War, Colonialism and the British Experience: The Redefinition of Christian Missionary Policy, 1938-1952." *Kirchliche Zeitgeschichte* 5:2 (1992): 269-88.

———. "Religion and Empire: British Expansion in the Long Nineteenth Century 1780-1914." *Journal of Imperial and Commonwealth History* 20:3 (1993): 370-90.

———. "Cultural Imperialism and Protestant Missionary Enterprise, 1780-1914." *Journal of Imperial and Commonwealth History* 25:3 (Sept. 1997): 367-91.

Powell, Avril. *Muslims and Missionaries in Pre-Mutiny India.* London, 1993.

Raiser, Konrad. *Ecumenism in Transition: A Paradigm Shift in the Ecumenical Movement.* Geneva, 1991.

Randall, Ian. *Evangelical Experiences: A Study in the Spirituality of English Evangelicalism 1918-1939.* Carlisle, 1999.

———. "'We All Need Constant Change': The Oxford Group and Mission in Europe in the 1930s." *European Journal of Theology* 9:2 (2000): 171-85.

Ranger, Terence O. "Connexions between 'Primary Resistance' Movements and

Modern Mass Nationalism in East and Central Africa." *Journal of African History* 9:3 (1968): 437-53, 631-41.

———. "Missionary Adaptation of African Religious Institutions: The Masasi Case." In *The Historical Study of African Religion, with Special Reference to East and Central Africa,* edited by T. O. Ranger and I. N. Kimambo, 231-51. London, 1972.

———. "Religious Movements and Politics in Subsaharan Africa." *African Studies Review* 29:2 (1986): 1-69.

———. "From Command to Service: Trevor Huddleston in Masasi 1960-68." In *Trevor Huddleston: Essays on His Life and Work,* edited by Deborah Duncan Honoré, 35-52. Oxford and New York, 1988.

———. "Missionaries, Migrants and the Manyika: The Invention of Tribalism in Zimbabwe." In *The Creation of Tribalism in Southern Africa,* edited by Leroy Vail, 118-50. Berkeley, 1989.

———. "'Taking on the Missionary's Task': African Spirituality and the Mission Churches in Manicaland in the 1930s." *Journal of Religion in Africa* 29:2 (1999): 175-206.

Raychaudhuri, Tapan. *Perceptions, Emotions, Sensibilities: Essays on India's Colonial and Post-colonial Experiences.* New Delhi, 1999.

Richter, Julius. *Geschichte der Berliner Missionsgesellschaft 1824-1924.* Berlin, 1924.

Rhoodie, N. J., and Venter, H. J. *Apartheid: A Socio-Historical Exposition of the Origin and Development of the Apartheid Idea.* Cape Town and Pretoria, 1960.

Rich, Paul B. *White Power and the Liberal Conscience: Racial Segregation and South African Liberalism, 1921-60.* Johannesburg, 1984.

Rickets, Eva. *Light on the Horizon.* Upton-on-Severn, 1995.

Ritter, Ernst. *Das Deutsche Auslands-Institut in Stuttgart 1917-1945. Ein Beispiel deutscher Volkstumsarbeit zwischen den Weltkriegen.* Wiesbaden, 1976.

Roberg, O. Theodore. "Marcus Ch'eng (c. 1883-1963): Apostle or Apostate? Relations with the Covenant Mission in China." M.A. thesis, North Park Theological Seminary, Chicago, 1982.

Rorty, Richard. *Contingency, Irony, and Solidarity.* Cambridge, 1989.

Rosenberg, Emily S. *Spreading the American Dream: American Economic and Cultural Expansion, 1890-1945.* New York, 1982.

Rotberg, R. I. *The Rise of Nationalism in Central Africa: The Making of Malawi and Zambia, 1873-1964.* Cambridge, Mass., 1966.

Sachs, William L. *The Transformation of Anglicanism: From State Church to Global Communion.* Cambridge, 1993.

Sanneh, Lamin. *Translating the Message: The Missionary Impact on Culture.* Maryknoll, N.Y., 1989.

———. "World Christianity and the New Historiography." In *Enlarging the Story: Perspectives on Writing World Christian History,* edited by Wilbert R. Shenk, 94-114. Maryknoll, N.Y., 2002.

Scott, J. C. *Domination and Arts of Resistance: Hidden Transcripts.* New Haven, 1990.

Seal, Anil. *The Emergence of Indian Nationalism: Competition and Collaboration in the Later Nineteenth Century.* Cambridge, 1968.

Senfu, Yang. *Zhongguo jidujiao shi* (History of Christianity in China). Taibei, 1968.

Shell, Robert C.-H. *Children of Bondage: A Social History of the Slave Society at the Cape of Good Hope, 1652-1838.* Hanover and Middletown, Conn., 1994.

Sinha, M. *Colonial Masculinity: The "Manly Englishman" and the "Effeminate Bengali" in the Late Nineteenth Century.* Manchester and New York, 1995.

Smith, Alec. *Now I Call Him Brother.* Basingstoke, 1984.

Smith, H. Maynard. *Frank Bishop of Zanzibar: Life of Frank Weston, D.D., 1871-1924.* London, 1926.

Sovik, Arne. "Church and State in Republican China: A Survey History of the Relations between the Christian Churches and the Chinese Government, 1911-1945." Ph.D. thesis, Yale University, 1952.

Stanley, Brian. *The Bible and the Flag: Protestant Missions and British Imperialism in the Nineteenth and Twentieth Centuries.* Leicester, 1990.

———. *The History of the Baptist Missionary Society, 1792-1992.* Edinburgh, 1992.

Stark, Rodney. "Atheism, Faith, and the Social Scientific Study of Religion." *Journal of Contemporary Religion* 14:1 (1998): 41-62.

Strayer, R. W. *The Making of Mission Communities in East Africa.* London, 1978.

Stuart, John. "'A Measure of Disquiet': British Missionary Responses to African Colonial Issues, 1945-53," *Currents in World Christianity Position Paper 109.* Cambridge, 2000.

Studdert-Kennedy, Gerald. *Providence and the Raj: Imperial Mission and Missionary Imperialism.* New Delhi and London, 1998.

Sundkler, B. G. M. *Bantu Prophets in South Africa.* 2nd ed. London, 1961.

———. *Zulu Zion and Some Swazi Zionists.* London, 1976.

Taylor, John V. *The Growth of the Church in Buganda: An Attempt at Understanding.* London, 1958.

———. "Selfhood: Presence or Persona?" In *The Church Crossing Frontiers: Essays on the Nature of Mission. In Honour of Bengt Sundkler,* edited by P. Beyerhaus and C. F. Hallencreutz, 171-76. Uppsala, 1969.

Taylor, John V., and Lehmann, Dorothea A. *Christians of the Copperbelt: The Growth of the Church in Northern Rhodesia.* London, 1961.

Tengatenga, James. "The Good Being the Enemy of the Best: The Politics of Bishop Frank Oswald Thorne in Nyasaland and the Federation, 1936-1961." *Religion in Malawi* 6 (1996): 20-29.

Throup, David. *Economic and Social Origins of Mau Mau.* London, 1988.

Thunberg, Lars. "Redemption for the Wrongs of History." In *The Church Crossing Frontiers: Essays on the Nature of Mission. In Honour of Bengt Sundkler,* edited by P. Beyerhaus and C. F. Hallencreutz, 209-25. Uppsala, 1969.

Tilgner, Wolfgang. *Volksnomostheologie und Schöpfungsglaube. Ein Beitrag zur Geschichte des Kirchenkampfes.* Göttingen, 1966.

Tripp, Aili Mari. "A Foot in the Door: Historical Dimensions of the Women's Movement in Uganda." In Tripp, Aili Mari, *Women and Politics in Uganda.* Oxford, Madison, Wis., and Kampala, 2000.

———. "A New Look at European Women in Colonial Africa: British Teachers and Women's Rights Activists in Uganda (1898-1962)." Unpublished paper, 2000.

Tucher, Paul H. von. *Nationalism: Case and Crisis in Missions. German Missions in British India 1939-1946.* Erlangen, 1980.

Tuck, Patrick. *French Catholic Missionaries and the Politics of Imperialism in Vietnam 1857-1914: A Documentary Survey.* Liverpool, 1987.

Turner, H. W. "A Typology for African Religious Movements." *Journal of Religion in Africa* 1:1 (1967): 1-32.

Ustorf, Werner. "Anti-Americanism in German Missiology." *Mission Studies* 11 (1989): 23-34.

———. "'Survival of the Fittest': German Protestant Missions, Nazism and Neocolonialism, 1933-1945." *Journal of Religion in Africa* 28:1 (1998): 93-114.

———. *Sailing on the Next Tide: Missions, Missiology, and the Third Reich.* Frankfurt am Main, 2000.

Uya, O. E. "Alexander Crummell: Apostle of African Redemption through Religion." *West African Journal of Religion* 16:2 (1975): 1-12.

Uzoigwe, G. N., ed. *Uganda: The Dilemma of Nationhood.* New York and London, 1982.

Uzoukwu, E. E. *Liturgy: Truly Christian, Truly African.* Eldoret, 1982.

Wachanga, Kahinga. *The Swords of Kirinyaga.* Nairobi, 1991.

Waliggo, John. *A History of African Priests.* Katigondo, Uganda, 1988.

Walls, Andrew F. "Africa in Christian History: Retrospect and Prospect." *Journal of African Christian Thought* 1:1 (1998): 2-15.

Ward, Kevin. "The Church of Uganda amidst Conflict." In *Religion and Politics in East Africa: The Period Since Independence,* edited by H. B. Hansen and M. Twaddle, 72-105. London, 1995.

———. "The Church of Uganda and the Exile of Kabaka Muteesa II, 1953-55." *Journal of Religion in Africa* 28:4 (1998): 411-49.

Ward, Kevin and Stanley, Brian, eds. *The Church Mission Society and World Christianity 1799-1999.* Grand Rapids and Richmond, Surrey, U.K., 2000.

Warren, Max. *Social History and Christian Mission.* London, 1967.

Watt, C. A. "Education for National Efficiency: Constructive Nationalism in North India, 1909-1916." *Modern Asian Studies* 31:2 (1997): 339-74.

Watt, Gideon van der. "GBA Gerdener: Koersaanwyser in die Nederduitse Gereformeerde Kerk in Sending en Ekumene." D.Th. thesis, University of the Orange Free State, 1990.

Watteville-Berkheim, Diane de. *Le Fil Conducteur.* Caux edition. Caux-sur-Montreux, 1973.

Weber, Charles. "Christianity and West African Decolonisation." North Atlantic Missiology Project Position Paper 80. Cambridge, 1997.

Webster, John C. B. *The Christian Community and Change in Nineteenth-Century North India.* Delhi, 1976.

Welbourn, F. B. *East African Rebels.* London, 1961.

———. *Religion and Politics in Uganda 1952-1962.* Nairobi, 1965.

Weller, John. "The Influence on National Affairs of Alston May, Bishop of Northern Rhodesia, 1914-40." In *Themes in the Christian History of Central Africa,* edited by T. O. Ranger and John Weller, 195-211. London, 1975.

West, Charles. *The Power To Be Human.* New York, 1971.

White, Gavin. "Frank Weston and the Kikuyu Crisis." *Bulletin of the Scottish Institute of Missionary Studies,* n.s. 8-9 (1992-3): 48-55.

Whyte, Bob. *Unfinished Encounter: China and Christianity.* London, 1988.

Wickeri, Philip L. *Seeking the Common Ground: Protestant Christianity, the Three-Self Movement, and China's United Front.* Maryknoll, N.Y., 1988.

Wilson, G. H. *The History of the Universities Mission to Central Africa.* London, 1936.

Wolffe, John. *God and Greater Britain: Religion and National Life in Britain and Ireland 1843-1945.* London, 1994.

Wright, Marcia. *German Missions to Tanganyika, 1891-1941: Lutherans and Moravians in the Southern Highlands.* Oxford, 1971.

Yates, Timothy. *Christian Mission in the Twentieth Century.* Cambridge, 1994.

Ying, Fuk-tsang. "Bensehua yu minguo jidujiao jiaohui shi yenjiu." ("Indigenization and Studies of Chinese Church History in the Republican Period.") *Journal of the History of Christianity in Modern China* 1 (1998): 85-100.

Yip, Ka-che. *Religion, Nationalism, and Chinese Students: The Anti-Christian Movement of 1922-1927.* Bellingham, 1980.

———. "Education and Political Socialization in Pre-Communist China: The Goals of San Min Chu-I Education." *Asian Profile* 9:5 (Oct. 1981): 401-13.

———. *Health and National Reconstruction in Nationalist China: The Development of Modern Health Services, 1928-1937.* Ann Arbor, 1995.

Zha Shijie. *Zhongguo Jidujiao renwu xiaozhuan* (Concise biographies of important Chinese Christians). Taibei, 1983.

———. *Minguo Jidujiao shi lunmin ji* (Essays on the history of Christianity in the Republican period). Taibei, 1994.

Index